THE PLOT TO
DESTROY
DEMOCRACY

THE PLOT TO DESTROY DEMOCRACY

HOW PUTIN AND HIS SPIES ARE UNDERMINING AMERICA AND DISMANTLING THE WEST

MALCOLM NANCE

FOREWORD BY ROB REINER

hachette
BOOKS

NEW YORK   BOSTON

Hachette Books
Hachette Book Group
1290 Avenue of the Americas, New York, NY 10104
hachettebooks.com
twitter.com/hachettebooks

Originally published in hardcover and ebook by Hachette Books in June 2018.

First paperback edition: June 2018

Hachette Books is a division of Hachette Book Group, Inc. The Hachette Books name
and logo are trademarks of Hachette Book Group, Inc.

The publisher is not responsible for websites (or their content) that are not owned by the
publisher.

The Hachette Speakers Bureau provides a wide range of authors for speaking events. To
find out more, go to www.hachettespeakersbureau.com or call (866) 376-6591.

LCCN: 2018939279
ISBN: 978-0-316-48483-1

Printed in the United States of America

LSC-C

10 9 8 7 6 5 4 3 2 1

Contents

SECTION III   America Under Siege...from Within

Foreword

In 2016 the United States was attacked by a foreign enemy power. Unlike the Japanese attack on Pearl Harbor or al-Qaeda's attack on the World Trade Center, the attack by the Russian Federation struck at the core of our democracy: our free and fair election system. The purpose was to destroy our system of self-governance that we have cherished and held up as an example to the world for over 240 years. Carried out in stealth, using state-run news media and intelligence agencies, Russia managed to influence the election with the express purpose of aiding their preferred candidate, Donald J. Trump. The Kremlin took advantage of our open society. And through social media and agents of influence they deployed ex-KGB spies to spread blackmail, forgery, and propaganda. Putin loyalists (neo-Nazis, fascists, and racist xenophobes) had and continue to have but one mission: Use the freedoms afforded to us to halt, attack, and destroy democracy from without and within.

With the election of a childish, self-dealing, autocratic narcissist, we see evidence of the Kremlin's success. Donald Trump's contempt for our inclusive values, our norms, and the rule of law, along with his weak support of NATO and the European Union, has elevated Russia on the global stage.

One of our founding fathers, Benjamin Franklin, once wondered why Benedict Arnold would sell out 3 million Americans to King George for 20,000 pounds. Today we face another question: Why would a failing real estate developer turned reality show host cozy up to an autocrat who rules over a kleptocracy? Will we come to find that 320 million Americans have been sold out to the Kremlin for 20 billion rubles?

As of this writing, the United States and Europe have been standing up to the attacks on the pillars of democracy. But we the people must be the strongest pillar of all. And we must heed the warnings of the risks to our beloved system of government that continue to come. To that end, we can have no better Paul Revere than Malcolm Nance.

—Rob Reiner

Introduction

O ne of the greatest dreams of the old Soviet Union was to put a highly suggestible American ideologue into power who would do the bidding of the Kremlin. For nearly a century, Russia wanted to change American policy in such a way that its economy and alliances with NATO would be so damaged that the Soviet Union would become the preeminent superpower in the world. The idea of a Kremlin-controlled President would live on after the death of the Soviet Union.

In 2012, the plan to subject the 2016 United States election to a massive cyber influence operation, possibly in coordination with the Trump campaign, was launched. It ostensibly started with the hacking of the Democratic National Committee's servers in order to steal critical information to knock Hillary Clinton out of the running for President of the United States. The plan would eventually work to the benefit of Russia's chosen candidate, Donald Trump.

On November 8, 2016, the American presidential election culminated into what could arguably be called the greatest intelligence operation in the history of the world. In the Russian attack on the American election, a strategic adversary influenced enough voters through manipulation of the internet to get their preferred candidate chosen—and convinced more than 40% of the American population that they had nothing whatsoever to do with it.

I was determined to track down other information to illustrate where Russian intelligence used cyberwarfare to influence elections, referenda, and political opinion to their advantage. My investigation showed that Russian intelligence had been using these advanced malware suites to attack other nations for almost a decade. The 2016 election hacking was just window dressing on a larger goal. I found there were many activities where the Russian CYBER BEARS—a collective name for their national, criminal, and intelligence hackers—were involved in shifting the goalposts. The 2016 hacking was the start of a global campaign to imagine a "New World Order" and make it a "Russian World Order." The Federal Bureau of Investigation (FBI) and the Central Intelligence Agency (CIA) code named the Russian operation against the United States GRIZZLY STEPPE. In my last book, *The Plot to Hack America*, I referred to it as Operation LUCKY-7, considering the amount of luck the Russian spies would need.

The next phase of their campaign—the plot to destroy democracy—would be better described as GLOBAL GRIZZLY. The best plan would be to resort back to a goal from the Soviet era, discredit and destroy Western-style democracy altogether. This time Americans would be curried through their hatred of Muslims (and their first African-American President, Barack Obama) to align themselves through cultural similarities, as opposed to Cold War politics. In the GLOBAL GRIZZLY plan, tribal commonalities among white ethno-nationalists would be cemented through a political order based on authoritarianism, anti-liberalism, and anti-globalism, and leverage the success of the super-rich.

By 2016, Operation GLOBAL GRIZZLY was occurring right before our eyes. It was the full-scale implementation of a new form of asymmetric warfare. Although Russia was a military superpower, it remained an economic dinosaur, with the exception of fossil fuel production. In order to defeat a superior economic entity like the United States, Russia embraced a new battlefront that could cripple a democratic adversary. It would exacerbate the domination of the information battle space.

In *The Plot to Destroy Democracy*, I will reveal the strategy the Russian Federation put into effect to defeat the world's biggest democracies and challenge principal governance structures of the Western world. The singular beauty of this plan, which has roots far back into Stalin's Soviet Union, is that the Russian political chess players have harnessed the West's own technology and liberty as daggers to be plunged into the heart of democratic governance. Russia saw opportunity to co-opt American and European political parties to destroy democracy itself.

At its heart, *The Plot to Destroy Democracy* is a fast-paced cross between a spy thriller and a National Intelligence estimate that provides a deep-dive assessment of the dangers that surround the nation where the enemies are both foreign and domestic. However, the game remains in motion. All the pieces are still visible, and a bulldog of an investigator, former FBI Director Robert Mueller, is on the hunt. Make no mistake: Democracy in the era of Trump and Putin is in retreat and has been targeted for extinction. With the right amount of public awareness, determination, and dedication to the principles we hold dear and love, it can be stopped.

Cyber Bears

CHAPTER 1

Shots Fired

On November 8, 2016, Vladimir Putin became the first Russian President of the United States. What could arguably be called the greatest intelligence operation in the history of the world had been executed and the result was that the candidate Moscow had supported had won. Putin didn't care what happened next. He was certain that with Trump in power, the American public would be so enmeshed in chaos that they would be completely indifferent on how to respond, if they responded at all. That was the weakness with democracy; it required consensus, process, and time. Putin relied on none of that. He had ordered and executed a daring political mission. His cyber spies, state-run news media, and his elite global rich—the oligarchs—had successfully influenced the American public's mindset so deeply they were in total denial that it had been done at all. As both Baudelaire (and Keyser Söze) said, *"La plus belle des ruses du Diable est de vous persuader qu'il n'existe pas!... The best trick of the devil was to convince you he didn't exist."*

The political party controlling the US Congress, the Republican Party, had dedicated itself for eight years to destroying any positive action by President Barack Obama. Hillary Clinton, his Secretary of State, was likely to be the Democratic Party's frontrunner and even more likely to be the next President of the United States. Putin's personal hatred of both seemed to be the key motivating factor that caused him to intervene. But luck was on his side in 2016 because all of the actors and stages that the Russian Federation had cultivated over a decade were in place to effect a change bigger than a US President. Russia had taken a modest distrust of Hillary Clinton and had used the Republican Party's own argument, "But…Hillary's emails," and had turned it into a weapon. Russia capitalized on the repeated investigations into Clinton's emails that were found on a secure server in her Secret Service–protected home. It was an easy target. When the election was done, America had fractured.

Russia had exerted its asymmetric power to elect Donald J. Trump to the highest office in the West and it had succeeded beyond its dreams. With this, they'd get the Magnitsky Act and Crimea sanctions lifted. Russian investments would become highly desired vehicles again, but to sustain Putin's dream, the real goal must be attained: Put an end to liberal democracy in America and Europe and bring about a worldwide conservative renaissance.

It wasn't a very difficult job, despite the perils of running an integrated intelligence mission against the world's premier superpower. Like the 9/11 attacks, American politicians and the public just did not have the imagination to believe that Putin would dare do something so intrusive. US Intelligence did have the imagination—as well as the information—that both Moscow and Beijing could pull off such a stunt, but the military and intelligence leadership was responsive to politicians. One could warn till one is blue in the face, but intelligence produces warnings; politicians must act on them.

In the end, Putin won with the aid of Americans who had turned on their own values. The news media assisted greatly by elevating stolen innocuous emails from an insecure party server to a national crisis in which the victims were treated as suspicious. To Trump supporters it validated everything they ever suspected about Hillary Clinton—she hid emails, which meant she was a liar. No matter that Trump voters elected a man who openly embraced white supremacy, rejected diversity, abhorred global engagement, ignored his own corruption, and enlisted his own family and staff as royalty to be worshipped. Trump voters saw these traits as perks. They viewed nepotism, largesse, and excess as virtues of a business and political shark. If he vocally stood against virtually all gains America had made in equality and global economic expansion since 1964 and it got him elected, then all the better that he hold those positions. *By all means necessary* was Trump's apparent motto for the 2016 election. Russian intelligence lived by that motto too. The spies of Red Square were shameless enough, but the real scandal was that Team Trump saw nothing wrong with it.

Trump voters had blindly elected him despite knowing that Russia had intervened in the electoral process. They cared not that Trump's own surprising level of slavish devotion to Putin was suspicious. It. Did. Not. Matter. Trump had created a cult of personality in the white lower class so that they worshipped his every word and challenged the veracity of anything negative said against him. This worked out well for Putin.

For the new Russian President of the United States, the original goal had been to just make America consume itself in partisanship and beat them on the global market to return to economic supremacy. Now with the election of Trump, America would become fundamentally dysfunctional. More importantly, Russia would gain an ally that would release its illicit billions stolen from them by the Obama administration through sanctions. It had taken a decade to earn those hundreds of billions of dollars through the theft of former Soviet assets. Liquidating Russian shipyards and airports, and selling off everything from tanks to chemical factories, had been a tough business where only the toughest could survive. Led by an ex-KGB officer, Russia was about to embark on a path to a new era of global leadership. Yet Americans were fickle, and the "Yes, We Can!" of Barack Obama had splintered the nation to the point that just a few subtle strokes of assistance—financial and ideological—would shift the US into Moscow's orbit. It was a tough shot, and if it failed the damage could become permanent, but Vladimir Putin dared to take it—and in the 2016 American election it paid off.

Fresh Bear Tracks

The plot to hack America, given the FBI code name Operation GRIZ-ZLY STEPPE, was executed early in the summer of 2015. Russian

Military Intelligence hackers executed a long-term plan to penetrate the servers of the Democratic National Committee (DNC). It was technically simple. The GRU, an acronym for *Glavnoye Razvedyvatel'noye Upravleniye,* or Main Intelligence Directorate, used the lax computer security of the Americans, which allowed their spies to gain access to the servers. The Russian army spies ran rampant for as long as seven to ten months before the threat was detected. They copied what they wanted and left no part of the DNC untouched. Someone in the US intelligence community must have noticed the attempts. In September 2015, the FBI sent the DNC a notice that their computer systems were being probed by an undesignated foreign actor. The DNC did perfunctory checks and detected nothing out of the ordinary. They would already be too late. The Russian army spies were well into the system and operating almost invisibly. They were using a suite of cyberware known as Advanced Persistent Threat-29 (APT-29). It was a well-known hacking suite that had been nicknamed by many companies but the one that stuck was coined by the cybersecurity company CrowdStrike: COZY BEAR. The people behind the software were a cell of Russian army intelligence soldiers using a highly sophisticated suite of malware in their attacks. This wasn't the first time the GRU had deployed COZY BEAR. It had been used many times around the world and had been used to penetrate the White House and Pentagon servers in 2014 and 2015. It was the GRU's go-to penetration system. To get into a civilian agency such as the DNC, it was child's play. In the past, they had gotten into White House staffers' log-ins, so an American political party was cake.

Yet while the GRU was successful in owning the DNC, a very specific attack was carried out by another spy entity known as APT-28 and nicknamed FANCY BEAR. This malware belonged to the cyber spies of the Russian intelligence agency, the FSB. The Federal Security Service—the FSB—was heir to the entire legacy and corporate knowledge of the villainous Soviet spy agency, the KGB. (They changed their acronym after the USSR fell.) In fact, once Russia lost its Communist ideology, the former KGB became far more powerful in computing power. In the cybersecurity world, FANCY BEAR was well known to be controlled by the FSB. The only difference between the modern-day

FSB (and its overseas clandestine service branch, the SVR) and the ruthless KGB is that the FSB has a much bigger budget and more latitude for overseas operations.

THE FSB IGNORED the GRU team in the DNC hack and stole a single yet specific folder of opposition research in their FANCY BEAR software. An opposition research folder is all the dirt a political party collects on another party's opponent. The Republicans had 17 candidates and the Democrats had folders on each, but the FSB stole the folder for one specific person: Donald J. Trump.

In June 2016, the CEO of CrowdStrike, Dmitri Alperovitch, published the findings of the DNC hack. The paper is titled *Bears in the Midst: Intrusion into the Democratic National Committee* and it publicly accused Russian spies of conducting the DNC hacking. It was well received in the cybersecurity community but detractors in the Republican Party, particularly those of the now-frontrunner, Donald Trump, did not agree with the Russian findings.

A few days after the CrowdStrike report, a WordPress blog written by someone using the name "Guccifer 2.0" appeared on the internet. The entity claimed that he had penetrated the DNC by himself, a "lone hacker." Cybersecurity experts were immediately suspicious because that name was apparently an homage to "Guccifer," a prolific Romanian hacker who repeatedly read and published the emails of Colin Powell and other luminaries. Since the real Guccifer was sitting in a US prison and cooperating with the FBI, who was this guy? Journalists and cybersecurity experts quickly surmised that the person on the blog was likely a Russian citizen due to a poor understanding of Romanian language and their use of a Russian language keyboard. No matter, Guccifer 2.0 started to publicly release data stolen by the COZY BEAR/FANCY BEAR hacks. He started by releasing DNC financial reports, a "dossier on Hillary Clinton," and other materials that could only have come from DNC computer servers. However, the Guccifer persona was met with skepticism and derision. Apart from in the cybersecurity world, the story was not making headway. That changed immediately when Julian Assange's WikiLeaks organization announced it had the DNC emails. The effect was galvanizing. The entire global media stood up and paid attention.

ON JULY 22, 2016, WikiLeaks flooded the global media with 19,252 stolen DNC emails from senior DNC staff, including the communications director and the senior finance team. The materials appeared to focus on discussions designed to split the Democratic Party by revealing then-chairperson Debbie Wasserman Schultz's views on Bernie Sanders and Hillary Clinton. Schultz was a close personal friend of Clinton's, so it was no surprise she supported her, and the release of the emails was timed to occur just before the Democratic National Convention in Philadelphia. The intent of the leak was clear—split the Bernie Sanders faction from the Democrats and damage Hillary Clinton among independent and progressive voters. It worked like a charm. The first morning of the convention, Bernie Sanders supporters walked out, staged loud protests, and even publicly shouted Donald Trump's schoolyard nickname for the nominee: "Crooked Hillary."

The Friday before the Democratic Party's convention in Philadelphia, I was in New York City to provide analysis and commentary related to possible terrorist and security threats to the convention. As the counterterrorism analyst for MSNBC, I was kept hanging around their makeshift studio. The temporary studio had an elevated and breathtaking view of Independence Hall. I felt the pride of Jefferson, Franklin, and the others who had come to that spot to tirelessly create history. In the air was a feeling of jubilation and the inevitability that America would overwhelmingly reject the hatred, bigotry, and mean-spiritedness of the previous week displayed at the Republican convention.

The Republican convention in Cleveland, and its process to nominate self-described billionaire Donald J. Trump as their candidate for President, was a visceral parade of grievance, rejection, and near-open appeals to racism. It became apparent to everyone watching, even a lifelong Republican myself, that the party would show a willingness to fight as dirty as possible and go as deep into the mud as one could go—and maybe a step lower. The convention was accurately reported as a massive grievance fest.

While the Republican convention unfolded, numerous shenanigans to get rid of Trump were floated and shot down among the party establishment. In the end, the Republicans nominated arguably the most divisive person to run for President since Abraham Lincoln—and we all know how that ended.

Consequently, the Democratic Party was poised to stand on a platform of cooperation, strength through diversity, compassion, and love. First Lady Michelle Obama's slogan "When they go low, we go high" would resonate with Hillary Clinton's supporters. It would allow Bernie Sanders's following to come together with Clinton's and close ranks in the way she'd done with Barack Obama's nomination in 2008. Everyone looked forward to a rousing party.

At my Independence Hall standby location, I kept watch just in case a terrorist group or individual would attempt to break up the Hillary lovefest with guns, bombs, or worse. There were no indications of a terrorist threat, but for almost four months I had been aware of a different kind of threat. As part of my continuing counterterrorism study, I had been drafting a manuscript for a new book titled *Hacking ISIS*. I was writing it with my chief researcher and coauthor Chris Sampson. We had been working on the manuscript for more than a year to provide the deepest dive on the terrorist group's success at hijacking social media. While researching ISIS's tactics, we came across two efforts that seemed at odds with the terrorist's capabilities: the hacking of TV5 in Paris, a major television network that broadcasts internationally to the entire francophone world, and the Warsaw Stock Exchange. On the surface, both of these efforts were carried out by hackers of the Islamic State terrorist group, but forensic analysis showed that the entity used in conducting the attack was confirmed to be FANCY BEAR. I watched with interest when news of the WikiLeaks trove came out. One glance at the data revealed to me that they had the stolen DNC information that had been taken by COZY BEAR and FANCY BEAR. WikiLeaks was clearly acting as a Russian laundromat for stolen material.

It immediately became clear to me, and my brothers and sisters in

US Intelligence, that a massive cyberwarfare operation was afoot. I had been the first to publicly declare on national television that the United States had been subjected to a wide-ranging cyber-and political warfare attack. My breathless warning was, in reality, an intelligence estimate. My call to alarm was based on my background as a career cryptologic collections operative in Naval Intelligence. I was heir to the legacy of the codebreakers and analysts who had seen the bread crumbs that led to numerous victories, such as the Battle of Midway and Operation Desert Storm, and failures including Pearl Harbor and 9/11. Although my career background was in Middle Eastern state sponsors of terrorism and warfare from Libya to Syria to Afghanistan, I was a child of the Cold War spy world. When I was first read into the Top Secret code word world, the first briefings were not about Libyan spies, Saddam's assassins, or Iranian VEVAK agents—it was a massive counterintelligence indoctrination on the activities and operations of the former Russian intelligence agency, the *Komitet Gosudarstvennoy Bezopasnosti* (the KGB). The KGB was a worldwide threat during the Cold War that enveloped every intelligence operative and analyst in the West. Their ability to identify, seduce, and turn intelligence professionals into spies who betray their own nation was legendary. The counterintelligence motto was "Beware of the Bears. The Bears are Everywhere!" Their military forces were our primary targets but their spies were far less visible and insidious. The motto was true. Throughout most of my career, the KGB (and its successors the FSB and SVR) was literally everywhere our missions took us. A souk in Marrakech, a café in the Casbah in Algiers, a men's room in Naples, or a bar in Port Said: There they were. The KGB knew where Americans were and had assets or agents looking to surveil, engage, and recruit. KGB officers and propagandists routinely criticized our military activities, funded terrorists from the Irish Republican Army (via one of my targets, Libya), and ran Palestinian insurgency training camps in the deserts of Syria and the refugee camps of Southern Lebanon. They facilitated dictators and despots across the Eastern Hemisphere. Annually we were briefed on Russian intelligence operations that were enmeshed with our targets everywhere, from Iraq to Spain.

When I added one and one together with the DNC hack, the Guccifer 2.0 blog, and the WikiLeaks data dump, it was an obvious large-scale, old-school KGB-style Russian information warfare operation. It could have but one goal—elect Donald Trump president. It was bold. It was daring and it could only have been directed by Vladimir Putin. I said this loudly and repeatedly throughout the campaign. However, there was much skepticism. I was not alone in my analysis of the bread crumbs. But the news media were interested in the emails and not the source. The more stolen data that were released, the more voraciously the media covered the story. Television and internet news consumed with reports of "emails" had little critical analysis. The actual emails revealed nothing. But the word was in the air. After a month's hiatus (to turn the data over to WikiLeaks), Guccifer 2.0 popped back up to work in concert with WikiLeaks. They released freshly stolen documents that revealed another Democratic Party institution had been hacked. This time it was the Democratic Congressional Campaign Committee (DCCC). In addition, a disturbing pattern was emerging: When Donald Trump gave speeches complaining about a certain subject, within days entire dumps of DNC and DCCC emails on that subject would hit the news media from both Guccifer 2.0 and WikiLeaks. For example, emails on Pennsylvania and Florida primaries were released soon after Trump mentioned them. When he disparaged Nancy Pelosi, a huge tranche of documents on her was released. The flood continued with the entire DNC databases for New Hampshire, Ohio, Illinois, and North Carolina hitting the streets—all Democratic battleground states that Trump eventually won. I spent days on television warning that there was a cyberwar designed to destroy the Democratic Party and tilt the election in favor of Donald Trump. Aside from MSNBC, the news media largely ignored the spy story unfolding before their eyes and breathlessly awaited new stolen tranches.

On August 21, Roger Stone, the Nixonian Republican dirty trickster, hinted that he had advance information about the WikiLeaks releases on John Podesta, the campaign chairman of the Clinton team. He tweeted that "Podesta's time in the barrel will come."[1] A statement such as this was perplexing at the time, but it appeared to be

Stone's classic foreshadowing of a dirty political trick. A few weeks later it would become one of the first of many signs of possible collusion between Trump supporters and Russia via their laundromat, WikiLeaks.

Like clockwork, in mid-September 2016 a new website, DCLeaks, suspected of being another Russian front, published email chains from John Podesta. Some of which included messages to Hillary Clinton but did not expose anything more sinister than a risotto recipe. That was the least of it. September and October brought an endless flood of leaks. DC Leaks released the schedules of key Clinton staff and a copy of Michelle Obama's passport.[2] Each of them appeared to be timed to whatever bad news the Trump team was facilitating at the time.

The impact of the stolen email flood was to keep the US news media fed with day-after-day coverage of Democratic Party emails. It didn't matter that they were extremely benign or that none of them was from Hillary Clinton's email server; the media ate it up.

Spy Hunters of the World, Unite!

Soon after the release of the Guccifer 2.0 data, a serious question was being asked aloud by the more enlightened global punditry: Was Trump's team working with Russia? The fact that the Trump team insisted on removing a core platform piece on the arming of Ukraine made many eyebrows rise. That was a key Russian desire that had never been entertained. But now...?

Coordinated or not, both Russia and the Republicans played the email scandal brilliantly. Initially conceived as a ploy to hammer Clinton on the grounds of national security during the Benghazi hearings, Republicans would come to work in sync with the conservative media on the matter of emails. Websites such as InfoWars and Brietbart News claimed all the releases showed criminal intent. They saw each email release as proof that the Clinton machine was corrupt beyond all reason.

On October 4, 2016, just as Donald Trump was accusing the Clinton Foundation of corruption, Guccifer 2.0 claimed to have hacked the

Foundation's servers. The documents were actually from the DCCC batch, but the Republicans and the news media treated it like gospel. Trump hyped this news even as his own foundation was revealed to have been used to funnel money into his family coffers.

If Trump was not in conspiracy with Russia then his mouth did him no favors. As early as July 27, 2016, just 48 hours after the disastrous DNC opening day, Trump appealed to Moscow to hack and release even more emails. Trump said, "By the way, if they hacked, they probably have her 33,000 emails. I hope they do. They probably have her 33,000 emails that she lost and deleted.... Russia, if you're listening, I hope you're able to find the 30,000 emails that are missing."

To US intelligence and counterintelligence agencies and professionals, this statement would be a key point from which to piece the data together that would lead to the most serious national security investigation in American history. The question on the table became: Were Americans working in concert with a foreign intelligence agency to elect a President? Unbeknownst to Donald Trump and the American public, the spy hunt for a conspiracy with Russia was already under way.

Trump was suspected to be a Russian asset much earlier than his "Russia, if you're listening" speech. One person with doubts was John Brennan, the soft-spoken but tough Director of the CIA who had worked for the clandestine service for over 25 years. He held the position of CIA station chief in Saudi Arabia and specialized in counterterrorism. However, he was an old-school spy. He was well schooled in Russian intelligence operations. As the CIA Director during the 2016 elections, any information related to Russian shenanigans during the election would have fallen under his purview. Early in 2016 he would be informed of the DNC hack and Russian efforts to co-opt members of Trump's campaign. Brennan would task his agency's Russia team to work with the National Security Agency to scrub what information they had so President Obama could be briefed. He sent out feelers to intelligence agencies around the world for information. Soon, three allied foreign intelligence agencies would bring him and the Director of National Intelligence, James Clapper, unambiguous intelligence that Russia was going in strong to win the election for Donald Trump.

US Intelligence and the counterintelligence spy hunters of the FBI now understood they were dealing with something completely different than the cyber-espionage officers assisting in the DNC hack. We intelligence officers are suspicious of coincidences. In the spy world, coincidences just don't exist. I coined the phrase "Nance's Law" to remind new operatives that, in the shadows of espionage, "coincidence takes a lot of planning." By midsummer, the intelligence community was awash with more than coincidences: They had "Red Flags." Red Flag was a Cold War–era counterintelligence term that meant Russian intelligence active measures were suspected or detected. One set of Red Flags stood out: The FBI and other agencies had learned that members of the Trump campaign were meeting with Russians virtually everywhere. Worse, they were denying the meetings had happened. By election time, there would be at least 12 senior administration or campaign officials who held 19 face-to-face meetings and/or had more than 51 communications with Russians associated with the Kremlin. Most of them would deny these contacts until confronted and then would claim coincidence. Obviously, they were hiding something. But what?

The Storm of Chaos

The FBI's National Security Branch (NSB) is a group of highly specialized counterintelligence officers who seek out enemy spies and terrorists in the United States. For almost 80 years, the NSB and its predecessors tracked down espionage threats when they arrived on American shores. From Soviet Communist agents sent by Stalin, Nazi saboteurs landed by Hitler, or al-Qaeda and ISIS sleeper cells, the NSB does one thing: watch, hunt, detect, and capture enemy agents.

Early in spring 2016, intelligence was flowing in from the CIA and NSA that something was afoot with the hacking of the DNC. Reports that Americans were in contact with known Russian assets and agents soon followed. British news media reported that Signals Intelligence (known as SIGINT) was coming in from the British counterpart to the American NSA—the British Government Communications Headquarters (GCHQ).[3] NATO sister agencies in Europe were also warning that they had solid intelligence that Americans were in communications with known Russian intelligence officers. The director of GCHQ had personally passed this information on to DNI Clapper, CIA Director Brennan, and NSA Director Admiral Michael Rogers.

It was in March 2016 that a young man named George Papadopoulos came to the attention of the FBI and the CIA. Papadopoulos was a senior foreign policy advisor to Donald Trump who had been present at a meeting with Trump and Jeff Sessions in mid-March 2016. According to the *New York Times*, Papadopoulos inadvertently revealed his role in a plot when he bragged about his Russian connections while drinking in London with Australian diplomat Alexander Downer. Papadopoulos told Downer that Russia had thousands of Hillary Clinton's emails and intimated that they were going to benefit the campaign. Papadopoulos had found himself in contact with a Maltese citizen, Joseph Mifsud. Mifsud had met Papadopoulos in early March but had ignored him. Once Mifsud discovered Papadopoulos was a Trump campaign advisor his interest changed. They worked out a scheme to arrange a meeting between Trump and Putin. Mifsud coordinated a meeting with a young woman he called his "niece," Olga Polonskaya. She was accompanied by Ivan Timofeev, the head of a Russian academic forum tied to the Kremlin's foreign ministry. The Australian was alarmed that an American would be caught in such an obvious spy trap. Downer would report back to his superiors, who would then pass it on to Australian agents and US Intelligence. The FBI started to investigate Papadopoulos as a potential Russian asset. Eventually, Papadopoulos would be questioned about these contacts, and like virtually every other member of the Trump team, he would lie.[4] Only when arrested by the FBI would he confess the plan.

At nearly the exact same time, another Trump foreign policy advisor, Carter Page, was claiming to be a global expert in the Russian energy industry even though no one had heard of him. Page claimed to have worked for seven years for Merrill Lynch in London and Moscow. He also claimed to have been assigned to Lynch in New York as "Chief Operating Officer of the Energy and Power Group." What is known is that Page did work for three years in Moscow coordinating the merger of Gazprom and RAO UES. These relations were critical to convincing Trump of his bona fides. Trump brought him onto the campaign as an expert on Russia. Trump even mentioned him by name when asked who was on his foreign policy team. By September 2016, his name would figure highly when it was cited in a secret dossier developed by former British Secret Intelligence Service agent (MI6) Christopher Steele. Steele developed a 35-page package of rumors and observations about Donald Trump and his campaign based on information gathered by his former spy contacts. He worked these tips up into a dossier for Fusion GPS, a political research group hired first by conservative donors working for Ted Cruz and then Democrat donors. In the Steele dossier, Page's name came up in relation to an oil deal between Exxon and Russian oil giant Rosneft. When this became public, Page quickly left the campaign.

Upon further inquiry, the FBI spy hunters would find these two low-level staffers were the least of the contacts. An investigation by the *New York Times* of Trump's campaign manager, Paul Manafort, would expose his ties to the Kremlin through his illicit dealings in Ukraine. Former Director of the Defense Intelligence Agency Michael Flynn earned tens of thousands of dollars speaking to *Russia Today*. He even sat next to Putin at their 10th anniversary dinner along with American Green Party head Jill Stein.[5] Other higher-ranked Americans had met secretly with Russians and were caught lying about it, including Attorney General Jeff Sessions and the President's son-in-law, Jared Kushner. They were all found to have been in contact with Moscow. US Intelligence and the FBI were now on the case.

While the news media mused about the coincidences, the global intelligence community was hard at work running down the perpetrators of the hacks. One agency was the Dutch General Intelligence and Security Service (*Algemene Inlichtingen en Veiligheidsdienst*, or AVID). AVID was a European intelligence ally that maintained a highly regarded cyberwarfare division. It was a small, classified program that developed a highly specialized computer warfare capability to counter Russian intelligence operations. AVID was part of an international intelligence-sharing agreement by NATO nations that allocated targets set by the two major signals intelligence powers, NSA and GCHQ. Each nation had its strengths and weaknesses. Where highly refined exploitation was required, every nation in NATO contributed. In cyber operations, AVID was exceptional and was given one of the toughest nuts in the world to crack—they hacked Russian intelligence's own offices. The story of how the Dutch managed to exploit the FSB was broken by national newspaper *de Volkskrant.* For several years AVID had been focusing on Russian cyberwarfare operations related to the FSB.[6] As a counter to Russian hacks against NATO, the Pentagon, the White House, and France, the Dutch had developed highly specialized exploitation tools and techniques that allowed them to geographically track Russian Army intelligence systems. The Dutch formed a Joint SIGINT Cyber Unit made up of federal civilian and military intelligence staffers tasked with attacking hostile networks. Their specialty was COZY BEAR. Using secret methodologies, they were able to pinpoint the location of the servers to a building in Moscow. In a stroke of brilliance, they counter-hacked the security cameras on one particular floor of the building and observed the Russian spies using the system.[7]

CIA Director John Brennan reported the AVID and other agencies' intelligence on the Russian campaign to James Clapper. The intelligence picture was disturbing. It revealed Russia was conducting a massive active-measures operation against the United States election. As information started to pour into the major intelligence agencies, John Brennan was made the point man for processing the traffic by President Obama. DNI Clapper was the overall coordinator and policy manager for the 17 US intelligence agencies that were collecting the information. Brennan and Clapper agreed the Russian attack required a forceful American response. On August 4, 2016, at the direction of Obama, Brennan personally telephoned the director of the Russian intelligence agency, FSB chief Aleksandr Bortnikov. According to his testimony before the House Intelligence Committee, Brennan warned Bortnikov that the United States was aware of their operations and that it would damage relations between the two countries. Apparently, Putin knew Americans better than that. By September, Russian WikiLeaks email releases accelerated. The ex-director of the CIA would later tell the

House Intelligence Committee, "It should be clear to everyone Russia brazenly interfered in our 2016 Presidential Election process and that they undertook these activities despite our strong protests and explicit warning that they do not do so...."[8]

Brennan was then tasked by Clapper and President Obama to notify the key members of Congress—the "Gang of Eight"—of what was going on.[9] When Brennan brought him the indicators that a Russian active-measures operation was occurring on a large scale, he was assigned by the White House to coordinate with the intelligence community on the extent and impact of Russia's influence. Brennan complied and gave a series of briefs and phone calls to convince the senior national leaders that the United States had been attacked.

According to the *New York Times*, only Senate Majority Leader Mitch McConnell demurred. He actively worked to keep Russia's name out of a joint letter denouncing intrusion. McConnell, like Trump, refused to believe much of the underlying intelligence on the hacking.

By the end of July, suspicions had set fire to former intelligence professionals working in the news media and on the Clinton campaign. Though many of us did not have access to what was known at the CIA and NSA, it was apparent that the bread crumbs we were seeing in the media and the whispers from former colleagues of suspicious activity were setting off alarms.

Michael Morrell was a former Deputy Director of the CIA. He had also been acting director of the agency for three years until John Brennan took over the job. Morrell was a studious man and, though he was an informal advisor to the Clinton campaign, he had kept his opinions to himself. By August 2016, he too was seeing the writing on the wall. Trump's incessant positive references to Vladimir Putin and covering for Russia's hacking led Morrell to publicly endorse Hillary Clinton in the *New York Times*. In his op-ed, he suggested that Trump was an "unwitting agent" for Russian intelligence. Morrell went further, adding that Trump is "not only unqualified for the job, but he may well pose a threat to our national security." Those were big words from a CIA officer, but as a former acting director he was part of an extremely small club of directors who still have access to classified information—and one another. He was dropping more than a hint; he was offering an unclassified assessment of the same CIA/NSA intelligence projection that would land on the desk of President Obama just 30 days later. Morrell warned that Russia wanted Trump as President.[10]

On October 31, 2016, President Obama had became so concerned he made a bold move. He picked up the "Red Phone," the war decon-fliction hotline between the United States and Russian leaders, and he personally warned Vladimir Putin that America was aware of their operation and that any acts on Election Day would be seen in the harshest light. Putin did not care. The mission was to hack the minds of the American public and it was a complete success.

On October 7, 2016, President Obama had decided that the nation needed to know about the intelligence he had about the DNC hacking. He appeared on national TV and declared that Russia had conducted the DNC hacking and that the election was at risk. Clapper's statement said, "The U.S. Intelligence Community is confident that the Russian Government directed the recent compromises of e-mails from U.S. persons and institutions, including from U.S. political organizations...."[11] He continued, saying that the unnamed Vladimir Putin had ordered these reports. "We believe, based on the scope and sensitivity of these efforts, that only Russia's senior-most officials could have authorized these activities."[12]

Later in 2017, a member of the House Intelligence Committee asked John Brennan if he saw collusion between the Trump campaign and Russia and he answered, "I saw information and intelligence that was worthy of investigation by the [FBI] to determine whether or not such cooperation or collusion was taking place....I encountered and am aware of information and intelligence that revealed contacts and interactions between Russian officials and US persons involved in the Trump campaign."[13]

Unfortunately, the news of the day was not that Intelligence and Homeland Security leadership were accusing Russia of intruding in the American election, but of the *Access Hollywood* tape. That same day, news broke of a tape made years earlier of Trump confessing to sexual assaults and affairs. Trump bragged about conquering women and how one should "grab 'em by the pussy." Not 25 minutes after Trump's tape was revealed, WikiLeaks started pumping out newly stolen Podesta emails. But to no avail: The media was in a tizzy over the "pussy" comments. A national warning had been sounded but thanks to the salacious nature of the news media, the American public didn't really hear it.

Trump remained loyal to his commitment to protect Russia. When asked two days later about Russian hacking he said, "...maybe there is no hacking!" While Trump was in denial about Russian interference a new threat to the election was emerging. Thirty-six hours after the *Access Hollywood* tape reveal, investigators at the Federal Election Commission, DHS, and FBI would announce that Russia had hacked into the servers of a subcontractor handling voter rolls in Florida.[14] In the end, more than 25 other states had learned of attempts to penetrate their voter roll databases as well.[15] Russian access to the voter rolls could allow them to change party affiliation and registration status, which could disenfranchise hundreds of thousands of voters and tilt a close election to a preferred candidate. The hyper-partisan nature of the campaign led many Secretaries of State to deny the attempts. All of this worked to the advantage of Russian operations to sow chaos into the narrative of the 2016 election. In the campaign, the heat of the Russian investigation was starting to take its toll. During the final presidential debate Hillary Clinton directly stated that Putin wanted to install Trump as a "puppet" and Trump's only rebuttal was to childishly repeat over and over, "No, you're the puppet!"[16]

WikiLeaks's impact on the news media contributed greatly to the perception that Hillary Clinton was unfit for the presidency due to repeated stories about her emails and secure server. A Google word cloud for news coverage of Clinton during the 2016 campaign showed that one word blotting out all others: "E-MAILS."[17]

On November 8, 2016, nearly 139 million Americans voted. Late in the evening it became apparent that Donald J. Trump would become the 45th President of the United States. Hillary Clinton had blown Trump away in the popular vote, winning that by 2,864,974 more votes, but it mattered not. America uses the Electoral College system, in which a certain number of votes are allotted to each state. The candidate who wins 270 of these votes is the winner, no matter what the popular vote. Trump won 306 Electoral College votes. When the votes were finally tallied, Trump won three critical Electoral College–vote-heavy states by flipping just 77,000 former Obama voters in Pennsylvania, Michigan, and Wisconsin. When the election night dust settled, he was the President-elect.

The unlikely victory of Donald Trump for President of the United States astounded the world. No one thought it possible that he could overcome the long odds and rise from reality TV star to become the most powerful man in the world. It was an unthinkable possibility that had unfolded. Trump brought a wave of "populism" from the American hinterlands. It played in the global media as the stirring story of a groundswell of American conservatism and the ultimate rejection of liberal values and policies. In Trump's vision of America, the election was a referendum on the nation's true heart. The rural American "silent majority" had risen and rebelled against the harsh economic tides and desecration of traditions and sought nothing more than to make itself great again. During his campaign, Donald Trump promised a nationalist "America First!" movement that would take them back to an America they could recognize—an America that existed before civil rights, urban riots, and political correctness. Trump's America had not existed since 1963; the year before the Civil Rights Act gave blacks and women full equality, and where coal and steel was the heart of the American engine. He resolved to take it right back there.

In the eyes of his voters, the promise of a renewed America under Donald Trump would return the nation of Washington, Lincoln, and Reagan to a greatness lost under Barack Obama. It was a fantasy based on pure hatred of the first black President. The first dark sprouts of an authoritarian ideology presented themselves in Trump's inauguration speech. He described a dark vision of the United States as he saw it in his mind, not as it was.

Trump's reliance on the poor and uneducated would become a hallmark of his campaign. He mobilized a base of white hatred not seen since before WWII, when the original "America First" movement wanted closer ties to Nazi Germany and refused to accept Jewish refugees into America. When he told the world at a press conference at the Nevada primary, "I love the poorly educated," he was mobilizing a new base that had long been forgotten by the GOP establishment and who would never vote Democrat—poor, racist white men and women.

Trump's gambit relied on ignorance, hatred of fellow countrymen, and a silent belief by his voters that White Nationalism was a right. Trump deemed them "The Silent Majority," which was typified by 19th-century Prussian philosopher Alexander von Humboldt. "The most dangerous worldview is the worldview of those who have not viewed the world."[18] It signified that a large swath of the American public had abandoned core values such as freedom for all, inclusiveness through diversity, and the power of the American Dream for immigrants. The election of Trump was an open effort to move the United States away from a democracy that protected the rights of the minority, the literal definition of a republic, and toward a nation ruled by "a strong man"—an autocracy.

CHAPTER 2

Reporting to Moscow

Democracy is the belief that together we can make each generation better than the last. Trumpism is the belief that only one man, actin' in his own best interest, will miraculously make our lives better.

—T-Pain

D onald J. Trump is a millionaire developer who fancied himself a billionaire; a malignant narcissist whose sole concern was for his money and his ego. Trump was easily led by a golden nose ring when he was complimented on his business prowess, flooded with beautiful women, and shown riches that he could never attain. He held a devilish aspect that was belied by his real idiocy and poor-little-rich-boy appeal to the "common man." He was the archetype of the American that Putin's old organization, the Soviet-era KGB, had been turning into spies, assets, and useful idiots for over 70 years.

The mindset of Russian intelligence is that Americans are full of themselves; over-preening fools who believe they alone can change the world, yet always need someone else's money to do it. It is a sucker's nation without strength of character or manliness. Had the Soviet Union had the financial resources to be on par with the United States, America's downfall would have happened before the USSR itself fell. If the USSR had acquired Western wealth, America would have been eaten hollow like Swiss cheese at a mouse convention. When the Soviet

Union fell and the Russian Federation gained billions in oil wealth, Putin would set out to do just this.

By 2000, Soviet Communism was out and mass consumerism was in, fueled by selling off massive parts of the Soviet economy. The new Russian Federation was a hybrid of the old Soviet Union, with a love of authoritarianism and modern economic power. By 2007, Vladimir Putin would have the technological means to make use of a player like Donald Trump.

Russian intelligence transformed from a paper-based organization of old, wily alcoholics to a younger, faster, technologically savvy organization. However, some skill sets were core-valued—foreigners were evaluated and made ready to be Moscow's spies. The potential spies and assets they contacted and recruited were collected like trinkets and, when their time came, they would be turned, given orders, and deployed to spy on their own nation. Intelligence officers are trained to handle each potential asset differently. A good human intelligence officer could handle a person like Donald Trump, where he or she would get the person to do his or her bidding unknowingly while he—the poor victim—remains unknowledgeable about who he or she works for and the real objective of the spy's mission. In intelligence work, these are called the *Unwitting Assets*. If an asset figures out that a spy is handling him, but the rewards make it worth his while, he becomes a *Witting Asset*. Other assets need much more subtlety. Some personalities will do work for a spy or a propagandist without any prompting, particularly when they share common ground with spies. Often these persons will contribute to the cause without concern so long as they benefit, especially if their efforts are paved with money; they are called *Useful Idiots* by the intelligence community. The Useful Idiots are often manipulated with financial payments or recognition for their influence. Those who seek no reward but cooperate purely for shared ideology are the *Fellow Travelers*. Under the Soviet intelligence system, Fellow Travelers were the least desirable of the assets. They were fickle and because they believed what you believed, only with more fervor, they were often pushing a more ideologically pure line. Worse, if they turned on officers, they could cause serious damage should they go public and reveal your operations. Their repentance would be solidified by their depth of knowledge. They can burn you with credibility, but the influence of Fellow Travelers is deep and can reach areas no foreign intelligence officer could touch in some societies. If carefully handled, they could become a perfect *Fifth Column*—workers on the inside who corrupt and sabotage their own countries. Between 2010 and 2016, Russia would successfully craft a league of Fellow Travelers in the West including a whole new branch of Fifth Columnists in America.

So what about the hapless American President? What category does he fit? It will be easily revealed that to Russia, Donald Trump started as a Useful Idiot, and then became an Unwitting Asset, but quickly became a Witting Asset once he realized that Russia was working in his best interest.

Trump's usefulness to Moscow was critical to their goal of breaking links between America and its traditional allies. Trump has lived up to that expectation. Within the first year of his presidency, Trump managed to insult virtually every ally, neighboring country, international treaty body, and all of Africa, the Middle East, and Asia. Yet Vladimir Putin held such sway over him that it would take almost 15 months and a brazen chemical weapons attack to offer the first mild criticism.

This sycophancy had an effect. By early 2018, as much as 65% of America is permanently alienated from Trump's administration, as it has become increasingly clear that he is determined to rule only for his 35% core constituency. No matter, Trump views anyone who did not vote for him as alien: Non-voters and opposition are unworthy of his attention. He wants to lead and reward those who elected him and no others. Policies have been designed to punish the major Blue States that had the nerve to vote for Hillary Clinton. His only piece of major legislation, a massive 1-trillion-dollar tax cut to the ultra-wealthy, included many provisions that raised taxes on states like California and New York, and cut them for the impoverished deep-Red States like Alabama and Mississippi.

A figure like Trump was bound to come up in American history: a man who rigged the system for his own benefit and rode the wave of populism to win. The Founding Fathers warned of such an event. Over two centuries ago, in 1792, Alexander Hamilton predicted Trump's strategy to divide America. The new nation was an agrarian society that had just come through a baptismal fire. It had beaten a massive army and formed a new type of governance. However, those who won this victory were relatively uneducated, prone to conspiracy theories, easily led by false-hoods, and generally a rabble that looked to the educated and wealthy to navigate the political waves. The brilliance of those educated men of enlightenment, for all their flaws, shone a light on America's susceptibil-ity to being conned by a fraud. Hamilton said, "The truth unquestionably is, that the only path to a subversion of the republican system of the country is by flattering the prejudices of the people, and exciting their jealousies and apprehensions, to throw affairs into confusion, and bring on civil commotion...."[1] Throughout American history, those confusions and commotions have sprung forth in the form of rebellions, clashes, and civil war. Yet America had never been tested with a leader who had the same mindset of King George III; a monarch who ignored the voice of the majority, who ruled as he lived above the rest, and cared not a whit about the traditions of the free society in America.

Trump lived for the con man's game. He also brought the persona of a larger-than-life cartoon—the "professional" wrestler—to the cam-paign trail. Before he entered politics, he was a man who had appeared on wrestling shows and enjoyed the spectacle of riling a crowd of young children and the great blue-collar worker. Trump played him-self, an indifferent rich guy with a giant fake million-dollar check to the delight of the audiences. He understood the pantomime of giving the public heroic characters and evil villains. All these Punch-and-Judy traits helped propel him into the White House.

Within a few months of the election, what was a once a recog-nizable republic was backsliding down the guardrails of law and jus-tice, and careening toward a totalitarian family and single-party nation much less like King George's monarchy and more like the Borgias—a medieval papal crime family that held power through nepotism, mur-der, corruption, and deceit.

In less than a few months, Trump had done more damage to America's political world order than any event since WW II. Diplomacy was dead.

His chosen Secretary of State, Exxon CEO and friend of Vladimir Putin Rex Tillerson, lasted only one year. When Tillerson publicly criticized Russia on a chemical weapons assassination in London, Trump fired him by tweet. Jared Kushner, Trump's son-in-law, and his wife, Ivanka, were sent to address state issues that bypassed all of America's diplomats. To fill the void, the military was ordered to step into the breach as the principal voice of American power. The nation went from managing a dying terrorist insurgency to talks of a sneak attack nuclear war on the Korean peninsula or a disastrous war with Iran. The State Department's website removed "spreading democracy" from its mission statement.

Trump's standing with the American public went into immediate free fall. By January 2018, 53% of the nation rated his administration as a failure, 57% said the country was headed in the wrong direction, and 61% would assert that he had divided the country. Majorities disapproved of his handling of virtually every policy he had proposed, from immigration to foreign policy. His personal approval rating of 37% was rated as a historic low, beating George W. Bush, who had one of the worst rankings after his disastrous invasion of Iraq, which had smashed the last vestiges of stability in the Middle East. America's worldwide standing plummeted as well, and the US under Bush was rated at 39% approval. Under Barack Obama, the ratings had risen to 55%. Trump almost equaled Bush's status when it dropped to 42% approval in less than 12 months.

Yet for Donald Trump, planned and unplanned chaos is his guiding star. In his mind, his style of daring risk-taking honed in the New York City real estate market would translate well to big wins politically and admiration globally. That was not to be, but in the hermetically sealed world of conservative politics he only saw success where the world saw a disaster. Trump saw his first year in office as a smashing success because when he visited towns like Altoona, Pennsylvania, he was cheered by people who looked like him and clung to his every word. Praise on Fox News, public applause, and laurels given in his presence were his measures of success. The reality of the nation's descent would be precipitous, terrifying, and maddening—but only for the 260 million Americans who did not vote for him.

Erasing the Bear Tracks:
The Firing of FBI Director Comey

Now that Trump held the reins of power, he thought that he was capable of hiding any offenses he might have made in his past life or his relationships with Moscow. He took his first step to hide his relationship with Putin early in February 2017, when FBI Director James Comey was invited by Trump to the White House for a dinner. During the meeting, Comey claimed that President Trump asked him more than once to consider stopping the investigation into General Mike Flynn. General Flynn, the former Director of the Defense Intelligence Agency, was under a National Security investigation related to the lies he told about his phone calls with the Russian Ambassador in December 2016. Acting Attorney General Sally Yates had informed the White House that Flynn was at risk of blackmail since only the Russians knew what was said in the conversation and could hold it over his head. Trump said to Comey, "I hope you can see your way clear to letting this go, to letting Flynn go....He is a good guy. I hope you can let this go."[2] Comey was noncommittal, and after leaving the meeting he immediately drafted a memo detailing what Trump had said and informed his deputies what had transpired.

A few months later, on May 9, 2017, in a surprising move the White House announced that President Trump had fired James Comey. The firing required Deputy Attorney General Rod Rosenstein to find cause to remove him from office. Rosenstein was directed to draft a 2½ page memo with the justification. Comey's letter of removal was delivered to the FBI headquarters by Trump's longtime bodyguard Keith Schiller. The memo noted that Comey had fumbled "handling of the conclusion of the investigation of Secretary [Hillary] Clinton's emails." This accusation was outrageous since Trump himself benefited from said handling. Clinton believed the "Comey statement" in the last week of the election was critical as it gave the impression that she was under investigation, which was not true. In fact, the Trump White House was also furious at Comey for not revealing to Trump his testimony in advance of a hearing on the Flynn and Russia investigation.[3] More likely Trump was angry because he could not stop the Russia investiga-tion or the inquiry into Mike Flynn's susceptibility to blackmail.

The backlash was withering. When the news hit the wires, Trump was deluged with negative comments. His staff said he was personally taken aback by the outrage. He tried to justify the firing. "[Comey] wasn't doing a good job, very simply. He wasn't doing a good job." In his letter to Comey, Trump claimed the FBI Director had told him "on three separate occasions, that I am not under investigation."[4] Trump assumed that like on his reality TV show, he could fire people at will. It also stunned him that Democrats, who had severely criticized Comey, were not siding with him and cheering him on. He tweeted, "The Democrats have said some of the worst things about James Comey, including the fact that he should be fired, but now they play so sad!"[5]

Trump's tweetstorm continued with a lie that was equally as outra-geous. "Comey lost the confidence of almost everyone in Washington, Republican and Democrat alike. When things calm down, they will be thanking me!"[6] Displeased with the public backlash, Trump resorted to fantasy and made up fantastical, near-pathological lies. "He cried like a baby and begged for forgiveness...and now he is judge & jury. He should be the one who is investigated for his acts."[7]

Amazingly, the day after firing Comey, Trump kept a meeting with Russian Foreign Minister Sergey Lavrov and Ambassador Sergey Kisl-yak at the White House. Though the optics of meeting with Russians the day after attempting to stop an investigation into his contacts with Russia were alarming, even more surprising was that US news media was forbidden to cover the meeting. But Trump allowed a Russian news media photographer into the Oval Office.[8] During the meeting, Trump bragged to Lavrov about how he got rid of the FBI Director, "I just fired the head of the FBI. He was crazy, a real nut job...."[9] As if to impress the Russians, he blurted out, "I faced great pressure because of Russia. That's taken off." The Russian photographer took pictures of Trump huddled together with the two diplomats as if sharing a joke. It was no joke when, soon after, reports emerged that during that same meeting Trump had compromised a highly compartmented top-secret Israeli spy mission in Syria to the Russians.[10]

If there were doubts about Trump's intention to cover up the Russia investigation for the Kremlin and himself it was wiped clean within 48 hours. A few days later Trump granted an interview with NBC News's Lester Holt. During the interview Holt asked a series of questions about the firing of Director Comey. Trump was nonplussed. If he had stayed on message with the story the Attorney General had helped him manufacture he would likely have gotten away with it. But Trump has a predictable pattern of masticating the truth. His usual pattern is to 1) Lie; 2) Dissemble; 3) Spread Disinformation; 4) Confess; 5) Threaten. After trying numerous stories about why Comey needed to be fired because he was hated by the FBI, "He's a showboat, he's a grandstander, the FBI has been in turmoil" (lie), he then claimed that he only went by the recommendation of Rod Rosenstein (dissemble). Trump attempted to spread more false stories about Comey (disinformation): "You know that, I know that. Everybody knows that. You take a look at the FBI a year ago, it was in virtual turmoil, less than a year ago. It hasn't recovered from that." Finally Trump, not realizing he was committing perjury, told the truth:

TRUMP: What I did is, I was going to fire Comey. My decision.
   It was not—
HOLT: You had made the decision before they came in the room.
TRUMP: I was going to fire Comey. There's no good time to do it, by the way.
HOLT: Because in your letter you said, "I accepted their recommendation."
TRUMP: Well, they also—
HOLT: So, you had already made the decision.
TRUMP: Oh, I was going to fire regardless of recommendation.[11]

Trump seemed to be completely unaware that he had contradicted days of statements. He also seemed unaware that firing an FBI Director to stop an investigation into potential espionage was the textbook definition of "obstruction of justice."[12]

Trapped by the news media, Trump then claimed that there were tapes of the conversation in an effort to intimidate Comey. He didn't seem to understand that this also was a potential additional obstruction of justice charge. "James Comey better hope that there are no 'tapes' of our conversations before he starts leaking to the press!"[13] The White House would eventually have to admit there were no tapes.

Trump was hell-bent on defending himself from the accusation of collusion but never disputed the fact that he wanted to be friends with Putin. If his co-option by Moscow was unwitting then it could have been seen as an acceptable reflex to protect himself. But Trump's behaviors and defenses went far beyond a man out to defend his honor. He made it clear that he would defend Moscow—even above himself—at every turn. Whatever effect he thought he would achieve by firing Comey was then magnified when Deputy Attorney General Rod Rosenstein would submit to political pressure and appoint a Special Counsel to investigate Trump's ties to Russia. No better investigator could have been chosen for the task. Robert Swan Mueller III was a Vietnam War combat veteran, Silver Star winner, federal prosecutor, and Director of the FBI for three Presidents. He reorganized and revitalized the bureau after 9/11 and was deeply admired throughout Washington. He was the last man Donald Trump would ever want investigating him.

The Special Counsel wanted to know if Trump and his team had been party to a foreign intelligence operation that may have damaged American democracy. All the evidence pointed to a tribe that was active in conspiracy with the Kremlin and with financial ties that were beyond suspicious. Mueller reviewed Comey's notes and set about hiring a Murderer's Row of top financial and espionage prosecutors to fill his staff. Trump was now in mortal danger from his own government, so he set out to do the only thing he knew how—he tried to fire Mueller.

According to the *New York Times*, less than 30 days after the Special Counsel had been appointed, Trump tried to fire him. White House Counsel Donald F. McGahn II was called in and informed that Rod Rosenstein was to fire Mueller.[14] Trump threatened that if Rosenstein balked, he too would be fired and the number-three official, Associate

Attorney General Rachel Brand would be appointed in his place to carry out the order. Trump argued that Mueller needed to be fired due to a conflict of interest. Trump said Mueller disputed golf fees at a Trump National Golf Club in Sterling, Virginia, and that disqualified him from investigating the administration. Trump also asserted that Mueller had worked at a law firm that represented his son-in-law, Jared Kushner. McGahn tried to disabuse the President of this course. As a lawyer he was well aware that if he carried out this order he would be participating in a crime. McGahn refused the President's request and told the President he would resign instead.

Trump backed off his demand, and when asked he lied to the press that firing Mueller had never been considered. Still, Trump decided that the Special Counsel had to be stopped. He cared not that firing FBI Director Comey had been incredibly damaging. Trump was the firing kind. A month earlier, Trump had expressed frustration that Attorney General Jeff Sessions had recused himself from the Russian probe. He later told the *New York Times* in an interview that he was frustrated with Sessions over the Russia issue. Trump said, "Sessions should have never recused himself, and if he was going to recuse himself, he should have told me before he took the job and I would have picked somebody else...."[15]

Why Did Russia Do It?

The Director of National Intelligence's report on Russian hacking concluded that "Russia's goals were to undermine public faith in the US democratic process, denigrate Secretary Clinton, and harm her electability and potential presidency.... We further assess Putin and the Russian Government developed a clear preference for President-elect Trump."[16]

Those goals were each achieved, but the larger question looms over the entire controversy: What did they intend to do by making Donald Trump President? The answer is simple: For decades, Soviet Communists in the Kremlin had spent billions of dollars and countless intelligence operations trying to achieve one goal: to reveal to the world that

American democracy was an old, dead system of government that had to be replaced. The Soviet Union could never do it, but in 2016 the Russian Federation had brought America to its knees at the speed of an election while America and its officials were still at home watching cable TV and trying to figure it out. Russia is a dictatorship led by a single, ruthless autocrat who simply had to give an order to change the fabric of the Western world. According to Russia, Trump's true destiny was to be an inaugural member of the world's newest alliance—the Axis of Autocracies.

The election of Trump led to an explosion of activity from the Russian government, including coordinating direct meetings with transition officials. All of them were designed to be hidden from US Intelligence and law enforcement. Within days of Trump's taking office, it became clear that the White House was behind Putin's number-one goal—all sanctions against Russia would be lifted. The common denominator associated with every aspect of the Trump-Russia investigations was that Moscow was desperate to get the crippling financial and personal sanctions against Vladimir Putin and his oligarchs lifted. Each investigation starting with ex-FBI Director James Comey, Special Counsel Robert Mueller, and the House and Senate Intelligence Committees found strong indicators that this was one of the core reasons for the attack on the United States.

For example, the US State Department under Rex Tillerson started seeking ways to lift the Obama-era sanctions designed to punish Russia for espionage, hacking, and violations of international law, including the invasion of Crimea and fostering an ethnic Russian insurgency in Ukraine. Retired diplomat Dan Fried told *The Hill* that almost immediately after the administration made its principal staff appointments to Foggy Bottom, "There was serious consideration by the White House to unilaterally rescind the sanctions...."

The American sanctions were not hurting the Russian economy; they were hurting the personal finances of Moscow's most elite citizens—and Vladimir Putin personally. To the Russian oligarchy the Americans were stealing bread from the mouths of their children. Granted, the bread was handcrafted *pain a l'ancienne* from their châteaux outside

Monaco, made by a French master baker who studied all the recipes of Marie Antoinette and used a 600-year-old stone oven, and was flown into Moscow 30 minutes before each meal by their own Gulfstream G650 executive jets—but it was their bread all the same. The Russian oligarchy needed American interference with their dirty money to stop the sanctions, and an ally in the Oval Office who would assist them in this endeavor. They found this in Donald Trump.

By the fall of 2017, news reports would find that virtually all of Trump's senior staff and family had numerous contacts with Russia, which were nothing short of suspicious. Less than three weeks into the job, General Michael Flynn, former Director of the Defense Intelligence Agency (DIA), would resign due to lying about secret phone calls with Russian Ambassador Kislyak. That incident would eventually have him confess and plead guilty to criminal charges of lying to the FBI. Others were quickly implicated, including Jared Kushner, husband of Ivanka Trump. He would be found to have asked Russia for a secure communication network within the Russian embassy to communicate without interception by the NSA or the CIA. He would later claim it was an innocent proposal to get Russian military information about operations in Syria to Trump. It was suspicious because the US military already had a formal liaison mission working with the Russians at their secret base near Qamishli in Northern Syria. Attorney General Jeff Sessions was found to have lied about meetings with Russians, including Kislyak, before his Senate confirmation hearing. Paul Manafort and Rick Gates, Trump's mafia consiglieri–like campaign manager and deputy campaign manager, were both so under Russian influence that they were indicted for laundering funds believed to have come from a pro-Moscow Ukrainian strongman.[17] Manafort was so uncooperative early on that the FBI carried out a predawn raid on his home to secure documents that would lead to his charges. Gates would plead guilty. George Papadopoulos was charged with lying to a federal officer and pled guilty along with Michael Flynn. Many reports would emerge about Trump's son, son-in-law, and senior advisors willfully participating in schemes to get dirt on Hillary Clinton and unwittingly repeat the Kremlin's finely tuned propaganda.

Even with all of this emerging evidence, Trump's daily refrain for almost a year was "No collusion. No collusion. No collusion." Not only was America not going to do nothing about the Kremlin's intervention in its affairs, they had two wings of the government dedicated to assisting them—through inaction and disbelief. In the House of Representatives, Devin Nunes, Trump's lackey on the House Permanent Select Committee on Intelligence, even issued his own unilateral report exonerating Trump from any collusion, while agreeing with all other intelligence findings that Russia rigged the election for him. So long as Donald Trump and his allies worked with Moscow and had control of Congress, there was little anyone else could do to stop Putin's march to do the same worldwide.

CHAPTER 3

Make Russia Great Again

The plan for winning the United States was well executed. Now, with Trump in power, Putin would facilitate the rise of other conservative political parties in Europe and would try to take control of multiple governments, starting with France. Once his plan was achieved, France, Austria, Hungary, and others would withdraw from the European Union and NATO. These new conservative parties would reestablish Europe as a bastion of Western white Christianity led by Vladimir Putin, the Charlemagne of Red Square. Marine Le Pen was his greatest hope, but even with her failure in the French election in 2017, others were rising across Europe. Just as in the US, these white Christian populists were a mélange of fascists, neo-Nazis, and racists who rode a wave of hatred for immigrants from Africa and the Middle East. Fortress Europa required strong white leaders. Moscow would engineer their rise.

Trump's success was the North Star for European and American political leadership to embrace the extreme Conservative Right. These white conservatives would take over the Western nations and reengineer the old democratic institutions and ally themselves as light autocrats. Moscow would facilitate that power with ideological guidance, money, and whatever else was necessary. Together America, Europe, and other strongmen around the world would form a political alliance. This alliance of like-minded conservative nations and their oligarchies would end the old political order that had existed since 1945. In Putin's estimation, the West, starting with the United States, would be degraded by sowing chaos, acrimony, and internal division though disruption of the electoral processes. The best way to do this would be to hijack and weaponize social media and then release it in a blizzard of attacks at the heart of the American presidential campaign. Natural enemies of liberal democracy would be elevated. This American self-destruction would allow a firmly led Russia to figuratively step over the grave of the dysfunctional United States. Russia would show staunch, unwavering leadership. Promising to other nations, such as Turkey, Egypt, Libya, and the Philippines, opportunities for future riches if they partnered with the nation that would pick up the markets when America goes to pieces.

From Peter the Great to Putin

Russia's desire to control the destiny of the Western world has existed since before the birth of the Soviet Union. Its attempts to integrate and manipulate empires have always been dynamic and prone to confrontation. The Tsars had periods of expansion where they pushed the limits internationally and repressed domestically. Russia's imperial desires expanded in the 19th century and came into direct conflict with British power in what would be called the Great Game. The Great Game was the military's diplomatic and intelligence proxy wars for control of trade routes through Central Asia, with Afghanistan at the center to South Asia. One main British goal was to stop Russia from gaining ports in the Persian Gulf to protect British trade routes from India and Arabia. Both Russia and England used military power, diplomatic missions, bribery to buy kings and warlords, and Islamic fanaticism in order to expand zones of political and economic influence. By the beginning of the 20th century, the Game had tapered off through agreements that gave Russia the dominance in Central Asia. After the birth of the Soviet Union in 1917, those regions would become Soviet Oblasts, or administrative states. The Communist leadership of the Soviet Union held dictatorial sway over Russia and sought to expand its influence worldwide by projecting its ideology. By the late 1930s, the three political ideologies that dominated the world were Communism in Russia, fascism in Germany and Italy and their ally, imperialist Japan, and

American democracy. Constitutional monarchies and liberal republics existed, but most fell under or in alliance with one of the three big ideologies. Adolf Hitler's and Mussolini's Fascists would launch a global attack to seize the world's economic leadership away from America, put an end to the British Empire, and destroy Soviet Communism.

The modern Putin foreign policy is steeped in his own history and that of the Soviet Union. Yet Putin may see himself as more of a Russian ruler of the classical period. He is not a Josef Stalin, the Communist mass-murdering dictator. He views himself more akin to Peter the Great.

Peter I was a child who came to power through palace intrigue and army revolts, but he would eventually make Russia a great diplomatic and naval power. He would also instill in Russia a near-insatiable, centuries-long desire to have access to warm water ports. As a young man, Peter wanted to understand the dynamics of other nations. He would travel clandestinely across the United Kingdom and Western Europe and live undercover as a common worker in shipyards, factories, and other points of growing technology to see firsthand how Western industry worked. He foresaw a time when Russia would be the incubator of new technology and eclipse the scientific advancements of Europe. His later military campaigns against Turkey and Persia, and a 21-year-long naval campaign in the Baltics, showed his desire to expand Russia's role among the great powers. After assisting in the rescue of drowning sailors in the Gulf of Finland, Peter would later become ill over the course of a year and die. Peter I was a man of action. A man Putin revered and who built his hometown, St. Petersburg, into a modern "Window to the West." A man Putin could admire and use as a role model. Putin wants the Russian public and his opponents to believe he is equal to the legend. Scholars on Russia's internal workings, Fiona Hill and Clifford Gaddy, believe that "Putin is less interested in presenting a particular version of reality than in seeing how others react to the information."[1] Now he portrays himself as the leader of a greater, more respected Russia. He understands the psyche of his people and appeals to them by exhibiting the best (and worst) characteristics of the greatest Russian leaders, both Communist and classical.

After the French revolution, some Russian elites thought westernization was the right course. Tsar Alexander III attempted modest liberalization of Russia in the way of the European courts. He came to power after the assassination of Alexander II by anarchist terrorists. Alexander III's heavy hand on peasants would lead to the formation of terrorist groups such as Sergey Nechayev's *Narodnaya Volya* (People's Will)—Russian anarchists who sought to spark revolt against the Tsars through selective bomb assassinations both in Russia and across Europe. The 19th-century Tsars' disastrous military operations (e.g., the Crimean and Russo-Japanese wars), and unpopular autocratic rule led to a wave of terrorism and revolution. Russia fell to a people's uprising led by the Communists and the Soviet Union replaced centuries of Tsarist rule. Vladimir Putin may have been educated by the Communists, but he presides over a relatively rich nation where a large measure of personal freedoms has been restored. Yet he moved to ensure that Russia was operating closer to the autocratic political strengths of Alexander's time. While 19th-century France was adopting "Equality. Fraternity. Liberty." Tsar Nicholas I established the official ideology of "Orthodoxy. Autocracy. Nationality." Today, Putin's national core values would be best described as "Autocracy. Oligarchy. Global Money."

Russia in the beginning of the 21st century was rich with natural resources and weapons sales flowing into the global market. It was a nation respected for its wealthy ruling class after it had cast off the constraints of Soviet Communism. Early on, many saw Putin's pragmatic cooperation with the West as helpful in building the fledgling economy. Russia was open to money, fast cars, and culture, but remained cautious of foreign encroachment. Putin's early view was that he would cooperate with the West and limit confrontation. There were places Russia found where they could work closely with the United States. The asymmetric terror capability shown by al-Qaeda in the 9/11 attacks was sure to provide a template for Chechen terrorists. It was in Russia's interest to learn what they could. However, when President George W. Bush ordered the invasion of Iraq in 2003, it brought with it old Kremlin fears of an America set on regime change. Under his successor, Dmitry Medvedev, Russia appeared to moderate, but it would be Putin's return to Red Square in 2012 that was the tipping point where that pragmatic cooperation began to erode.[2] It had become a nation led by an ex-KGB officer. Putin had personally experienced the difficulties of wrestling with foreign powers that wanted to dissect Russia, encroach on its borders, and infect it with democracy.

Another core concern for Russia was its insecure borders and large non-Russian populations. Russia had been victim to invasion for centuries. Wars, insurrections, and religious insurgencies had plagued the nation. Russia's massive oceans, freshwater seas' coastlines, and its natural treasures were often violated by foreign encroachment as well. Russia's history was rife with rulers fighting foreign invasions, whether it was the Tsars cleansing the Khanate of Astrakhan; Catherine II fighting off the Ottoman invasion in the Russo-Turkish War, or staving off Swedish fleets; Napoleon knocking at Moscow's gates; or the Soviets battling Hitler's attempt to take all of western Russia. Conflagrations crossing their borders repeatedly consumed their people and resources; they also often led to Russia's already limited access to the unfrozen seas being severed. The challenge of secure borders was doubled under Soviet Communism. The Kremlin used their secret police and border guards ruthlessly to keep the dangerous outside influences of American and European democracy away from their own people. The motto of the secret police was simple: "Nobody gets in. And definitely nobody gets out." Sealing Russia off from the outside world continued after the fall of Germany in 1945. The Soviets seized control of all nine nations they occupied and half of Germany. Under this system, people were said to live behind "The Iron Curtain." To the Soviets the corrosive influence of individualism and free will offered by democracy was their greatest threat. Western ideology became a threat equal to physical invasion. American and European liberal ideas and culture would skirt their border via Radio Free Europe and Liberty, the BBC, and even Armed Forces Radio and TV. They would combat America's effect through the aggressive use of propaganda, political intrigue, and lies.

Team Putin

Vladimir Putin would make the new Russian imperial vision possible. With almost two decades in power, he is the longest-running ruler since

Stalin. His popularity in Russia remains high with an 82% approval rating. He remains the supreme leader. As many Russians mourned the solidity of Communist authoritarianism, Putin stepped in to provide a Communist-like firm hand but with Western cash and goods. The most popular leader in Russia's last century, Putin has honed a firm belief that his destiny is aligned with Russia's. He also believes that only through his guidance can Russia's third-rate economy rise to be the top superpower. When a journalist questioned him about dominating his country's leadership, he responded with "I do not need to prove anything to anyone."[3] The words of a first-rate autocrat.

Putin is also the leader of a pure oligarchical kleptocracy. He was ranked by *Forbes* as Most Powerful Person in the World four times, and his official biography was a masterful work of hagiography designed to paint a picture that every Russian could love. Raised by a single mother, he was a loyal son and good boy whose greatest desire was to serve the nation in the KGB. The apocryphal tale is that a 13-year-old Vladimir Vladimirovich saw a public presentation by KGB officers. He told them he wanted to join. They laughed at his fervor and they advised him to go get a law degree first. He did just that and earned a law degree from Leningrad State University. He was selected for training at the Andropov Red Banner Institute of Intelligence, named after the Soviet Premier Yuri Andropov, a former KGB officer who rose to the top of the Supreme Soviet. There he learned the art of espionage. As an intelligence officer, he would need to know surveillance, psychology, recruiting, and how to manage foreign spies in the West. The basics of intelligence tradecraft included hand-to-hand combat, and Putin excelled at judo. After training, he would be assigned to the KGB offices in Dresden, East Germany. He would work there for seven years, doing the mundane day-to-day work of monitoring both West and East German governments. He would later be tasked with recruiting Germans with access to the West to steal or illegally purchase and smuggle computer technology for the KGB's use. Advanced computer technology, even the rudimentary systems of the 1980s, would revolutionize reporting and databasing for the KGB. It would also give Putin very early insight into how technology could be used against the Soviet Union's opponents.

After the fall of the Soviet Union, Putin returned to Leningrad, once again called St. Petersburg, where he helped his friend Mayor Anatoly Sobchak gain control of the mafia and sell off billions of dollars in city assets. Hill and Gaddy believe he was seen by the Yeltsin administration as a man who showed loyalty and used it to climb:

> "Mr. Putin paid close attention to individuals who might further his career. He studied them, strengthened his personal and professional ties to them, did favors for them, and manipulated them. He allowed—even actively encouraged—people to underestimate him even as he maneuvered himself into influential positions and quietly accumulated real power."[4]

Putin would bring his expertise in liquidating Soviet assets as Boris Yeltsin's Deputy Chief of the Presidential Property Management Department. There he learned a valuable lesson about corruption. As a Soviet intelligence officer, he identified the need to concentrate that illicit wealth into a stovepipe of money that only a few should share. Anyone who didn't play by his rules would be cut out...or killed. It was simple, refined, and extremely KGB-like in execution. His reward was to be named Director of the Federal Security Service (FSB, the KGB's successor) by Yeltsin. After excelling in rebuilding the spy networks he would be appointed Yeltsin's Prime Minister, which put him in line to rule Russia. Putin rocketed to the top of the polls when he entered the presidential race. He no longer presented himself as the shy, unassuming spy-turned-bureaucrat, but as the hard-hitting anti-terrorism strongman. Putin promised brutal retribution against the Chechens, whom he blamed for a series of mysterious apartment building explosions that killed several hundred people in Moscow. (The attacks may have actually been the convenient handiwork of his FSB officers.) With the exception of the four years that Dmitry Medvedev held his seat, Putin has become the longest-serving leader in post-Tsarist Russia. Even the Communist Premier Leonid Brezhnev's 18 years are fewer than Putin's long reign.

Putin has carefully crafted his image as an ordinary Russian man who built his own path to the presidency through sheer focus, hard work, and an undying commitment to the Soviet Union and then the New Mother Russia. The Russian Orthodox Church was key to his success. Early on as Director of the FSB, he bought their favor by renovating the Russian Orthodox Cathedral of St. Sophia of God's Wisdom on the infamous Lubyanka Square, located next door to FSB headquarters. A far cry from the Soviet era when churches were turned into government facilities and priests were murdered in Lubyanka prison or forced to become informants. After almost a century of murder and repression, Putin knew the powerful draw of God in the post-Soviet world. He portrays himself as a man of God quite publicly, often praying in front of television cameras. He puts the church on a pedestal, but it's a portrayal crafted for his own political purposes. Like all autocratic leaders and skilled propagandists, he also likes to produce a constant stream of masculine, macho imagery that portrays him as a virile leader who hunts whales, wrestles with bears, rides motorcycles with biker gangs, scuba dives to rescue antiquities, and plays with tigers…usually shirtless.

The *Kursk* Incident

On August 12, 2000, a Russian Oscar-class guided-missile nuclear-powered submarine, hull number K-141, christened the *Kursk*, left the Russian Navy submarine base in Murmansk. The double-hulled submarine, built in the 1970s, was out of port and under the freezing Barents Sea on a training exercise with the North Banner Fleet. The boat carried a full complement of torpedoes and its main arsenal of the 24 SS-N-19 SHIPWRECK anti-ship guided missiles. At 11:27 a.m., a torpedo suffered a malfunction and exploded in the torpedo room at the bow of the sub. The explosion set fire to the compartment and killed the weapons department crew. Fire on a submarine is far more dangerous than even a nuclear power plant malfunction—smoke can kill the entire crew in minutes; radiation takes days. The submarine's torpedo room filled with tens of thousands of gallons of seawater, which led to flooding throughout the boat, dragging it toward the bottom of the sea nose-first. The captain tried to inject air into the ballast system in order to blow water out of the tanks, which would make the submarine shoot to the surface—an "emergency blow"—in an attempt to get to the surface at all costs. Unfortunately the boat suffered a catastrophic failure of control systems and crashed down to the seabed. Then the remainder of the torpedoes and cruise missiles exploded. The blast measured 3.5 on the Richter scale and was detected by earthquake sensors worldwide. All the men aboard were thought to be lost.[5]

The Russian navy submarine command in Murmansk had some clue that a critical incident was occurring on the *Kursk*. A message from the captain that a torpedo had malfunctioned and was seeking permission to launch it was garbled but received. Then all routine communications stopped. The Kremlin was notified and news of the tragedy was given to the families in the Navy village of Vidyayevo. As the news broke publicly, speculation started about what had caused the blast. Many in Russia were saying that it was caused by a collision with an American or British submarine. Yet all Western submarines were accounted for and without damage. The Kremlin ordered the Navy to attempt rescues but they were unable to attach to the boat. NATO had far more sophisticated equipment that could be brought in, but Moscow had not called for assistance. The Kremlin did not publicly speculate as to the cause of the disaster, but the collision with an American submarine was trending in the news.

The Soviet Union had fallen only a decade earlier and their trust of administrations was near zero. Any and every conspiracy theory was to be believed. Speculation on the disaster's cause was being picked up by the relatively free news media in Russia. Several outlets would publish stories about survivors tapping from inside, and that the Russian fleet had evidence of an American submarine in Scotland with hull damage but were hiding it. Though it was denied by the Kremlin, messages found on the corpses show that the first claim was true. After salvage, the story would soon come to surface that 23 of the 118-man crew managed to evacuate to the nuclear reactor and engineering section at the rear of the submarine as the boat sat on the seabed. It would be four hours before they slowly died of lack of oxygen. One officer wrote numerous notes and recorded their impending doom in a logbook. Others wrote their goodbyes to their families on scrap paper and their bodies.

The TV news in Russia began to say that Putin's Kremlin was incompetent and engaged in deliberate disinformation. That hit Putin the hardest. Russians had lived under the Soviet Union and knew a Kremlin *dezinformatsiya* when they heard it. But now that they had free speech and free press they could air those grievances. Deputy Prime Minister Ilya Klebanov was forced to come out before the nation and publicly deny that the Kremlin had carried out a planned disinformation campaign.

The *Kursk* incident was what made the Russian Federation believe that free press and free speech in a fledgling democracy was unacceptable. Putin knew that he could not just grab the news media and take it away. This wasn't the Soviet Union anymore—but to Putin, the unwelcomed level of news and media transparency that criticized him was unacceptable. They would have to be reined in. The easiest way would be to essentially step backward to a Soviet solution—make the news media state-run outlets. His former advisor Gleb Pavlovsky recalled on *FRONTLINE:*

> "I think that he began to think that everything can be manipulated. Any kind of press, any TV program is all about manipulation. It's all paid for by someone.... And when following that, TV channels—liberal TV channels—started criticizing him, he decided that... this was a war against him, and he was going to take the challenge."[6]

In the new Russia, the media was privately owned, but with the right impetus of billionaires or FOVs (Friends of Vladimir), he could pool resources and buy out the Russian media, one TV network and newspaper at a time. Over the next few years, he did just that.

The Colour Revolution

By 2010, American and NATO expansion in Eastern Europe and Ukraine was starting to irritate Putin. In his first term, he had brought Chechnya to heel and installed a reliable warlord as governor. Stability was returning with increased oil and gas exports to Europe, which buoyed the economy, but it was not steady. Despite oil and gas making up 50% of the country's revenue, the average Russian family remained economically depressed. But Putin was very wary of turning to the West for help. Even though Russia under Yeltsin had participated in the Partnership for Peace, a NATO initiative that brought Russia into a tacit alliance with the US, Putin felt the United States was playing heavy-handed politics now that the Soviet Union was gone. It was intervening wherever it wished, such as in Bosnia-Herzegovina in the 1990s. As I mentioned, the decision by George W. Bush to invade a former client state, Saddam Hussein's Iraq, eroded the US/Russia relationship. Putin believed that America should not act unilaterally and challenged the Bush administration's goals. Many Russian political elites felt the Bush administration had not consulted with Russia on the matter as his father, George H.W. Bush, had during the first Iraq war.[7]

Some of Russia's few remaining allies were being seduced by calls to join the West while others like Ukraine were being used as buffers between the two opposing spheres of influence. Democracy was spreading faster than Putin would like and these nations' alliances with Washington were sapping the leverage Russia had over them as former Soviet states. A series of cultural revolutions called "Colour Revolution" quickly took former Soviet states out of Moscow's sphere and into NATO's. That worried Putin. The first was the Rose Revolution in the former Soviet Republic of Georgia in 2003. A predominantly Orthodox nation, they sought extremely close ties to the United States, which they received. It was quickly followed by the 2004 Orange Revolution in Ukraine. This wave of desire for Western-style freedom and democracy soon spread to the Russian-occupied Baltic countries. In quick succession, Latvia, Lithuania, and Estonia declared independence from the Russian sphere of influence. As a buffer to future interference from the Kremlin, they all joined both the European Union and NATO in 2004.[8] Kyrgyzstan's Tulip Revolution happened in 2005, though it didn't drive as large a wedge in US-Russia relations as the previous two; Putin's military influence forced the US to evacuate its base at Manas airport in 2013.[9]

Putin was particularly concerned about regions in Europe with ethnic Russian or pro-Russian Slavic populations. One group was the Slavs in the former Yugoslav nation of Serbia. They had suffered a humiliating political defeat in a war with NATO that had injected democracy into their political system and had displaced the two Serbian ultranationalist leaders, Slobodan Milosevic and Ratko Mladic. Both would be hunted, captured, and sent to the International Criminal Court in The Hague for genocide trials. The Serb grip on Croatia, Bosnia-Herzegovina, Macedonia, and Montenegro had been broken due to NATO, and Moscow did not like it. In 2008, adjacent Kosovo declared independence and was occupied by NATO forces. Once again, to Putin this was a nearly intolerable encroachment by NATO on traditionally Slavic parts of Europe. It was bad enough that Poland, Latvia, Lithuania, and Estonia had joined NATO and were on his borders with his allies in Belarus and Ukraine. 2008 led to numerous clashes with Russia in "unrecognized breakaway regions" such as South Ossetia and Abkhazia in the Republic of Georgia.[10] Though the elected President of Russia in 2008 was Dmitry Medvedev, he was just considered a placeholder by most Russians until the Constitution could be changed for less frequent elections so Putin could return to his post.[11] While Medvedev acted as a seat warmer, Putin's spies in the FSB, GRU, and SVR were exercising his new strategy of Hybrid Warfare, an amalgam of cyber, special operations, and intelligence activities. They were to carry out political warfare missions just short of open war and push back NATO's influence. Georgia was the first unit on the test bed of hybrid war.

In 2008, Georgia had restarted trade with Abkhazia, the small seaside oblast to their northwest after the government of former Soviet Foreign Minister Eduard Shevardnadze had folded. Eduard Shevardnadze had started making overtures to the United States and NATO. Georgia has always laid claim to Abkhazia and the Georgian government beefed up its military presence there. Abkhazian separatists armed and started to ethnically cleanse Georgians from the region. This led to Georgian forces engaging in combat against them. At the request of the Abkhaz, Russia decided to intervene and assisted their side in the 13-month war that followed. Russian military forces fought alongside the separatists with tanks and aircraft. But during the Russian attack a new dimension was added, Russian intelligence cyberwarriors cut off all of Georgia's internet access to the world.[12] Foreign Minister Sergey Lavrov tried to justify the actions of the Kremlin. He claimed they needed to protect ethnic Russians living in South Ossetia and Abkhazia. But it was due to both irredentist motives and a warning shot to stop Georgia from joining NATO. Putin believed that the democratic movements that were building in these former Russian states were orchestrated and/or supported by the US via the CIA and nongovernmental organizations. He openly claimed they brought with them NATO troops and cultural changes that Russians found distasteful. America had dedicated itself to pushing liberal democracy worldwide since the end of WWII, and Russia had succumbed to the demand for freedom. Look what it wrought: America's embrace of ethnic diversity, a gay sexual revolution, and slovenliness had sought to wrench Russia apart. To Putin, America and Europe represented weakness. They had sought to remove from his people the national rigidity in the once strong Soviet Union. Putin's advisor Gleb Pavlovsky characterized how he was seen as a savior and problem solver for the population once he pushed back against America, "We saw some fluctuations after Putin's strong actions. We saw that people became pathologically addicted to Putin. In case of any crisis, people would look up to him."[13]

The Ukrainian Orange Revolution began in 2004 when people demonstrated in the streets at Maidan Nezalezhnosti (Independence Square) after an election, when it was found that the results were rigged in favor of Victor Yanukovych, a pro-Moscow strongman whose campaign was financed with Russian money. Putin funneled an estimated $500 million into his election campaign and provided "campaign helpers" who "fixed the election." The election was held again and Yanukovych's opposition, Viktor Yushchenko, won. However, before he won the runoff election Yushchenko was poisoned by a powerful chemical, TCDD, a potent form of dioxin, and the handsome Ukrainian's face was horribly disfigured—a warning from Putin. In 2010, Yanukovych ran for president again and won by a slim margin. He continued the corrupt practice of using the state-owned gas company for personal ben-efit. Russia kept Ukraine within its influence using the price of gas it supplied to Ukraine as an incentive to create favorable policies related to Russia. It should be noted that one of Yanukovych's principal foreign advisors was an American named Paul Manafort.

In 2008, Ukraine had begun discussions with the European Union to create an Association Agreement that would ultimately allow Ukraine a special trade arrangement with the EU. In 2013, under Yanukovych, negotiations intensified with the EU, which had certain requirements prior to proceeding; meanwhile, Putin offered large gas discounts and loans to Ukraine if Yanukovych didn't sign the deal. In February 2014, when Ukrainians learned the news that Yanukovych dropped the deal, the number of protestors who had been camping out in Maidan Nezale-zhnosti Square grew to tens of thousands. This would become the colour revolution Putin worried about, famously known as Euromaidan. After a serious crackdown on protestors that left many bloodied and included government-controlled snipers killing over 100 protestors, Yanukovych agreed to new elections, but the next day he fled to Russia.[14]

After the fall of Yanukovych, Russia moved troops into East Ukraine and provided heavy weaponry to Russian-supported militants in Luhansk and Donbass both were ethnically Russian border areas, Russian-armed and agitated for these fighters to seize and separate these regions from Ukraine. After Russian separatist fighting com-menced with Ukrainian army forces, the US and EU added a second level of sanctions against Moscow. On July 17, 2017, with Moscow's direct assistance, Russian-backed militants targeted and shot down a Malaysian airliner, an MH-17 that was flying from Amsterdam to Kuala Lumpur. The plane crashed and killed 303 passengers and crew. The US and EU added more sanctions against Russia. This was the final straw for Putin. He was determined to seize Crimea from Ukraine, sanctions be damned. Gleb Pavlovsky told American television

"…Putin said, if Ukraine is to join NATO, it will join NATO without the Crimea. And when he came back from a meeting with Bush [in 2008], Putin started developing a plan for taking

Crimea. It's not that he did it personally; the chief of staff was given this task and they developed a plan, and that plan stayed in the safe box for seven years."[15]

In 2014, Russia sent Special Forces without insignia to take over governmental administrative buildings in Crimea. Crimea was a peninsula that was part of Ukraine but had an ethnic majority of Russians. Claiming that they were assisting Russians in crisis, Putin held a referendum that violated the Ukraine constitution, and annexed the territory through armed force. The UN did not recognize the annexation of Crimea as Russian territory, and Russia's actions resulted in EU and US sanctions against the Russian government.

According to the United Nations Human Rights Office of the High Commissioner (OHCHR), as of May 2017, the death toll due to the Crimea conflict is at least 10,090 people. Additionally, over 2,777 civilians have been killed and almost 24,000 people injured. The UNHCR estimates that there are more than 1.6 million people who have been internally displaced. This brought about another round of crippling sanctions from President Obama and the European Union. The game was now set as to which side would prevail. Russia wanted to expand, stop, and get its money back. Obama held NATO, the EU, and its sanctions over their heads like the sword of Damocles. Putin decided to change the nature of the game entirely. If he could not get rid of sanctions, he would get rid of the political systems that imposed them.

The New Politburo

If a secret cabal was going to be formed in order to push the election of Donald Trump, then Putin's personal star chamber of close friends would make the judgment on what actions to take. Putin has a small group of advisors, all ex-KGB spies and natives of St. Petersburg known as the *Siloviki*, but they could be best described as the "Four Horsemen of the KGB."

The first of Putin's loyalists is Igor Sechin, the chairman of Rosneft, an oil company owned by the Russian government. In the oil industry, he is called the "Darth Vader of Russian oil." Putin appointed him in 2004.[16] When Putin was deputy mayor of St. Petersburg, Sechin worked as Putin's Chief of Staff[17] and was the leader of the former intelligence officers who surrounded Putin. He served in Africa as a KGB officer and military operations translator in Angola and Mozambique in the 1980s.

In 2011, Sechin secured a deal with then-CEO of Exxon (and, recently, ex-Secretary of State) Rex Tillerson for an agreement between Rosneft and Exxon to drill in the Arctic. Tillerson's Exxon-Mobil had previously been negotiating this deal with Yukos, the Russian oil and gas exploration company. According to Mikhail Khodorkovsky, the former oil oligarch in charge of Yukos, it was Sechin who drove the effort to destroy Yukos, which resulted in Khodorkovsky being forced to sell his shares to the Kremlin and flee Russia. He was also accused of having a hand in the arrest of Vladimir Yevtushenkov, owner of oil and gas company Bashneft. Like Khodorkovsky, Yevtushenkov was arrested and imprisoned until he turned over his shares of Bashneft to the government.

Sechin's net worth is close to $200 million, but the actual value of his worth is considerably higher thanks to his proximity to Putin. Not one for criticism or public scrutiny, Sechin famously sued Russian media outlets *Vedomosti, Novaya Gazeta*, and RBK because they identified that he and his wife, Olga, luxuriated on a 280-foot, near-$200-million-dollar Dutch-built yacht named *St. Princess Olga*. Sechin was awarded $49 million in fines against the paper for "libel." However, all the newspaper did was publish the boat's owner's details.[18]

The second horseman is Sergei Borisovich Ivanov, who served as Chief of Staff to the Presidential Executive Office from December 2011 to August 2016, a seat previously held by the Russian clandestine foreign intelligence agency (SVR) chief Sergey Naryshkin. Also a former KGB officer, he attended the Red Banner Institute in the early 1980s and spent nearly 20 years in the 3rd Department of the First Main Directorate focused on the UK, Australia, New Zealand, and Scandinavia. This led him to field intelligence assignments in Finland and Kenya. Under the Russian republic, he served in the SVR as First Deputy Director of the European department. In 1998, he went to the

FSB to serve as deputy to then-director Vladimir Putin. His duties brought him to lead the department of analysis, forecasts, and strategic planning. When Putin became Prime Minister, he joined as head of the Russian Security Council and as Putin's envoy to US President George W. Bush.

A longtime Putin loyalist, Ivanov served in several positions of trust. From 2001 to 2007 he served as Minister of Defense. From 2005 to 2007, he filled the role of Deputy Prime Minister, then as First Deputy Prime Minister from 2007 to 2008. In the first Medvedev administration, he returned as Chief of Staff from December 2011 and remained under Putin until 2016. Soon after the hacking of the DNC was exposed, he was replaced by Anton Vaino in August 2016 in an inglorious announcement: "Russian President Vladimir Putin has decreed to relieve Ivanov of his duties as head of the Russian presidential administration."[19] It was reported as a firing, but among old KGB officers this may have been a tactical reassignment to show he had nothing to do with the operations. He was subsequently assigned a post for transportation and environmental policy.

The third horseman is former KGB and FSB officer, Viktor Ivanov. He served as the Director of the Russian Federal Drug Control Service (FSKN) from 2008 until it was dissolved in 2016.[20] He served as a KGB and FSB officer from 1977 to 2000. He served as chief of internal affairs and was appointed deputy director of the FSB under Vladimir Putin from April 1999 to January 2000. He was made deputy head of the presidential administration on January 5, 2000, serving until he was made assistant to the president in April 2004. Ivanov was accused of using his power and influence to control Putin's rivals. This included the effort to take down Mikhail Khodorkovsky. Khodorkovsky was once named the 16th Richest Person in the World by *Forbes* and was one of the wealthiest oligarchs in Russia until the company was dissolved in 2007.[21] Ivanov was also known for ordering the killing of former KGB officer turned Putin critic, Alexander Litvinenko, in which a rare radioactive substance called polonium-210 was used. Litvinenko had accused Ivanov of being involved with organized crime, notably with the involvement with the Tambovskaya mafia gang led by

Vladimir Kumarin. Ivanov was accused of leveraging his power to help the Tambovskaya gang fight their rival, the Malyshevskaya mafia. In a dossier prepared by Litvinenko's colleague, Yuri Shvets, he says that sources claimed Ivanov was "a hand, which puts things in order." Shvets said that Ivanov was notably vindictive against anyone who exposed information about him or, more importantly, Vladimir Putin.[22]

Nikolai Patrushev is the fourth member of the *Siloviki*, or horsemen. He is an ex-KGB officer and the successor to Putin at the Russian intelligence agency, the FSB. It was Patrushev who was chief of the FSB when "terrorists" blew up apartments around Russia that killed hundreds and conveniently allowed Putin to easily win the presidency on a counter-terrorism platform. It was also his men who were captured planting one of those bombs. He was a chief of dirty tricks and carried out some of the most aggressive punishment campaigns against Putin's enemies. He coordinated with Ivanov on executing the assassination of ex-FSB officer Alexander Litvinenko using the radioactive isotope polonium-210, and was known for killing journalists and opposition members. He was an officer of the hardest KGB school of intelligence. "Death to enemies of Russia" is his apparent motto. He dubbed the Russian intelligence operatives the "new nobility" of the Federation and, along with Putin, takes a devil-may-care attitude toward their active measures in the West. After a decade running the FSB he became the head of the State Security Council, where he advises Putin and gets the intelligence agencies and the oligarchy to do Moscow's bidding without question.

Putin has used members of security services in almost all key positions in government and the oligarchy since his first term. His trust of ex-KGB and FSB officers would give the new government the feeling that the intelligence community was running Russia. Intelligence officers filled key positions in the national reindustrialization and modernization program under Putin. There was no need for political commissars as they ran the ministries and industry. Olga Kryshtanovskaya, director of the Center for Elite Studies at the Russian Academy of Science Institute of Sociology, told Radio Free Europe what this advisor board of spies desires most: "They want an authoritarian modernization. They want a strong authoritarian state of the Soviet type without the Soviet idiocy," said Kryshtanovskaya. "The idiotic Soviet economy and the idiotic Soviet ideology were minuses. All the rest they want to bring back and preserve: a state system without a separation of powers."

YEVGENY PRIGOZHIN, ALSO nicknamed "Putin's Chef," is a colorful ex-criminal who came to operate a catering company named Concord Management and Consulting, LLC. Concord did in fact provide catering, but apparently Putin wanted a loyalist who could operate a non-attributable "off the books" intelligence support agency. Prigozhin started in St. Petersburg as a hot dog seller and grew to open the most exclusive restaurant in the city as well as a fast food chain. His entry into Russian government operations came when he was awarded a $1.2-billion-dollar contract to cater food for the Russian army. Putin must have had a soft spot for chefs because his father, Spiridon Putin, claimed to have been a chef for both Lenin and Stalin in the Soviet Union. At some point, the former convict who spent nine years in a Soviet penal colony and grew his company in just 11 years, became involved in multiple covert operations for the Kremlin. His foray into information warfare began when he opened a fake news factory called Kharkiv News Agency. In 2013, Kharkiv was designed to create false pro-Moscow "people" who would hijack website comment pages and disparage the Euromaidan movement, the Ukrainian popular protests, to move away from Moscow and toward Western Europe. Putin tapped Prigozhin to set up and operate all of Russia's off-the-books black operations under the guise of the civilian news company. He would also establish the primary generator of fake news in the West, the secret Russian Federation's Internet Research Agency (RF-IRA). Prigozhin also runs private security contractors in Syria and Ukraine, and is linked to armed militants in Russian-dominant ethnic regions such as Donbass and Luhansk in Ukraine. These secret contractors have been linked to a secret Russian training base, similar to Blackwater's former North Carolina facility that has been connected with Russian military intelligence. These same mercenaries would eventually come to grief by daring to attack a US Special Forces base in 2018.

Among Putin's Russian knights, all were ex-KGB except for the former criminal turned gray zone dirty tricks man Prigozhin. Putin and his advisors aligned for a mission on the US—a win to be gained by acting as case officers and coaches to Donald J. Trump. Trump was brash, arrogant, and a colorful character. He could be just the man to help lift the crushing sanctions imposed by Obama and Europe. All evidence from the KGB era and FSB collection would show that he was an easily led person. He had an insatiable desire for respect he was not afforded. With the right whispers in the right ears, perhaps Moscow could get him to adopt positions that most American Republicans would find odious. NATO was knocking on Russian borders and this had to be stopped. The European Union as a body made Russia's economic life difficult. If the EU could be disassembled through alluring offers of unilateral trade agreements with Washington, then all the better for Moscow. Donald Trump was a unique character to Russia as well as the world. His TV show *The Apprentice* was loved in Russia. He had come to Moscow's 2013 Miss Universe pageant seeking to kiss the ring of Vladimir Putin. Putin would return the favor by making him President of the United States. The Four Horsemen knew he would be an easily handled asset.

Based on my knowledge working in this field for years and the secret intelligence manuals of the KGB, Trump was the kind of quality recruit that spies always sought. Every Russian spy knew that it was the greedy, narcissistic, and self-absorbed conservatives that made for the best assets. Almost invariably, they thought they could handle any situation and rarely looked deeper than their financial pockets. Putin was going to push back against any chance that Hillary Clinton would become President. If that meant having to risk going from a cyber-war to a hot war, so be it. Maybe it was time to just introduce a little chaos in America. The American Republican Party had been shifting to the far right for more than two decades. Many of them supported a strong man and powerful national leader like Vladimir Putin. Putin's own contacts with the religious right presented him with the opportunity to co-opt an entire party. It was far too tempting to avoid. If it could be done in the United States, it could be done everywhere else in the world—save China. A successful co-option of the American right would lead to an entire wing of supporters operating the most powerful nation on earth and viewing Putin as its closest ally. Russian intelligence would go back and scrub every document and contact about Donald Trump from his overtures made in the late 1980s. If they could pull it off, why not try?

Planning Operation GRIZZLY STEPPE

GRIZZLY STEPPE, the operation to destabilize the West and bring Russia to power, would have three legs:

1. Russia would use its intelligence services and Prigozhin's gray market civilians to steal information, develop *Kompromat* (the use of compromising materials), and prepare the political propaganda warfare battlefield for intervention in the 2016 election cycle. This planning started in late 2012 and would accelerate in 2013. If Putin's preferred candidate, Donald Trump, didn't rise to the top, then activities would be launched to create chaos and allow the Republican Party to savagely attack the likely choice, Hillary Clinton, and hound her for the rest of her administration.

2. Russian oligarchs and diplomats would spread into the field and determine who the frontrunners would be and where Russian influence, money, and friendship would be spread. With major financial decisions such as the Exxon deal in the balance, there would be many Americans more than willing to assist Moscow.

3. Kremlin-aligned Russian citizens and like-minded social groups would spread their influence to see if they could co-opt Americans from the far right. Groups that were mired on both sides of the Atlantic included the National Rifle Association, biker gangs, and strongman Americans such as actor Steven Seagal, who, along with others, will extol Russia support as being a net positive for any conservative. It would mean delicate but open support for extremist far-right conservatives such as the California and Texas separatist movements, Russian exiles living in the United States, and radicals

such as the neo-Nazi movement and Ku Klux Klan, if they could all be brought into a powerful unofficial coalition. They would align America's cultural losses with the white Christian nationalism they admired in Russia.

To begin his mission, Putin would use diplomats to give his plan the social acceptability for upper class Republican politicians. As all diplomats in the Soviet era were principal points of contact for identification, recruitment, and handoff to the KGB, so were the modern-era diplomats for the FSB and SVR. Diplomats would be the first to look for Americans who were of interest to Russia, and who could be exploited by the intelligence services. The top diplomats who have contacts with the Americans would be brought in to ensure a smooth transition. Donald Trump had been fascinated with injecting himself into American diplomacy since 1987. He had met the Russian Ambassador and made overtures to coming to Russia to build hotels. His visits during the Soviet era found his affability always increasing when he was in the presence of diplomats. This was to be exploited. Additionally, diplomats were no longer seen as an intelligence threat in America. That oversight would also assist in the recruitment of high-level Americans who could assist without knowing that they were involved in a massive intelligence operation against their own nation. Others, once given promises of access to oil money, wouldn't care. If the Americans were reliable about any one thing it was that assets, and even agents, were always easy to buy with Russia's cash.

The job of the American-wrangling diplomats would be to ensure that they understood Moscow's position and how it could benefit them personally if they were to make these positions certain in the Republican Party. The point man for this operation would be the Ambassador to the United States, Sergey Kislyak.

Sergey Kislyak served as the Russian Ambassador to the United States from 2008 to 2017. He had served as Deputy Foreign Minister under Sergey Lavrov. In 1977, he had joined the Foreign Ministry and worked his way up through the ranks as a trade representative during the Soviet era. He became the first secretary at the Embassy in

Washington, D.C., and soon after that became a trusted negotiator for nuclear arms control treaties with Ronald Reagan's administration. His education as a nuclear physicist gave the Americans trust in his ability to understand complex problems. As with any Soviet-era diplomat, he was required to carry out espionage-related duties. Former Ambassador John Beryle said, "In modern Washington, he had to do [almost] nothing, as Americans fell all over themselves to become friends with Vladimir."

If Kislyak was the operative on the ground, then Sergey Lavrov was the heavy above him who was linked directly to Putin. Lavrov was a quiet, unassuming man of considerable girth. As Russian Foreign Minister since 2004, he was the principal point of diplomacy for Moscow. However, he had other duties assigned. Lavrov was a lifelong career Communist functionary. Born in 1950, he was a child in Stalin's Soviet Union and became the secretary of his local Komsomol, the Young Communist League. He studied and graduated from the Moscow State Institute of International Relations in 1972 and was assigned to the Russian Foreign Ministry under Premier Leonid Brezhnev's regime. In 1994, he was posted to New York as the Russian Federation representative to the United Nations. He earned his stripes during the Obama era as the vocal mouthpiece of Putin's ire. His diplomatic demeanor is that of a big fat bulldog, but he can be blunt, direct, brash, and very Russian in countering US positions. In a *Newsweek* article, John Negroponte, the former US Ambassador to the United Nations, referred to Lavrov's style as, "His two objectives were always the same: veto things for the greater glory of Russia and to take the Americans down whenever possible...."[23] This was how Lavrov earned his nicknamed "Mr. No."

Every intelligence operation would need funding. Putin had just the man: Sergei Gorkov was the head of a Russian state investment bank, Vnesheconombank (VEB). Gorkov graduated in 1994 from the same KGB school of intelligence as Putin. He never went into active field operations, which made many believe that after basic service, he was tasked to become a banker-spy in a NOC position—Non-Official Cover. These were the deepest of spies, as they had no visible ties to their agencies. He worked his way up through Russian banks including the Menatep Financial Group under Mikhail Khodorkovsky. This included the oil giant Yukos. In 2002, he attended the GV Plekhanov Russian Economic Academy. During his time at Menatep-Yukos, he emerged clean from a massive tax scandal that rocked the industry. Khodorkovsky had publicly fought with Putin over corruption and bribes in the government. Putin filed charges against Yukos for tax evasion, fraud, and corruption. Khodorkovsky was arrested and imprisoned for eight years. His oil company assets were nationalized. Gorkov walked away free and became a close ally of Putin.

In 2008, Gorkov worked for Sberbank, Russia's state-owned bank. Not surprisingly, Sberbank is represented in the US by Marc Kasowitz, President Trump's attorney, who was named lead attorney in defending the company in a federal civil lawsuit.[24] In 2016, Gorkov was appointed to head VEB. The VEB is considered Putin's personal bank for special projects. It is also under US sanctions related to Russia's invasion and annexation of Crimea and for its reputation as "The Bank of Spies." Many Russian intelligence activities were funded from their coffers.

Putin's team of wranglers would support the operations that were necessary to stop the encroachment of the United States—and particularly that odious Democratic frontrunner, Hillary Clinton. The days of second fiddle to Obama and his incessant talk of spreading democracy would end in 2016 one way or another, and the sanctions would be released. Russia would not respond to America's shoves. Putin did have a vision to destabilize the West. It was a long-ball plan. It would happen when he, Vladimir Vladimirovich Putin, chose. When the plan was executed he would Make Russia Great Again.

CHAPTER 4

Putin's Philosophy

Russia has long been in flux, with mixed beliefs on the most advantageous system for a nation in which three-quarters of its land mass is in Asia, while three-quarters of its population lives in the European quarter. Since the time of Peter the Great's European illumination, the question of the Russian cultural identity has risen to the forefront of discussion. In the age of Putin's neo-Tsarist empire, the question is this: Does Russia accept the status quo of European and American dominance of the world order, or does it take measures to upset the global center of gravity and forge its own strategic culture?

Putin is at a crossroads that many Russians struggle with. For a century, Russians have been conditioned to believe that Western democracy is destined to fail, but when given the chance to embrace it they did—and many do not like the messy results. Many former Communist philosophers emerged from the Soviet debris field and embraced a wild mélange of beliefs about the future of Russian identity. Some have emerged as thought leaders who have not only influenced Russia's elite ruling class but have jumped the Atlantic and acted as polestars for American conservatives. To many neo-Tsarist Russian philosophers, the Soviet Union's traditional leftist and European socialist partners, who were horribly liberal, failed them in the battlefield of ideas. Hence, liberalism of any kind is a mortal enemy that must be vanquished. They embrace the conservative right and teeter close to fascism.

Putin is an autocratic ruler and, like every Tsar and dictator before him on the global stage, it is imperative that he control the narrative with an intentional philosophy. Gleb Pavlovsky describes it as, "He acts as a professor, as a lecturer. He [explains] to us what Russian history was like, what values we have, what we should believe in."[1] But, furthermore, under Putin lies a pantheon of new philosophers who are helping craft the future narrative of both Russia and America.

VLADISLAV SURKOV WAS a Russian businessman and politician of Chechen descent who served as the Deputy Prime Minister of Russia from 2011 to 2013. He was also Putin's "right hand man" as the first Deputy Chief of the Presidential Administration of Vladimir Putin. His career first started as a bodyguard in the 1990s for Mikhail Khodorkovsky.[2] Under Putin, Surkov was more widely known as a Kremlin propagandist. According to *Atlantic* magazine's Peter Pomerantsev, he is nicknamed "Political Technologist of all of Rus." Many have assumed that Surkov is an éminence *grise*—a behind-the-scenes mastermind who pulls the levers of power. As a political technologist, he strengthens Putin's control in Russia through media power. Russia's democracy is a "Sovereign Democracy," a Surkovian term—via media intervention, it assures that Russia's democracy has a different set of philosophies than other democracies, which under Putin bears a striking resemblance to the true democracy that was always proclaimed under the Soviet Union:

> "It is a society of true democracy, [a] political system which ensures effective management of all public affairs, ever more active participation of the working people in running the state, and the combining of citizen's real rights and freedoms with their obligations and responsibility to society. Democracy in capitalist countries, where there are antagonistic classes, is, in the last analysis, democracy for the strong, democracy for the propertied minority. In the U.S.S.R., on the contrary, democracy is democracy for the working people, i.e., democracy for all."[3]

Vladimir Ilyich Lenin, founder of the Soviet Union and Marxist-Leninist Communism, wrote in a 1917 treatise *The Transition from Capitalism to Communism*: "Democracy for an insignificant minority, democracy for the rich—that is the democracy of capitalist society."[4] However, instead of being a bastion of balance and tolerance, Surkov's version of democracy is crafted by a centralized control system for information and narrative manipulation through the use of mind control and influence techniques, and where certain words and images were repeated, mantra-like, over and over. Surkov was focused on ideology. He created covert fake opposition parties, not just in Russia but in Ukraine as well. He would stage liberal art shows in order for them to be attacked by Russian Orthodox priests. In 2013, Peter Pomerantsev interviewed Surkov in an *Atlantic* article titled "The Hidden Author of Putinism or How Vladislav Surkov Invented the New Russia" where Surkov introduces himself as, "I am the author, or one of the authors, of the new Russian system."[5]

Surkov has given talks at prestigious universities and public forums worldwide despite the fact that he was linked to Nashi, aka the Ours! movement,[6] a group labeled the Russian pro-Putin version of the Hitler Youth. Surkov organized the group in 2005. He is also renowned in Russia for burning books by democratic authors (deemed "unpatriotic writers") in Red Square.[7] His biggest efforts at censorship involved suppressing liberal media outlet rankings in Yandex, the most widely trafficked search engine in Russia.[8] Since 2009, he has written at least two post-modern ideology novels. Though in 2012, he denied ever having penned them. His first book, *Almost Zero*, blames liberal society for the bad state of Russia during the fall of Communism and rise of capitalism, and his second novel, *Mashinka and Velik* (*The Little Car and the Bicycle*), introduces a worldview where intellectuals, mafia, sadists, ex-clergy, and professors are all pedophiles and exploiters of children—many disappeared—all on the same side—the left.[9] He also published a short story "Without Sky" in March 2014, a futuristic work complete with technology, robots, warfare, mutants, and underworlds, etc. He published it under the pseudonym, Nathan Dubovitsky, a nom de plume based on his wife's maiden name, Natalia Dubovitsky.[10]

Surkov was allegedly fired by Putin's Kremlin officials in 2011, though it was stated that he had resigned. In Putin's second run for president, Surkov had surprisingly backed Medvedev. He had been verbal with the Russian elite that he supported the liberal Medvedev instead of Putin. He was dismissed from the Putin Administration. Considering that Medvedev was a political placeholder for Putin, if they had a falling out, there must have been another reason.

In 2016, Surkov was put on the US sanctions list for his role in helping fashion the rebellious Donetsk and Luhansk "People's Republics" and agitation in Eastern Ukraine. His role was exposed by a group of Ukrainian hackers known as "Cyber Junta." Central and Eastern European correspondent Shawn Walker wrote in *The Guardian*, "It is possible that going after Surkov is the first salvo in what the CIA promised would be 'unprecedented cyber covert action against Russia' in the wake of alleged Russian hacking of the Democratic Party's computer networks."[11]

Aleksandr Dugin was a former professor of sociology at Moscow State University and an advocate of neo-Eurasianism, a geopolitical policy that advocates for the seizure of former Soviet Union territories. He has been referred to as "Putin's Rasputin" by Breitbart News[12] and has become the loudest voice of the Russian fringe as it reflects the global conservative themes prominent in right-wing circles in America and Europe. He was the leader of the National Bolshevik Party, National Bolshevik Front, and Eurasia Party. Dugin created the International Eurasia Movement in 2000[13] and idealizes the Eurasia concept that Russia is more aligned to the Asian continent. With this philosophy, he seeks to expand Russian control over not only the former Soviet Union territories but other Asian countries as well.[14] He sees Russia as having gone through a national awakening under Putin's leadership, a Russian Spring. "I think that the new Russian identity and ideology will be constructed on the basis of people as the central political reality—not ethnic or racial, but the people as a community."[15] According to Dugin, unipolar globalization brings "sociopolitical, ethnic, religious, and national infrastructures into one system." Neo-Eurasianists believe it is Russia's destiny to smash the "one nation state" of globalization that is consuming the world into that American trans-atlantic paradigm above. It's a Russian take on "New World Order," and it has many American adherents, including Donald Trump and his supporters.

Dugin is said to be inspired by the writings of Adolf Hitler and the German philosopher Martin Heidegger. Ironically, he is a staunch advocate against governments and people he calls "globalists" who, in his words, "are in the process of destroying any identity except for that of the individual." His followers include combined tribes of anti-globalists and nationalists.[16] Dugin calls for revolutionary ideas that bear a striking resemblance to a conservative version of the Capital-ist (owner) versus Proletariat (worker) rhetoric of Communism under which he was raised.

He has advocated for a shift to traditional conservative politics to restore the place of the Russian Orthodox religion in public policy. Regarding the United States, Dugin has stated that liberalism in the West has come to an end of its political cycle and a return to conser-vative policies was inevitable. For instance, he strongly protested the acceptance of the LGBT community and other policies commonly associated with liberalism. His stances mirror characteristics of Amer-ican conservative extremists. However, Dugin has no problem rec-ommending unbridled use of the Russian military force that he often complains of. In 2008, Dugin called for the seizure of Ukraine and Georgia and to bring them back into the post-Soviet sphere of influ-ence. He has espoused the view that the former Soviet states belong to Russia. These statements are alarming to small NATO nations such as Estonia, Lithuania, and Latvia, which only recently liberated them-selves from Russia.

Dugin's brand of radical, almost fascist conservative populism is very popular in pro-Trump circles. He endorsed Donald Trump for president in 2016 in an article titled "Trump Is Real America," in which he postulated that Trump was a common man of the times and thus a challenge to the "global elite."[17] In his YouTube videos, he loudly proclaimed his support for the billionaire, "Donald Trump is the most right-wing candidate of the Republican Party, but not like the insane disabled McCain or the ex-Trotskyist neoconservatives, obsessed with the idea of world dominance."[18] He claimed that Trump would reverse the policies that support the transatlantic ties of America and Western Europe. "Trump is the voice of the real right-wing in America, which, in fact, doesn't care about foreign policy and American hegemony."[19] On the election of Donald Trump, Dugin pushed his agenda to promote this ideology:

> "November 8th, 2016 was a most important victory for Russia and for him (Putin) personally."[20]
>
> "This is the real America, the America of realism which has chosen its president and not succumbed to the false propaganda of the globalist liberal media."[21]
>
> "More than half of the US population believes only itself, not the lying liberal globalist propaganda of the transnational elites. This is brilliant news. Dialogue can be held with this kind of America."[22]
>
> "There is nothing more stupid and fake than the American vote counting system. It is a disgrace, and not a democracy!"[23]

Born July 3, 1974, Konstantin Malofeev has been likened to "Putin's George Soros," but without the empathy and dignity. He had 15 years of experience in the world of private equity and investment banking. As founder of Marshall Capital Partners, an international investment fund group, he has amassed a vast fortune in real estate, agriculture, telecommunications, technology, and media investments. He ran the advisory board of St. Basil the Great Charitable Foundation, Russia's largest charity, and St. Basil the Great Grammar School, a school he founded in 2007. He is on the board of trustees for the Russian non-government nonprofit Safe Internet League, which led to the drafting of Russia's original internet censorship law.

As president of right-wing think tank Katehon, Malofeev founded and subsequently funded Tsargrad TV & Tsargrad Media Group. He advocates for a new Russian empire and, in doing so, hosts a media platform for the far right. It includes voices like American conspiracy theorist Alex Jones and Aleksandr Dugin, as well as a former Fox News anchor Jack Hanick; Aymeric Chauprade, advisor to Marine Le Pen; Austria's Prime Minister Heinz-Christian Strache, formerly the Freedom Party leader, among others. On Twitter, @Katehon was the entity pushing Dugin's "Drain the Swamp," a mantra during the election that would become a phrase used by presidential candidate Donald Trump and his followers.

In 2014 the Russian opposition hacking group, Shaltai Boltai (Humpty Dumpty) released emails between Malofeev and Georgy Gavrish.[24] The emails revealed a massive effort to prop up extremist right-wing ethno-nationalist groups throughout Europe, including in France, Germany, Italy, Greece, Hungary, Poland, Romania, Slovakia, Croatia, Serbia, and Turkey. Efforts were also underway outside of Europe in Argentina, Chile, Lebanon, and Malaysia.[25] Malofeev was sanctioned by the Obama administration for being the principal funder of the Ukrainian separatist groups fighting in Donetsk that helped facilitate the seizure of Crimea.

Another of Putin's philosophers was Igor Panarin, a Russian intelligence officer and former KGB analyst who worked for the Federal Agency of Government Communications and Information (FAPSI), then the Russian equivalent of the NSA. In 2003, FAPSI dissolved and became the Special Communications and Information Service. He went on to receive a doctorate in political science with a focus on geopolitics, social psychology, and US economics and information warfare. Panarin is most widely known for announcing his prediction at the Information War Conference held in Linz, Austria, on September 9, 1998, nearly seven years after the fall of the Soviet Union, that the US would face a similar Balkanization fate within the decade, and no later than summer 2010. It was at that conference where Panarin planted the seeds of what many would later come to view as the basis for Putin's disinformation campaign against the United States. Panarin calculated that fear of mass immigration, moral decay, and economic uncertainty could spark disunity within the United States. These factors could result in a civil war/culture war that could discredit the stability of the US dollar on an international level while undermining globalization.

Panarin predicted that "there is a 45%–55% chance that disintegration will happen."[26] It was met with great skepticism at the conference as he unveiled a map showing the United States—then still in a trade partnership with Russia—broken into six parts due to the fact that some economically sound US states would aim to unleash themselves from control from the federal government. At the same time, Alaska, which is only 90 miles from Russia's nearest point, would once again, according to Panarin, become part of Russia, while Hawaii would become a protectorate territory of either Japan or China, and "The Californian Republic" would be under Chinese influence (Calexit). Additionally, the northern states that Panarin refers to as "the Central North American Republic" would be taken over by Canada.[27] Not surprisingly, by 2015, the Kremlin would come to financially back some American separatist groups in order to effect this prediction. Panarin's warning to the United States was based on what happened to the Soviet Union. Panarin wrote that Americans expect miracles from President Obama "but when the spring comes, it will be clear that there are no miracles." Panarin cited that the collapse of the Soviet Union was predicted in 1976 by French political scientist, Emmanuel Todd, and that people laughed at him as well.[28]

Steve Bannon, the American Goebbels

Steve Bannon is the American politician whose ideology has bridged the philosophies of the new Kremlin thinkers with the masses in America. He rose to prominence under Donald Trump, and at a time when Trump looked like he would falter, Bannon led his campaign to victory in the 2016 elections. But once he opened his mouth about his true feelings of Trump's incompetence, while extolling himself as a brilliant king-maker, he would fall in disgrace. That disgrace did not last long. Bannon started crisscrossing Europe to act as the networker-in-chief to bring his Trump-style authoritarianism to European populist groups.

In power or not, Bannon would come to be the shining star in the Putin plan to bring America into an alliance of autocratic thought leaders. His ideologies were deeply rooted in Duginism, and that gave him a place in the manipulation chain in the global game of information warfare. If the Americans under him proved as malleable as they were when it came to Moscow's money, then perhaps it was appropriate to cultivate the entire American conservative movement into Moscow's unwitting assets. Bannon saw the alt-right as conservative storm troopers who would assist Trump with changing the United States into a pro-Moscow wing of the world nationalist conservative network. When Bannon emerged on the political scene, he had worked in the investment banking, entertainment, and gaming industries. He became executive chairman of the ultra-extremist Breitbart News. His personality has been described as everything from pathological to dangerous. He is a man with no fixed address, though he has residences in Florida and California. He also claims to be a resident of Washington, D.C., New York, London, Los Angeles, Laguna Beach, and Miami.[29] During his time in the Trump administration, he lived on and off with his third ex-wife. She allegedly smuggled drugs and a cell phone into prison to a lover, who was not Steve Bannon. On the other hand, Bannon was accused of violently abusing his ex-wife. He is alleged to have destroyed a leased home in Miami where the Jacuzzi bathtub had been ruined by a corrosive acid and every room was festooned with padlocks, including the bathroom door. In the entire maelstrom that would become the 2016 campaign, these bizarre characteristics and foibles were not considered a problem for a man working in Donald Trump's White House.

As Trump's chief campaign advisor, one would have thought Bannon had been a political operative his entire life. But he came to the political forefront in a unique way. Bannon wasn't of the manor-born. He was the son of an AT&T telephone company lineman and a stay-at-home mom. "I come from a blue-collar, Irish Catholic, pro-Kennedy, pro-union family of Democrats.... I wasn't political until I got into the service and saw how badly Jimmy Carter f—ed things up. I became a huge Reagan admirer. Still am. But what turned me against the whole establishment was coming back from running companies in

Asia in 2008 and seeing that Bush had f—ed up as badly as Carter. The whole country was a disaster."[30]

Bannon attended Virginia Tech and graduated in 1976. He was an officer in the US Navy for seven years, serving on the destroyer USS *Paul F. Foster* and later at the Pentagon as a special assistant to the Chief of Naval Operations. He then went on to Georgetown to earn a Master's degree in National Security Studies. In 1985, he earned an MBA degree with honors from Harvard. His military service, by many accounts, shaped his worldview. After his military stint, he worked at Goldman Sachs as an investment banker, working to expand their presence in the entertainment industry. In 1990, he and some colleagues from Goldman Sachs launched a private investment company specializing in media. He was an executive producer of 18 films before 2016. He ended up with a financial stake in comedian Jerry Seinfeld's TV show *Seinfeld*, from which he still receives residuals.

In 1993, Bannon left Goldman Sachs to become acting director of the ecological self-reliance research project Biosphere 2. In 2007, he cofounded Breitbart News with Andrew Breitbart. Breitbart had originally conceived of the site during a trip to Israel as a website that would be "unapologetically pro-freedom and pro-Israel." Andrew Breitbart died unexpectedly of a heart attack in March of 2016, and Steve was named the chief executive officer.

In 2006, in a move that would later help to cultivate just the kind of young, intelligent, anti-feminist, gun-loving, disaffected white male that would help elect Trump, Bannon persuaded Goldman Sachs to invest in Internet Gaming Entertainment, or IGE, a company that sold virtual goods to gamers including magical swords and costumes and ways to cheat. There was, however, a significant problem with this Hong Kong–based enterprise: The companies that made video games like *World of Warcraft* considered IGE's business model illegal. The entire reason Bannon agreed to be the Vice Chairman of IGE was to gain acceptance of the moneymaking scheme with gaming companies. It was another big challenge with a huge potential payoff. Gamer credits were rewards for players who invested in games such as *Medal of Honor* and *World of Warcraft*, but Bannon weaponized the credit system by using cheap Chinese computer players in sweatshop environments to earn credits for online computer games. It was brilliant because there was a huge global market in online games, and players could buy enhancements with these credits. Bannon's company, IGE, then sold the harvested credits to gamers around the world for hard cash. When one considers that there are tens of millions of people playing these games in real time 24/7, even a single, dollar sale could generate millions monthly. IGE worked hard to hide their activities from the large computer game design companies who were seeking to shut them down. In 2007, facing a class action lawsuit and an investigation by authorities in Florida, Bannon steered IGE away from its virtual credits business and changed the name of the company to Affinity Media Holdings. Authorities dropped the investigation in 2008 after being convinced IGE had gotten out of the business of selling virtual goods. Affinity Media Holdings stabilized under Bannon's leadership and was sold for $42 million.

Bannon's working-class background, military service, financial shrewdness, and digital media acumen helped him to see an opportunity in Donald Trump's candidacy. He understood that a large part of America believed immigration, gender equality, diversity, political correctness, feminism, secularism, trade agreements, and Islam were the greatest threats to the American way of life. He hoped to harness a new power with gamers through Breitbart News. Regarding the gamers, Bannon said, "These guys, these rootless white males, had monster power."[31]

Bannon is a loyal follower of Aleksandr Dugin, who glorifies the lost Tsarist Russian empire, just as Bannon glorifies the racist, genocidal Jacksonian America of the 19th century. Both men have a stringent belief that the true struggle is not between Russia and the United States but between ethical Judeo-Christian capitalists on one side and global crony capitalist bankers and multinational corporations on the other. Bannon believes in the strength of the nation-state—which is precisely what Putin's Kremlin is promoting as it backs anti–European Union candidates in elections across the West. "I happen to think that the individual sovereignty of a country is a good thing and a strong thing.... If we do not bind together as partners with others in other countries then this conflict is only going to metastasize."[32] He was referring to a conflict he perceived between Judeo-Christian values and what conservatives call Islamic fascism. He praises both Vladimir Putin and Dugin's brand of Russian neo-Eurasianism, though he views Putin with suspicion. Bannon believes Putin is standing up for traditional institutions, and he's trying to do it in a form of nationalism. Bannon told Ronald Radosh at *The Daily Beast* that "Lenin... wanted to destroy the state, and that's my goal too. I want to bring everything crashing down, and destroy all of today's establishment."[33]

The greatest success of Dugin was to find a disciple in Bannon, the man who would become the strategy advisor for Donald Trump and editor of the ultranationalist web-based news source, Breitbart News. Bannon likened himself to Dugin in the belief that American democracy was doomed, and that the world should be led by autocrats and oligarchs in alignment with nationalist beliefs. They believed the East and West money class would join their easily led nations in a global alliance. Despite the fallout from his high-publicity firing, Bannon still believes that Trump is the natural leader of the worldwide populist, anti-globalist movement.

CHAPTER 5

A Rising Russia, a Failing America

Putin was committed to a quiet but decisive plan to revive the national standing of the Russian Federation. He may have used his quiet demeanor to make many in Russia believe he was just a plodding bureaucrat. Still, he was bred in the Communist security state ethic of "Love the State. Kill for the State. Make Russia Great." The KGB addendum would be "... *by all means necessary*." This would include in dealing with his opponents: the assassination of Boris Nemtsov; the beating and imprisonment of the band Pussy Riot for exercising free speech when they allegedly defiled an Orthodox church by playing music in it; and forbidding electoral candidates to run against him. If an acceptable "opponent" is found, it's because he created them. He puts them into the fray and the slightest investigation will find they are secretly Putin loyalists. During the 2018 election cycle, Russian exile Garry Kasparov quipped, "Putin is so popular that anyone who challenges him must be murdered, exiled, or banned. Anyone who treats these 'elections' as anything other than a dictator's theater is a fool."[1]

His popularity did not match the poor state of the Russian economy. Russia's move to a free market economy from a centralized state distributions system that was antiquated, incompetent, and corrupt was positive for many. Basic food items, like milk, canned goods, bread, and clothing soon flooded the nation. Yet, the fire sale–like liquidation of the national assets created massive inequality and a class that hadn't existed before—the insanely rich oligarchy. Under the Soviet system everyone worked for the state and those in the Supreme Soviet could skim and graft along the edges. Perhaps there were millionaires in that system among the top leadership and mafia, but Putin's Russia created wealth along the lines of the Romanovs. Unfortunately, just like with the Tsars, the wealth rested in the hands of a few.

Vladimir Putin wanted Russia to prosper with a global tour de force oil economy like no other, but oil and gas sales to Europe aside, it is an economic backwater. In 2008, a reserve fund was created preemptively in the event of market volatility in oil prices. Russia nearly depleted this fund, subsequently tapping into the social services budget. Consequently, by 2016, Russia's economy was half of the State of California's, and the drop in oil prices really hurt the social and infrastructure sectors of the economy. It did not help that Russia remained one of the most corrupt countries in the world. According to Transparency International's 2017 Corruption Index, Russia ranked as 135 out of 180 countries with a score of 29 out of a range of 0 through 100 (with 0 value being no corruption). Lawlessness and corruption in a kleptocracy are what have contributed to little faith in the Russian economy and investment.

Today there are Russian billionaires worth tens of billions of dollars each. Industries such as oil and natural gas, television media and newspapers, as well as mining uranium or shipbuilding, were divvied up and over time fell into the hands of Vladimir Putin's closest allies. Technically, everyone in Russia would come to work for them in some way or another.

———

THE MILITARY WOULD also be a step toward a greater Russia. Putin has always been an outspoken critic of NATO, but he was particularly troubled by its expansion into the post-Soviet Baltic states. In January 2016, Putin signed off on the National Security Strategy, a policy that repositioned Russia's national security posture from one of observation to a more confrontational stance. Putin's policy list is a litany of grievances he held against the West and the United States in particular: "the intensification of military activities of member countries," "further expansion of the alliance," and "moving military infrastructure closer to Russia's borders."[2] He declared the United States and NATO as the main "threat to national security" of the Russian Federation.

A key component in the strategy to restore Putin's Russia to a position of prominence was redevelopment of the armed forces. The Soviet armed forces were noteworthy for two reasons: First, the equipment, particularly tanks, were tough but impractical for the survival or comfort of its operators. Russian tanks and trucks were tested in Cold War proxy battles but would only sell in the cheapest markets. The quality of Soviet-era aircraft was poor compared to NATO's. Submarines were good but the technological edge in the West made them a last choice for other navies. Apart from the ubiquitous AK-47 weapons and the RPG-7 rocket launcher, Russian sales were limited to repairs and resupplies of ammunition. After the fall of the Soviet Union, Russia embarked on a complete upgrade to quality and cost-effective weaponry. Putin gained credibility in counterterrorism by taking over the failed conflict in Chechnya. While labeled "counterterrorist and counterinsurgent" operations,[3] Putin let the Ministry of Defense have free rein to kill whomever they pleased. The Russian military received a free hand to bomb, rocket, and decimate Chechen towns with impunity. These were not surgical operations in the American model, they were a massive land and air war within its borders along the model of the Nazis besieging Stalingrad in WW II. These tactics, though effective, worked at the cost of many lives. Yet Putin and his generals brought Chechnya to its knees in the early 2000s and made the Russian populace bordering Chechnya and Ingushetia feel safer from terrorist attacks. Their beloved military, with the help of state television, saved face after the disastrous Beslan massacre and the terrorist takeover of a theater in Moscow where almost all hostages died.[4]

On the heels of the Beslan massacre and the *Kursk* submarine disaster, Putin and his cabinet then wanted to "modernize" the Russian military, which meant new weapons to replace Soviet artifacts, and policies that would counter NATO forces, and to gain the perception that Moscow was again a top-tier world power.[5] The Kremlin spent the past two decades attempting to modernize the Russian military from the antiquated Soviet model to one with a qualitative edge over Western forces. Russia wanted to be recognized as a global military power once again and has indeed managed to move on from outdated military policies and structure, but remains unable to be a global force as it was during its Warsaw Pact heyday. It has concentrated on working its way up from an intimidating regional power to attempting American-style power projection in the Middle East. That modernization is evolving, and the desired perceptions have started to gain traction. It helped that the Kremlin has continued to punch above its weight in Syria, but, with the exception of their airpower, they have not changed their target for military power. But Moscow has certainly tried. In the Mediterranean, Syria under Bashar al-Assad has used military force to flex its muscles by launching cruise missile and ballistic weapons attacks from within Russia to strike both ISIS terrorists and anti-Assad revolutionary targets in Iraq and Syria.

The regional military advance in Georgia in 2008 allowed Russian forces to show they could take territory and stand up to international condemnation. Where annexing South Ossetia and Abkhazia showed the brute force of Russian power, the later annexation of Crimea in 2014 demonstrated a new form of Russian warfare—hybrid warfare.[6] Hybrid warfare is the Kremlin strategy to use an amalgam of operational techniques, such as hard weapons, kinetic combat, unmarked special operations raids, covert espionage, and unbridled cyberwarfare. They battle-tested it against Ukraine along with a light signature special operations presence to begin eventual operations to seize the Crimea peninsula. Moscow's grander goal was a total collapse of the pro-European Kiev government, but for now the hybrid warfare shows the Russian military has a recipe for success in regional conflicts.[7]

However, these are small successes. Russia has shown in Georgia and Ukraine that it can take territories where it has placed assets and has long-standing historic ties. What has yet to be tested is Moscow's military willingness to take and hold an entire country in which NATO has a stake, such as one of the Baltic states. There is no sign Moscow can do that successfully or has the strategic willingness to test Western militaries' appetite for open conflict.

Which is not to say Russia has learned over the past years how to integrate command and control, intelligence and surveillance, and use of precision weapons. Moscow has learned from Western militaries—especially the United States—that Unmanned Aerial Vehicles are a combat multiplier of the highest order and have tried to mimic what we have done. The more the Kremlin can learn from initial usage of these assets, the more they can work on adapting that for geostrategic goals.[8] Russia most recently tested this theory by placing a large garrison inside Syria,[9] where it has long had military relations with the Assad government.[10] That contingent has done anything but serve as a "peacekeeping force." They are in Syria and engaging in full-scale combat missions to assist the Assad government in targeting opponents to the regime. Their presence also tests US and Allied forces' willingness to engage with their troops.[11] Much like the operations in Chechnya a decade earlier, Russian forces engaged in indiscriminate and brutal attacks against Assad-chosen targets. The wanton and deliberate destruction of hospitals, public utilities, and homes of civilians was a Nazi technique designed to empty cities. It was learned well. It is now the regional model applied to others.

Despite Moscow's goals, there have been few improvements to the nation's military. The command structure remains top heavy and enlisted troops are more likely to face brutal hazing[12] than they are to have opportunities to lead missions. The military is still unable to conduct combined or joint operations with any precision. While Russian media present these joint and combined exercises as feats of strength, the reality is they are anything but. The footage is chosen ahead of time and is meant to show power but it's not reflective of any cohesiveness.[13] Open conflicts with powerful militaries would expose these shortcomings.

The Russian military has begun to understand its limits and remains able to flex its muscles throughout the region. The threat of military force—especially Moscow's missile, submarine, and bomber forces—remains a challenge NATO nations must concern themselves with. The specific use of special forces, military intelligence, and cyberwarfare has proven an exceptional edge to gain small swaths of territory while political machinations are more effective to undermine targeted governments.[14] Russian military power remains ferocious and concerning. However, internal organizational problems and historic inabilities to operate on a truly global scale render the current Russian military a shell of its Soviet glory. Kremlin planners have adapted to this by using political and economic levers to undermine NATO and Western nations because the military does not yet represent a true threat. But the longer we remain at the current status quo, the longer Moscow has to improve these deficiencies.

Because the Baltic Sea is strategically important to Russia as a trading route and buffer from the West, Russia moved the SS-26 STONE, aka the 9K 720 Iskander-M, an intermediate-range nuclear-tipped ballistic missile, to Kaliningrad in 2010 and later installed air defense systems there. Kaliningrad borders Lithuania, further inflaming a security dilemma for the Baltic countries.[15]

Russia's aggressive actions in Georgia in 1998 and invasion of Ukraine in 2014 have further influenced the Baltic countries' national security policies. Because Russia uses hybrid warfare tactics, leaders in the Baltic countries have become increasingly concerned about a potential invasion by Russia.[16] NATO subsequently stationed a small battalion of troops in the Baltics as deterrent to Russia. Every few years, Russia performs large-scale military exercises near the Baltic countries, with scenarios such as using tactical nuclear weapons, which further increases tension in the region.[17]

Russian Political Parties and Organizations

To assist the Kremlin in integrating European and American groups into the anti-West program, Russian parties and organizations work as advisors to advance Moscow's goals. United Russia was formed in 2001 and led by Russia's President, Vladimir Putin. Dimitry Medvedev was its Chairman and Vladislav Surkov was its First Deputy Chief of Staff to the President. Russians refer to United Russia as "the Party of Power." Other nations refer to it as "the Party of Crooks and Thieves."

In exchange for financial support, Putin's party controlled power by giving out contracts, bribes, and kickbacks. Across the country members of the party were routinely accused of corruption, drug trafficking, racketeering, vote-rigging, and murder. Yet, once in office they would not only escape prosecution, in some cases they were awarded medals for their service. Being a member was almost a get-out-of-jail-free card, unless you crossed the party itself. United Russia was Russia's answer to unity after a period of chaotic displacement after Yeltsin and the fall of the Soviet Union. As of early 2018, United Russia held the majority of seats at the Duma.

For the 2018 Presidential election, Vladimir Putin ran as an Independent.[18] He did this in 2004. But his words are just puffery. He poses as an "independent" to project the idea that he belongs to all of Russia. He ran essentially unopposed by other candidates and won with 75% of the country voting for him.

Motherland-National Patriotic Union, aka Rodina, was founded by Dmitry Rogozin in 2003. It is popularly believed that the creation of Rodina was the work of Putin advisor Vladislav Surkov, as an effort to erode the voting base of the Communist party before the 2003 elections in the Duma.[19] Surkov is supposed to have established Rodina to make Putin's United Russia party look moderate next to the ultranationalist coalition of the right and left that is represented by Rodina.[20]

In 2005, the party had two actions that led to its dissolution. The first was a petition to the Prosecutor-General to ban Jewish organizations from operating in Russia. The second was a campaign ad to incite racial hatred when a political advertisement showed swarthy men eating watermelon and throwing the rinds on the ground in front of a white woman. Dmitry Rogozin is seen in the background watching and he steps forward to tell the four men to clean it up. The ad ends with "Очистим Москву от мусора!" or "Let's clear Moscow of garbage!" The Liberal Democratic Party filed a complaint and, consequently, Rodina was banned from participating in many regional elections in 2006.

In March 2006, Rogozin left Rodina and was replaced by Alexander Babakov, a relative unknown. The party ceased to exist temporarily as members joined the Party of Life and Party of Pensioners for Social Justice to form a new party, A Just Russia. The A Just Russia party lasted from 2006 through 2012 before Rodina re-emerged under the leadership of Rogozin's ally Aleksey Zhuravlyov. Many political observers say the party is still controlled by Dmitry Rogozin.[21]

The new party was more focused on militarism, uniting nationalist movements, and cooperation with Putin's All-Russia People's Front. Rodina member Fedor Biryukov organized a forum in St. Petersburg on March 22, 2015, that brought together far-right movements from around the world. They called for the establishment of a World National-Conservative Movement (WNCM). Additionally, the group has ties to and has encouraged separatist movements in the United States.[22]

It should be noted that though Rogozin left Rodina, he moved onto more sinister work. Dmitry Rogozin sought to get protection for Russian spies Eduard Shirokov and Vladimir Popov over terror charges levied in a failed Montenegro coup attempt.[23] The two GRU officers were arrested and accused of attempting to assassinate the Prime Minister of Montenegro, Milo Djukanovic.[24] The officers allegedly planned to launch a massive attack on the country's parliament.

Political party youth organizations stretch back to the early days of the Soviet Union, when Lenin advocated the inclusion of young people into the role of social order. Thus the Communist Party established its first youth groups: the Komsomol, the Young Pioneers, and the Little Octobrists.

The Komsomol was established in October 1918 in the early days of the post-Tsarist Russia. It trained and indoctrinated youth up to the age of 28 into the objectives of the Communist Party of the Soviet Union. The term Komsomol came from the first letters of the phrase "kommunisticheskiy soyuz molodyozhi" or the "Communist alliance of young people." Under the Komsomol were two younger groups, the Little Octobrists, who ranged from 7 to 9 years old, who would then graduate into the Young Pioneers, which was for 9- to 14-year-olds.

Though scouting groups existed before the Soviet Union, the

Komsomol was specifically aimed to promote the ideological demands of the Soviet Union. Any scouting groups that didn't fall in line under the Soviet rules were driven underground and essentially eliminated.

In the era of Putin, the Nashi replaced the Komsomol. They were known for their public displays of affection for Putin and their public scorning of the designated enemies of the state, which included journalists, human rights activists, or anyone who was a critic of Putin and Kremlin policies. They would parade through the streets with signs featuring the faces and "crimes" of these dissidents, with the youth scorning their names. The first event, on April 15, 2005, was called "our victory" or *nasha pobeda* and on the same day of the rally Garry Kasparov accused the kids of attacking him with a chessboard.[25] Yearly, the group organized an event called the Russian March, which had large turnouts. In 2009, an estimated 30,000 people attended, mostly bused in from the Moscow suburbs. These events were used to bolster nationalist sentiment and attack the Kremlin's enemies as "Russia's enemies."

The Nashi were also quite skilled at disrupting other groups and spent many hours planning to disrupt rallies of groups critical of Putin. When they would learn of an event being planned, they would fill the space of the event like a flash mob, thus preventing it from taking place. They were known for the rigidity of their doctrine. The group had a list of "Commandments of Honor" written by Ruslan Maslov, who may have stolen them from Nazi propagandist Joseph Goebbles:[26]

1. Your fatherland is Russia. Love it above all others, and in deed more than word.
2. The enemies of Russia are your enemies.
3. Every compatriot, even the lowliest, is part of Russia. Love him like you love yourself!
4. Demand only duties of yourself. Then Russia will regain justice.
5. Be proud of Russia! You must honor the fatherland for which millions gave their lives.
6. Remember, if someone takes away your rights, you have the right to say "NO!"

7. Uphold what you must without shame where Great Russia is concerned!
8. Believe in the future. Then you will become the victor!

An alternative to the Nashi is the Eurasian Youth Union (EYU), which was created in February 2005 to combat the Ukrainian Orange Revolution. Like the Nashi, they were there to espouse a pro-Russian nationalism but with the Eurasian flavor that was typical of their leader, Aleksandr Dugin.[27] They were more tolerant of working with openly racist groups like Aleksandr Belov's Movement Against Illegal Immigration. In November 2005, the two joined up for a rally that quickly became more identified with neo-Nazi antics. The group was sanctioned by Ukraine, Canada, and the United States for participating in fighting in Ukraine.[28] The EYU also created "war camps" outside of Moscow to prepare to fight in Ukraine or beyond.[29] Dugin's effort to stoke the fires of conflict were mirrored in his impatience with Putin's efforts in Ukraine. "When we are hesitating, we are losing," said Dugin, who never served in the military.

The Gray Zone

Under the Soviets, the KGB oversaw training of leftist terrorists as a method of frightening and destabilizing the West. They formed and funded groups such as the Baader-Meinhof Gang and its successor Red Army Faction, France's Action Directe, Belgium's Communist Combatant Cells, Greece's 17 November, and the Irish Republican Army. The Russians also backed anti-American dictators such as Muammar Gaddafi and Saddam Hussein. Their intelligence agencies were encouraged to conduct acts of terror. This led to great massacres such as the bombing of Pan Am flight 103 over Lockerbie, Scotland, and UTA 772 over the Sahara, together killing over 400 passengers.

The 1970s and 80s were awash with assassinations of diplomats and military members, kidnappings of Americans, and bombings of embassies and military bases. Russian- and Cuban-backed insurgencies spread to Nicaragua, El Salvador, Colombia, Peru, Mozambique, Angola, Eritrea, and Yemen.

The Russian terror strategy was a major component of their active measures. But when the fall of the Soviet Union occurred, the terror methods were placed into secure storage. The Communist Alliance no longer existed. Russia had shifted from collectivists to capitalists. They also embraced their new religious orthodoxy and cultural conservatism. Under the strategy of neo-Eurasianism and the growth of the internet, the Russians found right-wing groups, even some that were explicitly neo-Nazi, were better examples of Fellow Travelers. Gone were the days of leftist liberals, and European socialists with their peace, love, and happiness claptrap. Russia was to be a mighty bear allied with others in Europe and America who saw it their way. This ideological jump from hard left to hard right occurred over 10 years. What it led to was a need for conservative agitators and paramilitaries ready to carry out Moscow's will in forging a new Russo-European-American axis upon which to confront the Muslim world.

Ultranationalist groups like the Russian Imperial Movement (RIM, or RID, *Russkoe Imperskoe Dvizhenie* in Russian) were encouraged to open and grow their membership. The RIM is believed to be a Russian paramilitary group that organizes pan-European groups for militant purposes. The group runs paramilitary training camps they referred to as "clubs" and a combat program called "Partisan." With it, the RIM recruited and trained people from around the world.[30] The Partisan camp is run by a former Russian army soldier named Denis Gariev. Gariev formerly served with Russia's strategic missile troops. He is a graduate of history studies from St. Petersburg.[31] Gariev claims to have been the leader of the Imperial Legion, the paramilitary arm of the Russian Imperial Movement. Stanislav Vorobyov, leader of RIM, said men of the Imperial Legion were combat veterans of the pro-Moscow Ukrainian rebels fighting in the breakaway regions of Donetsk and Lugansk.[32] Vorobyov would be seen on social media arriving in Crimea. He wrote on a blog:

"I accompanied an airplane to Crimea that carried Russian military instructors who were to organize the local resistance movement. I remember one night the SBU guys [Ukrainian security officers] burned documents in their yard—then I understood that we were going to annex [Crimea]."[33]

The Partisan training "club" was located in the Udelnaya district of St. Petersburg. They claimed to have another camp near Kaluga, southwest of Moscow. According to Gariev, they train 10 to 15 members at a time. By 2015, they had graduated over 100 members who paid 250 euros to attend.[34] Vorobyov wrote in his blog that the group was maintained by donations that were used to purchase equipment—clothes, radios, bulletproof vests, etc.—and to pay instructor salaries. In keeping with their racist core, he also wrote that they would not train Muslims.

Other extremist groups had trained with Gariev's crew, including the ultranationalist Stiag (or Flag) Slovak Revival Movement and Nordic Resistance. Nordic Resistance organized a summit in 2015 led by Vorobyov. István Győrkös, former leader of the Hungarian National Front, a neo-Nazi group, killed a police officer in October 2016.[35] Győrkös is said to have practiced paramilitary exercises with members of Russian military intelligence.[36]

Private Military Contractors

The American war in Iraq brought about the rise of the private military corporation. Many Russian soldiers served with Western security companies. Post-war Russian energy companies such as Lukoil and Gazprom won contracts in Iraq and formed their own Russian security forces. The war in Ukraine led to Russia using asymmetric forces such as local militias and intelligence subcontractors. Russian hybrid warfare strategy uses special operations forces without markings and flags, or they deploy local surrogates. When they seized Crimea, these off-the-book special forces were called "little green men." In Syria and Ukraine, contractor companies formed to fill the roles of special action groups so they could provide deniability for their patrons, Russian intelligence. The military intelligence agency GRU is said to operate a contractor training base near Krasnodar where these forces are prepared, armed, and deployed. In a study of Russian private military corporations, journalist Pierre Sautreuil wrote in the blog *War Is Boring* that one in particular, ChVK Wagner, had extra special sanction:

> "In eastern Ukraine in 2015, several local separatist warlords died violently in apparent assassinations. The deaths ensured the unquestioned authority of Igor Plotnitski, the Kremlin's strongman in the region. Interviewed by the author, numerous separatists point to a single culprit—the ChVK (that's Russian for 'private military company') Wagner, a band of Russian contractors who allegedly also took part in the battle of Debaltseve in February 2015."[37]

Some efforts are not sanctioned by the Russian government—for example, the Slovanic Corporation.[38] This organization was a Hong Kong–based Russian company formed in 2013. This group formed to protect assets in Syria for pay. In comparison with the situation in Syria, it was widely considered a joke.[39] Two hundred and fifty men self-organized to come to Syria after responding to advertisements that they were there to conduct "offensive" military operations à la the American Blackwater corporation. This group claimed to have top-tier equipment but found trash kits, broken weapons, and no armor as promised. One contractor reported they were given buses with steel plates welded on. The role of the Slavonic Corporation was to seize oil fields in the vicinity of Deir ez-Zor, which is in the middle of ISIS-held territory and over 500 km from their base camp. Without any planning or fire support, Slavonic militia convoyed out to the east and were quickly ambushed by an al-Qaeda-linked militia. They were saved from massacre by a blinding desert storm. The company quickly went out of business.[40]

From the ashes of the Slavonic Corporation, the company ChVK Wagner, or Wagner Group, emerged. Wagner was a new model of security contracting. Formed by Dmitri Utkin, they were designed to fill the "little green men" role, with complete deniability of the Russian government. It did not work well, as in 2015 Utkin was sanctioned by the US Treasury for seizing Syrian oil and gas fields for oil giant Evro Polis.

Journalist Denis Korotkov told the *War Is Boring* blog "…now [it] seems the ChVK Wagner is building on the Slavonic Corps' misfortune. Indeed, many members of this mysterious organization, as well as its leader—a former major in the Spetsnaz and ex-employee of Moran Security—were also members of the luckless 2013 expedition in Syria."[41]

The Syrian army had difficulty meeting its manpower, so instead of recruiting directly into the army, an all-volunteer force made up of tribal units and militias was formed called Fifth Corps. Their nickname, adorned on their black circle logo with a white human skull, was "the ISIS Hunters." Apparently, the contractors from Wagner were attached to Fifth Corps and were operating in the vicinity of Deir ez-Zor. It is rumored that Wagner Group technically a sister company of Evro Polis, like Slavonic before it, had signed a contract with the Syrian regime. According to the *New York Times*, "In the petroleum deal, Evro Polis, a corporation formed last summer, will receive a 25 percent share of oil and natural gas produced on territory it captures from the Islamic State, the news site Fontanka.ru reported."[42] Evro Polis was a shady oil management company that was operated by the owner of Wagner and director of covert operations for Vladimir Putin, Yevgeny Prigozhin. Prigozhin's disguised "offensive" contractor operation to seize the American/SDF-held oil field would be literally blown to the winds by direct contact with the US Army Special Operations Command and the US Air Force.

Sometime on the morning of February 17, 2018, US Intelligence, supporting Special Forces detachments operating in partnership with the Syrian Democratic Front (SDF) Kurdish fighters in Deir ez-Zor, observed Russian armored vehicles amassing on the opposite bank of the Euphrates River. US forces deconfliction liaison officers notified Russian army command in Syria and asked if they were conducting offensive operations near US units. The Russians officially stated that no Russian army forces were near the Americans, as they were completely unofficial.

I have personally participated in US intelligence-gathering operations where an unknown enemy is amassing. The myriad of national and tactical intelligence systems that we can bring to bear is staggering. US Intelligence would likely have assessed that the Russians were security contractors working for the Assad regime and operating in cahoots with the Syrian militias. Observing them from satellites, drones, reconnaissance aircraft, and on the ground, the Special Forces commander would have made sure enough air assets including F-18 Strike aircraft, AC-130 gunships, AH-64 Apache helicopters, and even B-1 Lancer bombers were on station to deter or defeat an actual attack. US Marine Corps artillery operating the M777 long-range heavy artillery and US Army HIMARs truck-mounted battlefield tactical missiles would also have been ready and available. All that would be left to do is brew a new pot of coffee and see if the threat develops or evaporates. The bottom line for the Special Operators was that the Russian massing up in dozens of tanks and armored personnel carriers were private military contractors with ChVK Wagner. The Syrians supporting them were the uncontrolled locals under the Syrian Fifth Corps.

According to survivor accounts, Wagner had indeed organized a massive armored force spearheaded by highly modernized T-72 tanks and BRDM armored cars to seize the al-Jabar oil fields. The fields in the Deir ez-Zor region produce 40% of Syria's oil reserves and the allied SDF forces had captured this facility in late September 2017.

US force commanders contacted the Russian army's deconfliction liaison officer in Syria. This liaison was set up to stop accidental exchanges of fire between the US and Russia. The Russian liaison said that no Russian forces were anywhere near the American positions. That meant whoever was coming had gone rogue and was not under Moscow's control—or were they?

The joint Russian and Syrian forces started their armor assault to take the American-Kurdish positions. Well before they reached their first objective, crossing a pontoon bridge over the Euphrates, an ominous sign occurred: A large American stars-and-stripes flag was raised over the most forward position. It was not for the Russians—it was to make sure the incoming American airstrikes knew their precise location. The Russians did not know it yet, but they were already dead.

Recorded phone calls from the battle shared with US media showed the mercenaries were completely decimated by US air power, with special forces Joint Terminal Attack Controllers (JTAC) calling in precise strikes.

In one extended telephone call that was played in Russian on Voice of America a survivor described the flow of the battle once they launched their attack on the Special Forces outpost:

> "The reports that are on TV about...well, you know, about Syria and the 25 people that are wounded there from the Syrian [fucking] Army and—well...to make it short, we've had our asses [fucking] kicked. So, one squadron [fucking] lost 200 people... right away, another one lost 10 people...and I don't know about the third squadron, but it got torn up pretty badly, too....So, three squadrons took a beating....The Yankees attacked...first they blasted the [fuck] out of us by artillery and then they took four helicopters up and pushed us in a [fucking] merry-go-round with heavy caliber machine guns....They were all shelling the holy [fuck] out of it and our guys didn't have anything besides the assault rifles...nothing at all, not even mentioning shoulder-fired SAMs or anything like that....So they tore us to pieces for sure, put us through hell, and the Yankees knew for sure that the Russians were coming, that it was us, [fucking] Russians....Our guys were going to commandeer an oil refinery and the Yankees were holding it....We got our [fucking] asses beat rough, my men called me....They're there drinking now...many have gone missing...it's a total [fuck] up, it sucks, another takedown.... Everybody, you know, treats us like pieces of [shit]....They beat our asses like we were little pieces of [shit] but our [fucking] government will go in reverse now and nobody will respond or anything and nobody will punish anyone for this....So these are our casualties...."[43]

Syrian Fifth Corps would later claim they were attacking a joint SDF unit working with ISIS, as Syria maintains that all US operations are in support of the terrorists, not liberation forces. Unofficial counts would say up to 300 Russians and Syrians were dead.[44]

The Russian Foreign Ministry spokesperson, Maria Zakharova, claimed the attack was nothing like the US Central Command described:

> "Material about the deaths of dozens and hundreds of Russian citizens—it is classic disinformation. It was not 400, not 200, not 100, and not 10. Preliminary figures indicate that as a result of the armed clash that took place, the causes of which are now being investigated, we can talk about the deaths of five people, presumably citizens of Russia. There are also wounded, but all this needs to be verified—in particular, and first and foremost, [their] citizenship; whether they are citizens of Russia or other countries."[45]

US intelligence agencies learned that Yevgeny Prigozhin, who has contracts with the Russian Defense Ministry, spoke with Kremlin officials before the attack. Prigozhin, who is close to Putin, received permission from a Russian minister to move forward with a "fast and strong" initiative in early February, then later spoke with Syrian presidential aides to coordinate. In the end, Prigozhin's bid ended in wholesale slaughter. The 12 or so American special operators on the ground called in nearly three hours of airplane, artillery, and helicopter strikes against the Russians that obliterated the entire assaulting column. For now, Russia's ambitions to seize Syria oil were as dead as their mercenaries.

Bullets, Lies, Laptops, and Spies

CHAPTER 6

Active Measures

Evidence that Vladimir Putin's Russian intelligence agencies, including state intelligence FSB, clandestine service SVR, and military intelligence GRU, as well as national cyber-contractors and the state-run news media, used well-cultivated espionage methods developed under the Soviet Union to carry out the cyberattack on the 2016 United States election is overwhelming. The espionage methodology that they used for these operations is called *aktivnyye meropriyatiya*, or "active measures." In a House subcommittee for foreign affairs, at the peak of the Cold War, Robert Gates defined it as "Covert operations designed to shape public opinion in foreign countries on key political issues. These measures are targeted at opinion-makers, such as political leaders, the media, and influential businessmen, as well as the public at large."[1]

Active measures are the dirty tricks of the intelligence community, done on a political or personal stage using a myriad of methodologies, including assassination, forging documents, and the arranging for them to "surface," and making legitimate documents appear insidious or incriminating. Other methods include fabricating and planting rumors so that they enter the media stream as news; distributing carefully crafted false narratives or disinformation; and writing and printing books, pamphlets with disinformation themes, and fabricated stories. Some of the most effective use stolen or false information or imagery to compromise or blackmail an individual to do one's bidding (Kompromat).

Even famous dissidents living in the West were under attack. Aleksandr Solzhenitsyn, the famous writer who exposed the Soviet gulag prison systems, has been a target of active measures.[2]

Starting in 2013, the Russians launched massive active measures against the United States and Europe. Using compromised assets, blackmail, media manipulation, and quite possibly a number of assassinations, Russian intelligence, at the direction of President Putin, have exploited political division through propaganda campaigns, spies, and disinformation. Russia continues to use these measures against the United States and its allies, including the use of hacking, cutouts, spies, and unwitting assets to advance its goals worldwide. Russian intelligence employs subversive social media campaigns, fake news, troll armies, and propaganda to subvert the democratic process in the US and European democracies. It continues to this day.

None of this is new. From the early days of the Soviet Union to today, the Russian espionage craft is alive and well. Deployed against the United States and Europe in 2016 and 2017, Russian active measures have been explained by former Russian intelligence officials as the use of all actions short of including overt military operations to influence an enemy nation or to gain an outcome favorable to Russia. Gleb Pavlovsky says that this new animosity to America began in 2012 when Putin returned for a second term:

> "I think in the early Putin days as president, and then certainly when Medvedev was president and Putin was prime minister, Russia was not what it is today. We were interacting with them in a much more normal way—we being the United States and Europe. It was only when Putin came back the second time as president, that the behavior started to turn, and turned significantly back towards what was essentially Russian behavior during the Cold War, which is challenge the United States everywhere you can in the world, and do whatever you can to undermine what they're trying to accomplish. Do whatever you can to weaken them."[3]

Weakening one's enemies is precisely what active measures are for.

History of Active Measures

Active measures of every sort are part of the operational menu for bringing about results that could not be achieved elsewhere. The first Russian secret police, the Cheka, were established in 1917 by the Bolsheviks and were primarily used to thwart opposition to the Bolshevik ideology and "enemies of Bolshevism."[4] The Cheka were disbanded and reestablished as the State Political Directorate (GPU) in 1922, and then renamed under Stalin as the People's Commissariat for Interior Affairs (NKVD)—used in Stalin's "Great Terror" in the 1930s.[5] After Stalin's death, Khrushchev established the KGB in the early 1950s.[6] According to a House Intelligence report on active measures:

> "Soviet bloc disinformation operations were not a rare occurrence: more than 10,000 were carried out over the course of the Cold War. In the 1970s, Yuri Andropov, then head of the KGB, created active measures courses for operatives, and the KGB had up to 15,000 officers working on psychological and disinformation warfare at the height of the Cold War. The CIA estimated that the Soviet Union spent more than \$4 billion a year on active measures operations in the 1980s [approximately \$8.5 billion in 2017]."[7]

Active measures were and remain an offensive instrument of Russian policy.

Tennent Bagley, a former CIA officer assigned to handle high-value Russian defectors, wrote that in 1923, under the OGPU, one of the earliest Soviet active measures groups, they had three principal objectives:

> "1. discover what the enemy of the revolution knew, what they were seeking

2. create and disseminate false information to project the desired image of the Soviet leadership and

3. to disseminate that disinformation into the press of various countries."[8]

The Stanislav information warfare active measures group was the *Komitet-Informatsii* (KI) or Committee of Information. It operated between 1947 and 1951.[9] The committee was formed in July 1947 as a centrally organized information warfare and intelligence exploitation group. It merged the Russian military intelligence (GRU) and the early Stalinist Ministry of State Security (MGB) into a unified foreign intelligence service.[10] It was created in response to the American National Security Act of July 1947, which created the CIA. The first leader was Vyacheslav Molotov, Minister of Foreign Affairs. Eventually, the personnel from the KI were peeled away back to the GRU and MGB until it was dissolved in 1951.[11]

General Ivan Ivanovich Agayants was one of the early commanders of the KI and is a legend in Russian intelligence. He began his career in espionage, disinformation, propaganda, and active measures in 1930.[12] As a spy from 1937 to 1940, Agayants was stationed in France to conduct operations supporting the anti-fascist brigades in the Spanish Civil War. After the invasion of France, he went to Iran.[13] In 1943, when the Soviet Union became a part of the anti-Nazi alliance, he was brought back to the Mediterranean—Algiers—to serve as an envoy to the French provisional government led by Charles de Gaulle. After the defeat of the Nazis and the creation of the KGB, he served as the first resident (chief of station) in France. Agayants often traveled around the world to assist or oversee operations throughout the Cold War.[14]

In 1959 at the height of his stellar career, he sent a memorandum to the then KGB chairman, Aleksandr Shelepin. He proposed a new department that would specifically plan, manage, and execute active measures. It would become the KGB's Active Measures department—Department D. By 1962 they had 40 officers; by 1967, the staff had more than doubled to over 100 officers. By the end of the Cold War it was nearly 15,000 people.[15] The Department was divided into five parts: political, economic, scientific and technical, military, and counterintelligence. Eventually, the department rose to a level of prominence and was rebranded "Service A."

The KGB's Service A was the key department of the First Chief Directorate responsible for active measures. It managed dirty tricks activities around the world, including disinformation efforts, making forgeries, arming insurgents, sending weapons to terrorists, or deploying assassins. It was this group with ruthlessly evil KGB characters depicted in the James Bond film *From Russia with Love*.[16]

Under the Soviet system of government, the chain of command started in the Politburo, the policy-making committee in the Communist Party, then below them was the central committee. Within the Supreme Soviet was the International Department, which handled the United States–Canada Institute, pro-Soviet Communist parties, front groups, and "Liberation Movements," aka insurgent or terror groups. Until WWII, the United States was an "important target" for Russian intelligence officers, but afterward it became the "main enemy" for Department D, including NATO and followed by China. The CIA and its sister intelligence agencies of the West were a constant target. Security and defense contractors were targets for agent recruitment. In one of the more famous cases, Andrew Daulton Lee and Christopher Boyce worked with the KGB to steal information on US spy satellites from the TRW Defense and Space Systems Group in 1977.[17] The two were arrested and sent to prison. They were later portrayed by Timothy Hutton and Sean Penn in the movie, *The Falcon and the Snowman*, which was based on the book by Robert Lindsey. However, all industry companies were targets. The KGB had spied on international oil companies in San Francisco using microwaves to capture voices during their corporate meetings.[18]

Since the day the Soviet Union officially ceased to exist, December 25, 1991, Putin has not changed those task orders for the FSB and SVR.

Though most active measures operations were coordinated from the Kremlin and were deployed directly by Moscow efforts, the nine Warsaw Pact nations in the Soviet bloc carried out operations based on their own agendas. Doing so provided cover for Kremlin activity abroad. This allowed the reach of Kremlin aims to migrate west. Such efforts were still ultimately relayed back to Soviet authority.

The directives of the active measures teams were derived from Soviet national objectives. Their long-term goals were to work on lifting sanctions and keeping NATO influence and member states away from Russian borders. All other activities below that were generally performed in piecemeal fashion to address a small component of these larger goals. Often these missions would be part of the jigsaw puzzle to weaken Russia's opponents and to create a favorable environment for Kremlin policy. They'd do this by creating a newspaper or hosting an international peace conference with American political groups who wanted a connection to Russian money, but did not have a direct contact. Much of the time was spent discrediting and vilifying opponents and dissidents.

When it came to targeting the CIA for disinformation, the KGB went for a direct attack. They used allies, politicians, and political dupes to villainize the CIA and its operations. Almost all KGB defectors agreed that the overall mission focus for attacking and damaging the CIA was to demoralize, expose, and undermine the effectiveness of the agency. The KGB did not leave the US Department of Defense alone on this field. Their global political and propaganda warfare teams would develop themes, organize protests, and ensure that American forces overseas were always uncomfortable.

Though intelligence agencies were high priorities, the highest goals were to undermine the American political process. The Russian interest in damaging American politics goes back to its earliest Bolshevik days. For almost 70 years, democracy in America was often portrayed as false while Soviet democracy, as they called it, was promoted as "true democracy"—since supposedly everything belonged to everyone. Yet the Supreme Soviet spent inordinate amounts of time and money trying to ideologically destroy the United States and European liberal democracies. The KGB and all state media were tasked to ensure the following strategic objectives were carried out:

1. Infiltrate the decision-making process of the American bureaucracy.
2. Influence, insinuate, and use the American media.

3. Promote smear campaigns against politicians who were obstacles to Russian objectives, including presidential, congressional, state or local officials, or public policy figures.
4. Fuel racial division and resentment.[19]

Where the direct contact with Russian intelligence might have been a turnoff for potential assets, use of operatives from other countries and intelligence organizations were more effective. During the Cold War, Czech, East German, Angolan, Egyptian, Syrian, Afghan, and Cuban officers were able to conduct operations that would have otherwise been hindered by a Russian contact. Russian liaison officers kept these satellite services in order and conducted counterintelligence spy hunts for infiltrators from Western agencies. All important decisions required their approval.[20] Though their prime ministers and interior ministers were aware of what their agents were doing, Moscow kept a tight rein on their work.

Training for satellite intelligence services in all aspects including propaganda, disinformation, forgery, and other active measures were handled by the KGB. The nationalities were divided up into different camps; their countries covered the cost of the training, but the KGB determined the spy craft curriculum.

After the fall of the Soviet Union, active measures continued under intelligence officer Sergei Tretyakov. According to Tretyakov, a colonel for the modern-day Russian clandestine service SVR, KGB Service A was never disbanded but was simply rebranded as Department MS, or "Support Measures."[21] Department MS changed with the times. They would avoid tying activities to the diplomatic missions to avoid counterintelligence efforts by the FBI. The advent of advanced computing communications and mobile telephones made linking Russian spies to the Embassy and their agents harder to prove, though they had to keep using the Embassy as a secure base of operations.

Disinformation Warfare

Disinformation is the art of using false or misleading information and injecting it or getting it credited by legitimate and credible sources.

The false information must be logical, believable, and acceptable to gain the confidence of the target population of an adversary nation. Like all good lies, the material must be crafted to play to the biases and accepted norms of the target audience, even if the information is horrible or distasteful to others not of that tribe. If the target audience disbelieves the message because it violates the consistency of accepted reality, then the disinformation campaign will be ineffective or fail. However, the accepted reality can be bent so that eventually, as the disinformation campaign plays itself out, a grand lie will be accepted as truth. That is the art of disinformation.

During the Cold War, Russian disinformation campaigns were used to frame the world according to the Kremlin. They have also been used to project the power of Russia's military capabilities, hype the living conditions and joyfulness of Russian citizens, and to manipulate relations between other countries. Guided visits in Russia by foreigners were arranged to give them a view of the prosperity of Russian people or to cover the abuses of Russian citizens.

Extremists strong in biases and prejudice were considered the easiest targets for disinformation. Those who seek to gain their information from biased sources without critical skepticism were preferred targets for campaigns of disinformation. The rise of partisan news only magnified the problem as each played to the biases of their crowd and thus were easy targets of disinformation.[22]

One prominent disinformation agent was Vitaly Yevgenyevich Lui, who got published in the *New York Times* and the *Washington Post*, and was featured on CBS News and other notable credible news agencies, under the name Victor Louis.[23] His efforts were used to attack dissidents like Solzhenitsyn or Stalin's daughter, Svetlana Alliluyeva. In one case, he was used via the *London Evening News* to spread disinformation aimed at China claiming the Soviets were planning a preemptive nuclear attack.[24]

Ex-spy Sergei Tretyakov explained that disinformation products crafted in Moscow were surreptitiously transmitted to Russian FSB/SVR officers in the US who would use public internet access, such as the New York Public Library internet terminals. From there the propaganda warfare staff would propagate articles that purported to be educational or scientific reports that were created to be believable works of reputable academics with names that sounded respectable.[25] Those reports would then be passed to organizations that were known for criticizing the US government.

According to the famous ex-KGB trained Czech officer-turned-dissident and author Ladislav Bittman, Russian intelligence saw each mission from smallest to strategic as having three necessary characters:

1. The Operator: The operator as the Russian intelligence officers and producers of the disinformation (called the "product").
2. The Adversary: The adversary was spy-speak for the target of the operation. It could be anyone or anything. Most often it was a national political goal or policy, a specific politician or political party, a public figure, or even the entire population of a target country.
3. The Unwitting Agent: The unwitting agents were the unaware participants used to attack the adversary either directly or indirectly. They were unwitting, as the operator usually covered his true nationality, intent, and sources of payment. Often UAs believed they were working in a common interest with the operator.

In his classic book on Cold War active measures, *KGB and Soviet Disinformation*, Bittman spelled out the details of the Active Measures Campaign and how this organized method leads to chaos for the adversary and the unwitting agent.[26]

"1. The unwitting agents were used to attack the adversary in a direct role as a proxy for the operator. The unwitting agent believes the actions were self-initiated.

2. The operator directly attacking the adversary but, in a way, that the adversary retaliates against the unwitting agent. Doing so would leave the adversary and unwitting agent to fight it out without noticing the operator.

3. The operator directly attacking the adversary but, in a manner, that the adversary doesn't perceive the action as an attack or were led to rationalize the actions.

4. The operator attacks both the adversary and unwitting agent with the aim to pit them against each other."

In the early days of the Soviet Union, the Cheka used these methods against Russian exiles in Western Europe to retaliate against those who left the ideological fold. These efforts were driven by ideological demands of the revolutionaries and focused on circles of former Russians and foreign Communist parties.[27]

The goal of strategic disinformation was necessary to sow doubt, suspicion, and conspiracy theory for enough time that the Russians could execute a full-scale invasion. By extension, the Foreign Ministry was responsible for holding the propaganda and disinformation line at all costs. Like old Politburo statements from the Soviet era and even when the truth is easily observable, and the party line was disprovable, diplomats and apparatchiks would insist up was down. For example, when Russia invaded the Ukrainian peninsula of Crimea, hundreds of sources witnessed and videotaped the takeover of key government buildings by Russian Special Forces soldiers (RUSOF). The men wore RUSOF uniforms. They carried RUSOF guns. They spoke Russian. They flew in on Russian aircraft. They were Russian except for one glaring piece of kit…they had removed their Russian army flags and name tapes from their uniforms. Foreign Minister Sergey Lavrov was confronted about Russian forces in Crimea spearheading a military operation. He came forward on international TV and claimed that the "little green men" were not Russian Special Forces.[28] In fact, he insisted they were locals who just happened to have the most advanced weaponry and kit in Eastern Europe. Speaking from a conference in Madrid, Lavrov stated, "If they are the self-defense forces created by the inhabitants of Crimea, we have no authority over them. They do not receive our orders."[29] In 2015, Putin would boldly admit that Russian Special Forces had indeed spearheaded the invasion of Crimea. They needed to control the local government infrastructure, so no Ukrainian terrorism could occur.

In the early days of the post-revolution Soviet Union, Operation Sindikat and Operation Trust were some of the first active measure campaigns in Soviet history. Trust was carried out by the Red State Political Directorate (OGPU) spies to trap a dissident Russian writer named Boris Savinkov and his handler, a former British agent (and alleged con artist) Sidney Reilly. Reilly was a WW I British espionage officer who went to Russia as an independent contractor after the revolution. He supported anti-Soviet causes and operations of the White Army. He is most notably portrayed in popular fiction and the BBC TV series *Reilly: Ace of Spies*.

The Red Army Bolshevik counterintelligence created the appearance of their agents acting as if they were an anti-Soviet counterrevolutionary "White Army" organization called "The Trust." Using this lie, the OGPU lured Savinkov and Reilly back to Russia and captured them. Savinkov was sentenced to prison but forced to write against his former White Army comrades for Russian and European publications. Savinkov was later killed at the hands of the Soviet revolutionaries.[30] Reilly also did not fare well. He was taken to a forest and executed by firing squad. Like all good Russian propaganda, the death of a famous British spy was given an exciting cover story that was in itself a propaganda product. Russia claimed his death was at the hands of simple, trustworthy Soviet border guards who shot him as he tried to cross from Finland into the glorious new Soviet Union.

Document theft and dispersal to a hungry news media, à la the 2016 election, were precisely what Russian intelligence did in 1927 to discredit Japan and stop its imperial machinations. Russian intelligence officers from the Stalin-era Chekist intelligence agency, the INO (*Inostranny Otdel* or Foreign Department) carried out a brilliant operation that penentrated the heart of the Japanese imperial government. The INO was formed by Felix Dzerzhinsky to give the Cheka access to overseas intelligence. The INO officers recruited a Japanese government interpreter who had very high-level access to the offices of the Japanese government. He was tasked to steal a strategic war plan allegedly written by Baron Tanaka Giichi, the then–Japanese Prime Minister. The stolen documents were returned to Russia and leaked to the American and Chinese press in Nanking by the spies. The "Tanaka Memorial Imperialist Conquest Plan" called for the Japanese invasion of Manchuria and Mongolia. This action was part distraction as it was meant to have the appearance of being stolen by American spies.[31] To this day, its authenticity is under dispute.

Russian intelligence were masters of forgery in active measures. Sometimes the forgeries were mixed with real documents to spread "black propaganda" or fake news stories. Under the KGB the 1950s and 60s were great times for forgeries. Their usage dropped off in the mid-1970s but in 1976, rudimentary computers and faster IBM electric typewriters facilitated the resumption of anti-US campaigns. Computers would come to replace them soon enough. Not all forgeries were meant for public consumption. Undetected forgeries can still do damage privately, particularly when they show up in classified information as "leaked." The KGB, and then the FSB, carried out thousands of micro campaigns of propaganda and forgeries. From trying to discredit the US-backed government in Ghana to making documents appear suggesting that West Germany and America wanted racist South Africa to acquire nuclear weapons. In many cases, these campaigns are so pervasive that the lies continue on the internet.

Kompromat

Kompromat refers to the use of "compromising materials" that were used to impugn the reputation of a target. The materials may have been real or forged, but were designed to attack politicians, officials, media or entertainment personalities, or business targets. The materials came in a variety of types—documents, photographs, or videos. In the early days, the KGB sought to find and use Kompromat on Eastern bloc defectors and dissidents.

The Russians used Willy Brandt. Brandt was Germany's first

left-of-center Chancellor, part of the Social Democrat Party (SDP), and a Nobel prize–winner for improving East-West relations in Germany. Brandt was elected in 1969 and was extremely popular in Germany and the West. The KGB gave him the target code name POLYARNIK.

A major active measure was executed against Brandt in the form of getting Günter Guillaume, a deep penetration agent for the Stasi—East Germany's secret intelligence service—to discredit Brandt. Guillaume was a trained German agent and former Nazi who had been infiltrated into the West in 1956 in order to subvert the political parties. Guillaume worked his way up the ranks and became a close personal aide to Brandt. In 1973, West German counterintelligence was tipped that Guillaume was an East German spy. Brandt was informed and changed no routines in order to capture the spy. Guillaume was caught in 1974 and tried for treason. He was later exchanged for Russian spies. Brandt resigned over the affair of having a KGB/Stasi spy as his right-hand man.[32]

In 1961, former British naval officer and politician Anthony Courtney was caught in an early Kompromat operation using a KGB officer as a sex partner. When he ran for office and won, he was a staunch critic of the exploitation of diplomatic privileges by the Russians. His effectiveness in spreading anti-Russian sentiment caused the KGB to expose him in the British media. The Russians released photos of him having sex with a Russian Intourist guide named Zinaida Grigorievna Volkova, who was working for the KGB. The sexy photos were taken during his visit to Russia in 1961. Needless to say, he was quickly forced out of Parliament.[33] An adaptation of this scandal was used in the James Bond film *From Russia with Love*, when Bond is filmed from behind a double-sided mirror wall, with KGB officers filming his sexual liaison with a Russian Embassy codebreaker.

The FSB under Putin used Kompromat extremely effectively in the highly charged anti-corruption atmosphere of Post-Soviet Russia in 1997. A video surfaced, purportedly of Russian justice minister Valentin Kovalev in a sauna with five naked women. The video was allegedly taken by the Solntsevo criminal gang. The videotape was found after a search of a banker's house. The banker, Arkady Angelevich, was under investigation.[34] The tape is widely believed to have been made by the FSB, planted, and "found" during the investigation.

Russian lawyer and former Prosecutor General, Yuri I. Skuratov, was shown in a pornographic video with two young women who were supposedly prostitutes. Skuratov had been part of a corruption case against Russian president Boris Yeltsin, Putin's new boss.[35] In January 1999, Skuratov had been called to meet Yeltsin, who then showed him a video and asked him to resign. Later, Putin, then Russia's Prime Minister himself, called for Skuratov to resign again and threatened criminal prosecution.[36]

Ilya Yashin, a Russian opposition activist and friend of slain activist Boris Nemtsov, was caught in a video titled "The Word and the Deed."[37] The video attempted to show the men bribing police. The video also featured Mikhail Fishman, editor of *Russian Newsweek*, and Dmitry Oreshkin. Another video also included footage of Fishman with cocaine and a young woman titled, "Fishman Were an Addict." The video featured Fishman snorting drugs with "Katya." Ilya Yashin recognized the girl and the location.[38] Victor Shenderovich was trapped in a 2010 Kompromat operation where a video of his liaison with a young woman forced him to go public. The Russian satirist had to admit in a blog post he also had sex with the young woman named "Katya" after being told a video of him had surfaced on the internet.[39] He was married and a father; it effectively shut him up.

In 2015, Vladimir Bukovsky was set to testify in the case of murdered KGB officer Alexander Litvinenko when he was arrested for having child pornography on his computer. His house was raided before he could testify.[40] He subsequently sued UK prosecution, claiming his innocence.[41] It is widely believed that the Russian intelligence hackers may have planted the pornography surreptitiously without ever entering his home.

In 2016, Russian television network NTV broadcast a video of Natalia Pelevina having an affair with Mikhail Kasyanov. Pelevina says the video was set up by the FSB under orders from Putin. She was an activist focused on the Magnitsky Justice Campaign. This campaign led to American sanctions that tied up billions of dollars of oligarch money. Mikhail Kasyanov was married, and the video was filmed in a private apartment he owned. Kasyanov was chair of PARNAS, an opposition party to Putin. The video was seen by millions of Russians on NTV.

These activities were not limited to Russian opposition. Attempts on American diplomats continue, including the active measure run against US State Department political officer Brendan Kyle Hatcher. Hatcher focused on human rights in Russia and was subjected to intense surveillance and a Kompromat campaign. In 2009, a heavily edited video was posted to a Russian website for the newspaper *Komsomolskaya Pravda* attempting to show Hatcher with a prostitute. What the video does show is Hatcher, who is married, on the street talking on a mobile phone under FSB surveillance. The video then shows his hotel room, with him in it alone, filmed with hidden cameras from all angles. It cuts to the same darkened room with supposedly a man and a woman having sex but there is no way to tell whether it's Hatcher. The State Department came out and declared the video a cheap forgery and continued to support Hatcher as a "good officer."[42]

Kompromat was acquired traditionally through photography, videos, theft of letters, and audio recordings. In the modern world, it would be the advent of computer technology and digital mobile technology in which anyone could be a victim of Kompromat. Additionally, modern computer networks were susceptible to theft. Everyone stores email, personal photos, and organizational secrets on computer networks, and those, if hacked, would be a treasure chest Russian intelligence would want to access. Hacking computers, cracking secure encryption networks, and phreaking telephone systems was a specialized active measure that was the domain of two Russian intelligence organizations, the FSB and the GRU.

The Soviet Union historically lagged way behind the American technology curve when it came to computers. For the Soviets, the first computers were utilized for missile control and cryptography. In 1948, Soviet scientist Sergey Alexeyevich Lebedev directed the design of the first Soviet computer, called the "small electronic calculating machine," or MESM. By 1950, the 6,000 vacuum tube–filled machine was operational.[43] Despite the advance in computing, the mindset of the Kremlin under Stalin was aimed at human intelligence and openly disdainful of the use of computers. Decades later, the first Russian internet service provider, DEMOS, was established in 1989. This was 20 years behind the Western establishment of the internet created by DARPA and Stanford University. In Russia, the first networks connected research organizations only. The Soviets' first contact with the global internet occurred on August 28, 1990, with an email exchange between Kurchatov Institute and Helsinki, Finland.[44] The first Soviet Union domain (.su) was registered September 19, 1990.[45]

The First Hacking Campaigns

The first well known hacker of US assets for the KGB was a German named Markus Hess. He had been tapped by the KGB to steal technology secrets in the mid-1980s. Hess hacked into the Lawrence Berkley National Laboratory (LBL) systems from his location in Hanover, West Germany. Using his access through the LBL systems, he went on to compromise additional systems, including computers belonging to the US Army, Air Force, and Navy. He was caught after being tracked by a systems administrator at LBL named Clifford Stoll. Stoll baited the unknown attacker with a honey pot plan. The plan involved planted documents that would lure the attacker into sustaining a data connection that allowed investigators to trace the origin of the attack. This led to the arrest of Markus Hess, Dirk Brzezinsky, Karl Koch, and Peter Carl in March 1989. Koch would die in May 1989 before trial, and the remaining three were given suspended sentences.[46]

The four men were loosely affiliated with a group of hackers called the Chaos Computer Club (CCC), the oldest and largest organization of hackers in Europe. Dating back to 1981, the CCC was focused on exposing information of governments it deemed intrusive. In this capacity, the CCC was a perfect target for the KGB to seek recruitment that would give plausible deniability and a Useful Idiot to take the fall. Decades later, much of the philosophy that drove the CCC could be found in one of the attendees of its 2007 conference, a former hacker named Julian Assange. Assange presented his idea of WikiLeaks to the CCC's yearly congress accompanied by his server tech partner, Daniel Domsheit-Berg.[47]

Operation Moonlight Maze

Author Fred Kaplan wrote the book *Dark Territory: The Secret History of Cyberwarfare*, a true-life spy story of how a massive Russian intelligence network hacked US Defense computers and were caught in an operation known as MOONLIGHT MAZE. In 1997, eight years after the first Russian ISP was launched, the first substantial Russian cyberattack against the West via computer systems involved a massive campaign to infiltrate computers in various educational, government, and military systems stretching around the United States.

The connections were happening outside normal business hours and from networks around the world. What investigators noticed was that the attacker had a particular goal in mind, was patient about getting to the targets, and demonstrated sophisticated though not perfect operational security (OPSEC). This included attempts to obfuscate or eliminate the tracks of entry. As analysts and investigators were working to detect the source of a series of breaches, the NSA set a trap for the hacker. Using a technique developed by Clifford Stoll, the man who caught the German hackers years before with a honey trap, the new plan involved adding code to the NSA program that would respond like a beacon. The effort ultimately resulted in the NSA tracking the stolen material back to a Moscow IP emanating from the Russian Academy of Sciences.

In 1999, because of these events, Deputy Secretary of Defense John Hamre would say, "We're in the middle of a cyberwar."[48] Little did he know the United States was barely at the beginning of a protracted, decades-long online war without an end in sight. Targeting the United States would include not only the use of military and government agency hackers, but also the use of proxies like independent hackers, hacking groups, and criminals from multiple countries; but the largest and most aggressive was the new Russian Federation. Using both criminal and contracted proxy hackers would be cost effective and would give the government plausible deniability.

Independent hackers were driven by their own economic agendas and thus the government wouldn't have to support them. This would allow Moscow to build an unpaid army of hackers, trolls, and propagandists who could be driven by their own ambitions and yet interfere with attribution. In cyberwarfare, attribution is key to identifying the target for defense or retaliation campaigns.

One seemingly unique characteristic of Russian hacking efforts was the fusion of government, business, and criminals into the CYBER BEARS. While it was not unheard of to have a former hacker go to work for the United States after serving time or paying a penalty, in Russia it was a full-blown art. Hackers in Russia had a single rule to live by: Hack whoever you want, so long as you don't hack a Russian. Doing so would guarantee a knock on the door by the FSB.

One hacker became notorious in the game of nation-state cyberbattles: Evgeniy Bogachev. Bogachev was named in a report by US intelligence agencies about the Russian effort to hack the 2016 election. With a list of hackings that dated back to at least 2006, Bogachev was accused of stealing millions using a Trojan malware named Zeus, and a ransomware set called CryptoLocker. The Zeus Trojan was used to steal credentials that were ultimately used to access financial institutions. Bogachev was accused of using a botnet named Gameover ZeuS to spread CryptoLocker across the web. It was taken down in an international effort dubbed Operation Tovar. Operation Tovar was one of the largest international campaigns to disrupt criminal cyberactivity and included law enforcement from eleven countries and numerous private cybersecurity companies.

Known under his screen names "lucky12345" or "slavik," Bogachev was just one of many Russian criminals believed to have ultimately helped the Russian government in its efforts to penetrate US and European assets. Another hacker who was allegedly recruited by the Russian government was Alexey Belan. Belan was accused of stealing Yahoo! user credentials in 2014. Bogachev was indicted in August

2012.[49] Belan was indicted and listed on the FBI's most wanted list in March 2017.[50] Both Bogachev and Belan were allegedly recruited by FSB officers Dmitry Dokuchaev and Igor Sushchin, according to an indictment released March 15, 2017.[51] These hackers represent a fraction of the hackers who conducted activities for Russian intelligence over the last 20 years. For the Russian effort to flip the West into its column in the 2016 American and 2017 European elections they would employ the entirety of their national active measures. Every resource was applied from hacking to Kompromat to their national specialty, employing fake news.

"Wet Work"—Murder by Assassination

Assassinations had been a key part of Russian active measures since the birth of the nation, but the Soviet Union made it an art form. From the pre-Soviet days, officers of the Tsar were murdered as an act of "capital punishment" for crimes against the people. For example, several attempts were made to kill the Tsar's family advisor, the strange mystic Rasputin. After attempts to murder him by stabbing, and then with poison, he was ultimately shot and dumped in the Malaya Nevka River.

The first leader of the Soviet Union, Vladimir Ilyich Lenin, was targeted for assassination just after the 1917 Revolution. In January 1918, shots were fired at his vehicle, allegedly by members of the White Guard, on his way to Smolny Palace. His life was saved by Swiss Communist Fritz Platten, who was riding alongside Lenin's vehicle. He shielded Lenin from the gunfire with his own body. In August 1918, Fanny Kaplan also attempted to assassinate Lenin. Though Kaplan seriously injured Lenin, he survived; Kaplan was tried and executed.

Thus, a revolution born of blood would continue with more blood— as Josef Stalin eventually took the helm of Soviet power. Over 30 years he used both mass executions and targeted assassinations as a means to control opposition who were dubbed "enemies of the people." Dating back to 1926 when Vyacheslav Menzhinsky set up the "Administration of Special Tasks," the Russian intelligence services have been carrying out Wet Jobs. "Wet Job," or *mokroye delo* was the term used by the KGB to define assassination operations.[52] The department was responsible for assassinations, kidnappings, and sabotage. Special tasks, as they were called, were handled by the KGB's Operations and Technology Directorate (OTU).[53]

"My task would be to mobilize all available NKVD resources to eliminate Trotsky, the worst enemy of the people," said Pavel Sudoplatov in his book *Special Tasks*. "I was responsible for Trotsky's assassination."[54] And eliminate Trotsky they did. On August 21, 1940, in Mexico City, Trotsky died after being repeatedly struck with an axe by Ramón Mercader, an NKVD agent originally from Spain. Trotsky was one of many who were targeted by Stalin as he sought to destroy all opposition to the Kremlin's ideologically driven objectives.

After the fall of the Soviet Union and the rebranding of the KGB to the FSB and SVR, the tasks of targeted assassinations continued unabated. From the 1990s on, the "special tasks" were aimed at critics of the Kremlin and the aligned oligarchs as the country shifted from its Communist days to the corrupt "mafia state" as it was called by former KGB/FSB officer, Alexander Litvinenko.

Alexander Litvinenko and Boris Berezovsky

Alexander Valterovich Litvinenko had served in both the KGB and FSB in multiple roles but mainly in counterintelligence. In the 1990s, Litvinenko was tasked with assignments focused on organized crime, a role that would become more important after the fall of the Soviet Union as crime bosses vied to take control over resources and officials. Additionally, he was tasked with responsibilities that took him to the heart of the Chechen war as he shifted from his KGB role to one in the FSB.

One key role that would foreshadow his fate was his work as security for Boris Berezovsky, a Russian oligarch who made his wealth in the early days of the post-Soviet era. In 1994, Berezovsky's life was nearly ended when he was targeted with a car bomb that killed his driver. Litvinenko was tasked with investigating the attack. Ironically,

Berezovsky was accused twice of ordering assassinations, including the murder of the mayor of Moscow, Yury Luzhkov.[55] Berezovsky had known Putin for many years, and in the 1990s was clearly close to the former KGB officer turned FSB head. But later Berezovsky openly criticized Putin over his increasingly authoritarian policies and specific events like the death of Russian sailors in the *Kursk* submarine. As a result, Berezovsky went into exile, and Putin's government ate up all of his media and oil businesses. But back home, this didn't stop Putin from hunting him, as he was charged with embezzling and being a crime boss. Despite these charges, it was Berezovsky who called Putin a "gangster" and "terrorist number one." He said he intended to topple Putin and force a regime change. As a result, Berezovsky became a target for assassination. In 2003 and 2007 he was targeted again—each unsuccessful.[56]

Litvinenko had grown more critical of the corruption of Russian law enforcement. The very agencies tasked to control crime were now cooperating in a full-on Mafia state. It was Berezovsky who had introduced Putin to Litvinenko in the late 1990s as Putin became leader of the FSB. Yet when Litvinenko turned to Putin about cases of corrupt officials, he was not only rebuffed, but hampered in his investigations. He went public with accusations about this corruption on November 17, 1998, with fellow officers and was subsequently fired for his bold act.[57] Putin proudly took responsibility for firing Litvinenko in an interview.[58]

Subsequently, Litvinenko sought and was granted exile in the United Kingdom in May 2001. But back in Russia he became an enemy of the state. In his new life, Litvinenko would begin working with British intelligence to expose the Russian corruption, which increased his risks as a target. In Russia, nothing would be worse than a former FSB agent cooperating with MI6. Now the world would hear from yet another Russian defector about the efforts of Russia to sow terror around the world. He echoed the words of others who tied Russian intelligence with terrorists around the world. His book, *Blowing Up Russia: Terror from Within*, was an exposé on the use of terrorism to bolster Putin's grip on Russian authority. As more terror events unfolded in Russia, Litvinenko would be quick to tie them to the FSB.

Journalist Anna Politkovskaya was targeted several times for assassinations, including being held in 2001 and subjected to a mock execution. After she repeatedly wrote about the human rights abuses and handling of the Chechen war, she survived a poisoning attempt during a flight on the way to help those taken hostage in Beslan. Chechen leader Ramzan Kadryov told her, "You are an enemy, to be shot." She was assassinated in her Moscow apartment elevator on October 7, 2006. She had been shot twice in the chest, once in shoulder, and finished with a coup de grâce to the head.

After Politkovskaya was murdered, Litvinenko pointed the finger at Putin for her assassination. On November 1, 2006, he turned violently ill. On November 23, he died of poisoning. At some point an assassin had given him the radioactive isotope, polonium-210, which he unknowingly ingested. Subsequently, the British authorities launched a massive investigation and held public hearings to discuss the death of the former FSB officer. The two suspects were named: Dmitry Kovtun and Andrei Lugovoi. In January 2007, British investigators formally indicted the assassins, but despite requests to extradite the suspects, Russia refused to turn them over. Years of investigations went by until the British government accused Nikolai Patrushev and Vladimir Putin of ordering the assassination in 2015.

Back in Russia, the Putin propaganda machine had their own suspect. They blamed Boris Berezovsky. Though they offered no proof of these claims. Even though traces of polonium were found in Berezovsky's office, it was not surprising since Litvinenko had visited the former oligarch after he was already ill. After he was accused of murdering his friend, Berezovsky sued the Russian television channel, RTR-Planeta, and was awarded damages in 2010.[59] Ultimately, like his friend, Berezovsky was killed in March 2013. His body was found hanging, and though the coroner found that the death was a suicide, another pathologist hired by his family claimed that upon closer examination the death didn't appear to be a suicide.

Journalists were a ubiquitous target for assassinations. Anna Politkovskaya was just one example. Natalya Estemirova was abducted and murdered on July 15, 2009, after having covered the human rights abuses in Chechnya, including kidnappings, torture, and executions by the Russian government. Yuri Shchekochikhin was an investigative journalist who covered government corruption and human rights abuses, and like Politkovskaya and Estemirova, the Chechen wars. He was poisoned in June 2003 and died weeks later on July 3, 2003. It was suggested to many that he, like Litvinenko, was poisoned with radioactive materials, though the Russians would never release his autopsy records.[60]

Other political critics of Putin have been murdered, including liberal politician Boris Nemtsov. Nemtsov had been an activist for decades before he was murdered on February 27, 2015. From his early days protesting the disastrous Chernobyl meltdown to his opposition of Viktor Yanukovych, Nemtsov led a lengthy career of calling for reform. He served as a governor for Nizhny Novgorod oblast after being appointed by Boris Yeltsin in late 1991.[61] He was later elected to the Federation Council in 1993, and by 1997, had risen to become First Deputy Prime Minister.

But after Putin came to power, Nemtsov would become one of his chief critics. With other critics like chess master Garry Kasparov and Vladimir Kara-Murza, Nemtsov repeatedly called out Putin as an autocrat. In 2007, he was going to run for President of Russia, but withdrew and threw his support to Mikhail Kasyanov of the People's Democratic Union. The same month, he joined Kasparov in creating the Solidarity (*Solidarnost*) movement. Shortly after, he was attacked by three men who were in the Nashi youth movement.[62]

After Nemtsov signed on with the Putin Must Go manifesto in March 2010 and helped develop a report, "Putin: Results-10 years," the website hosting the report was targeted with a DDoS attack.[63] When Nemtsov and his allies levied their criticisms at Putin, he responded with claims that they were attempting to fill their pockets. This didn't dissuade Nemtsov, who again accused Putin of corruption during the Sochi Olympics with claims of embezzling the funds that were meant for security.

After the Russian invasion of Crimea, Nemtsov published an op-ed in the *Kyiv Post* blaming Vladimir Putin. He said, "Putin is trying to dissect Ukraine and create in the east of the country a puppet state, Novorossiya, that is fully economically and politically controlled by the

Kremlin." *Novorossiya* translates to "New Russia" and is one of the call-ing cries of the pro-Kremlin nationalist groups, including the Rodina party. But Nemtsov went further to point out that the real reason had more to do with the natural resources in the area: "It's crucial for his clan to control metallurg in the east of Ukraine, as well as its military-industrial complex," and that "Ukraine is rich in shale gas which would create real competition for the business of Putin's Gazprom."[64]

Nemtsov was keenly aware that he was a target. He had been arrested many times under Putin's regime, including in 2007, 2010, and 2011. Just like Putin critic Alexei Navalny, Nemtsov was arrested for "unauthorized protests," which only proved his lingering point that Putin was an authoritarian. He stated he was afraid for his life but that it wouldn't dissuade him, "If I were afraid of Putin, I wouldn't be in this line of work."[65]

Nemtsov's fears would materialize on the night of February 27, 2015, when he was gunned down on the Bolshoy Moskvoretsky Bridge in Moscow, right in front of the Kremlin. The reaction around the world was strong, with activists and leaders issuing strong rebukes and point-ing the finger at the Kremlin and the FSB. But officially the Kremlin blamed five Chechen men who worked for Ramzan Kadryov.[66]

While there are many who were murdered by the Kremlin, not every attempt proved successful. Notably, Boris Nemtsov's friend, Vladimir Kara-Murza, was targeted at least twice and both times the Kremlin failed.[67]

Oleg Erovinkin had served with the KGB starting in 1976. He was mysteriously killed in Moscow and found in a Rosneft company car, a black Lexus, on December 26, 2017. Erovinkin had been serving as Chief of Staff to Igor Sechin since May 2008, when he was appointed by Vladimir Putin.[68] It was also suspected that Erovinkin had been a source for the Steele Dossier, which exposed the Trump campaign's Russian efforts.[69] In the Steele Dossier, one entry mentioned a source who was in contact with Igor Sechin. The July 19, 2016, entry said, "a Russian source close to Rosneft President, PUTIN close associate and US-sanctioned individual, Igor SECHIN, confided the details of a recent secret meeting between him and Carter Page, who was acting as an advisor to Donald Trump."[70] However, the official cause of death was listed as a heart attack. His death happened well after the news and details in the Steele Dossier were released. If it was true that Erovinkin had discussed the meeting with Steele or other conduits, this would have been a threat to the Kremlin's operational security as it sought to cultivate Carter Page to be used as an agent of influence over Trump.

On March 4, 2018, former Russian spy Sergei Skripal and his daughter Yulia were found by police slumped over each other on a bench with their eyes rolled back in their heads in a Salsbury, England, park. Skripal was a colonel and former Russian military intelligence officer of the GRU who retired in 1999. During his time at the GRU, he was recruited by British Intelligence, where he worked to identify FSB, SVR, and GRU intelligence agents. He was later found out and arrested in Moscow in 2004 and charged with high treason for being a spy for MI6, the British intelligence service. He was sentenced to 13 years in prison, but was likely being held as a bargaining chip for other Russian spies. In July 2010, that chip was cashed when Skripal was handed over to the UK as part of a spy swap that returned ten Russian "illegals" captured in the US, including celebrity spy Anna Chapman. Experts say Skripal was poisoned with a military grade nerve agent known as Novichok. This class of chemical weapon is eight times more deadly than VX, which can kill in less than a minute.

In addition to Skripal, three responding police officers were hospitalized. Twenty-one others who came into physical contact with them or surfaces they had touched were affected by the Novichok chemical agent. Skripal was a close friend of Christopher Steele, famous for his work on the "Trump dossier." Some have suggested the attack was a result of this association, as it appeared that Vladimir Putin was cleaning up former Russian intelligence officers who may have betrayed the Kremlin's interests.[71]

Prime Minister Theresa May went before Parliament and excoriated Moscow. May said, "Either this was a direct action by the Russian state against our country, or the Russian government lost control of its potentially catastrophically damaging nerve agent and allowed it to get into the hands of others."[72]

On March 22, 2018, the British government responded by kicking 23 Russian diplomats out of the country. British officials also said other diplomatic activities would be suspended. Under Article 5 of the NATO charter, the UK was within in its power to call upon allies to respond against Russia. In the United States, Donald Trump was relatively silent on the issue. His normal barrage of tweets had no mention of the case. The soon-to-be-fired Secretary of State Rex Tillerson said that the attack "clearly came from Russia," and that the United States would react to the event. However, White House spokesperson Sarah Huckabee Sanders failed to hold the Russians to task on the matter. After days of criticism, UN Ambassador Nikki Haley finally agreed with Britain that Russia was responsible, but Donald Trump refused to mention Russia and Putin by name.

The Russian response was a mixture of mockery to the British claims. It was a reminder that the Kremlin never forgives. "Traitors will kick the bucket," said Putin to a television audience in 2010.[73] In a March 2018 interview with NBC host Megyn Kelly, Putin said, "not everything can be forgiven…in particular betrayal."[74] That same day on Russian television, TV anchor Kirill Kleimenov said that Skripal was "by training, a traitor to his country," and warned that "being a traitor is one of the most dangerous professions in the world."[75] British officials who were stunned that state TV would brag about their deed threatened to remove the RT network from British airwaves in response to the Skripal attack.[76]

It took a state-sponsored chemical weapon of mass destruction terrorist attack on the territory of our closest NATO ally to understand that Putin was now using all tools at the state's disposal to punish traitors. Like a professional terrorist leader, Putin understood that the intended audience of the attack was not the immediate victims—it was anyone who dared cross the spymaster-in-chief, including all Russian diaspora. The other part of the message was that if Russia calls on anyone, including its spies and assets to assist the FSB or GRU, they had better understand the stakes of refusal.

CHAPTER 7

Fake News

> "Give a man fake news, and he'll fool you for a day.
> Teach a man to fake news, and he'll lie to you for
> life."
>
> —J.M. BERGER

The history of Russian disinformation campaigns is loaded with stories that are bizarre fabrications, fantastical yarns, the worst of conspiracies, and Trumpian outright lies. Russia has always been a nation predisposed to believe almost anything, but under the Communist rule they were immersed in the policy of "Make a Big Lie, Call It the Truth" for three-quarters of a century. Needless to say, it made them experts at detecting a lie, but also of fabricating a bigger one.

In the digital era, the ability to generate stories with no basis in reality went beyond the KGB officers in Service A of the First Chief Directorate, spreading the incredible lie that AIDS was created to kill blacks and gays. Of course, this was helped by the global news media and fringe commentators. Now you could read about how the Democratic Party had a campaign staffer murdered or how Hillary Clinton and John Podesta ran a child sex trafficking ring from the imaginary basement of a Washington, D.C., pizza parlor, or how the most liberal Pope in history, a Hispanic one at that, had a change of heart and happily endorsed Donald Trump wearing a MAGA hat and all. Every one of these stories was "reported" during the 2016 campaign and sent to hundreds of millions of watchers as the truth. That every one is also a blatant lie is beside the point. It was sent out using a global propaganda distribution system, picked up by US social media and mainstream press and then turned into a debate as to its veracity. Mission accomplished.

Russian military intelligence officer Colonel Vladimir Kvachkov, writing in the GRU's white paper on propaganda and political warfare said, "A new type of war has emerged, in which armed warfare has given up its decisive place in the achievement of the military and political objectives of war to another kind of warfare—information warfare."[1]

Kvachkov is correct about information being a new domain of warfare. Propaganda, fake news, and influence operations are the modern era's most advanced weapons systems. Bombs are not persistent, but they create damage and have a terminal effect. Fake news can persist throughout history and has the ability to change both minds and the perception of reality.

The Russians incorporated social media into their strategic planning for information warfare. Their strategic doctrine states:

> "Confrontation between two or more states in the information space to damage the information systems, processes and resources, which are of critical importance, and other structures, to undermine the political, economic and social system, and effect massive brainwashing of the population for destabilizing the society and the state, and also forcing the state to make decisions in the interests of the confronting party."[2]

Note that the Russians specifically use the words "massive brainwashing" in their armed forces doctrine when discussing social media information warfare. Their propaganda are cyber weapons flooded into the global information dispersal domain (the internet) and flows through the information battle space (news and social media) to influence or change perceptions in the primary target (your mind) or create secondary results in the impact zone (your mobile phone or television). Social media propaganda harnesses human curiosity to make you look closer.

During the Cold War, Russian intelligence conceptualized, developed, and deployed a perfect Communist propaganda weaponization system that harnesses 1) what you know; 2) what you've learned; 3) what you hear; and 4) what they want you to believe. With this, they crafted a wholly false but generally believable story. Russia was not the only nation to do this, nor the first. In WW II, America and its allies had entire ministries dedicated to propaganda.

Deputy Defense Minister of the Russian Federation Andrey V. Kartapolov was a pioneer in creating cyberwarfare operations into a new kind of hybrid warfare. He wrote:

> "... the main aim of information psychological conflict is regime change in the adversary country (through destroying the organs of government); by means of mass influence on the military-political leadership of the adversary achieving as a minimum an increase in the amount of time available for taking command decisions and lengthening the operational cycle; by means of influence on the mass consciousness of the population—directing people so that the population of the victim country is induced to support the aggressor, acting against its own interests."[3]

Putin's Russian intelligence has taken finely crafted fake news stories—what psychological warfare experts called Propaganda Products (PPs)—and deployed them into the information domain using a myriad of injection systems: Facebook, Twitter, Sputnik, *Russia Today*, individual bloggers, conspiracy theory websites, mainstream media comment sections, and even mailing propaganda postcards to journalists. This system disperses the ideological products from Russian philosophers like Dugin and Surkov, and American fellow travelers like Steve Bannon and Donald Trump.

The command post for the Russian cyber active measures onslaught is a Russian intelligence subcontractor with thousands of English-speaking computer operators called the Russian Federation Internet Research Agency (RF-IRA). Former acting Director of the CIA, Michael Morrell did not see the weaponization of social media coming, "So, I have little doubt that we, the intelligence community, didn't see from a strategic sense the weaponization of social media....I didn't see...a warning about the possible use of social media to attack us."[4]

A Brief History of Russian Propaganda

Since the fall of the Soviet Union, journalism remains a key state information battle space. The news media's "fake news" is the preferred method for the production and dissemination of Russia's information. Virtually every "journalist" was first and foremost a state propagandist. Reports from that era say that as many as 70 to 80% of the TASS news bureau personnel were intelligence officers. Being a journalist was a wonderful way for KGB officers to insinuate themselves into circles of power or of interest to the Kremlin. Information KGB agents were deployed around the world under the guise of being journalists to surface forgeries, publish or influence articles favorable to Russia, or engage in disinformation campaigns. Agents would be under the directive of the Information Directorate, the International Information Department, or KGB. The agent could build the same relationships a legitimate journalist might with political or economic figures who could either share valuable information or be subjected to directional information meant to manipulate their view on topics that mattered to the Soviets.[5]

Russian-run press agencies were used to spread rumors and float forgeries. For example, an old magazine established in India, *Blitz*, was used by Russians to out CIA personnel, spread disinformation, and drop forgeries. Others, such as the Soviet's *New Times Magazine*, was founded in 1943 as a vehicle for Communist propaganda posing as journalism. Its mission was to filter state lies into the global news media information stream. It was the publication that KGB defector Stanislav Levchenko worked for when he was stationed in Japan.

Levchenko was posted as a journalist for *New Times* in Tokyo starting in the early 1970s.[6] According to US Congressional testimony of the 14 correspondents in the office, 12 of them were KGB staff officers. He spoke fluent English and played the role of a legitimate journalist, which led the Japanese to let him further into backgrounders without people realizing he was a Russian agent. Generally, only when defectors like Levchenko expose them were these media organizations outed as fronts for spies.

Former Soviet Premier Nikita Khrushchev summed up Russia's use of state media succinctly, "Just as a soldier cannot fight without ammunition, the party cannot conduct a war without print. Print was our main ideological weapon, and we cannot pass it into unreliable hands. It must be kept in the most reliable, most trustworthy hand which could use this weapon to destroy the enemies of the working class."[7]

Fake News of the Old Kremlin

One of the most important operations in the history of active measures was *Operation Infektion*. This fabrication was so effective that it persists among conspiracy theorists even today. As mentioned, when the HIV/AIDS epidemic was identified, the KGB fabricated a story that the AIDS virus was part of a biological warfare program created by the United States.[8] In 1984, on Independence Day, *Patriot*, an Indian newspaper, published a story claiming that the virus was created at the United States Army Medical Research Institute of Infectious Diseases (USAMRIID) at Fort Detrick, Maryland.

Another Russian-designed propaganda weapon had deadly results. The Grand Mosque in Mecca, the point of pilgrimage for all Muslims, is located in Mecca, Saudi Arabia. It was seized in 1979 by Islamic extremists seeking the return of the Mahdi (savior) for the 1,400-year anniversary of the birth of Islam. Taking advantage of the Middle Eastern penchant to believe in conspiracy theories, Russian intelligence created a region-wide campaign to claim the United States orchestrated the seizure of the Grand Mosque of Mecca and had bombed it with fighter-bombers. It was a highly successful lie. Even

Iran's Ayatollah Khomeini repeated it. Following the reporting, when TV media showed Saudi aircraft bombing the terrorists, riots broke out in Pakistan, including an attack on the American diplomatic outpost, leading to the deaths of two US servicemen defending the Embassy, which was burned to the ground. Playing both sides and to add further chaos, the Russians sought to incite anti-Muslim bias in the US. Soviet agents spread the lie that Pakistan's army was responsible for attacking the US Embassy in Islamabad and not a mob enraged by Russia's own false report.[9]

The 1980s Strategic Defense Initiative (SDI) was a space-based missile defense system proposed by President Ronald Reagan, nicknamed "Star Wars." This system was going to get multibillion-dollar funding to overtake Russia's ability to defend against a space-based laser and kinetic anti-missile system. The Soviet Union could ill afford to try to match the United States, so they embarked on a global campaign to remove all support for the system away from America.

The Soviet Union organized a massive global campaign to discredit the policy, technology, and safety of the planned system. Though the US would be decades away from experimental stages of the system, the Soviets blitzed the global media. According to Congressional testimony, they took an innovative step of using actual scientists to lead the argument against deployment of such a system. "To make their criticism of SDI more authoritative, the Soviets are using scientists to take the lead in defining the SDI issue." Anti-SDI–themed propaganda was introduced from daily news reports, UN conferences, festivals, cultural exchanges, non-governmental organization meetings, and white papers, to even the photos at innocuous international commemorations such as the 40th anniversary of VE day.

The anti-SDI campaign was a massive effort that involved thousands of people informed of the Kremlin's wishes through tens of thousands of wire or telephone transmissions daily to coordinate a global campaign. A modern effort could be pulled off with as few as 5 people with some desktop computers and a green screen. The modern effort could reach billions as opposed to thousands on its best day.

But it is General Ivan Agayants's assessment of political propaganda warfare that is most noteworthy. Before he died in the mid-1960s he said, "Sometimes I am amazed how easy it is to play these games, if they did not have press freedom, we would have to invent it for them."[10]

For a snapshot of a historical fake news campaign we look at India during the 1970s. India was a massive propaganda market for the KGB. India was considered a point-of-entry country to get fake news and propaganda into the Western media information stream. Russian secret agents would buy newspapers, journalists, and entire printing presses. In an extremely slow age of news communications by Teletype and couriers, each propaganda article had to be meticulously crafted in such a way that it was plausible and checkable with carefully positioned sources. It would take weeks or months to position propaganda then, whereas today it would take less than a few seconds to transmit a whole year's supply of fake news articles. For example, in the first two months of 1977, the KGB spent over 3 million rupees (approximately $100,000 or $929,000 in today's dollars) to bolster the election campaign of the Communist Party of India.[11] As an allied political group, this kind of expenditure was expected as a usual donation to the Communist International (COMINTERN) ally. In India, the KGB's intelligence infiltration of the global news world was overwhelming. Over the years, the Indian press was flooded with KGB propaganda products from ten Russian allied or operated newspapers and one press agency. During the Indira Gandhi era (1971–1977), the following number of anti-Western, pro-Communist propaganda articles were introduced into the media stream through plants in India:

- 1972, 3,789 articles (10 per day)
- 1973, 2,760 articles (7 per day)
- 1974, 4,486 articles (12 per day)
- 1975, 5,510 articles (15 per day)

When Gandhi declared a state of emergency in 1976, which included a press crackdown, Russia had a harder time planting fake stories, but they still managed to get 1,980 articles out in 1976—still 5 per day. By 1977 the Russians realized that India was no longer a favorable entryway. Gandhi had tightened the reins on Communist propaganda and it withered down to only 411 articles that Year.[12]

State-Owned Media

The entirety of the Russian state media, from its founding numerous agencies, magazines, and newspapers, including the most notable newspaper in the world that was so detached from reality that its name became equivalent to the meaning of a lie: *Pravda* (Truth). Other Soviet-era agencies were the TASS, Novosti, and Sputnik news services, and radio stations such as Radio Moscow, Radio Peace and Progress, and RIA Novosti.

When the Soviet Union collapsed, all of these agencies were up for sale to the person with cash in hand. Novosti News Service continues as a state news agency, and has been supplemented by companies that started off as free and independent media, but were quickly bought out and converted by Putin or his allies back to state news à la the Communists. So pervasive is Russian state media that now more than 80% of all television in the country is state-run. The other 20% is satellite TV.

Alexander Yakovlev, founder of the International Democracy Institute and a Putin critic, sagely noted that under Putin state television and controlled social media are the big drivers of Russian opinion. He said: "To take the Kremlin, you must take television."[13] That television is firmly in the hands of the President and his friends.

Russia's present international television channel, Russia Today (now referred to by its initials, RT), and other stations including Channel One, Russia One, and Gazprom oil company–controlled NTV, continue in the tradition of *Pravda* by providing a seemingly legitimate face to what were state-run agencies subordinate to the national leadership and intelligence agencies.[14]

Former Putin loyalist Gleb Pavlovsky told PBS television documentarians that Putin coordinated the state disinformation campaigns. The inner circle made conscious decisions about what to expose, who to attack, and what narratives would work best. Considering that Putin's

Four Horsemen advisors were all ex-KGB officers, it should come as no surprise. Pavlovsky said:

> "We had meetings every week, and during the election campaign, we had meetings every day, and it was decided what TV channels would show what news, what kind of articles would be published in different newspapers, what would be posted at different websites. This was a strict plan that was executed precisely. Putin decided that this was the case everywhere."[15]

On the other hand, free independent media companies that crossed Putin would be targeted for destruction or purchased by the oligarchy and turned into state allied media. For example, Dozhd (TV Rain), the formerly free and independent news and information channel, was cut off from access to the Russian people after they infuriated the Kremlin with an online poll about surrendering Leningrad (St. Petersburg) to the Nazis in WWII to save lives. After a majority of pollsters agreed, it was shut down. One can only see it on the internet behind a paywall. Russia allows it to operate along the Fox News model, to keep one free voice in opposition so they could say they are "fair and balanced." It's run by journalist Natalya Sindeyeva, and provides an outlet for those who desire greater freedom and democracy but also know that by visiting the site they will be monitored by the state.

Spearheading Putin's national disinformation agencies is Dmitry Peskov. Peskov is the Presidential Press Secretary and the Deputy Chief of Staff of the Presidential Executive Office. Born into the Soviet Union, he graduated from Moscow State University in 1989 and was assigned to the Foreign Ministry. During the fall of the Soviet Union and transition to an uncertain democracy, Peskov remained in the Russian Embassy in Turkey until 1994. Under Boris Yeltsin he was brought into the press service just in time to work for Putin in his first term. He grew close to Putin and has been the Presidential Press Secretary since 2012. Under Peskov, the propaganda image of Putin as statesman, masculine leader, and clever spy was crafted. Peskov has the ability to create narratives that do well in Russia precisely because they can be created out of whole cloth. In the Soviet era, journalism was the preferred cover story for the production and dissemination of information warfare products. Today RT, Sputnik, Newsfront, and other channels continue that tradition.[16]

Founded in 2005, Russia Today was a television and website voice of the Kremlin, based in Moscow. Consistent with the Kremlin disinformation history of sowing doubt in credible news sources around the world and in government institutions of the West, its motto was "question more." RT broadcasted in multiple languages including English, French, Arabic, and Spanish. It had multiple channels including RT Arabic, RT en Español, RT America, RT UK, RT Documentary, RT Deutsch, and RT en Français. It was broadcast on cable stations in the United States, Canada, UK, Australia, Portugal, Mexico, the Netherlands, Poland, Serbia, Italy, Israel, the Philippines, Singapore, India, Pakistan, Indonesia, and Sri Lanka.

RT regularly covered stories of interest to the Kremlin with a slant designed to support the pro-Russian narratives including coverage of the Ukrainian revolution, the seizure of South Ossetia in Georgia, the seizure of Crimea, and the downing of Malaysia Airlines Flight 17. The broadcasters regularly praise Vladimir Putin and criticize the leaders in the West.

RT promoted anti-American views by bringing on hosts and guests who could be relied upon to discuss American policies in negative terms. Fringe voices or hosts who had lost their seats in American media soon found a comfortable seat in the RT studios, including Larry King, Ed Schultz, and Julian Assange. The same year WikiLeaks founder Julian Assange claimed he was going to expose Russian leaders and oligarchs for corruption, he was given a show on RT called *World of Tomorrow*. In 12 broadcasts, Assange conducted interviews with various political voices including Hassan Nasrallah, Slavoj Žižek, Moncef Marzouki, Alaa Abd El-Fattah, Noam Chomsky, and Tariq Ali.

Former American hosts like Liz Wahl have shared their stories about being fed narratives that were clearly Kremlin-biased or untrue.

Liz Wahl resigned from RT during a live broadcast in March 2014, and later became a chief critic of the news outlet.[17]

In response to the active measures Russia had been conducting against the United States in 2016, RT was forced to register under the Foreign Agent Registration Act (FARA) for being "Russia's state-run propaganda machine."[18] The designation requires RT to disclose its financial information. RT editor Margarita Simonyan claimed that in response, American staffers were quitting out of concern that they would be charged for working with the Kremlin-controlled propaganda organization.[19] In retaliation, the Russian government passed a law in November 2017 aimed at Voice of America, Radio Free Europe, Current Time TV, and other outlets that were forcing them to register as foreign agents.

Sputnik was a news website that replaced the defunct RIA Novosti in 2014. RIA Novosti had been the worldwide Russian news agency until it was dissolved in December 2013. When it was launched by the Kremlin via Rossiya Segodnya, its new general director, Dmitry Kiselyov, said it was being launched to challenge "aggressive propaganda that is now being fed to the world."[20] Andrew Feinberg told Politico that he thought working at Sputnik was going to be a good job for a freelance journalist. Yet in no time he was asked if he'd report on items that were not true.[21]

Most NATO cyberwarfare experts believe that Sputnik was set up to be a propaganda warfare distribution system. The indictment of the Internet Research Agency by the special counsel Robert Mueller in 2018 seems to indicate that the shift from RIA Novosti to Sputnik was a deliberate reengineering to prepare a specific fake news distribution system for the 2016 election operation to elect Donald Trump.

The Atlantic Council's Digital Forensic Research Laboratory described accurately RT TV broadcast operations as a key component of hybrid warfare combat support. RT was not just used to spread propaganda, but it shaped the perceptions of the viewing population in and around Ukraine at key times in the invasion.

"At critical moments, RT's support for Russian government positions has become even more explicit, adopting almost identical language to

Kremlin statements. This is the most overt form of propaganda, literally propagating the government's messages in the very same words in which they are given. For example, throughout March 2014, the Russian government referred to the new Ukrainian government in ways which denied its legitimacy. Some of the terms used by the Foreign Ministry included 'the Kiev regime,' 'the current "Ukrainian government,"' the 'current Kiev authorities,' 'the people calling themselves the Ukrainian authorities,' and 'the coup d'état in Ukraine.'"[22]

These terms transmitted nonstop by RT became a way of signaling to pro-Moscow Ukrainians the official talking points that were expected to be used in and around media. As local ethnic Russian Ukrainians/Crimeans repeated these terms, they became part of the common parlance for all discussions about Ukraine. This created a cycle of common discussion points heard from the man on the street in Kiev, Sevastopol, and Moscow, and were mainstreamed in any discussions about Ukraine. This uniform speech pattern essentially brought the user into a continuous cycle of verbal brainwashing, whether they were aware of it or not.

The DFRL also did an extensive study of German social media nets linked to the Kremlin: @RT_Deutsch, Sputnik Deutsch (@de_sputnik), and NewsFront Deutsch (@newsfront). These Kremlin organs not only spread propaganda, they acted as megaphones to amplify messages and act as links for real life individuals to share ideological materials and rally points for extremists. The DFRL noted "[Our] analysis shows that the most active amplifiers of these outlets do, indeed, include apparent bots, but they are not the most important factor. The signals are significantly boosted by pro-Kremlin activists, far-right users, and anti-migrant users, who have been known to work together to harass critics."[23]

Putin and his state media often use "analogies" in their influence operations on the world stage, particularly when disparaging NATO. One example is the Russian state-controlled media narrative that emerged during Putin's invasion of Ukraine. He evoked images of Nazis and fascists in Ukraine using WWII photos to manipulate Russian public opinion about his military incursion into Ukraine. Robert Donaldson noted:

"Analogies can reflexively serve as a strong unifying force. Putin often uses analogies against the international community. He stated on several occasions that Russia's incursion into Crimea was little different from NATO's incursion into Kosovo. He forgot to add, of course, that Russia consumed Crimea, while no NATO country incorporated Kosovo."[24]

The DFRL identified patterns of propaganda and fake news reporting when Russia seeks to discredit NATO operations and exercises. They identified consistent metanarratives used by Russia. They included themes that:

1. NATO is unwelcome and NATO troops are occupants
2. The [insert geographic region here] are paranoid or "Russophobic"
3. NATO is provocative and aggressive
4. NATO is obsolete and cannot protect its allies
5. NATO [insert geographic region here] are sympathetic to the Nazi ideology.[25]

IN LATE MAY 2006, a contingent of 227 reservists from Marine Wing Support Group 47 (MWSG-47) went to Ukraine to participate in the annual US-Ukrainian military exercise "Sea Breeze." This is an annual naval and capacity building exercise held in the Black Sea. The Marines were reservists from Michigan who were deployed to Ukraine to construct dining tents, latrines, and other housing for the multinational forces.[26]

The Marine contingent arrived on board a contracted container ship, *Advantage*, and docked in the port of Feodosia. The American State Department was informed locally that Russian officials had spread rumors among the local Russian-speaking population that the boats carrying the Marines contained "poisonous substances" to be used in Crimea. They also told locals that the Marines carried materials to build a permanent NATO base in the area.

Forty-eight hours after arrival, protesters blockaded the port and shouted anti-American and anti-NATO propaganda at the troops. The troops tried to move to the Ukrainian naval base near Stary Krym to start work on a barrack facility they were rehabilitating. Over 2,000 protestors organized by Russia and the local pro-Russia Party of Regions and the Natalia Vitrenko Bloc besieged the convoy, rocking the buses the Marines were riding in and smashing windows. The Marines were forced to take shelter in a military hospital until they could be evacuated back to the United States. As they left, protestors lined the roads with signs saying "Yankee Go Home."[27]

DURING THE 2014 Russian invasion of Crimea, the Russian TV news spread a series of calculated fake news stories to lay the groundwork for popular acceptance of the coming invasion. Putin's state news services put out a flood of fake news reports that ethnic Russian citizens in Ukraine's Donbass region and Crimea were being persecuted in Ukraine. Invariably the news reported that pro-European "Colour Revolution" or "Euromaidan" protesters, who took power back from the pro-Moscow government, were paid agitators working for NATO and the CIA. Another propaganda story spread by Russian television and Facebook reported that Ukrainian soldiers had crucified a Russian-speaking toddler. News reporters breathlessly reported on a mass of ethnic Russian refugees fleeing Eastern Ukraine for Russia.[28] For people living in the region, the Russian media gave the impression a major war was on the verge of breaking out. Populations of both countries were bombarded with fake news injected into real reports to shape the narrative around the coming conflict.

The RAND Corporation conducted a study of Russian propaganda in the lead-up to the invasion of Crimea. They found the propaganda streams were "'high-volume and multichannel' while disseminating messages not grounded in reality. The propaganda media is also 'rapid, continuous, and repetitive,' and 'lacks commitment to consistency,' which makes it difficult for nation-states to counter it."[29]

This extensive preparation of the political, psychological, and propaganda battlefield allowed Moscow to take territory and hold it because

Russia and its allies were prepared to accept it as a just military operation or a fait accompli, depending on the point of view.

The Russian propaganda warfare arms attack virtually all NATO operations and exercises to keep the metanarrative of the inherent evilness of the Atlantic alliance. In 2015, US soldiers deployed to "Operation Atlantic Resolve" in Ukraine had details from their personal lives publicized by Russian officials. The agents discovered information on their social media accounts and broadcast chosen details. These came after allegations of US Army officers raping children.[30] In Latvia, Russian propaganda efforts portrayed NATO servicemen in the country as raping women or living in luxury apartments paid for by local taxpayers.[31] A Russian website mimicking a Finnish government research site presented patently false and misleading headlines like one claiming a Finnish cyber threat center had a direct link to the CIA, accusing it of waging "hybrid war" against Russia.[32] In 2016, the Bulgarian prime minister canceled a joint exercise with NATO forces because he did not want to risk war with Russia after it produced propaganda about the naval exercise.[33]

Moscow dipped into the heart of NATO in January 2016 when it helped drive a fake story about the rape of a 13-year-old Russian-German girl. Moscow used the internal divisions against immigrants to shape the story, then used its intelligence and media arms to drive the story. Russian television outlets including both Sputnik and Russia Today ran near-constant reports on the story, Russian hackers drove the story through social media, and eventually the Russian foreign minister questioned the ability of German officials to keep citizens safe.[34] While the story eventually proved false, the Kremlin was able to take that pause to further drive divisions within even a relatively stable Western democracy.

In contrast to their influence operations in the West, Russian mass media inside their borders are under the control of the state. The Kremlin agency Roskomnadzor manages all access to the internet for its citizens. At any moment, the Russian state can monitor, limit, block, or cut off anyone who incites dissent or even disparages the Kremlin in any way. Numerous independent voices have been blocked without explanation by Putin.

The favorite tool of the state for limiting or blocking "free speech" is to say that the organization, website, or individual has used "illegal information," a veiled charge that threatens use of the state's secrets laws. The Kremlin can identify and cite virtually any speech as illegal and often claims it is part of an espionage operation supported by American Intelligence.

CHAPTER 8

Internet Research Agency & Russian Cyber Weapons

Russia may not have been the first nation to weaponize information. They were not even the first to turn modern social media into a propaganda platform, recruiting sergeant, and fear projection tool—that would be the Islamic State terrorist group. While ISIS was using the precedents for weaponizing social media that exploded during the 2011 Arab Spring, Russian intelligence was watching and fusing their techniques with their near-century-old political and propaganda warfare legacy from the KGB. The Russian goal was to quickly harness the power of personal access that social media gives and craft metanarratives and distribute them in such a way that the enemy population can be turned against their own government. Opinion polls, news coverage, and street talk can be shifted by changing the perception of the populace. Social media not only weaponizes opinion, it gives the attacker the ability to act as puppeteer for an entire foreign nation. Two Russian information warfare officers wrote a treatise describing the combat effects of weaponized news and social media:

"The mass media today can stir up chaos and confusion in government and military management of any country and instill ideas of violence, treachery, and immorality, and demoralize the public. Put through this treatment, the armed forces personnel and public of any country will not be ready for active defense."[1]

Additionally, the Russians make no distinction between using these activities in wartime and "peace." The Russian Federation will deploy information warfare and propaganda persistently in a constant effort to keep adversaries off balance. When it comes to information warfare, such distinctions of peacetime and wartime fade away.

One key distinction that should be drawn is the difference between strategic tasks aimed at people and those aimed at technology. Deploying tasks against people involves psychological operations meant to affect the mindset of citizens, politicians, and military forces, whereas tasks aimed at technological assets are meant to undermine the structures used to collect, process, or share information, including networks, computers, or the data itself.

The United States and Europe will be involved in a psychological engagement until the fringes of their society turn to Moscow. The attack will be persistent, intense, and subversive. It's a Metanarrative Cold War: Democracy or Autocracy?

Techniques of cyber operation resemble non-cyber techniques in many ways. Sabotage for instance, will now be aimed at digital infrastructures. Sending tons of data at a server, known as a Denial of Service (DoS) attack, or when sent from multiple sources, a Distributed Denial of Service (DDoS) attack, is much like jamming radio or radar signals in the past. DDoS attacks the opponent blind. While they can be carried out by non-state hackers for many reasons, in the hands of a nation-state, a DDoS attack can immobilize a nation. Similar sabotage techniques were used in combination with other tactics like in December 2015 when Russian hackers deployed BlackEnergy 3 and KillDisk, two malware tools, to take down power plants in Ukraine. The first took control of the systems and allowed the hackers to essentially flip the breakers, while the second, KillDisk, wiped the code of the computers' operating systems. The plant had to go on full manual control and rebuild all the computers. This attack showed that Russia could take control of Ukraine's biggest power plants and flip them off like a light switch.

Subversion Station: The Internet Research Agency

A "troll" is a person who maliciously engages in a conversation with the intention of disruption. Internet trolls have been a part of internet culture since near the beginning of public access. Like the obnoxious dirty little gnomes that live under the bridge in the Brothers Grimm fairy tales, they interrupt your existence and threaten to eat you. The life of human trolls is to be overbearing, intrusive, and mean-spirited. They are also designed to stop you from performing normal activities on the web. The use of trolls in modern active measures resembles the use of human agent provocateurs during the pre-Bolshevik era to incite riots that legitimized action against revolutionaries.

The headquarters of the global troll activity under control of Vladimir Putin was the Russian Federation Internet Research Agency (RF-IRA), originally located on 55 Savushkina Street in St. Petersburg. The RF-IRA headquarters was the largest of what may have been the start of many of the paid troll factories operating in Russia to provoke and inflame discussions in the US.[2] The network was under the special activities umbrella of Putin loyalist Yevgeny Prigozhin, the director of Black and Grey area civilian operations who worked directly for the Kremlin.

Mikhail Burchik was alleged to be the head of RF-IRA. Previously, he owned information technology companies. He was supervised by Putin loyalists, including Prigozhin, and Oleg Vasilyev.[3] The "American Department" (Americanski Otdhel) of what was code-named the "Translator Project" at the Savushkina location reportedly started with 80 to 90 permanent employees. It would expand to several hundred including subcontractors. The group produced thousands of fake news and propaganda items per week. By 2015 they could generate 20 to 30 million views on items per week. Their products are tied to bots that can resend their obnoxious messages by the millions per hour.

The Mueller special counsel indictment as well as Russian and other journalists have discovered the salaries and structure of the Internet Research Agency. The lowest level content creators: $1,000 per month, community administrators: $1,538 per month. Department heads make $2,051 per month. Purchasers of SIM cards, proxy servers, IP addresses, and other IT support is $3,481 per month, likely per work station, and social media advertising is $5,000 per month.[4] The Mueller investigation found that as much as $1,200,000 was spent on their operations per month.

Alex Stamos, Chief Security Officer of Facebook, told Congress that the RF-IRA spent more than $100,000 on Facebook political ads between June 2015 and May 2017.[5] This amounted to approximately 3,000 ads from 470 fake accounts and pages. A quarter of these ads were "geographically targeted" with an uptick in 2016 over 2015.[6] Stamos stated that the "behavior displayed" was intended to "amplify divisive messages." In addition to these numbers, Stamos said that accounts with "very weak signals of a connection" or "not associated with any known organized effort" amounted to $50,000 spent on approximately 2,200 ads, including ads purchased from US IP addresses.[7]

These advertisements, tweets, and Facebook posts were seen by as many as 150 million Americans during the 2016 election. The Oxford Internet Institute studied the election and found that on Twitter and Facebook people shared almost as many fake news stories as they did real ones.[8] By 2018, Twitter would be forced to notify 677,000 users that they were exposed to Russian propaganda during the campaign, but not what kind specifically.

In February 2018, the United States District Court for the District of Columbia filed an indictment in the United States versus the Internet Research Agency, Concord Management and Consulting, LLC, and Concord Catering. The indictment alleges that the internet research organization is a Russian organization engaged in operations to interfere with elections in political processes. According to the indictment, beginning in late 2013, the organization hired staff and planned to manipulate the US Presidential election by creating false personas of American citizens. They would set up social media websites, group

Facebook pages, and Twitter feeds to attract US audiences. They name 13 Russians who are the key managers of the organization, starting with Yevgeny Prigozhin.

The Mueller indictment wasn't the first to identify the activities in these troll factories. One former employee of the RF-IRA named Lyudmila Savchuk attempted to expose the troll factory despite the risk of retaliation. She and others claim that the Russian government protects the organization. She sued the RF-IRA in Russia over worker conditions and pay, working with a lawyer named Ivan Pavlov from an NGO called Team29. Team29 represented Savchuk and another employee, Olga Maltseva, in her case against the RF-IRA.

Cambridge Analytica—Reengineering the American Psyche?

Russian hybrid warfare and its ability to develop propaganda to craft beliefs and change minds was the heart of their perception management campaign against Europe and the United States. Though their operations were conceptualized in the Soviet era and engineered during the first Putin years, they were operationalized as a response to the Colour Revolution in Ukraine, the Baltics, and central Asia. The Russian perspective was being lost and the only way to stop it was to craft a new view of Moscow through information warfare.

To apply this against hardened political structures such as those in the United States and Europe would take a new system of mind warfare. The most difficult political analysis was how to steer an undecided bloc of voters into believing what a candidate offers in the most efficient manner. In America, the king was television advertising. Billions were spent on 30-second advertisements. It was tried and true, but this was the second decade of the 21st century. Social media was even more influential. A political analyst who understood the modern social systems would be savvy enough to understand the distribution system depended on word of mouth. That was the entire basis of social sharing networks on Facebook and Twitter. The Muslim world showed the exponential power of social media during the Arab Spring of 2011.

Egyptian protesters created rallies and sit-ins—agitation and political action seen across the world using applications such as Facebook, WhatsApp, and Viber. They streamed live video of the marches, which were picked up by international news media from Al Jazeera to CNN. When the Egyptian government shut off television broadcasts to halt the throngs, the street protesters transmitted videos and live streams of their protests. These protests and public outrage at the government forced the army to intervene and remove the Mubarak family. This would play out again in Libya, Syria, and Tunisia. Why could it not be co-opted and turned back into a propaganda warfare tool?

To work in the West would take a more sophisticated type of social engineering. In 2013, a British company called Strategic Communication Laboratories formed Cambridge Analytica in order to win contracts with the Republican Party leading up to the US elections. Cambridge also was said to have helped in the Brexit Leave.EU campaign. The company was partially funded by the extremely conservative Mercer family and their super PACs. Steve Bannon and Jared Kushner were on the board of advisors.

After the election of Donald Trump and the suspicions that he had been assisted by the Kremlin, Cambridge Analytica would quickly come under investigation by American Special Counsel Robert Mueller. Konstantin Rykov, Putin's head of propaganda and author of the infamous Rykov confession (where he asserts Trump worked with Russia to win the election as early as 2013), stated that Trump had been working with Cambridge to create "psychotypes, or psychological profiles," to influence voters. Rykov said that "British scientists from Cambridge Analytica offered to make out of 5,000 existing human psychotypes—the 'perfect image' of Trump's possible supporter. Then... put that image back on all the [profiles] and thus find the universal key to anyone and everyone."[9]

Cambridge Analytica would also say the same. They could predict personality types and the political leanings of an individual based on data factors called OCEAN—Openness, Conscientiousness, Extroversion, Agreeableness, and Neuroticism. With this data they could then target specific types of individuals with the proper advertising.[10]

Alexander Polonsky of Bloom Consulting told the *New York Times* that, "It goes beyond sharing information.... It's sharing the thinking and the feeling behind this information, and that's extremely powerful."

At the exact same time that Cambridge Analytica was forming, Putin's two loyalists, Rykov and Yevgeny Prigozhin, were forming the Russian Internet Research Agency (RF-IRA) to distribute Russian propaganda warfare content to the United States and Europe. Is it a coincidence that both CA and RF-IRA started their efforts in 2013 to impact the US elections simultaneously and independently? Accidents of destiny such as this raises eyebrows. They validate Nance's Law: Coincidence takes a lot of planning. A historic intersection of these two entities was just too incredible to be believed.

In 2017, it would be discovered that the CEO of Cambridge, Alexander Nix, secretly reached out to Julian Assange at WikiLeaks by email to try to acquire the 33,000 emails that Clinton had deleted from her server and which WikiLeaks allegedly had in their possession. Assange turned Nix down, claiming he would sort through them himself.

However, Assange did not have the actual Clinton emails Nix wanted. In fact, no one did. On May 9, 2016, Fox News's legal analyst Judge Andrew Napolitano claimed that Putin and his top advisors had 20,000 of Hillary Clinton's deleted emails and were having an internal debate about whether to release them to the West. Napolitano said, "There's a debate going on in the Kremlin between the Foreign Ministry and the Intelligence Services about whether they should release the 20,000 of Mrs. Clinton's emails that they have hacked into...."[11] The source of that story was an obscure website called whatdoesitmean.com and an even more enigmatic conspiracy theory writer using the pseudonym "Sorcha Faal."[12] David Corn at *Mother Jones* also found the same story planted at a conspiracy news dump called the *European Union Times*. Both sources and the story are likely highly refined inventions of the RF-IRA and had the exact effect they desired. Moscow was not a hero in the conservative anti-Hillary world, and they had the goods Republicans needed. The supposed existence of the 20,000 emails took on a life of its own when Trump publicly asked Russia to release them. However, Nix's request was a sign that Cambridge was not just a data analytics company—they were a part of the Trump campaign's political warfare and dirty tricks group.[13] The question that has yet to be answered is whether Cambridge Analytica is the "bridge of spies" between the Trump campaign and Russian intelligence's information warfare groups. The Mueller investigation is trying to determine if Cambridge knowingly provided the RF-IRA or Trump team with that extra bit of data targeting the 77,000 voters of Pennsylvania, Michigan, and Wisconsin that gave Trump his victory. The data flow was so precise that there is no way Russia could know which specific voters in those states would be open to their propaganda. Only Americans on the ground could know with that level of specificity. If Cambridge or its staff passed the specific individual voter data collected for the Trump team on to Moscow so that the RF-IRA could target its messages to a specific bloc of voters, they may be exposed to much, much more than embarrassment, as both England and the United States laws would consider working for the Kremlin an act of espionage.

The Internet Research Agency and other troll farms weren't the only Russian intelligence subcontractors in the 2016 election. Media investigations found that there were young, English-speaking men in Macedonia generating nonstop pro-Trump fake news stories for purely economic reasons. They would then feed these stories to Facebook pages and collect revenue via Google AdSense. They also created pro-Trump websites with domain names like DonaldTrumpNews.com, WorldPolititcus.com, and USADailyPolitics, which were then filled with fake news from numerous sources in the Russian information sphere. In a town with very little economic potential for young men, $5,000 per month is a lot of money.[14] They did not have to maintain a news staff as their content was appropriated from other fake news sites from the United States. They found that posting pro-Trump materials were the most profitable, but had no vested interest in his success during the election of 2016. However, they profited Donald Trump and Vladimir Putin to no end.

The motivation for creating fake news ranges from an intentional desire to mislead people for political reasons to a raw desire for money from the ad revenue generated by ad clicks. In web speak, "click bait" refers to content that is manufactured purely to get viewers to click the "read more" link. The content may be partially true and misleading or completely made up.

Ad-based revenue can generate thousands of dollars for site owners who create or aggregate fake or misleading partisan news. Using ad services like Google AdSense, content creators can monetize these manufactured stories. Fake news ads can generate lots of views on Facebook. For $33, a single ad can reach up to 60,000 Facebook users per day.[15]

Approximately 12% of the tweets posted from these accounts also attempted to mask the origin of the account by using VPN (Virtual Private Network) access. VPN allows users to access content indirectly to appear to be coming in from another location. For example, a death threat against the author used a VPN to access American servers. Once on the internet, it appeared to be in Denver, Colorado. VPN isn't a guaranteed method to disguise the user's origin, as counter hackers discovered the death threats actually originated at the RF-IRA in St. Petersburg, Russia.

RF-IRA Gets Indicted

On February 16, 2018, Special Counsel Robert Mueller filed an indictment at the US District Court for the District of Columbia titled The United States versus the Internet Research Agency [RF-IRA], Concorde Management and Consulting, LLC, and Concorde Catering. The indictment alleged that the "research" organization was in fact a "Russian organization engaged in operations to interfere with elections in political processes." According to the indictment, beginning in late 2013, the organization was formed, hired staff, and planned and received orders to manipulate the US Presidential election through the largest Russian intelligence active measure ever conducted against the United States—a broad-based information warfare campaign to change the minds of American citizens. In addition to the RF-IRA setting up tens of thousands of social media websites, Facebook groups and pages, and Twitter feeds designed to look like American citizens posting information to attract conservative American audiences, they used "marionetting," where they pretended to be US citizens, and organized protests with civic groups who were convinced that they were communicating with legitimate people, not Russian agents.

The heat from the Mueller investigation and the FBI on RF-IRA for the activities during the American, French, and German elections proved too much. By 2017, they had been forced to shut down, change their name to "Teka," and move to a new location on Beloostrovskaya Street in St. Petersburg. Then they resumed operations once Trump was in office—they attacked Robert Mueller, the FBI, and any critic of Donald Trump or Vladimir Putin.[16]

Propaganda products, fake news articles, and crazy Russian death threats are not mass broadcasted tens of thousands of times a day by a real human being. The human element drafts the product but uses a self-replicating, self-transmitting piece of computer software called a "bot." A bot refers to the use of software that posts, reposts, and interacts like sentient human users. It's a takeoff from the word robot. In propaganda warfare bots are automated software weapons designed to disperse propaganda and fill blank spaces with their own message like the particles in a mist of influence warfare. They are the cockroaches of computational propaganda as they can invade any crevice no matter how seemingly secure, and cannot appear to be eliminated entirely. By using bot-deploying technology to influence target audiences, the RF-IRA became a globally unique information force in modern active measures. Had Stalin or Hitler had bot dispersal systems, they would currently be ruling the world.

Creating accounts or organizations that appear to share topical or partisan affinity mixed with hashtag promotion allowed bots to drive public opinion. People tend to enjoy spreading messages they agree with, no matter how obscure the source or crazy the claim. Human curiosity and gullibility are the dispersal agents of the bot. Russia became aware of this and turned it into an idea-changing weapon. Russians did not just attempt to rig elections in the United States, France, and Germany, but also influence operations like the policy debates of Brexit, immigration, or the Russia probe in the United States. The first place they experimented was on the Russian people. Recall that Yevgeny Prigozhin himself created the Kharkiv News Agency and used bots to flood it with fake news and horrible comments using fake individuals to push the Kremlin's view.

Another tool in the Russian arsenal was the use of fake news fire hydrants called botnets. A botnet is comprised of a string of connected computers and devices that run automated software (bots) for a particular task. When used by a nation-state, it can act as a virtual army that transcends the attackers' point of origin. Imagine every fire hydrant in a city exploding and flooding the streets: The botnet would be the water main system feeding those hydrants. Botnets might be used to conduct Distributed Denial of Service (DDoS) attacks in which internet access is clogged by flooding data; brute-force log-in attacks where massive computer power tries billions of attempts to log in to server or website administration log-ins; or to spread malware, ad-clicking fraud, and email spam. Botnets were first deployed in the early 2000s and continue to expand in complexity and capabilities over the years.

Every bot has a job, and in many ways they mimic roles previously carried out by human beings in the espionage world. Those people were called Agents of Influence, Agents Provocateurs, and Chaos Agents. Today bots fill these roles. Botnets could include millions of messages of every type that are usually focused on one propaganda objective.

In the weeks leading up to the 2016 election, Russian-linked bots retweeted 47,846 @HillaryClinton tweets while tweets from @realDonaldTrump were retweeted 469,537 times. Similarly, @HillaryClinton tweets received 119,730 likes from Russian-linked bots compared to 517,408 likes of @realDonaldTrump tweets by Russian-linked bots.

Twitter also examined content being shared from known and alleged Russian cutouts including from WikiLeaks, Guccifer 2.0, and DCLeaks. They noted @WikiLeaks posts were retweeted 196,836 times,

@Guccifer_2 tweets were retweeted 24,000 times, and @DCLeaks tweets were retweeted 6,774 times by Russian-linked bots.

A unique bot seen in the 2016 election could be called the Agitation Bot. In human terms it would be an agent provocateur, where it would pose as a local resident and exhort followers to show up at a protest or real-life street action. Of course, a bot can be used to organize the place and time of an event such as a protest. We use them all the time on our mobile phone schedulers. The trick is to make real people think it is a real person scheduling the event. Once people show up in real life, even without a bot organizer, they generally will spontaneously continue the protest activity. The Internet Research Agency created 129 Facebook events between 2015 and 2017.[17] Facebook reported to the Senate Intelligence Committee that the posted events were viewed by over 300,000 users, and that around 62,500 planned to attend the events and 25,800 were interested in attending the event. All these Americans were being manipulated like marionettes by puppeteers in St. Petersburg, Russia.

For example, Russian accounts used Facebook to promote Pro-Trump rallies like the "Florida Goes Trump" rally on August 20, 2016. The rally was promoted on the Facebook page created by username "march for Trump." The page called "Being Patriotic" promoted this event along with a "Down with Hillary!" event in New York at the Hillary Clinton campaign headquarters.[18]

Another example: the trolls posted opposing events for May 21, 2016, in Houston, Texas, around the opening of an Islamic Center library. Both sides, including "Stop Islamization of Texas" protesters and "Save Islamic Knowledge," were actually Russian entities trying to create mayhem. Some comments related to the event issued threats of violence aimed at Muslim Americans.

In January 2017, a more unusual case of Russian intelligence "marionetting" of an unwitting innocent citizen using a hybrid mix of bots, human, and web propaganda, involved a martial arts teacher named Omowale Adewale. He was asked if he wanted to facilitate training self-defense classes to African Americans. Under the banner of "Black Fist

Self Defense Project," he conducted over a dozen trainings between January and May 2017 and was paid $320 via PayPal and Google Wallet for the sessions.[19] However, Adewale never met the people who were soliciting him to conduct the classes. Instead, the events were part of a campaign developed by Russian Intelligence and the Internet Research Agency.

Adewale was first contacted by a person who identified himself as "Taylor." Taylor asked him to collect information on the participants. In other examples, the name "Jackob Johnson" has been used. The group used a website, "blackfist.pro," to promote the trainings and even arranged interviews with podcasts like "No Holds Barred" with a host named Eddie Goldman.[20] The podcast discussions with Adewale were conducted by phone. Text of the interview was posted to the blog Sherdog.com.

"We all understand that since the election of Donald Trump there have been a lot of, I'll say, hate crimes against minorities. And so, we thought that it's a good idea where as Black people we could be able to defend ourselves. The main idea is not even the defense. It's just being able to be in a position to defend ourselves. And also we understand that self-defense is something that if you know, it boosts your own [self-esteem]. To accomplish this, this year they have begun holding a series of seminars and self-defense classes around the U.S. At this time, these classes have been held in New York and Florida, with more locations soon to be announced. The trainers include Omowale Adewale, a kickboxer, boxer, and MMA fighter based in New York.... In addition, we open with a commentary on the importance of using the combat sports to fight the rise of reaction we see today, and of following the time-tested slogan on 'an injury to one is an injury to all.'"

This was an active measure to create the impression that African Americans were preparing to focus their aggression through mixed martial arts–type street fighting. Had this succeeded, the propaganda would have been spread across RT, Sputnik, and Fox News to terrify white Americans who support Donald Trump.

When it comes to using bots, hashtags are relatively easy to program since they can be adopted, updated, and repeated. This made hashtags, symbolized by the #, a perfect companion to information warfare campaigns that were aimed to draw attention to themselves. The Internet Research Agency drove several propaganda campaigns in Europe well before the US election. They used hashtags #Frexit (French Exit the EU), #Grexit (Greek Exit the EU), #Brexitvote, #PrayForLondon, #BanIslam, and #Brexit. In the United States, they drove hashtags #CALEXIT (Northern California separatists), #TEXIT (Texas Republic separatists), #WhiteGenocide, and #BlackLivesMatter.[21]

In the 1960s, Service A (the disinformation service of the KGB) sought to sow racial division around Dr. Martin Luther King Jr. King was the target of active measures organized under KGB officer Yuri Modin. The KGB campaign to inflame racial tensions included sending fake pamphlets to black activist organizations meant to instigate tension with the Jewish Defense League. But decades later, it would be RF-IRA–driven trolls seeking to exacerbate tensions around the Black Lives Matter campaign. This time it would be a competing set of Twitter accounts joining the fight to instigate division between #Black-LivesMatter, #BlueLivesMatter, and #AllLivesMatter hashtags. A University of Washington examination of the accounts associated with the Internet Research Agency found that 29 of them were feeding the hashtag war on all sides.

In the lead-up to the 2016 election, the hashtag #DNCLeak was used. In the two months before the election, 26,500 users created 154,800 tweets with the hashtag #DNCLeak. This included 3% that were Russian-linked accounts. Clinton campaign chairman John Podesta's emails had been stolen after a successful spear-phishing attack by COZY BEAR. He was tricked when he clicked on a link that pretended to be a Google security alert. In the weeks before the election, WikiLeaks published 118 tweets with the hashtag #PodestaEmails.[22] Twitter said nearly 5% of the tweets with this hashtag were generated from Russia-linked accounts for a return of 20% of the impressions for the first week of posting.[23] Twitter estimated 64,000 users created 484,000 tweets with variations of this hashtag in the two months before the election.

Twitter later testified that it sought to reduce the exposure of these hashtags and limited their distribution. It drew an immediate outcry from not only right-wing and conspiracy theory sites in America, but also from Russia Today and the Sputnik website. Both groups called this "censoring."

In early January 2018, there was an effort by Chairman of the House Permanent Select Committee on Intelligence, Representative Devin Nunes, and other Republicans to discredit the investigation into Trump's relationship with Russia. A memo drafted by Nunes accused the FBI of abusing the FISA (Foreign Intelligence Surveillance Act) process to target Donald Trump and his campaign staff. Soon after rumors of this report surfaced, the Russian-originated hashtag #ReleaseTheMemo appeared on January 18, 2018. It was quickly shared over 3,000 times in a two-day period following the announcement of the memo's existence.[24] Other Deep State hashtags were launched to accompany this effort including #fisagate, #obamadeepstate, #wethepeopledemandjustice, #thememorevealsthecoup, and #obamaslegacyisobamagate.[25] In addition, #SchumerShutdown was launched in a failed attempt to rival another hashtag, #TrumpShutdown, after the administration allowed the government to shut down for two days. On many accounts, it was added to posts with #ReleaseTheMemo. So pervasive was the belief that Russia was pushing the hashtags, many real conservatives started posting #IamNotaRussianBot. It was amusing until RF-IRA posts used it as well.

In early 2018, Twitter updated its methods of detecting bots and Russian associated accounts after the election in response to demands to deal with the abuse of their platform. This included examining what qualifies as "Russian-linked" or "RF-IRA–linked." Criteria for this included determining where the account user was located, use of Russian email addresses, if the account was created from a Russian IP address, or if the account had been accessed from a Russian IP address.

In some cases, use of Cyrillic in usernames or display names or if Cyrillic was used in the sign-up interface was considered.

Hoaxes: 48 Hours in the Life of an Assassination Bot

Bots may be automated software spreading propaganda everywhere, but they can also be "retasked" by their human handlers to intervene and focus a hateful message against very specific people and try to bring about violence at the hands of their puppets. In late July 2017, Moscow decided that they had enough of my and Joy Reid's free use of television. In late July 2017, I was attending Politicon, the convention for politics in Pasadena, California. Two days before the scheduled panel on "From Russia with Trump," an account on Twitter began to issue death threats against both Joy Reid and me. The "person" promised an armed confrontation at the convention. But upon very close inspection it was determined this was a Russian bot programmed to pretend to act like an American citizen.

The account was named "Mario__Savio" (double underscores). It was found on Twitter encouraging people to confront me and others at the Pasadena Convention Center. When it was investigated, it appeared to be a legitimate account, but on closer inspection it was found that the Russian bot had "typo-squatted" and mimicked a real account right down to stealing the profile and photo. Typo-squatting is when an online name appears almost identical to another but distinguished by a hard-to-see typographic error. In this instance, the Russian programmer added an additional underscore mark (_) to the legitimate account Mario_Savio (single underscore).

A review of the bot's history found that it had been operating as an agent of influence bot using a series of attacks and attempts to pump up followers. For almost 90 days, it posted negative comments on Twitter about four TV personalities: Bill Maher, Joy Reid, Rachel Maddow, and Michael Moore. A shift came when it started to attack Republican Senator John McCain, who had criticized Donald Trump for his response to Russian aggression. In response to McCain, the account repeatedly attempted to associate the Senator with conspiracy theories about his funding ISIS and the war in Syria. Further back, the account had focused on Ukraine, Syria, and other topics that are typical of Russian geopolitical discussion. Forty-eight hours before the Politicon conference, the bot was re-tasked to agent provocateur mode. It started notifying a Southern California pro-Trump forum of my presence at Politicon and requested that followers go there. Twenty-four hours before the panel, it was re-tasked again and went into chaos agent mode. The bot started issuing death threats against Joy Reid and me. It started posting threatening posters of me with a sniper's crosshairs on it with the text "WANTED! For inciting #ISIS to "suicide bomb" a #Trump Hotel @FBI @Secret-Service." It also posted images of Joy Reid with Nazi paraphernalia and the word "Goebbels." This was likely an allusion to the "Baby Goebbels" joke I had made on *Real Time with Bill Maher* about White House speechwriter Stephen Miller. The bot stated, "I need all the publicity I can get before I come after Malcolm Nance. I'll be there after @JoyAnnReid at her gig #Politicon #Fakenews." Cybersecurity experts determined it was a bot not physically located in Denver, Colorado, as its Twitter profile showed, but that it was a VPN used for entry into the US internet. The bot's true location was then tracked back to St. Petersburg, Russia, likely the Internet Research Agency.

Though Twitter was alerted to this account on July 29, 2017, it took weeks for the same false username to be suspended, and only after it had made dozens of additional threatening posts calling for direct confrontation with me and others.

Another American fake news story pushed by Russia was the notorious hoax called #PizzaGate. After the release of emails attributed to former New York representative Anthony Weiner, a conspiracy theory emerged claiming that a pizza parlor, Comet Ping Pong, in Washington, D.C., was secretly a front for a human trafficking and pedophilia ring. The story claimed that the New York Police Department found evidence of a massive human trafficking racket based on inside sources in the department. The story was then picked up by Sean Adl-Tabatabai, who posted it to his fake news site, YourNewsWire.com, with the additional claim that he had confirmed the claims through an "FBI Insider." Adl-Tabatabai is the former webmaster for conspiracy theorist David Icke.

After the post was created, the 4chan message board picked up the story and began to feed on it. 4chan was one of the most popular genesis points for alt-right subcultures and was known for viral campaign generation. Driven by posts by anonymous users, 4chan is the web equivalent of the Wild West, with very lax oversight and a culture of feeding-frenzy behavior around fake news and rumormongering.

Conspiracy theorist Alex Jones's InfoWars and others carried the stories farther across the web, each with its own click bait–driven agenda. The spreading of the story didn't stop in the US, but was picked up by sites around the world, often with each adding its own spin, variation, or new material to the claims. In just days, the first claimant of the story had reposted a link to truepundit.com, who had echoed the original claims as a source of validating it. "My source was right!" claimed the Twitter account under the name "@DavidGoldbergNY."

The story wasn't true, of course, but that didn't stop self-appointed internet sleuths from continuing after the release of emails via WikiLeaks supposedly belonging to John Podesta, Hillary Clinton's campaign advisor. Various people began to pick apart the Podesta emails, looking for code words they claimed would substantiate the PizzaGate theory, especially code words related to food. "I'm dreaming about your hotdog stand in Hawaii…," wrote Mike Cernovich, alt-right leader and prolific fake news promoter. Under the hashtag #PodestaEmails28, users were combing through the WikiLeaks releases and picking out words like, "pizza," "cheese," "pasta," "ice cream," and "walnut" as code for little girls and boys or male prostitutes.

Ultimately, the story came to a crescendo when Edgar Maddison Welsh of North Carolina traveled to Washington, D.C., and opened fire inside the restaurant with an AR-15 on December 4, 2016. Welch was convinced that real crimes were being committed and decided to take matters into his own hands. He was charged in December 2016, entered a plea agreement on transportation of firearms and assault with a deadly weapon on March 24, 2017, and was sentenced to a fine and four years in prison.

Additionally, a Shreveport, Louisiana, man, Yusif Lee Jones, called in a threat to shoot up another restaurant just three days after the Welch shooting. Jones called the Besta Pizza restaurant in Washington, D.C., claiming he was going to "shoot everyone in the place" to "save the kids." Jones was arrested and pled guilty to issuing criminal threats against the restaurant on January 12, 2017.[26] Though the story had been debunked in plenty of outlets, the restaurant faced an onslaught of continued harassment. The owners and others are still repeatedly threatened via social media.

The story wasn't limited to fake news sites. Donald Trump's campaign team member and soon-to-be National Security Advisor, Michael Flynn, shared the story via his Twitter channel as did his son, Michael Flynn Jr., who added, "until #PizzaGate proven to be false, it'll remain a story."[27]

#PizzaGate may have been the most popularized fake news story of the campaign season, but not the most terrifying in terms of the number of people who were affected. In St. Mary Parish, Louisiana, residents were targeted with the fake news headline, "Toxic fume hazard warning in this area until 1:30 PM," which prompted calls to the local Homeland Security office on September 11, 2014. Though there were hundreds of Twitter accounts discussing the "powerful explosion" under the hashtag #ColumbianChemicals,[28] in fact, there was no emergency.

Despite the tweets and posts, the event was a hoax. Ultimately, Columbian Chemicals sent out a news release that there was no explosion and the reports were false. Despite it being a hoax, the non-event even had a Wikipedia page and a YouTube video purported to be an ISIS claim of responsibility with women in full burqa waving guns. On March 10, 2015, another similar hashtag, #PhosphorousDisaster was launched. It claimed that a large spill of phosphorus was dumped into American Falls (along with hashtag #AmericanFalls) in Idaho.

On October 4, 2014, a hashtag hit Twitter thanks to the Internet Research Agency. This time it was #MaterialEvidence. A Facebook event was inviting people to an art exhibit on West 21st Street in New York City with photos of Syria and Ukraine. When reporters from Gawker sought the funding source of the exhibit, they were told by the gallery source it was from a "silent guy" who "came back with a bag of cash and dropped it for them with no explanation."[29] The show ran from September to October 2014, and advertisements for the show were ubiquitously posted around the city on buses and subway posters. After emails were hacked by Anonymous International and leaked to the web, it was shown that among the financiers of this campaign was the Internet Research Agency of St. Petersburg.[30]

These are just a small sample of the efforts being conducted by the Internet Research Agency, not only in the United States but around the world. A review of the digital infrastructure behind these hashtag campaigns linked the Twitter accounts to a mass posting tool called "Masss Post" tied to a domain in Russia (Add1.ru). *New York Times* reporter Adrien Chen asked Mikhail Burchik, alleged leader of the RF-IRA troll farm, if he had registered the domain and Burchik denied it. Leaked emails stolen by the hacker activist group Anonymous tied Burchik back to the organization. Julian Hans of the German newspaper *Süddeutsche Zeitung* claims Burchik affirmed ownership of the leaked emails before denying it to Chen.

Frustrated with accusations that InfoWars was a Russian hashtag generator, Alex Jones posted a photo of his Russian business visa and tweeted mockingly, "Looking forward to Putin giving me the new hashtags to use against Hillary and the dems...."[31] Little did he know he was revealing something not far from the truth. Jones had been a highly reliable source of fake news for the Russian propaganda warfare structure and his conspiracy theories were hashtagged like crazy by the RF-IRA. His nutty commentary is widely admired by some of Russia's leading politicians, and thanks to his own tweet he revealed he had been issued a long-term business visa to keep his special brand of conspiracy mongering alive.

What Does the Fox Say?

Buzzfeed's Sheera Frenkel discovered that Russia Defense Minister Sergey Shoigu reported to the Duma that Russia was engaged in a propaganda war. Shoigu said that Russia's "[Cyber Army] are expected to be a far more effective tool than all we used before for counter-propaganda purposes."[32] The ability to use the worldwide web to execute many different avenues of attack would also explain why Russia chose WikiLeaks. They needed credibility on the world stage. Russian military strategists Col. Sergei Chekinov and Lt. General Sergei Bogdanov describe the efficiency of using non-attributable agencies such as non-governmental organizations to mask the work of intelligence operations in information war. They said:

> "It is preferable to have a foreign nonprofit, nongovernmental organization (NGO) that could best contribute to the attainment of the goal of a hybrid operation. It can be established beyond the Russian Federation under the rules of a foreign country [and] can draw its members from residents."[33]

Sergei P. Rastorguev, a Russian military hybrid warfare analyst, wrote an apocryphal story to illustrate the objectives of the coming cyberwarfare with America and Europe in *Philosophy of Information Warfare*:

> "Once there was a fox that wanted to eat a turtle, but whenever he tried to, it withdrew into its shell. He bit it and he shook it, but he wasn't getting anywhere. One day he had an idea: he made the turtle an offer to buy its shell. But the turtle was clever and knew it would be eaten without this protection, so it refused. Time passed, until one day there appeared a television hanging in a tree, displaying images of flocks of happy, naked turtles—flying! The turtle was amazed. Oh! They can fly! But wouldn't it be dangerous to give up your shell? Hark, the voice on television was announcing that the fox had become a vegetarian. 'If I could only take off my shell, my life would be so much easier,' thought the turtle. 'If the turtle would only give up its shell, it would be so much easier to eat,' thought the fox—and paid for more broadcasts advertising flying turtles. One morning, when the sky seemed bigger and brighter than usual, the turtle removed its shell. What it fatally

failed to [be understood is] that the aim of information warfare is to induce an adversary to let down its guard."[34]

With all systems in place, Russian assets of the FSB, SVR, GRU, the Military Intelligence Directorate, and Russia's NSA, the Special Communications and Information Service, were poised to strike a direct attack at the target they've been trying to hit for over 70 years—American democracy.

CHAPTER 9

Hail Hydra!

On July 22, 2011, 33-year-old Norwegian right-wing extremist Anders Behring Breivik set out dressed as a policeman to strike a blow against the ruling Norwegian Labor Party. Breivik had spent months building a 2,100-lb bomb that he placed in a large panel van. His plan was to explode it in the middle of the Norwegian governmental district, the *Regjeringskvartalet*. He intended to destroy the central building where the government bureaucracy was housed. If he was lucky, he would also kill the Prime Minister and everyone inside of the building. In his mind, the liberal Norwegian Labor Party had allowed Muslims into Norway, and that meant the purity of Norwegian blood would be corrupted by immigrant blood if mixed. To him, this government-sanctioned miscegenation was a crime against the white race. He blamed the Labor Party, and he was going to punish them.

Breivik forged a police identity card and uniform, drove the van into downtown Oslo, and set off the bomb, killing eight people. When the bomb went off, Oslo was in a panic. Terrorism had never reached its shores at this level and the world watched, thinking Islamic suicide bombers had chosen the soft Nordic nation for punishment. That was Breivik's intent. He wanted the world watching in one direction while he went off to perform a second act of White Nationalist terrorism. Breivik drove west out of the city into the wooded countryside. It is stunningly beautiful land filled with lakes, bays, and small islands. Still dressed as a policeman, he drove to Utoya Island. This was a small private island that was known for its gathering of the ruling Labor Party's Workers' Youth League Camp. When he arrived there, he loaded an American-made Mini-14 semi-automatic rifle. The rifle was a cutdown version of the US battle rifle from the 1950s, but its powerful 7.62mm NATO bullet could knock down a moose in seconds since it had a magazine capacity of 10 bullets. He also carried a Glock 17 pistol with multiple 15-round magazines. In preparation for his murders he scored the tip of every bullet, so they would break apart, then dipped them in nicotine tar to cause burning in the wound canal. He wanted to inflict maximum pain. But Breivik was not there to hunt big game; he was there to kill off the next generation of liberals in Norway.

Breivik rode to the camp on the boat designated to get attendees over to the island. Another passenger was the senior leader of the camp, Monica Bosei. Bosei, known as "the Mother of Utoya," was a beautiful, tall, striking brown-haired woman. She was also a brilliant scholar and director of the Norway Maritime Museum. She volunteered to run the program for the kids on the island. Breivik told her that he was going to the camp to protect the children. She noticed he was acting strangely and confronted him about what was happening in Oslo. He was evasive and did not seem to know even the basics of police procedure. As she disembarked on the island she knew something was wrong and sprinted off the boat to warn Trond Berntsen, a city police officer assigned to protect the camp. Breivik realized he was compromised. It was at that moment he definitively decided to murder her, the policeman, and all the others.

Breivik confessed to what he did with simplicity: "I was holding the pistol and there was a bullet in the chamber…and when I lifted the weapon Monica Bosei said I should not point the gun at the man in front of me. I then pointed the pistol at his head and shot him in the back of the head. Monica started to run and I shot her once in the head. Then I shot him twice in the head again. I went over to her then and shot her twice in the head."[1]

The island was his. No adults were left to stop him. According to his calm testimony at his murder trial, he thought to himself before beginning the massacre, "I thought this is now or never. There were a hundred voices in my head saying 'Don't do it. Don't do it.'" From there Breivik systematically started shooting every child he saw one by one. Children and teens ran screaming and hid, though they could barely escape him. He slowly and methodically walked to each, aimed the Glock at their heads and snuffed their lives out. For those who were too far away for an effective pistol shot, he methodically took aim with the high-powered rifle and shot them at their center of mass. In his trial, Breivik said he spared some young ones, but he would tell others he was a police officer, beckon them with a finger, and when they came within range, he would shoot for their heads. He seemed to be surprised that his victims stood totally paralyzed with fear as he raised his gun and shot them. By the time Oslo SWAT teams arrived he had shot and killed 69 teens and adults. Of course, like all cowards he feared death and surrendered knowing he would never pay with his life. He laughed to himself that Norway was too liberal for the death penalty. He said he mass-murdered the victims—who were between the ages of 13 and 22 years—because they were the next generation of "multicultural" liberals, whom he labeled Marxists. During his rampage he shouted at them, "You are going to die today, Marxists." Their parents had allowed a Muslim invasion of Norway and in his estimation he made them pay for their treason to the white race.

Anders Behring Breivik was the first of the foot soldiers of the white revolution being stoked by the neo-Nazi and fascist diaspora that was congealing in America and Europe. Surprisingly, these former Nazis and fascists were being funded and given ideological backing by Russia, a nation savaged by Nazis in WWII. Brevik left no stone unturned. To ensure he would be remembered by his White Supremacist brethren, he had written and left behind a 1,518-page manifesto in his home. As an international terrorism expert, a copy was sent to me on the same day it was found by Norwegian domestic intelligence officers. They wanted to know if this was the work of a madman or part of an international right-wing terror network. My assessment was that it was both. Breivik named himself a member of the "European patriot resistance move-ment." Some of what he assessed was a manifestation of ideas in his head, but it was a window into the mindset and links to a consolida-tion of anti-immigrant conservatives worldwide. They saw themselves as "Knights" of a Templar crusade cleansing Europe of blacks, Muslims, and liberals, but they were in fact storm troopers more akin to the mythical White Supremacist villains called Hydra. Hydra was the underground Nazi successor to the Third Reich, immortalized in the Captain America comic books, the Avengers movies, and the television show *Agents of Shield*. Only this was not an imaginary drama, it was precisely Hydra playing out across Europe and poisoning America. Their motto "cut off one head and another arises" was what Breivik and others dreamed. Even their post-Hitler Nazi salute "Hail Hydra!", a modification of "Heil Hitler!", would be later used by his American brothers, who would appropriate the salute with "Hail Trump! Hail Victory!"

Breivik may have gained his ideas from a myriad of American racists, extremists, and xenophobes, but he claimed he best identified with the Nashi—Putin's "Hitler youth"—as a model for the patriotic youth movement. Breivik wrote glowingly of his ideas on the growth of a conservative youth movement:

"We must spend the next 20 years wisely and continue our work on creating a pan-European conservative consolidation, a new conservative political ideology which has the potential to appeal to a MINIMUM of 20-35% of Western Europeans, including the bulk of our youth. The creation of cultural conservative student organizations in universities all over Europe must be a priority. In order to do this, we have to agree on a consensus for creating a modern, "un-tainted," cultural conservative, patriotic youth movement which will prevent our youths from joining NS or WN movements. This movement should be somewhat like the equivalent of Russia's Nashi. They were Putin's youth movement of 120,000 members aged between 17 and 25. They claim to be anti-fascist/anti-Nazi in name, but as "patriotic conservatives" they find themselves in league with both.

Breivik wrote a Q&A section in his manifesto where he asked himself who he most wanted to meet, he replied: "The Pope or Vladimir Putin. Putin seems like a fair and resolute leader worthy of respect."

Breivik was a canary in the global coal mine of right-wing conservative insurgency that was growing in the heart of Europe. By 2012, this virus of Russian-backed white ethno-nationalism would burn like an underground coal seam.

Austrian ultra-right politician Jörg Haider once said about European leaders worried about the rise of the right that "There is a lot of excitement in the European chicken pen—even though the fox hasn't even got in."[2] That idea is quaint. With Russia's assistance, the fox is not only in the pen, it is being elected by the chickens as the Rooster-in-Chief. Since 9/11, Europe has been slowly sliding toward more authoritarian governments. Many traditional former Warsaw Pact countries in Eastern Europe have pro-Russian government leaders including Bulgaria's Rumen Radev; Moldova's Igor Dodon, the pro-Russian leader of the Party of Socialists; and even pro-NATO Estonia's Center Party leader, Jüri Ratas. But the core of Russia's plan would be to harness the white ethnic extremists like Breivik in Western Europe and push them toward political activism. With the European political right in his pocket, Putin would make their autocratic nationalism the dominant political force in the West.

The hallmark of these European conservative demagogues was a single-issue hatred of Muslim immigrants, particularly since the Syrian and Libyan migration crises, which led millions of people to flee to Europe. Add to this the rise of ISIS in Syria that led Muslim nationals born in France, Belgium, and Germany to carry out terrorist attacks in their countries of birth. Divisive conservative politicians use this focused hatred to mobilize people based on their emotions. For example, the unabashed Geert Wilders in the Netherlands ran on a national campaign of the demonization of Muslims for decades. He has yet to win, but Muslim immigrant hatred is now the top European national security issue. However, over the last 17 years since the attacks on America, individual European politicians have turned these grievances into viable political parties that are gaining power.

What is at play here is that since 2001, Moscow has observed these nationalist racist trends and found they aligned with their own newfound cultural conservatism. They saw this as a chink in Europe's armor. Putin must have realized that by co-opting extremist European and American conservatives, who were naturally aligned with Russia. The Kremlin spent the last decade establishing a durable network of European populists who are fashioning themselves and their political parties in the same mold as Vladimir Putin and his United Russia Party. Putin's new Eurasian political fellow travelers are an amalgam of fascists, neo-Nazis, and nationalist political parties that for the last seven years were sidelined as they espoused the beliefs of Hitler, Mussolini, and the defeated demagogues of WW II. These shunned parties and personalities have suddenly found new life as nationalist Christian conservatives who want to destroy the status quo in Europe and eventually in the United States. The Europeans also understand that they have been held back by democracy itself and they admire the plan to use democracy to establish autocracies, led by themselves. From there they can assist Moscow in breaking America's "politically correct" democratic values of diversity, inclusiveness, globalization, and reliance on NATO and the European Union. The newly rehabilitated European fascists and Nazis also liked Putin's tough-guy image and confrontational tribalism as opposed to Barack Obama's studiousness and dealing with geopolitical power with thoughtfulness.

These European xenophobic parties have the universal characteristic of openly aligning themselves with Moscow and accepting their overt (and covert) political patronage, including being openly funded by Moscow. As a sign of their gratitude, Moscow has become the de facto capital of the anti-Atlantic, anti-globalization, white conservative world.

These groups all have the same ideological worldview. They see themselves as the opponents to the NATO-European world order. They want to realign the world with Moscow as the Christian cultural protector who helps them smash the establishments that have kept stability since WWII. As Aleksandr Dugin said when addressing the world after Trump's victory: "We, all together, should start the fight against the Russian Swamp, the French Swamp, the German Swamp, and so on. We need to purge our societies of the Swamp's influence.... So, let us drain the European Swamp. Enough with Holland, Merkel, and Brussels. Europe for Europeans."[3]

The pro-Moscow nationalist, anti-globalism, anti-NATO, and virulently anti-immigrant bodies in Europe are legion. To take an analogy from baseball, one really cannot understand the players without a roster. I will present here each nation's political parties that are being funded, co-opted, or that are in league with the Kremlin to destroy European democracy.

France

The National Front (aka FN, or Front National) was founded by Jean-Marie Le Pen in 1972. In 1974, Le Pen ran for President and lost with less than 1% of the vote to the socialist candidate, François Mitterrand.[4] Marine Le Pen was the 2017 candidate for the FN. Marine is the daughter of the party's founder, Jean-Marie Le Pen. A political heir, she joined in 1986. She rose quickly as a plainspoken champion of the conservative image of the French hinterlands. Le Pen ran for President in 2012 and came in third behind François Hollande and Nicolas Sarkozy. Her conservative voting bloc was the base for right-wing populism in France. Le Pen often called European populism the next wave in Europe's future. She once said, "What's populism? If it's someone who wants to defend government for the people, of the people and by the people, then yes, I'm a populist."[5] A reliable right-wing conservative who would sing from the Kremlin hymnal at every given opportunity, Marine was also an strident anti-globalist and an enemy of free trade. She once said, "Free trade is dead…and the world is turning a page. There's a new economic and cultural patriotism…and it's the way of the future."[6] Her remarks are ideologically in line with Putin, Dugin, Surkov, Bannon, and Trump.

Le Pen has a long-standing and close personal and financial relationship with Moscow. She was one of Putin's more reliable champions in Europe. She praised him in a 2011 interview with the Russian *Kommersant* newspaper, "I won't hide that, in a certain sense, I admire Vladimir Putin. He makes mistakes, but who doesn't? The situation in Russia is not easy."[7] In 2014, the National Front received $14 million from Russia through a Russian government finance front, First Czech Russian Bank.[8] Jean-Luc Schaffhauser, the FN representative to the

European Union for Île-de-France, helped to broker the loan between the party and Russia after failing to secure the funds from a UAE source.[9] The FN did managed to get a $2.5 million loan from sanctioned former KGB officer Yuri Kudimov, who ran the Russian "bank of spies," VEB Capital.[10] Kudimov also owned Vernonsia Holdings out of Cyprus. He was charged for spying in 1985 and expelled from the UK.[11] The FN then requested an additional $30 million from Russia in early 2016 to finance the 2017 elections. One could suppose that being lent so much money by Putin, he would easily earn Le Pen's undying admiration.

Marine's goal was to change France away from its centuries-long liberalism and make it the central pillar to the new European anti-Atlantic conservative alliance. She heartily accepted Moscow's money and vision for the realignment of the world away from Washington's influence. For this mission, Le Pen would choose the "blue rose" as the symbol of the FN. It symbolized the FN motto, *Possible l'impossible*, or "Making the Impossible Possible."

Le Pen openly and often expressed disdain for President Barack Obama and believed that all sanctions imposed after Russian's invasion of Crimea should be lifted. She promised that if she won the March 2017 French elections she would immediately withdraw France from NATO and the European Union in the name of "fiscal sovereignty"— knowing full well that France's withdrawal could damage NATO and spell the end of the EU. It was Putin who told Le Pen in a private interview that "France could become a colony of their former colonies."[12] She agrees her position on immigration is virtually identical to those of Putin, other Russian-backed populists, and Donald Trump:

> "We must curtail legal immigration to the very minimum required. Then we need to make sure that France has ceased to be attractive to migrants' country. Because now you come to France, even as an illegal, immediately get virtually the same rights as the French. [We] provide the benefit, social housing, free education and health. I am convinced that if we do nothing to offer migrants, they will stop coming."[13]

Le Pen fancied herself a new Charles de Gaulle, who had stood for an independent, patriotic France after WWII. When asked if France should withdraw from NATO, she said:

"Yes. I was initially against France's participation in the alliance....However, I am convinced that European countries should cooperate in the areas of security, but do not see any reason why Russia cannot be part of this process. European countries should cooperate with Russia to develop a plan to build a Europe of tomorrow."[14]

In 2015, Jean-Marie was banished from the National Front by his own daughter when he called Roma gypsies "smelly." Yet Jean-Marie Le Pen's racial rant is what many believed cost his daughter the Presidential election.[15]

The most recent addition to the family business is Jean-Marie's granddaughter and Marine's niece, Marion Maréchal-Le Pen. This young, attractive member of the National Front is considered the future of the party. Despite claiming she was taking a break from French politics, she spoke at the American Conservative Political Action Conference in 2018, where she charmed the alt-right with her fiery speech calling for a nationalist "first" policy. She said "I'm not offended when I hear President Donald Trump say 'America first.'...In fact, I want America first for the American people, I want Britain first for the British people, and I want France first for the French people." She finished very much like Trump voters with the battle cry, "Just like you, we want our country back."[16]

The Le Pen family remains the most militant pro-Russian Nationalists who have promised to forge ties with Moscow and help Putin integrate France into a network of neo-Nazi supporting counterprogressive Europeans—a Vichy French–like act which would surely have De Gaulle rolling in his grave.

The Le Pens are not the only xenophobes that helped forge France's special brand of racism. Bruno Gollnisch was a French Representative and Minister of European Parliament, a Catholic National Front member of the French National Assembly in the 1980s. Gollnisch was also a retired French Navy officer, lawyer, Holocaust denier, and the Alliance for European National Movement's President from 2010 through 2013. He was replaced by Bela Kovacs of Hungary's Jobbik Party.

In 2007, Gollnisch was arrested, tried, convicted, and issued a three-month suspended jail sentence for violating the Gayssot Act of 1990. This was for a Holocaust denial statement he made in 2004 just before the 60th anniversary of the liberation of Auschwitz. Approximately 3,000 French citizens who helped rescue Jews attended the Paris event and virtually everyone was offended. Gollnisch was also fined 71,400 euros with interest for payment to the plaintiffs. His racist and neo-Nazi friends were equally outraged. American racist and Ku Klux Klan leader David Duke called the charges against Gollnisch, "unrelenting persecution and character assassination." David Duke was a huge fan of his and wrote an article about Gollnisch on his blog after meeting him at his home in Lyon, France, and subsequently meeting Gollnisch's colleague Jean-Marie Le Pen on the same day of the interview.[17] David Duke wrote:

"The professor is a paragon of civility, but he has come to understand that unchecked immigration will constitute the destruction of European heritage and freedom. Dr. Gollnisch will not politely sit by while our European heritage is wiped away in France, the EU, and in the rest of the Western world."

As a faculty member at University of Lyon III, Gollnisch's collaborative efforts and active involvement with *American Renaissance*, a White Nationalist magazine, were never scrutinized nor deterred, while two years earlier, in 2002, a French government report affirmed that University of Lyon III had an established pattern of hiring Holocaust deniers.[18]

United Kingdom

Eurosceptic thinking is ever-present in the UK, but mainly in the voices of the Conservative Party. Anti-European think tanks like the Bruges Group, led by Robert Oulds, a member of the Conservative Party, help

guide their political allies. Bruges Group member Alan Sked, an economist and historian, founded the Anti-Federalist League in 1991 to block
the efforts of Britain joining the European Union. The efforts of Sked
were best summarized by the creation of two parties, the Anti-Federalist
League and the New Deal Party. In 1991, as Britain and Europe were
on the verge of creating a historical body to be known as the European
Union, Sked and others created a league of candidates who would com-
pete in the 1992 elections. Known as the Anti-Federalist League, they
were united in their effort to resist Britain's joining the newly created
European Union, which was established by the Maastricht Treaty. The
League would be defeated soundly in elections held in April 1992, but
instead of quitting, the Anti-Federalist League reformed as the United
Kingdom Independence Party, or UKIP, in September 1993.

The UKIP's founder, Alan Sked, had already begun losing control of
the party he created to the right-wing members around Nigel Farage. A
conservative Eurosceptic, Farage was a founding member of UKIP who
was elected into the European Parliament in 1999. Sked realized the
threat this presented and tried to push Farage out of the group. Farage
responded with a lawsuit.[19] As a result, it was Sked who was forced out
of the party by Farage with his fellow party members, Michael Holmes
and David Lott. Farage became the new unofficial leader while Michael
Holmes was formally elected the leader of UKIP, but he was soon forced
out by Farage and replaced with Jeffrey Titford. In 2006, Farage was
made the official leader of UKIP. Though he briefly resigned as the
party leader in 2009, he returned to the role again in 2010 and remained
in charge until 2016. He was replaced by Diane James in September
2016 for weeks before he replaced her briefly for a few months before
ultimately being succeeded by Paul Nuttall.

When it came to political successes, the UKIP had been in a steady
ascent from the moment it was seized by Farage. The big victory would
come in 2014 when the classic rivalry between the Labour Party and
the Conservative Party was rudely upset by the UKIP for the United
Kingdom's seats in the European Parliament. It had been a huge
advance from 2004, when UKIP placed 3rd, garnering just three seats,
and 2009, when they successfully grabbed 12 seats. These successive

victories fueled the party to advance its nationalist agenda, which had a target: leave the EU.

The British National Party (BNP) was a fusion of the English National Party of 1942 and the British Union of Fascists. First known as the English National Association of 1942 during WW II, it was full of fascists and Nazi sympathizers. Over time, they were viewed as extreme and never really carried favor within mainstream British politics.

The second incarnation came in 1960. The BNP was not all that influential, and so it died by 1967. However, it had become made up of the short-lived National Labour Party (1957–1960) and the White Defence League (WDL), a far-right anti-Semitic group whose symbol was a circle with a cross inside of it, and who had also been part of the League of Empire Loyalists (LEL), a Conservative Party affiliate who were against the WDL's ban on Jews. The WDL completely dissolved in 1960 and had no one else to represent them, so some of their members quietly snuck into the BNP.

The third and final incarnation came in 1982, when the new BNP was founded by neo-Nazi John Tyndall, a known leader in the violent British Movement of the 1970s. In its third incarnation, the far-right BNP had idealized their search for the white ethno-state. Like some in the Communist Party in America dovetailing on the Green Party's laurels, the new BNP were inconsequential groupies who piggybacked on the coattails of the UKIP after having kicked out Nick Griffin, the racist who did US college speaking tours sponsored by David Duke's colleague Preston Wiginton. Incidentally, Griffin (who may have been influenced by the White Defence League) was kicked out of the BNP for being too racist, and yet many refer to the BNP as being a fascist group. The new BNP were opposed to LGBT, Jews, Muslims, immigrants, etc. They were similar to the xenophobic Tea Party in the US, both racist and mostly middle-aged blue-collar white men in search of the white ethno-state. The BNP was never able to take off successfully given their history of various negative incarnations, so they evolved into the UKIP in 1993. And Griffin and populist racist Nigel Farage moved to the forefront in an attempt to mainstream Euroscepticism. They were originally the party of Margaret Thatcher with an emphasis on lowering immigration and multiculturalism—a seemingly futile effort in a country with a long and winding history of colonialism. Afterward, Nick Griffin formed the British Unity Party and helped create AENM (the Alliance of European National Movements).[20]

Few had heard of the group Britain First! until President Trump tweeted videos from the British far-right anti-immigration, anti-Muslim extremist group with the motto "Taking our country back!" It was founded in 2011 by Paul Golding and Jim Dowson. The group is known for anti-Muslim attacks and "patrols." Their deputy leader, Jayda Fransen, was convicted of religiously motivated harassment of a Muslim woman who was just walking with her four children—Fransen attacked her and pulled off her hijab. On November 29, 2017, President Trump reposted videos from their Twitter feed allegedly showing Muslim murders and atrocities under ISIS. The global outrage was instantaneous. British Prime Minister Theresa May stated through a spokesman, "The British people overwhelmingly reject the prejudiced rhetoric of the far-right, which is the antithesis of the values that this country represents—decency, tolerance and respect. It is wrong for the President to have done this."[21] On the other hand, Fransen told the *Washington Post*, "The British establishment no longer supports free speech, but the president of the United States, Donald Trump, clearly does, and that's why he tweeted, as a public display of support for Britain First and its deputy leader." Tommy Mair, the murderer of British MP Jo Cox, shouted the name of the group "Britain First!" when he stabbed and shot Cox to death. The group rejected all claims to Mair and the murder.

Germany

Germany's representatives in the Kremlin's European right-wing network are made up of three groups. The largest of the groups, and now represented in government, is the AfD (*Alternative für Deutschland*), or Alternative for Germany Party; second is the ultra-right National Democratic Party, the People's Union (NPD); and last is the anti-Islamic movement, the Patriotic Europeans Against the Islamisation of the Occident (PEGIDA), or *Patriotische Europäer gegen die Islamis-ierung des Abendlandes.*

The AfD was the German equivalent to Marine Le Pen's National Front or the base conservatives who elected Donald Trump in America. They held nearly an identical platform as American and French Conservatives on the major issues: Globalization (hate it!), immigration (hate them!), NATO (want out!), the European Union (break it up!), Russia (admiration), Russian sanctions (remove them!), and the Russian invasion of Crimea (boo-hoo, it's Russia's now!).

Like the French conservatives, the AfD senior leadership often made pilgrimages to the Kremlin seeking their support. Interestingly, the AfD's strongest base of power was in the former Russian-controlled East German provinces, where many had learned Russian as children and where economic equality had not completely made its way in since reunification. The symbol of the AfD is a broad red arrow swerving back to the right—in fact, it looks like it curves directly back to Moscow if one read it as a map.

The cofounder of the AfD is Dr. Frauke Petry, a doctor in chemistry and a successful entrepreneur; she would later step down from her post at the AfD because she wanted the pure "pursuit of Conservative politics."

Dr. Petry is best known in Germany for her condemnation and subsequent calls for the ban on minarets, or "Call to Prayer" spires. These are found on mosques that house the broadcast speakers for the Adhan, the Muslim call to prayer that occurs five times a day. Four million Muslims—roughly 5% of the population—live in Germany, where the Central Council of Muslims have compared the AfD's treatment of Muslims to that of Jews at the hands of the Nazis during WWII. Moreover, the AfD is against all male circumcision, but Dr. Petry has stated that nothing should disallow Muslims and Jews from having circumcision in Germany. These are issues that Dr. Petry has tried to soften given that the far-right Conservatives in Germany do not wish to lose political power or leverage. Despite this incongruity, Dr. Petry's views are anti-Muslim, stating that Sharia law and the wearing of burqa is also not compatible with Democratic and Western values and must be included in the ban.[22] Russia would play on those sentiments and concerns with vigor—they had little chance to topple Angela Merkel, but they could make a bruise.

In August 2017, the AfD held a Russian assembly in Magdeburg consisting of 300 members, half of whom spoke Russian. Here is what the speakers and guests said about Merkel: "Angela Merkel is an American puppet who wants to eliminate real Germans and replace them with Muslim invaders."[23] In an example of strategic patience meets 3D chess, the AfD was taking a decidedly pro-Moscow tilt—even their youth brigade had forged ties with Putin's United Russia Party youth branch.[24] The two sides were forging ties starting with teenagers.

Another German group is Pegida. It is best known for its far-right, anti-American, anti-Islam, and German Nationalist views. Pegida and the AfD are closely aligned in the sense that Spokeswoman and Treasurer Kathrin Oertel called Dr. Petry for advice on what to do with Pegida's former Chairman Lutz Bachmann. Bachmann was a convicted burglar who founded Pegida. He performed an act too disadvantageous and blatant even for the German ultra-right conservative cause in Germany—he impulsively posted photos of himself on Facebook dressed as Adolf Hitler. Dr. Petry suggested to Oertel that Bachmann step down for the good of all the right-wing groups. He stepped down in January 2017 but later stated, "I am an impulsive person....I regret I didn't resist my impulsiveness."[25]

The Czech Republic

Milos Zeman is the President of the Czech Republic. He is pro-Russian, is friends with Marine Le Pen and Nigel Farage, endorsed Donald Trump for President, and has ties to Hungary's Jobbik movement. Zeman has justified the civil war in Ukraine and has denied that Russia has a military presence there. He stated, "I take seriously the statement of Foreign Minister Sergey Lavrov, that there are no Russian troops [in Ukraine]." Zeman had been consistently verbal in his support for the lifting of Western sanctions on Russia and was against EU sanctions on Russia. He was re-elected President in January 2018 with 51.4% of the vote. He won the majority of the rural vote by exhorting a populist anti-immigrant slogan: "Stop Migrants and [opponent] Drahos. This is our land! Vote Zeman!"

Zeman's chief economic advisor is Martin Nejedly a former executive of Russian oil company Lukoil Aviation Czech. Lukoil was once the second-largest oil company in Russia following Gazprom. Nejedly was also owner of Fincentrum, a financial advisory firm with "more than 2,500 financial advisors" on its website with offices in Prague and Bratislava. The firm has a history of alliances with the Kremlin.

The Prime Minister of the Republic's coalition government is 63-year-old Andrej Babiš. He is a media and agribusiness mogul and the second-richest man in the Czech Republic. ANO is the Action of Dissatisfied Citizens Party founded by Babiš that holds a center-right populist platform like many European and American conservative right-wing groups. Its mantra is "Yes, it will get better." Stolen from Barack Obama's well known "Yes, We Can."

Babiš was a tough-talking populist who oozed rough charisma. He was entertaining to people bored by politics and charmed them enough to vote for change, even if it was linked to destabilizing uncertainty—no matter how nefarious its associations. Like Trump, he attracted the older rural populace and gained voters who had never voted before. Many of them had had enough with traditional politics. Others were impressed by his wealth without questioning his lack of transparency in corporate dealings.

Once again, like Donald Trump, Babiš "gamed" the anger of the Czech populace and inspired them to vote without having a consistent ideology; voters merely extrapolated the emotive sound bite they preferred, like fear of widespread immigration. Babiš steered this anger to the ballot box while they in turn ignored his questionable character of government corruption based on his misuse of EU subsidies. In addition, when the media investigated financial dealings of tax crimes in 2017 and his subsequent indictment in October of the same year, he had stated that he had been targeted by politically motivated disinformation...in other words, "fake news!"[26]

Filmmaker and social critic Michael Moore had often called Trump a "Molotov cocktail" to the American Republican political establishment; Babiš was the Czech Republic's Molotov cocktail, and Russia was behind his win, which garnered 30 percent of the vote.

Like Trump, Babiš was more liberal in his earlier years. He was a card-carrying member of the Communist Party for nearly the entirety of the 1980s before becoming a member of ANO from 2011 onward. This was after the dissolution of the far-right Nationalist Party and its paramilitary guard, which offered a "final solution" to Roma immigration.

Another extreme far-right party in the Czech Republic is the Workers' Party of Social Justice (DSSS, or *Dělnická Strana Sociální Spravedlnosti*). The DSSS refers to itself as "anti-Gypsy/Roma criminality." They posit that the majority of the Czech Republic's citizenry does not engage in political discourse. Only non-local foreigners do, and in doing so, they dismantle the ideals of the Czech people who believe in generations of tradition and its preservation. This is a powerful mantra heard throughout the conservative world.

Greece

Between 2010 and 2012, the Greek government suffered a debt crisis that led to a series of credit downgrades. This led to the Papandreou government implementing a series of severe austerity measures. In 2012, these measures led to disastrous consequences in the Greek economic system. Riots broke out in 2010 to protest these measures, and as the government tightened their belts, the riots increased over the next two years. Riots in central Athens became international news media spectacles showing the burning of buildings and police lines fighting Greeks who had lost their savings. The Greek parliament accepted one austerity measure after another, and still the credit ratings were downgraded.

The far-right Golden Dawn party was formed on January 1, 1980, by Nikolaos "Nikos" Michaloliakos, a mathematician with an ultra-nationalist, pro-Russia, neo-Nazi, and neo-Eurasianism ideology. Michaloliakos was in close communication with Aleksandr Dugin. Nikos maintained communications with Putin's top advisor, Dugin, by mail while Michaloliakos sat in his prison cell in 2013 on criminal organization charges following the death of a homosexual rapper/hip-hop artist by the name of Pavlos

Fyssas (aka Killah P). Fyssas was an anti-fascist who was murdered by Giorgos Roupakias, a member of Golden Dawn.

On November 1, 2013, Golden Dawn members Manolis Kapelonis and Giorgos Fountoulis were shot dead in their Neo Irakleio offices with a third Dawn member wounded. On television after the murder of Fyssas, Greek Prime Minister Antonis Samaras asked for the public to stay calm, assuring them that he will work to deter "the descendants of the Nazis from poisoning our social life, to act criminally, to terrorize and undermine the foundations of the country which gave birth to Democracy."

In July 2015, Nikos was released from detention, even though the verdict to many was "still out" and the trial was still in effect in 2017, four years after his initial arrest. Other members of Golden Dawn, Ilias Kasidiaris (MP), Ilias Panagiotaros and Nikolaos "Nikos" Michos, who were initially accused as accomplices in the murder trial, were later freed due to a lack of sufficient evidence for indictment. During this fragile time in Greek politics of corruption, hate speech, and austerity measures, protests had erupted on the street—the perfect chaos palette for Vladimir Putin and anyone looking to do artfully dodgy business in Greece after its economic collapse, which was blamed on liberals. The strength of the movement is relevant in that four years after the murder of the rapper, Golden Dawn retained its seventeen seats in Greece's Parliament. When sworn in, they stood and held their arms in the Nazi salute but with clenched fists.[27]

Unlike the more eccentric philosopher Aleksandr Dugin, it is unclear if Vladislav Surkov had any hand in making ties to the extremist rightwing Golden Dawn group in Greece after the financial collapse and austerity measures were under way. It seems likely, as Vladimir Putin was well received in 2016 by Golden Dawn. The Kremlin has since sponsored visits to Moscow for its leaders, as the mutual objective of their rise was the Greek-Russian alliance for trade, partnership, and security.

The Greek public and mainstream political establishment denouncement of their Nazi sympathizer ways has not weakened Golden Dawn in the eyes of their early supporters—it may even have emboldened them.

On February 11, 2018, *The Moscow Times* sported the headline, "Greek Election Wins Putin a Friend in Europe." It noted the win of the Coalition of the Radical Left, SYRIZA, winning the most recent election with a little over 36% of the vote. Greece's radical left party had decided to not interfere in Russian geopolitical objectives given Greece's financial situation. Even though SYRIZA was on the left, the pressure from the Golden Dawn movement gave Russia the European support it had been aiming for. Prior to SYRIZA's win, far-right Greek Prime Minister, Alexis Tsipras, had met with Putin to fix the financial situation of Greece while helping Russia attain European support against US sanctions. Even though Russia was in a recession with sluggish oil prices as well, Tsipras made the concessions he wanted. The Minister of Foreign Affairs under Greek Prime Minister Tsipras was Nikos Kotzias, a former Communist and good friend of Aleksandr Dugin. He also tried to raise Western sanctions against Russia.

Austria

The Freedom Party of Austria was founded by ex-Nazis in the 1950s. For decades they made little to no headway in Austrian politics, but in the 1990s the son of two ex-Nazis, Jörg Haider, was elected Chancellor (though did not ultimately serve in the role). Throughout his career he was an open admirer of National Socialism, the Nazi ideology, and a fierce critic of the European Union. He famously claimed that Nazi extermination and concentration camps were "the punishment camps of National Socialism" and "...in the Third Reich they had an 'orderly' employment policy..." as well as praising the veterans of the Nazi SS in a speech at their annual gathering, whom he referred to as victims, not criminals. He later went to say in a TV interview, "The Waffen SS was a part of the Wehrmacht (German military) and hence it deserves all the honor and respect of the army in public life."[28] Under his leadership, the Freedom Party of Austria (FPÖ) would win 27% of the general vote, shocking European politicians, who saw this sudden populist, pro-Nazi champion as having jumped onto their doorstep. His election would lead the European Union to impose sanctions against a member state for the first time. Unfortunately, Haider was not a flash in the pan but a symptom of a populist trend that he had harnessed.

Haider would merge his FPÖ with the Center-Right People's Party of Austria (ÖVP) for five years. Though he would die in an auto accident in 2008, his right-wing ideas did not die with him; they spread like wildfire. At the end of the October 2017 elections the ÖVP would win 31.6% of the vote and the FPÖ won 26.9%. Austria was now firmly in the camp of the right-wing with almost 57% of the population voting for the conservatives and only 9% voting for liberal groups such as the Greens or NEOS.[29]

The conservatives won on a platform of stopping immigration from Muslim countries. Not surprisingly, the day after the election the new Freedom Party leader, Heinz-Christian Strache, the young former neo-Nazi with a fashion model wife twenty years his junior, came to visit Trump Tower and met with the incoming National Security Advisor General Michael T. Flynn. Soon afterward, Strache signed a five-year agreement with Putin's United Russia Party on economic, business, and political matters to seal the bonds between the two parties. Sergei Zheleznyak, United Russia's Deputy General Secretary, signed for Putin.[30,31] This gave the appearance that Flynn had been key to an informal American-Russian-Austrian political alliance of conservatives. The *New York Times* wrote about the agreement: "Word of the agreement with Russia was the latest sign that the Kremlin is forging bonds with political parties across Europe in what some European leaders suspect is a coordinated attempt to meddle in their affairs and potentially weaken Western democracies."[32]

The Netherlands

Geert Wilders is a Dutch politician and leader of the Party for Freedom (PVV, or *Partij voor de Vrijheid*), a nationalist populist party dedicated to keeping the Netherlands free of Muslims. He fosters a naked hatred for Muslims and Islam as a religion. It grew from a one-man party in 2006 to winning 20 seats in 2017. It is now the second-largest party in the Dutch House of Representatives. The party platform is extremist and in line with the Kremlin's desire to withdraw from the European Union, as well as proposals to close all mosques in the Netherlands, forbid the use of the Quran, close all asylum centers, expel migrant "criminals," and forbid any further migration of Muslims into the country.[33] Wilders spoke in Milan in 2016, where he stated Europe was facing an existential crisis because of the "European elites." He proclaimed:

> "Our mission is to save and defend our nations and our Western civilization, built on the legacy of Rome, Athens and Jerusalem. The survival of our freedom, identity and values are at stake. My colleagues and I, we ring the bells of the revolution. A democratic and peaceful revolution to regain our national sovereignty. To stop the invasion. To protect our own people, our women, our culture. We have to become the masters again of our own borders, our own budgets, our own destiny. Our mission is to do what our governments fail to do. We say: *Basta! Finita la commedia!*"[34]

Wilders has always been a hard-line propagandist on his single issue of the de-Islamization of the Netherlands. Never mind the fact that his country, through the Dutch East India Company, traded and established Dutch colonies all across Africa and Asia. The Netherlands established forts and occupied parts of Muslim Malaysia and Indonesia, as well as outposts in India and East and West Africa, for more than 500 years. This occupation brought large numbers of Muslims to the Netherlands as citizens. Their Voortrekker descendants would even fight a war with England to maintain their racist control over South Africa. Yet many 21st-century Dutch want to restore the Netherlands back to a nation of only whites since the 1977 train siege by South Moluccan separatist terrorists killed two hostages. After 9/11, the anti-Muslim sentiment in the Netherlands exploded and was given voice through the renowned racist and xenophobe Geert Wilders.

Wilders led the global conservative anti-immigrant propaganda world almost by himself post-9/11. For example, he regularly tweets comments such as "The Netherlands must preserve their own national identity!" And he says that PVV stands for "Netherlands First," and "Our population is in danger of being replaced," "Together we will oppose Islam," and "It is time to de-Islamize the Netherlands." Like many European anti-globalists, he espouses a deep hatred of multiculturalism and takes the Putin worldview that "Western Europe is facilitating Islamisation." Oddly, Wilders follows one account @wilderspoezen, which tweets mixed-breed cat photos. This account may be a closeted nod to Art Spiegelman's MAUS, where the Jews and anyone non-white are depicted as anthropomorphized mice—the Nazis are cats and the Americans are dogs. According to the BotTracker, a site that analyzes the behaviors of Twitter feeds, that account, @wilderspoezen, is likely a Russian or neo-Nazi–programmed bot.

Hungary

The Hungarian link to the European pro-Russia, anti-NATO alliance is the Movement for a Better Hungary (*Jobbik*). Jobbik is led by Tamas Sneider. Like all Russian-backed leaders tasked with countering Western democracy, Jobbik is a Hungarian radical nationalist, conservative, and right-wing populist movement grounded in Russian-led anti-globalism, anti-Atlanticist rhetoric just like Pegida AfD, and numerous other conservative groups that worked to the benefit of Vladimir Putin by undermining NATO and the UN.

Gabor Vona had previously led Jobbik, and prior to that he had belonged to the conservative populist Fidesz Party (aka Alliance of Young Democrats) from 2001 to 2003. Fidesz was a Hungarian civic alliance founded in 1988. It subsequently morphed in 1995 into the Hungarian Civic Party. The Fidesz Party was started by university students who were forced to meet in secret groups to avoid being targeted by the ruling Hungarian Communist Party. Originally, the group was viewed as "liberal," given its focus on democratic ideals compared to Communism, but it soon became identified as ideologically conservative after the 1994 election loss with only 7.02% of the popular vote. They maintain a youth group known as Fidelitas.

In 2006, British-born Hungarian (now American) Sebastian Gorka spoke of taking fragments of Jobbik and Fidesz and forming a new group. According to Lili Bayer of the American Jewish magazine

Forward, in August 2007, Gorka appeared on Hungarian television openly supporting Magyar Gárda (aka the Hungarian Guard), an anti-Semitic militia founded by Gabor Vona that same year. The Hungarian Guard is a neo-fascist paramilitary group denounced by the Hungarian government and the European Court of Human Rights. It was subsequently disbanded in 2009 on legal grounds of promoting illegal institutionalized racism. In addition to their menacing, polarizing rhetoric, the Hungarian Guard was feared also because of their black storm trooper–like coats and vests emblazoned with the red and white Arpad flag. They evoked the symbolism of the Hungarian Nazis by adopting the Arrow Cross, a symbol of the pro-Nazi government of WW II. Gorka was dismissive of the suggestion when questioned on Echo TV in Hungary, stating that no one questioned the "fascist" black shirts of the Hungarian police. He also dismissed the concerns of Hungarian Jews wary of the anti-Semitic wave that had begun permeating once again throughout Europe.[35]

Gorka continued to say that the Hungarian Guard was an effort directed at a "big societal need," alluding to Hungary's official military as being anemic at best and a reflection of a sick Hungarian society. Banners appeared on Echo TV with the headline: "UDK supports the Hungarian Guard." UDK is an acronym for the New Democratic Coalition (founded by Gorka and colleague, Tamas Molnár). In September 2007, the UDK party issued a statement that critics of the Hungarian Guard were underhandedly propped up by Hungarian-born Holocaust survivor, US Representative and California Democrat Tom Lantos, and that accusations of anti-Semitism were "the very useful tool of a certain political class."[36]

In October 2017, Hungary also held a "conference for persecuted Christians." It was there that conservative supporters in both Hungary and Russia felt validated for their beliefs that Islamic immigration causes a denial of one's Christian roots and that multiculturalism was one of the restrictive confines of "evil liberalism." Vladislav Surkov and other friends of Gorka and Putin praised the conference arranged by the Fidesz Party and Nationalist Prime Minister, Viktor Orban, who appealed to many far-right American Putin-apologists as well. These are just a few of the current active measures in play.[37] The risks that Hungarian fascists posed to the United States became apparent when Sebastian Gorka was brought into the Trump White House as a tsar for counterterrorism. Fortunately, he was fired for a shady resume and his past ties to Nazis. He was immediately hired by Fox News.

Bela Kovacs was a Hungarian politician with a seat as Member of the European Parliament and a member of the far-right Jobbik party who was accused of turning into a Russian spy to further the Eurasian agenda. In April 2014, Kovacs was accused of being an agent of influence for Russian intelligence, a charge he denies. In addition to passing forgeries, Kovacs was accused of funneling Russian money into the Jobbik party.[38] In June 2017, he was charged with spying for Russia. He was a European Parliament Member since 2010 until he was stripped of immunity in October 2015, and is now awaiting trial.[39] He stepped down from Jobbik in February 2016.

Sweden

Sweden is a neutral but NATO-friendly Scandinavian country with a history of Cold War confrontations with Russia. Sweden has depth-charged, shot artillery, and confronted Russian Navy units and submarines since the 1960s. In 1981, the famous "Whiskey on the Rocks" incident occurred when Soviet Whiskey-class diesel-electric submarine S-363 from the Russian fleet in Leningrad ran aground in Swedish waters near Karlskrona Naval Base. The submarine had negotiated a series of difficult underwater obstacles and struck a large unmapped underwater rock, which forced it to the surface. As recently as 2014, a possible Russian Lada-class mini-submarine or a remotely operated submersible from a tanker was detected in Swedish waters. In many of these incidents, Sweden fired upon or depth-charged the suspected Russians to make them surface. The naval challenges between Sweden and Russia have existed since the 18th century, as they faced off as naval powers, and impose a major military obstacle to their access to the North Sea from the Baltics. For this reason Russia has always sought to shift internal political groups to their orbit.

The Swedish Democrat Party (SD, or *Sverigedemokraterna*) is an ultra-right conservative party with a history in advocating white supremacy, anti-globalization, and anti-immigration. The party formed from disenfranchised neo-Nazis, neo-Fascists, and Swedish ethno-nationalists. It is aligned with the pro-Russian European ultra-rightists across Europe and maintains a single issue as their platform—stop migration into Sweden and remove foreign immigrants. The SD logo is a blue daisy, which, like the French "blue rose" of the National Front, signifies "Making the impossible possible." They are unabashedly Eurosceptic but hide their pro-Moscow leanings. Their activities and opposition to the ruling Social Democrats is regularly pushed by Russia Today and Sputnik news.

Poland

The Law and Justice Party (PiS, or *Prawo i Sprawiedliwość*) was founded in 2001 by twin brothers, Lech and Jaroslaw Kaczynski. The Law and Justice Party's major amalgamation is populist far-right-wing Christian democratic Euroscepticism. The same year they were founded, they won 9.5% of the vote, adding 44 out of 460 Lower Chamber Parliamentary seats. Two factions made up the Law and Justice Party: the Solidarity Electoral Action (aka AWS) and the Christian Democratic Centre Agreement. "Law and Order" was the Kaczynskis' mantra. Their stated goal was to lock up the "bad guys"—any illegal immigrants. In 2005, the two Kaczynski brothers became a political powerhouse (with a first-place 27% of the Senate vote). Embracing the teachings of Catholicism, in 2006, Jaroslaw started the League of Polish Families and the Self Defense of the Republic of Poland.

In 2007, Lech became President of Poland and bequeathed party leadership to his brother Jaroslaw, who was appointed to Prime Minister. In 2007, PiS garnered 32.1% of the vote but were defeated by the Civic Platform Party with nearly 42% of the vote. In 2010, just three years after their rise to power, President Lech Kaczynski and 95 of his closest advisors and public notables were killed when his Russian-built Polish Air Force Tu-154 airliner crash-landed at Smolensk, Russia.

In late 2015, Eurosceptic President Andrzej Duda and his party had a majority parliamentary advantage, winning nearly 38% of the vote.[40] The *New York Times* summed up the turn from moderation in Poland with the headline, "As Poland Lurches to Right, Many in Europe Look On in Alarm." There were protests in the streets because the opposition groups believed that the PiS was plotting to destroy democracy.[41] PiS took several steps that did undermine democratic systems in Poland, including attempting to turn the TPV television into a party mouthpiece like Russia Today and passing a law that would dismiss all the judges on the Polish Supreme Court, though the effort failed.

In 2017, US President Donald Trump traveled to Poland at the invitation of President Duda to give a speech that was wildly criticized for its fostering the concept that the West and Islam were in a clash of civilizations. Trump sounded themes that appeared to foster the ethnonationalist belief that Western civilization (read as Christianity) was under attack from migrant cultures, largely believed to imply Islam. He said, "The fundamental question of our time is whether the West has the will to survive. Do we have the confidence in our values to defend them at any cost? Do we have enough respect for our citizens to protect our borders? Do we have the desire and the courage to preserve our civilization in the face of those who would subvert and destroy it?"[42] It was greeted with wild applause.

Soon after Trump's visit, Poland's conservatives put themselves back on the map as tilting hard to the right when they staged a march through the streets of Warsaw commemorating the 99 years since Poland's 1918 independence from the Austro-Hungarian empire at the end of WW I. Approximately 60,000 nationalists, carrying long flares and torches, marched through the streets and chanted "Pure Poland! White Poland! Refugees get out!," "White Europe," "White Europe of brotherly nations," and "Clean Blood." This march brought right-wing extremists and ethno-nationalists from all around the world. The governing Law and Justice Party seemed to encourage the display.

The Congress of the New Right (KNP, or *Nowa Prawica*), a Polish libertarian party, was formed in 2011 by Janusz Korwin-Mikke. This Eurosceptic party finished fourth in the Senate election with 7.2% of the votes.

Italy

Fascism has a deep history in Italy. *"Il Fascisimo"* was Mussolini's term to describe corporatist dictatorship of the extreme right. The Italian Social Movement was founded in 1946, to show support for Dictator Benito Mussolini. The Italian Social Movement-National Right, or *Movimiento Sociale Italiano-Destra Nazionale* (aka MSI-DN), was a fascist political party dissolved in 1995 when one of its leaders, Pino Rauti, disagreed with its moderate course of fusing into the National Alliance (after political defeats in the 1960s) and decided to branch out and create the Tricolour Flame (Fiamma Tricolore) Party instead. It was never a very popular party due to its attacks on civil liberties as the "Law and Order" party. As early as 2013, Valerio Cignetti, Italian MEP (Member of European Parliament), Secretary General of the AENM (aka Alliance of European National Movements), and MS-FT Party member was invited to partake at a round table of EU delegation members (including Bela Kovacs) set up by the Russian Parliament (aka United Russia Congress) to discuss Western sanctions in relation to the annexation of Crimea. Cignetti had very close associations with Jobbik's Bela Kovacs since he was in the AENM.[43] The New Force Party (aka FN, or *Forza Nuova*) formed as a far-right-wing group that is not ashamed of being fascist. They are an "openly fascist" group according to the Southern Poverty Law Center. Created by Roberto Fiore and the late Fascist Massimo Morsello, *"Forza Nuova* has been one of the persistent members of a series of alliances that mirror the Kremlin objectives in Europe. In saying that Moscow was now the protector of his values, he went further and said, 'It's not me saying this—it's God saying it.'"[44] Their US office is discreetly located in an undisclosed predominantly Italian-American demographic location in New Jersey. In the 2018 Italian elections, its right-wing authoritarian and fascist parties grew as well. The Five Star Movement received 32.22% of the vote, with a gain of 6.62% of the vote from the previous election. The younger demographic voter (under 30) without a college education voted for the Five Star Movement—similar to the rural 2016 electorate for Donald J. Trump. Similar to the 2016 US Presidential election, the Five Star Movement did poorly in 2018 with college graduates, especially in urban areas.[45] President Trump's former White House Senior Strategist and Chief Advisor, Steve Bannon, traveled to Italy to advise the Deputy Prime Minister and anti-immigrant fascist, Matteo Salvini, on the group that was previously known as *Lega Nord* (the Northern League), *La Lega*.[46]

Russia's European Alliances

Russia's European alliances formed roundtable groups such as Marine Le Pen's Eurosceptic European Alliance for Freedom meeting with Farage's Europe for Freedom and Democracy. Multiple inter-European groups were formed by these pro-Moscow groups to fuse the Eurosceptic, pro-Moscow, anti-immigrant, anti-NATO political parties and personalities into political and personal alliances including:

- European National Front (ENF)
- Alliance for European National Movements (AENM)
- European Alliance for Freedom (EAF)
- Movement for a Europe of Nations and Freedom (MENF)
- Europe of Nations and Freedom (ENF)
- The Alliance for Peace and Freedom (APF)

One of the largest organizing conferences was the International Russian Conservative Forum on March 22, 2015. It was hosted by Rodina leader Aleksey Zhuravlyov in St. Petersburg.[47] The forum was attended by:

- Rodina, Russian Imperial Movement, represented by Nikolay Trushchalov
- New Russia, Russian Institute of National Strategy, represented by Mikhail Remizov, Vadim Zazimko
- Forza Nuova, Italian Millennium Party, represented by Orazio Maria Gnerre
- National Independence Party (Finland), represented by Davidson Yukka

- Bulgaria's ATAKA
- Germany's National Democratic Party, represented by Udo Voigt
- Greece's Golden Dawn, represented by Georgios Epitidios
- Former French National Front member Olivier Wyssa
- Pro-Russian advocate from Ukraine, Alexey Zhivov
- Victoria Shilova, a pro-Russian Ukrainian, League for Life
- Former British National Party member, Jim Dowson
- Nick Griffin for the Alliance for Peace and Freedom

But this meeting wasn't only for Europeans—Americans Sam Dickson, former Ku Klux Klan attorney, and American Renaissance leader Jared Taylor were featured guests as well.[48]

The networks of the European right are clearly well established, and the United States was the Johnny-come-lately to the global conservative movement. But after the election of Donald Trump, the North American wing of the pro-Moscow conservative network was forming fast. In late 2017, Steve Bannon had a public falling out with Trump over his candid comments about the administration's competence and left the White House, but he set his sights on doing more than just parroting Trump. He saw himself as the leader of the global alternative right-wing movement and he was going to be the activist-in-chief for taking on the Western liberal establishment. He started crisscrossing Europe and advising election after election. He went to Italy and helped the populist Five Star Movement win a major victory and become the largest political party. He pulled no punches and advocated that European right-wing populists expose themselves for what they were at their core: racists. He told an assembly of the National Front, "Let them call you racist! Let them call you xenophobes! Wear it as a badge of honor."[49]

CHAPTER 10

The Axis of Autocracy

I f Putin could not take the United States out to limit their power and damage Europe, he would buy the loyalty of wannabe-oligarchs around the world. The 1990s and early 2000s had shown that poor Western politicians were just billionaires down on their luck—he would show them a way to improve their chances of becoming rich through Russia's oligarchy.

Throughout history, America's insistence on fair play, ethical conduct, and limiting kleptocracies had clearly become a liability for the Russian oligarchy. American democracy was the obstacle that led the uber-rich to steal, store, and transfer their illicit trillions across the globe. They wanted to spend it as they wished. American democracy was in the way, but with the right amount of warfare, Putin believed he could flip this to his own benefit. Done right, such an operation would be a global campaign. Why stop at America and Europe?

Intelligence officers understand that preparation of the battlefield is critical to achieving one's goals. Well before meddling in foreign elections, the Russian intelligence services would need to spread the belief that the old ways of NATO, America, and the European Union were bad for business. They saw the faulty lines in the Western economy growing deeper with time. America was getting older and the children of the greatest generation were drawing more conservative. The election of Barack Obama was anathema to them. Russia under Putin would not preach the gospel of Marx. There would be no appeals to brotherhood and collectivism. The mission would be to tear a deflated white America away from the rest and assist them in becoming the dominant political force. Liberals would dismiss it as racist craziness. Putin not only harnessed a base of rising white consciousness, he found that promises of Russian riches would bring those ideas directly to their elected representatives. When oligarch money was being represented, every one of them cleared their calendar to listen.

Russia would destabilize through the conservative right-wing. These millionaires and billionaires, particularly in the Trump campaign, working for their own self-interest, would advance the policies and goals of the Kremlin in exchange for a seat at the table with wealthy fellow travelers.

The Vote to Destroy Democracy

Democracy itself would be the weapon that would bring down democracy. The vote would be the infectious vector—so long as the people are of one mind, they would vote their own democracy out of existence. Politicians in America would help forge a global economic alliance based on personal financial gain and self-interest. And Europe would follow.

In America, the Mexican migration would become a horde of raping, pillaging invaders. In Europe, the Syrian and African migration would challenge the concept of being "European." These efforts to be inclusive, diverse, and liberal would be put to the test against the greatest psychological operations machine in history. With the right propaganda, fake news, and politicians willing to compromise their own national interest for the right amount of cash, the avaricious masses may be willing to reconsider autocracy as an alternative to democracy and the key to future advancement. Perhaps with the narrative framed properly, it would give them a new window from which to look for an exit. Promises of new riches in formerly closed markets such as Russia would make them embrace a more highly focused leadership and convert some of the inhibitions of democracy to global greatness.

The autocrat's argument is that one tribe—the dominant tribe—is better suited to lead the key nations of the West. The move would be to convince the Western conservative to embrace autocratic government as a hammer to build a cultural bridge of white Western conservatism from Eastern Europe, to Central Europe, and finally to the Americas. Together they would confront the challenges of the Muslim world.

The Clash of Civilizations

A core component to bringing Western European and American political establishments around to Moscow's way of thinking was to join the common cause against terrorism. Russia too had been subject to Islamic extremist terrorism. The 2004 Chechen suicide-hostage barricades at Beslan elementary school had ended with 334 women and schoolchildren dead. The village raids inside of Russia where men, women, children, and the elderly were roped together and forced to walk as human shields by Chechen guerillas had also killed hundreds. The Chechen Muslim extremists were hardcore, and Putin had stamped them out brutally in the second Chechnya war. That he committed atrocities not seen since WWII was beside the point.

Russia argued that the 9/11 attacks and Russia's own massacres were a common cause: Both Americans and Russians were locked in deadly wars to stamp out terrorists. Both Republican and Russian political bodies sought a higher meaning to the fight against Islamic terrorists. American Republicans saw it as a global crusade in the literal sense of the words. Many thought it was time for a religious reckoning with Islam as a whole. Many Russian and European right-wing politicians agreed. After nearly a decade of bloodletting (of mainly Muslim blood), some were calling on an alliance to fight Islam alongside Russia. They sought a clash of civilizations.

The concept of the West engaging in a clash of civilizations was deeply believed by Osama bin Laden. The 9/11 attacks in New York City, Washington, D.C., and western Pennsylvania; the 7/7 attacks in London and the 3/14 attacks in Madrid, Spain; the rise of the "Islamic caliphate" of the Islamic state of Iraq; and Syrian terrorist groups were born of the belief that the West must be forced to embrace their inner xenophobia. The efforts were in place to move the terrorist struggle from low-grade regional attacks to a broad global struggle where every Muslim would be called upon to defend the religion. Bin Laden's call for the clash of civilizations would intimidate all Westerners, Christians and Muslim alike. He sought to make them live in fear that a Muslim terrorist would kill them and their children while they slept comfortably in their beds at night. Bin Laden's insane belief lay in the fact that he understood the inherent bigotry of the West. In fact, it was necessary to make Christians view all Muslims as evil. It was critical to his plan of a worldwide clash of civilizations between Islam and the world. It required the demonization of every Muslim man, woman, and child. Hence, his disciples could say, did we not tell you that Christians hate us and were the actual evil?

After the invasion of Iraq, Saddam and bin Laden's terrorists knew America feared the *drip, drip, drip* of soldiers lost to suicide bomber terrorist attacks—so they put everything they had into creating the most spectacular attacks and distributing them through slick news media video releases. Their successor organization, the Islamic State of Iraq and Syria (ISIS), would take that to a completely different level by emphasizing brutality, blood spectacle, and mass murder. ISIS made videos and crafted their own global information distribution system where images of their men and women literally bathing themselves in the blood of their enemies would shock the senses. These spectacles would create a political backlash that would be exploited by Russia in 2016. Right-wing extremist groups all around Europe rallied to the "anti-Islam" movement after the million refugees from Syria were sent from Turkey and when immigrants and refugees were stopped crossing from Libya to Italy over the past decade.

A New Populist Axis

The terrorism we experience worldwide today is a direct reading of the ideology of Osama bin Laden and Abu Bakr al-Baghdadi, the leader of ISIS. Even with both men dead, the spark of an individual jihad designed to stoke hatred of Muslims required Western politicians to embrace that spark for their own political needs. Donald Trump and Vladimir Putin are two who have taken up the challenge. They believe that both Eastern and Western Christianity must come together with the objective to set aside the Old World Order created after WWII, and create three pillars of a new conservative Christian global leadership: 1) American conservatives would rule in the Western Hemisphere; 2) France would lead an anti-Muslim, anti-immigrant alliance of ultra-right-wing governments from Poland to Britain; and 3) in the East, the strong ultranationalists of Russia would support, finance, and defend this new alliance.

In a *Foreign Affairs* piece "How Democracies Fall Apart," authors Andrea Kendall-Taylor, Deputy National Intelligence Officer for Russia and Eurasia at the National Intelligence Council, and Erica Frantz detail how populism can easily lead to autocracy. They note the increase in democratically elected "strongmen" such as Putin, Duterte in the Philippines, and Erdogan in Turkey, is due to their ability to capitalize on citizen grievances: "These leaders first come to power through democratic elections and subsequently harness widespread discontent to gradually undermine institutional constraints on their rule, marginalize the opposition, and erode civil society."[1]

The world has been under threat of losing democracies to ideologies for decades. However, there has been a wave of authoritarian states growing and directly challenging the established norms. Kendall-Taylor and Frantz wrote, "In the last decade, however, populist-fueled authoritarianization has been on the rise, accounting for 40 percent of all democratic failures between 2000 and 2010 and matching coups in frequency."[2] They continued: "Data show that just under half (44 percent) of all instances of authoritarianization from 1946 to 1999 led to the establishment of personalist dictatorships. From 2000 to 2010, however, that proportion increased to 75 percent. In most cases, the populist strongmen rose to power with the support of a political party but then proved effective in sidelining competing voices from within."[3]

Venezuela is a good example.

Hugo Chávez of Venezuela came to power through a wave of

populism spouting whichever tropes worked at the moment that he spoke. He called his ideology Bolivarianism, named after General Simon Bolívar, who defeated the Spanish colonialists and is widely revered in Latin America. Chávez created a mélange of social justice, street action, and Marxist platitudes to be elected numerous times in a wave of populism. He slowly and systematically dismantled the democratic pillars of Venezuela before nationalizing all the country's oil industry. Once that was complete, he used state power and oil money to remain in power until his death. His successor, Nicolas Maduro, maintained the populist mantle has become a beacon of personal corruption. The nation is devoid of food, with people thronging the border to be able to buy even the simplest foodstuffs. The situation became so bad that in 2018 the international community and the United Nations offered to provide food aid, but like all dictators, Maduro refused unless the demoralized opposition accepted his government's national Constituent Assembly, a rubber stamp body that would invest in him all national power. This is the crushing power of a populist dictator. Invariably, their greatest enemy is democracy, which they always immediately seek to stamp out.

It should be noted that Russia is Venezuela's strongest partner in the oil trade and weapons sales. Russian military scholars have warned the Kremlin that Venezuela's unrest stems from the United States trying to overthrow the regime with a "Colour Revolution" akin to Ukraine.[4] Some have suggested that Russia step in to stop what they believe are American-backed revolutions.

Populist dictators and strongmen use divisive techniques and attacks to foster splits in their societies and to break the hold of establishment norms in order to rise to national leadership through a negative form of "people power"—to assert that the system "is rigged against you," where in many cases, the system is built and working properly for these very same people. The populist authoritarian is the master of the rant, a demagogue of the highest order, and runs an agenda which generally brings about ruin. German Foreign Minister Sigmar Gabriel openly warned the West of the dangers of the new populist movement washing around the world:

"With a few exceptions, that also applies to most authoritarian-led countries. Often, economically and socially weak countries are led by men who are only ostensibly strong. The assertion of power, the instigation of confrontations outside the country, often conceals even bigger domestic problems. There's a danger that this authoritarian style of politics is now making inroads into the Western world. And they all have in common the fact that they place their national interests over those of the international community. We Europeans do not do that. But that's also why we tend to be laughed at by these authoritarian-led countries. I am convinced that we are living in an era of competition between democratic countries and authoritarian countries. And the latter have already begun trying to gain influence in the European Union and to divide us. The first cracks are apparent in Europe. We will have to do far more to defend our freedom in the future than we have had to do in the past."[5]

CHAPTER 11

Operation GLOBAL GRIZZLY

In my preceding work, *The Plot to Hack America: How Putin's Cyberspies and WikiLeaks Tried to Steal the 2016 Election*, I outlined the resources that the Kremlin would have had to expend to achieve their goal of electing Donald Trump President. To further the goals of the Kremlin, they developed and carried out a strategic disinformation and influence warfare operation using computational strikes to the American social media system, whereupon they hacked the mindset of the American public. To describe Putin's larger strategic goals across Europe, the Middle East, and the Americas, I have code-named his effort Operation GLOBAL GRIZZLY. This plan was designed to use all assets in Russia's power, from foreign policy interventions and oil deals to spy agency assassinations and covert invasions, to bring the Axis of Autocracy to fruition. The strategy is called Asymmetric or Hybrid Warfare. All resources short of open warfare would be applied to restore Russia's power, world standing, and influence.

Putin's Axis of Autocracy strategy began with the hacking of the 2016 American election. Placing Donald Trump into the White House gave Russia a firm argument that we were at the heart of the new global populism movement. An inner circle of anti-globalist leaders who could be convinced to abandon the American–NATO–led worldview would assist in revealing the massive cracks in liberal democracy. By 2017,

NATO states including France, Spain, Turkey, Greece, Germany, the Netherlands, Britain, Poland, Hungary, and Ukraine would have major political parties poised to leapfrog into power under Putin's plan. To support these efforts, GLOBAL GRIZZLY resources are focused to support Kremlin-favored political parties and to push for nationalist referendums.

America was not alone in the political quagmire caused by Russian cyberwarfare operations. The Russian methodologies of intrusion into European politics from the Soviet period to today is not particularly different.

In the post-war period, Russian intelligence was locked in an ideological war with the West for control of Europe. Because of the ability of both sides to destroy the other with nuclear weapons, they faced off with conventional military forces and engaged in a global war of espionage and influence. This was the Cold War—a face-off between two massive armies along the West German border. The Communist East created an alliance of the eight Soviet-occupied nations to rival NATO. The alliance included half of Germany (called East Germany), Poland, Bulgaria, Hungary, Romania, Czechoslovakia, Albania, and the Soviet Union. Russia held these nations through military power and replaced their pre-war democratic governments with a local Communist totalitarian leader essentially chosen by Moscow. These leaders were kept in check by the KGB, who managed their local Communist intelligence agencies. Thus, half of Europe (including nations incorporated into the Soviet Union: Ukraine, Moldova, Belarus, Latvia, Lithuania, and Estonia) was occupied by Russia for 46 years. Russian was the lingua franca for military, government, and cultural affairs in the East.

The Baltic states of Latvia, Lithuania, and Estonia stick particularly hard in Moscow's craw. Invaded by the Soviet Union as part of the deal between Josef Stalin and Adolf Hitler in the 1940 Molotov-Ribbentrop Pact and then occupied afterward, these three tiny states were ardently pro-West and pro-NATO. They cut Russia off from the small ethnic Russian enclave of Kaliningrad. The first operations came at the hand of what could best be deemed MILITIA BEARS, or Russian citizen cyber-vigilantes.

The Test Bed States

Nations that crossed Putin were being attacked asymmetrically. For example, in 2007 Russia paralyzed Estonia with a national level Distributed Denial of Service (DDoS) attack when the local government wanted to move a WWII-era Soviet army statue, the Bronze Soldier of Tallinn. Though it is believed to have been started by cyber-vigilantes, the Russian intelligence agencies, the GRU and SVR, leaped onto the attack and shut that small nation's internet down...as a warning. Russian spies then started test-bedding more and more sophisticated cyber-attacks. Joshua Davies detailed in *Wired* what happened that day:

> "The future was looking perilous. Ago Väärsi, head of IT at the *Postimees* newspaper, watched as automated computer programs continued to spew posts onto the commentary pages of the *Postimees* web site, creating a two-fold problem: The spam overloaded the server's processors and hogged bandwidth. Väärsi turned off the comments feature. That saved bandwidth—the meter showed that there was still capacity—but what did get through tied the machines into knots and crashed them repeatedly. He discovered that the attackers were constantly tweaking their malicious server requests to evade the filters. Whoever was behind this was sophisticated, fast, and intelligent."[1]

The next year Lithuania passed an anti-Soviet memorabilia law and again the MILITIA BEARS struck. Led by a group calling itself "hack-wars.ru," they paralyzed the nation's access to the internet.[2] Former Estonian Prime Minister Toomas Hendrik Ilves, who was tasked to investigate how and why the Russians carried out these attacks, noted that "The Russians are very aggressive everywhere, across Europe, and this is a problem that each country is struggling with on its own....[W]hat they do to us we cannot do to them....Liberal democracies with a free press and free and fair elections are at an asymmetric disadvantage...the tools of their democratic and free speech can be used against them."[3]

The Estonian and Lithuanian cyberattacks presented a new clear and present danger to NATO operations. It was clearly an attack in which the organization would have to clarify if Article 5 of the treaty, the collective defense response, would be triggered by another event on a NATO nation. The headquarters in Brussels ordered a new cybersecurity warfare center to open in Estonia to be close to the threat, both physically and operationally.

At the National Day march in Red Square, Vladimir Putin insinuated that anywhere that the memory of the Soviet army was sullied, Russia would remember: "Those who are trying today to...desecrate memorials to war heroes are insulting their own people, sowing discord and new distrust between state and people...."[4]

That same year, the Republic of Georgia was struck by a DDoS attack too when armed clashes broke out in ethnic Russian regions of South Ossetia as pro-Moscow forces tried to ethnically cleanse Georgians. Soon after, Kyrgyzstan was struck with a DDoS attack for allowing American forces to use an airbase in the Afghanistan war. The base was quickly closed. The political success of these attacks was followed up with more attacks on Kazakhstan, Ukraine, France, and the United States. Russia had learned there was financial and political value in cyber punishment. Denying service was efficient for making a political point without launching a cruise missile. Stealing data for Kompromat was next-level, but cyber manipulations of social media with that stolen material? That was elite-level information war, a pinnacle goal of the Soviet intelligence apparatus—change minds to abandon their own governments. Now in the hands of Vladimir Putin, it would change the world.

Brexit—The British Guinea Pig

Britain was to be the test bed for the Russian strategy of perception management. Why did the Russians see an opportunity to influence the British? The systems being developed for the United States by Russian intelligence agencies would need a smaller test model to validate the programming of the bots and test the efficiency of the data collection process handled by Cambridge Analytica.

Britain was America's strongest ally and it was also a lynchpin for the European Union. Removing it from the Union would not seriously damage it like a French withdrawal. Britain would also not be likely to sever its ties to NATO. Russia saw that a successful British referendum would give the American right wing a symbol to point at and say, "If they can do it we can too." The European nationalist conservative networks had successfully permeated the belief that defending conservatives meant being anti-immigration, anti-Muslim, pro-white, and pro-Moscow. Disrupting Britain was the closest thing to disrupting the United States. For this, Putin would need allies in the UK, who would not even know they were working for him. If the British referendum could be made successful, then the RF-IRA and Russian intelligence operations would be expanded to attack the United States directly.

Euroscepticism in England dates back in many ways to the post–WWII effort to rebuild Europe after the destruction of the war. Winston Churchill suggested a "United States of Europe"[5] was called for, with France and Germany working together to create a way to ensure peace and cooperation. However, he did not necessarily envision the United Kingdom as a member of this new body.

From post-WWII until the 21st century, the relationship between Britain and the effort to unite Europe had been an intermittent love affair. The Treaty of Dunkirk united Britain and France in 1947. Then, in 1948, the Treaty of Brussels brought the UK into a defense agreement with Belgium, France, Luxembourg, and the Netherlands that created the Western Union Defense Organization, or the WUDO. In 1949, the North Atlantic Treaty Organization (NATO) was created with Belgium, Canada, Denmark, France, Iceland, Italy, Luxembourg, the Netherlands, Norway, Portugal, the UK, and the US.

In 1951, the economic needs of the European countries signed to the Treaty of Brussels were addressed in the creation of the European Coal and Steel Community (ECSC), with the signing of the Treaty of Paris by the same countries, but now joined by West Germany and

Italy. In 1957, the Treaty of Rome established the European Economic Community and the Euratom Treaty created the European Atomic Energy Community. These treaties helped form the first foundation of what would become the European Union. Subsequent treaties resolved jurisdictional and administrative issues, including the signing of the Brussels Treaty of 1965, the Schengen Agreement and Convention of 1985, and the Single Europe Act signed in 1986.

Led by Prime Minister Harold Macmillan, previous attempts by the British to join the European Community from 1957 to 1963[6] were rejected under pressure from French President Charles de Gaulle. De Gaulle considered the British too adversarial to the interests of the European Community to accept Britain being admitted.[7] After all, it was France and others who had led much of the existing progress in rebuilding Europe, with Britain abstaining from many important treaties along the way. But as Britain stood by to watch the progress of Europe under French and German recovery, its economy was becoming mired in stagnation.[8]

For all the effort of Harold Macmillan to join the European Community, however, there was Labour Party member Hugh Gaitskell, who opposed this entry claiming that it would rob the UK of its independence. This paradigm of choices would repeat itself for the next 20 years as the relationship between the UK and Europe continued to evolve.

In 1973, the United Kingdom joined the European Communities, a predecessor of the European Union with the ratification of the Treaty of Accession in 1972.

ONLY TWO YEARS after joining the European Economic Community (EEC), the British people were given a referendum to continue this new relationship within the EEC in 1975. Created under the Referendum Act of 1975, the June 5th vote was the first-ever countrywide referendum in the 20th century. Brits voted overwhelmingly to remain members of this new alliance.

In 1992, the Treaty on European Union,[9] also known as the Maastricht Treaty, established the framework for what would be called the European Union. Under the guidance of German leader Helmut Kohl and French leader François Mitterrand, the newly formed EU would advance European integration in banking and security, create European Union citizenship for citizens in member countries, and lead to the creation of the euro, the official currency of the European Union.

In late 2009, the Greek debt crisis had taken a toll on the Greek people; austerity measures and rioting by Golden Dawn, fueled by disinformation, gave momentum to the possibility that Britain would exit the EU, given that some economists believed Greece would be stronger without the EU.

In January 2013, Prime Minister David Cameron decided to call the question on whether Britain should remain in the EU after years of discussions, bickering, and pandering. He stated he would support putting it up for a vote. Again, in November 2015, he says that "Britain's best future lay within a reformed European Union" and that if re-elected he would keep the promise that "we would have an in-out referendum" on whether to stay or leave the EU.[10] This led to the European Union Referendum Act of 2015.[11] On February 22, 2016, Cameron announced the in-out referendum would occur on June 23, 2016.[12]

Driven by anti-immigrant sentiment, the Eurosceptic politicians like Boris Johnson and Nigel Farage pushed the referendum for the UK to leave the EU. Dubbed "Brexit," the effort was a portmanteau of "Britain" and "exit."

The push to leave the EU was largely orchestrated by two campaign groups, the Leave.EU group, backed by Nigel Farage,[13] and the Vote Leave group, founded by Matthew Elliot and Dominic Cummings in October 2015. Vote Leave had support from several parties and was led by former London Mayor Boris Johnson, a member of the Conservative Party.

But they were not the only groups. Better Off Out (BOO) had been around since 2006, pushing for a departure from the EU. Formed by the Freedom Association, a right-wing libertarian group that had been around since 1975, the group described itself as a "cross-party campaign group."[14] Others included Grassroots Out, or GO, led by Conservative Party leader Peter Bone, who went on to found Leave Means Leave in July 2016. Grassroots Out was largely run by Conservative Party members, but notably Russia Today host George Galloway's group, the Respect Party, joined in on February 22, 2016, as announced by Russia Today. The Respect Party dissolved in August 2016. Notably, former MP Galloway had interviewed Nigel Farage about the aspects of Brexit in an interview for Russian propaganda outfit, Sputnik.[15]

Some critics argued that the body of the EU formed a single market zone that controlled member countries and thus robbed Britain of its economic sovereignty. Additionally, they argued that immigrants could travel too easily between EU countries, putting British jobs at risk. They claimed that Britain was losing its identity, especially in terms of immigration. The most vocal proponents of this effort often invoked the idea that their culture was under threat and that removing the control from Brussels was the best way to handle this. They wanted to let Britain go it alone.

Arron Banks was the single largest political donor in UK history. The businessman from Bristol was co-founder of Leave.EU, and he put almost $10 million (£7 million) into the referendum to withdraw from the EU. He, along with Nigel Farage, former leader of UKIP, Raheem Kassam, London editor of Breitbart, and Andy Wigmore, Leave.EU's director of communications, called themselves the "bad boys of Brexit." Each in his way was a follower of Steve Bannon's Duginist philosophy of ending democracy via tying European and American extreme conservative groups into a worldwide network, in which Breitbart was the key node.[16]

On May 7, 2015, Brits elected a Conservative majority. By February 20, 2016, Cameron told the British media that the EU deal gave the UK "special status" in renegotiating trade deals. London Mayor, Boris Johnson, was the impetus behind the Leave.EU campaign on February 21.

On June 16, 2016, tensions were high in the UK over the referendum. A Remain advocate was out campaigning when confronted by an unemployed xenophobic gardener, Thomas Mair. Labour Party Member of Parliament Jo Cox was a young 41-year-old former humanitarian worker and mother of two children. The 52-year-old Mair laid in wait outside of a constituent meeting. He confronted her, and then stabbed her with a knife. Her aides tussled with Mair. He then drew a makeshift handgun and shot her to death. Thomas Mair was a National Front supporter and English Defence League member. The Southern Poverty Law Center says he was also a longtime supporter of the American neo-Nazi National Alliance, and had spent a total of $630 on their publications. One of the books was how to build a homemade single-shot pistol, the design of which killed Cox. Mair shouted "Britain First!" when he killed Jo Cox and repeated it proudly as police led him away.[17]

Seven days later, the Brit Leave.EU campaign irreverently won by 4 percentage points. The referendum saw over 30 million people turn out to vote in favor of leaving with 51.9% in support and 48.1% against. David Cameron was forced to resign as Prime Minister.

On July 11, 2016, Conservative Theresa May became Prime Minister. By October 2, 2016, she announced that the formal British exit from the European Union would begin in March 2017. Many Conservatives and Labour Party members never supported Brexit; it was an undesirable shock, like the 2016 election result in the United States six months later.

Now that the matter was settled, Prime Minister Theresa May had to follow the guidelines of Article 50 of the Lisbon Treaty of 2009.[18] The article stated that any member state could leave the EU, and the member country that wishes to leave must provide notice of intent to leave, then negotiations of withdrawal were to be arranged by members of the EU. However, the departing member state loses the option of deliberations of the European Council. The UK could not participate in rescinding this effort without approval of the remaining member states.

Brexit was the opening of a Pandora's box for the UK. Former US Ambassador to Russia Michael McFaul knew this and wrote an article in the Ukrainian paper *Kyiv Post* titled, "How Brexit Is a Win for Putin."[19]

McFaul stated that the success of the Leave.EU campaign was "a giant victory for Putin's foreign policy objectives."[20] Tempers flared.

Many could not believe that the extremists had won. There was a palpable feeling that democracy under fire and the murder of Jo Cox were signs of things to come. On the street, there was a rise in the demonization and harassment of Muslims.

According to the British Supreme Court, by January 24, 2017, a Parliamentary vote was necessary before Article 50 to leave the EU could be implemented by the British government. By March 13, 2017, British Parliament approved a bill to designate government authority for the use of Article 50.

The Brexit was coming. Theresa May did not dare cross the conservatives who had voted for the exit, even as UKIP fell completely apart and was almost consigned to the waste heap of history. On March 28, 2017, she signed the "official letter to European Council President Donald Tusk, invoking Article 50 and signaling the United Kingdom's intention to leave the EU." The following day in Brussels, the formal execution of Brexit was initiated as the Article 50 Implementation letter was handed by Tim Barrow, Britain's Ambassador to the EU, to Donald Tusk, European Council President.

Hang on a Tick

By June 2017, Twitter Inc. decided to be proactive by launching "the Global Internet Forum to Counter Terrorism" (the GIFCT), a partnership among Twitter, YouTube, Facebook, and Microsoft. The purpose of GIFTC was to "facilitate information sharing; technical cooperation; and research collaboration, including with academic institutions."[21] As a result of a fused network of research findings, Twitter announced on October 26, 2017, that they "would no longer accept advertisements from [Russia Today] and will donate the $1.9 million that RT had spent globally on advertising on Twitter to academic research into elections and civil engagement."[22]

Five days later, Halloween 2017 would prove scarier than normal. Twitter's corporate leadership informed the House Intelligence Committee of its suspension of 2,752 accounts in relation to the 2016 Presidential election, due to the fact that aggressive Russian digital interference had been noted.[23] That same day, the United States Senate Committee on the Judiciary, Subcommittee on Crime and Terrorism, reserved time for the testimony of Sean Edgett, Acting General Counsel of Twitter, to address the spam and automation of the social media platform and measures they took to investigate the disinformation campaign that utilized their platform. Edgett testified almost one year after the initial discovery of the keystone automated account @PatrioticPepe. This fake Twitter bot responded instantaneously to any and all @realDonaldTrump tweets. It was the nexus for flooding the network with obvious spam content. In technical speak the responses were:

> "…enabled through an application that had been created using [their] 'Application Programming Interface (API).'…We noticed an upward swing in such activity during the period leading up to the election, and @PatrioticPepe was one such example. On the same day, we identified @PatrioticPepe, we suspended the API credentials associated with that user for violation of our automation rules. On average, we take similar actions against violative applications more than 7,000 times per week."[24]

Figuring out @PatrioticPepe revealed that the Russians had figured out a way to game Twitter and amplify any message they wanted to that exceeded Twitter's ability to stop it.

British cyber and computer security researchers were alarmed. As the Americans found out too late, Brexit was most likely not a free and fair vote. Leading up to the referendum voting day, data researchers at the University of California-Berkeley and University of Swansea concluded that over 150,000 accounts traced to Russia posted Brexit Leave campaign content when they had previously posted content on Crimea. The pro-Russia, pro-Putin, pro-Brexit content was seen most often.[25] The British themselves retroactively investigated if a Russian hand had swung the internet in favor of the Leave campaign during the Brexit vote. According to the Director of Neuropolitics Research at the University of Edinburgh, Laura Cram, at least 419 Kremlin-linked troll accounts tweeted about #Brexit a total of 3,468 times.[26] Cram's research showed in the data from the 2,752 accounts (now deactivated) that were in possession of the US Congress, that the automated cyber-attacks on the UK (before the Brexit referendum) and on the US from 2014 up until the 2016 Presidential election were from the Kremlin-linked Russian Federation-Internet Research Agency (RF-IRA).[27] Russian Intelligence through the RF-IRA specifically targeting UK for Brexit with the numerous hashtags #Brexitvote, #PrayForLondon, #BanIslam, and #Brexit.[28]

On November 13, 2017, Theresa May accused Russia of "seeking to weaponize information" and to "sow discord in the West and under-mine our institutions."[29] Like in the United States, it was too little too late...but who knew at the time? The only common denominator was a company in Britain called Cambridge Analytica.

In 2017, Farage too was named as a person of interest in the possible conspiracy between the Trump administration and Russia. Farage held very close ties to Trump and Julian Assange, the founder of WikiLeaks. It should be noted in the immediate aftermath of Trump's victory, Farage was one of the first to fly to New York to guide Trump on his policies. Farage once said that Putin is "the statesman I most admire." He also had a dodgy relationship with Julian Assange. On March 9, 2017, Londoner Ian Stubbings was walking near the Ecuadorean Embassy where Assange was stationed when he saw Farage slip into the building. He tweeted that he saw him. A Buzzfeed reporter saw the tweet and arrived in time to catch him leaving the Embassy 40 minutes later. That both were now under US federal investigation into the electioneering by Russian intelligence is far more than coincidence.

The strategy of the Russians appeared simple: break up the United Kingdom and damage the EU. Russian agencies would stoke the Brit-ish Leave campaign and give it every assistance using cyberwarfare and perception management efforts. They would also sow discord and dissent in populations of white Britons who hated Muslims, immigra-tion, and saw White Christendom under fire. Done right, the referen-dum could force the breakup of the UK. Then when Scotland wanted leave the United Kingdom, the RF-IRA would use its web power to push the Scottish Referendum Leave narrative. Over a few years the effort would reduce the United Kingdom to just Wales and England. It almost worked.

Nicola Sturgeon, Scotland's First Minister, announced plans for a second Scottish Independence referendum sometime between late 2018 and early 2019. The incentive for the second referendum was more than likely fueled by Kremlin-paid trolls and automated bots, which is why digital researchers at Swansea University and the University of Edinburgh were motivated to sleuth as well. According to the *Sunday Post* in Scotland, 400,000 tweets on the second Scottish Independence Referendum were fueled by bots and trolls from spurious accounts. At Swansea University, it was noted by digital researchers looking for unusual activity in algorithmic sequences that from May 24 through September 24, 2017, an alarming pattern existed in the propping up of the Scottish independence narrative, "there were a total of 2,284,746 tweets containing at least one of the following keywords; 'scotland,' 'scottish,' 'sturgeon,' 'indyref,' 'scotref,' and 'snp.'"[30] A total of 388,406 were messages sent by bots, according to researchers. These findings corroborated the widely held suspicion that, like the Brexit referendum and the 2016 US Presidential election, bots and paid trolls were doing the dirty work of Putin's Kremlin.

Despite the best efforts to stave off a withdrawal from the EU, the referendum passed. The British market immediately suffered a 30% loss in its value, and since then corporations have started heading to the door to leave London and set up in Paris or Brussels. By all accounts the Leave campaign should have lost but, like Trump's election, it won by the slimmest of margins. Russian's amplification of the message that leaving the EU would help the British public was exponentially more impactful due to Russian enforcers rather than the strength of the argument. Those percentages would likely have been reversed had Putin not launched his information war attacks.

UKIP's promises of a new independent and wealthy Britain immediately vaporized the moment the referendum was won. Promises that the National Health Service would receive hundreds of billions to assist an aging population because of the withdrawal did not last 24 hours after the vote, and party bosses conceded that virtually nothing would happen except that the UK would now be "independent" of the common market. They somehow did not factor in the possibility that it could also lead to the breakup of the United Kingdom, as Scotland and Northern Ireland wanted to remain in the market and started eyeing their own independence. Propaganda always requires a bit of truth to hold a lie.

Britain was stuck with the disaster of Brexit but, unlike the American government, the British intelligence community was sounding multiple alarm bells that the process of independent information was under attack. Its new conservative leadership heeded the warnings. In December 2017, Prime Minister Theresa May told an audience that Russia was on notice for their activities:

> "This has included meddling in elections, and hacking the Danish ministry of defense and the Bundestag [German parliament], among many others...It is seeking to weaponize information. Deploying its state-run media organizations to plant fake stories and photo-shopped images in an attempt to sow discord in the west and undermine our institutions."[31]

Emboldened by the success of their influence campaign removing Britain from the European Union in the Brexit vote and their American victory, Russian intelligence now directed their efforts on European elections. The next election was France. If Putin managed to get his preferred candidate in power, the Western world order established in 1945 would quickly collapse. A win in France would break the primary pillars of American-European dominance: withdrawing France from NATO and breaking up the European Union. Brexit proved that a nation's democratic process could be changed by influencing social media at the margins, particularly when these elections would be won or lost within a point or two. In France the rules were different. Their information warfare teams could push a candidate, but the laws that blacked-out political campaign information from being released in the last 44 hours before an election would require a precision shot.

Russia was banking on being able to release Kompromat at the last possible second using third-party assets that were willing to use their social media distribution system to circumvent French laws. The last thing on the minds of the general French public will be whatever Russia chose.

2017 certainly was not the first time Russia interfered in a French Presidential election. However, the older traditional methodologies were slow, relied on print news media distribution, and centralized TV news media. In 1974, the KGB launched a covert propaganda campaign to disgrace the pro-NATO Gaullist Valéry Giscard d'Estaing and got socialist François Mitterrand into office.[32] In what was believed to be a victory for Moscow, Mitterrand brought into French government four French Communist Party members and made them ministers. American President Ronald Reagan was mortified until he learned that Mitterrand was running one of history's greatest spy missions inside of Russia. Operation FAREWELL was a French-paid spy in the form of KGB Colonel Vladimir I. Vetrov, who helped channel massive amounts of technical intelligence to France. Once Reagan learned of the Mitterrand operations, all was forgiven.

However, it was later learned that Russia wanted either of the two candidates and preferred the hard-line anti-Soviet D'Estaing. Their principal method of influence was manipulating journalists and news articles. In 1987, a former KGB political warfare officer, Ilya Dzhirkvelov, told the Paris-based magazine for the Russian émigré community, *Russkaya Mysl,* how it all played out:

> "In 1974, when the elections for a French President were coming up, at a meeting of the Central Committee, at which I was present, department chief and Central Committee secretary [Boris] Ponomarev said that we should make all possible efforts so that Mitterrand was not elected. These are not empty words. I will not name the newspapers and publications which we used, but we used two large French newspapers and three newspapers outside of Paris with publication of materials extolling Giscard

d'Estaing as a close comrade-in-arms of De Gaulle and a man striving for peace. I cannot say how much this material helped Giscard d'Estaing's election as President, but the fact itself is important. It surprised us, of course, that the Central Committee of our Communist Party was against the socialists and for the bourgeois party. Ponomarev explained to us that any bourgeois politician was much more useful than any social-democrat or socialist. We used newspapers not only in France, but also large newspapers in the United States, Italy, Japan, and Germany."[33]

The operations of old political war spies of the KGB were rudimentary, but for their era they were effective. Russia was no longer the Soviet Union, and technology was changing the speed of belief. However, the KGB had only changed names, and a young spy in East Germany who had been tasked with stealing that technology was now the ruler of Russia. He knew the old ways could bring brilliant results if executed with modern technology. His test beds convinced the Russians that elections could be affected, and he was determined to try to put his preferred candidate in power.

The 2017 French elections were held in two stages. The first round of voting occurred on April 23, 2017. The top two candidates facing off were the young Emmanuel Macron, and the mainstay of the French conservatives, Marine Le Pen. On May 7, 2017, the run-off election was held to choose between the two.

Macron was the leader of a relatively new party called *La République en Marche!* (LREM, or Republic on the Move!). He had worked as an economic advisor under President François Hollande for two years and served as an economy minister until 2016. He launched LREM in April 2016 as an alternative to the other major centrist and liberal parties.

Macron was young, 39 at the time of the election, very charismatic with boyish good looks and oozing with personality and charm. He had dispatched Jean-Luc Mélenchon of *La France Insoumise* (LFI) Party, and François Fillon of the Republican Party in the open primary voting. As the winner, he faced off with Marine Le Pen. As I mentioned, she built close ties to Moscow in what she referred to as "Regional Solutions." Her defense platform focused on working with Russia against Middle East terrorism. Second only to Donald Trump, she was the perfect Russian-backed candidate for Putin's vision of an autocrat-led Europe. But first, she needed to win.

Honeytrap

Just before the 44-hour political news blackout on the eve of the election, nine gigabytes of emails were allegedly stolen from the Macron campaign. The emails were quickly posted across the internet. Approximately 10,000 of Macron's personal documents and emails had been hacked and leaked by Russia. According to Macron's digital data team director Mounir Mahjoubi, most of the emails were innocuous documents including invoices, speeches, statements, and routine administration.[34] There was a reason for that. The French government's domestic intelligence agency, Directorate of Territorial Surveillance (DST), in cooperation with the American National Security Agency, had been laying a trap for Russian hackers.

Director of the NSA, Admiral Michael Rogers, spoke about the ambush they had laid out for the Russians:

> "We had become aware of Russian activity, we had talked to our French counterparts prior to the public announcements of the events that were publicly attributed this past weekend and gave them a heads up, 'Look, we're watching the Russians, we're seeing them penetrate some of your infrastructure. Here's what we've seen, what can we do to try to assist?' We're doing similar things with our German counterparts, with our British counterparts, they have an upcoming election sequence."[35]

Security firm Trend Micro also found the digital fingerprints of the Russian intelligence agency, Advanced Persistent Threat-28, the FSB's FANCY BEAR malware that was used in the attempted hacking of the US election just the year before.[36] The method of attack was phishing—a false link that takes the person signing in to what they believe is a trusted website but is in fact a Russian intelligence server. In this instance, a false Macron web server was established as a honeypot by the NSA and France's DST. When Russian cyberwar systems attacked they were actually being lured into a trap that France and the NSA controlled.

Interestingly, two American conservative extremists were implicated in the Russian operations. They seemed to have been standing by for the release of the Macron documents. Once released, they immediately created the Twitter hashtag #Macronleaks and started disseminating tweets to spread the stolen data. French Intelligence blocked their information and it played little, if any, part in the election narrative. Yet here was proof that Americans had teamed up with Russian Intelligence to impact a foreign election.

In the end, Macron won a majority margin by 66% and Le Pen lost with almost 34% of the vote.

After her failure to win and being disparaged publicly by her father, she stepped down as leader of the party.

Germany's Time in the Barrel

The Islamic State of Iraq and Syria was a terrifying and brutal terrorist group. They exercised national-level power when they created their small but less-than-resilient terror state. One area in which they did exercise a measure of success was their global cyber propaganda projection. They formed both centralized and vigilante social media distribution teams that spread their special brand of hatred across the globe. They were arguably masters of the cyber world. The CyberCaliphate Army (CCA) was led by a young British hacker named Junaid Hussain, a member of the Anonymous offshoot LulzSec, a black hat group that created cyber mischief. He migrated to Syria and was quickly chosen as the "cyber emir" who led the social media campaign for ISIS in 2014. For some time, the CCA dealt only in "script kiddie" (aka skiddie) or prefabricated and easily launched viruses. That was the limit of their capability; they had little evidence of real hacker skills.

Yet sometime between April and May 2015, 16 gigabytes of email data were stolen from the computer servers of the German Parliament (the *Bundestag*).[37] The ISIS flag logos and Arabic graffiti left on the Bundestag website was that of the CyberCaliphate Army, and for a period it was attributed to ISIS.

However, the follow-up forensic analysis indicated an old foe—the attack was unmistakably performed by the Russian military intelligence agency, the GRU. Cybersecurity researchers found electronic fingerprints associated with the GRU malware suite FANCY BEAR. The Russians were conducting a rare "False Flag" operation to make casual observers think ISIS was responsible and that they had simply performed web vandalism. The KGB had a name for it—*maskirovka*, masking the true perpetrator. The Russians stole data to weaponize it.

Not surprisingly, the hacked data were the emails of the political leftist bloc of the Bundestag, although all 20,000 computers were considered penetrated.[38] The attack was not focused on low-level staffers. The accounts associated with Chancellor Angela Merkel's offices and six members of parliament were infected.[39] The information that the GRU found must have been well worth the effort. In 2016, the center-left Social Democratic Party's parliamentary group in Bundestag and Merkel's conservative Christian Democratic Union in Saarland were attacked by the GRU.[40]

In the Bundestag attack, the GRU set up a fake server in Latvia and conducted a phishing attack. As before, they created a fake website to look like the Bundestag office website. The phishing emails encouraged German workers to click on the link and sign in—except they were signing in to Russian intelligence servers and giving away their passwords. This was exactly like the attacks the Russians used on the White House, the Macron election attacks, and dozens of others.

But these attacks were more like cyber cruise missiles. Angela Merkel was a strong leader. She was sharp and powerful. A skilled politician and a brilliant thinker, she was more like Hillary Clinton and reflected many similar policies. Merkel and Barack Obama were also ideological bedfellows. Bringing Le Pen into power would be a great blow to Europe, but getting rid of Merkel would be its death knell. By

2016, Putin thought he had a German beachhead to do what he needed to destabilize the political scene.

But Germany took election security seriously. Because the German election system uses paper ballots, there was no chance to hack and swing votes. Dieter Sarreither, President of the *Statistisches Bundes-amt*, the Federal Statistics office that monitors elections, said, "the entire network infrastructure has been overhauled and modernized since the last election in 2013."[41] Additionally, a highly conscientious office existed to monitor exterior threats. The German Federal Office for Information Security (BSI, or *Bundesamt für Sicherheit in der Informationstechnik*) and the SB agency monitor the system in real time.

With little chance to affect the vote directly, Russia's strategic goal was to encourage right-wing, conservative white voters such as the German populist Alternative for Germany Party. In their effort to swerve Germany back toward the Motherland, Putin would again harness social media, independent news, and, not surprisingly, Americans who supported Trump to damage Angela Merkel and make gains for the German right wing through active measures.

According to a Brooking University report titled "The impact of Russian interference on Germany's 2017 election," Russia was trying to punish Germany and, once again, it was about the financial sanctions America had spearheaded after the invasion of Crimea. The report stated that Germany "…orchestrated the European census on sanctions against Russia."[42] For Putin, that was enough to build a new right-wing political order that would overturn all the decades of liberal decadence and multiculturalism in this American-designed democracy.

With the German federal election scheduled to happen on September 24, 2017, the German government was on guard. France had just had a fortuitous bullet-dodge by working with the NSA and catching Russian attempts to use fake propaganda and distribute campaign materials just before the political news blackout. In Germany, the operations were more insidious and democratic. The Russian campaign appeared to be designed to turn out the Germans and ethnic Russians in the former East German states of the now-unified Germany.

The first signs that something was afoot were bots' repeated messages in German and Russian languages on German social media sites, particularly in the Eastern part of the country. A large bot network (botnet) was found on Russian-language Twitter accounts subscribing to Russian-educated Germans.

An analysis was done and revealed that 2,480 accounts were algorithmically found to be publishing exclusively pro-Kremlin propaganda. According to a report by the Institute for Strategic Dialogue (ISD), the Digital Forensics Research Lab at the Atlantic Council saw 60 of these pro-Kremlin accounts were reprogrammed to automatically pump out pro-AfD advertising of commercial or pornographic messages.[43] A seminal report issued by the ISD titled "Making Germany Great Again" noted the Russian hacker paid to distribute pro-AfD data asserted:

"15,000 pro-AfD posts and retweets would cost 2,000 euros; After negotiations, a discounted package included 15,000 pro-AfD tweets and retweets 'guaranteed' to make a pro-AfD hashtag trend. The hacker stated that the posts would 'come from at least 25% "high-quality" bots that would not be so easily identified as fake accounts.' He estimated he would need to send 80 tweets per minute to make a pro-AfD hashtag trend."[44]

A Russian hacker on *VKontakte*, the Russian social media version of Facebook, claimed that they sent out thousands of pro-AfD messages in the run-up to the election. He also claimed that numerous right-wing groups worldwide were coordinating to achieve a similar goal in their elections and were working together.[45]

Nikolai Alexander, the German far-right activist and internet social media star who posts videos under the name *Reconquista Germanica* (an allusion to a Germanic reconquest of Muslim lands by Christians), attempted to create an extreme-right channel on Discord, the voice and chat app, to disrupt the German elections. There are 33,000 Alexander followers all over the world on the Discord channel. The principal reason for this channel was to ensure a strong showing for the AfD in the Bundestag.[46] Alexander outlined the mission of the new channel:

> "The aim of the first campaign is to hoist the AfD as much as possible into the Bundestag. Today we will also start the meme war in the Bundestag against the race of mutts.... [and] to go after failed conservatives like [Markus] Pretzell and other hypocrites and strengthen the Höcke wing."[47]

Interestingly, Discord was used in 2017 to coordinate American neo-Nazis in the Charlottesville protests with their European counterparts to spread the message of a rising American neo-Nazi movement.[48]

On September 24, 2017, the German election was held. Chancellor Angela Merkel, leader of the center-left Christian Democratic Union/Christian Social Union, won a fourth term with 32.9% of the vote. The Social Democratic Party (SPD) won 20.5%. AfD won 12.6% of the vote and became the third-largest party in Germany.[49] The right-wing AfD now had 94 out of 630 seats in the Bundestag... for the first time since WWII.

Sweden—Attack of the Forgery Bears

Sweden may technically be neutral toward Russia, but Russia treats them like a major NATO country and has started to interfere in electoral politics using active measures. Swedish authorities have accused Russia of flooding the nation with fake news, disinformation operations, and attempting to smear the government with forged, false documents. The Russians' main goal is to discredit NATO and keep Sweden from formally joining the alliance.[50]

The Swedish Institute of Military Affairs published a study in 2017 detailing the effects of Moscow's active measures. They claim that "Moscow's main aim was to 'preserve the geo-strategic status quo' by minimizing NATO's role in the Baltic region and keeping Sweden out of the international military alliance."[51]

Interestingly, Russian Intelligence used forgeries of documents purported to be from the Ministry of Defense outlining a conspiracy between Sweden and NATO. Other forged letters included one to major industrial groups to implicate Swedish companies, such as Bofors, of selling weapons to Ukraine. No such weapons sales were happening. The documents were done on Ministry letterhead. Another was supposedly a letter from the Chief International Public Prosecutor dropping charges against a suspected war criminal. All 26 letters were "released" to Swedish and Russian language websites. Russian news media is a major component of spreading disinformation in Sweden. *The Guardian* reported 4,000 fake news stories were disseminated by Sputnik News in Sweden in just a one-year period.[52]

Swedish Prime Minister Stefan Löfven warned that Russia could directly interfere with the 2018 Swedish election. He told local media "We should not rule it out and be naive and think that it does not happen in Sweden. That's why information and cybersecurity is part of this strategy...."[53] Löfven detailed the eight biggest threats to Sweden and the first five were about Russia, with cybersecurity as second only to Russian military activity in Swedish waters. The government has gone so far as to propose creating a cybersecurity defense unit specifically to defend the integrity of their elections.[54]

The Montenegro Coup Attempt

A component of Russian hybrid warfare is to use all forces short of open warfare to effect a political result. In late summer 2016, two GRU Russian military intelligence spies, Eduard Shirokov (using the alias Shishmakov) and Vladimir Popov, were deployed to Serbia. On October 16, 2016, a group of Montenegrin and Serbian nationalists would storm the Parliament dressed as policemen, kill the pro-Western members, and seize control of the government. They would then ask for Russian assistance in consolidating control of the country. If successful, Russia would get a submarine-capable naval base and airbase, as well as an ally in the Adriatic Sea. Their mission was audacious and risked serious European-wide tension if discovered. If successful, they would shift the strategic balance of the Adriatic and Balkans dramatically.

Montenegro is part of the former Yugoslavia and was one of the small countries to declare its independence after the brutal Serbian wars against Croatia and Bosnia-Herzegovina. After the 1999 US-NATO-Serbian conflict, Operation ALLIED FORCE/NOBLE ANVIL, a pro-Western government in Serbia came into power and helped track down the Serbian leaders Slobodan Milosevic and Ratko Mladic. Both pro-Moscow leaders were wanted by the International Criminal Court for war crimes related to the Bosnian genocide. Montenegro left their union with Serbia in 2006 after a referendum for independence. They formed a pro-Western government that decided to join NATO while under constant bombardment of Russian threats. Pro-Russian ethnic Serbs make up 29% of the population of the nation and are concentrated along the Serbian and Croatian borders and Kotor Bay.

The coup was thwarted when an informant, former Montenegrin policeman Mirko Velimirovic, walked into the Ministry of Interior offices to confess that he had been hired by Russian nationals to participate in a coup. He was asked to purchase 50 machine guns with 30,000 euros and secure a safe house for Serbian nationalists. The Russians delivered the money. The mission was to help the Serbians storm the Montenegrin Parliament building, kill the legislature members, start an internal crisis that would stop Montenegro from seating the pro-West Prime Minister Milo Djukanovic, and install a pro-Moscow government. The government alleges that sophisticated Russian surveillance equipment was used to plot the movements of the Prime Minister to facilitate his assassination during the coup.

Anti-Western activist Aleksandar Sindjelic was part of the plot. He had volunteered as a fighter in eastern Ukraine. He claims the two GRU officers approached him in Ukraine and suggested the plan. The GRU officers came to Serbia and organized the attack. NATO intelligence agencies had the Russian under surveillance, and once the plot was foiled, they released photos of Sindjelic and Russian spies Shirokov and Popov conspiring in a park.[55] The Russians entered Serbia with official passports made out with aliases. Shirokov had once been made persona non grata and was expelled after being found conducting espionage in Poland.

The Russian spies gave the plotters three encrypted telephones with preprogrammed numbers. One of the participants said they were to not to use the second listed number. Velimirovic, the police informant, tried it and it was answered by a Russian in Russia.

The pro-Moscow political party, the Democratic Front, warned against joining NATO. The DF had received millions from Moscow. Russia itself had threatened Montenegro against joining the alliance. According to Velimirovic, two officers of the infiltrated Montenegro had contacted them. Members of the Democratic Front, the ultra-right-wing pro-Russian party, were part of the plot.

The plan was for members of the Democratic Front to stage a mass sit-in at the parliament. While police were distracted by the protest, the coup plotters would infiltrate the area dressed as police, then storm the government building, capture and kill the Prime Minister, and then declare a coup. The Montenegrin Minister of Defense said:

> "There is not any doubt that it was financed and organized from different sources or different parts of Russian intelligence, together with some Montenegrin opposition parties, but also under the strong influence of some radicals from Serbia and Russia."[56]

British Foreign Secretary Boris Johnson confirmed some of the details to the British press: "You've seen what's happened in Montenegro where there was an attempted coup in a European state and possibly even an attempted assassination of the leader of that state.... Now there's very little doubt that the Russians are behind these things."[57]

Animosity toward America and NATO by pro-Russia factions continues in Montenegro. On February 21, 2018, an unknown assailant tried to bomb the American Embassy in the capital of Podgorica with an explosive device, but it misfired and killed only himself.[58]

A New Pillar of a New Axis

These European cyberattacks happened nearly simultaneously with the American hacking and election, and it's not an accident. Russia reached back into the darkest depths of its history of Communist political and ideological propaganda warfare to effect a state plan where not just the United States would do their bidding, but they would reengineer Western conservatism to become willing assets who would create the conditions to put into leadership men and women who understand that democracy has had its day. The Kremlin would ensure that each nation under his tutelage would share a common bond that would erase borders, unify messages, and solidify a new order in Western culture. They would create an alliance of nations that would be led by strong authoritarian leaders. The alliance would use their own powerful tools of democracy—free and fair elections, freedom of speech, right to assembly, and other constitutional rights of citizenship to dramatically eliminate those same rights once in power. One by one the West would become a democratically elected version of Vladimir Putin's Russia. Once in office, their own financial self-interest and access to a super club of the elitest of the global elite would naturally override any guardrails their national laws could impose. Those rules, laws, and shouts would simply be ignored. With Moscow's cyber-espionage tools, Putin believed it was on its way to being reengineered from a squabbling coop of dysfunctional liberal democracies, into an economically powerful Axis of Autocracies. With an allied America and the Western pillar using Moscow's playbook, the end of the Atlantic alliance was now close to a reality.

America Under Siege…from Within

CHAPTER 12

Russia's American Beachhead

"Russian Officials Scramble as Plan to Delegitimize
Western Democracy Moving Way Faster Than
Intended"

— *The Onion*, FEBRUARY 2, 2017

M oscow's leader was a lifelong practitioner of judo. He would
continue executing GLOBAL GRIZZLY across Europe
and the Middle East while also carrying out his political
warfare operation against the United States, GRIZZLY STEPPE.
Attacking the United States was going to come in the form of a strategic flip against the anti-Atlantic alliance. Once pro-Moscow, right-
wing populist political parties took control of liberal governments in
the United States and France, they would have the ability to break up
NATO and realign the Western world toward Moscow.

Chief of the General Staff of the Russian Armed Forces, equivalent to the US Chairman of the Joint Chiefs of Staff, General Valery
Gerasimov, boasted of how Russia had created a strategy to foster fifth
columns in a nation. He believed that that Russian hybrid warfare and
active measures could do the job from within a nation without violating
its sovereignty. Gerasimov said:

"Of great importance here is the use of the global internet network to exert a massive, dedicated impact on the consciousness of

the citizens of states that are the targets of the aggression. Information resources have become one of the most effective types of weapon. Their extensive employment enables the situation in a country to be destabilized from within in a matter of days.... In this manner, indirect and asymmetric actions and methods of conducting hybrid wars enable the opposing side to be deprived of its actual sovereignty without the state's territory being seized."

Russia would create a literal fifth column of fellow travelers in the United States to become a critical pillar in Putin's Axis of Autocracy.

2016 WOULD BE a year of rebalancing the global spheres of influence. Russia had already spent a decade laying the groundwork for recruiting and seducing an entire American political party to support them. France was ready to be toppled. Austria was already in Putin's pocket. Poland, Hungary, Britain, the Netherlands, Italy, and even Sweden had significant gains for pro-Moscow groups. The end of NATO and the European Union was nigh.

Once Donald Trump was nominated, key Republican groups and personalities, along with Russia, quickly fell in line behind Trump. Despite the intense scrutiny of Trump's relationship to Putin, Republicans have already opened to Moscow's charms. The party was accepting donations from Russian Americans associated with the Kremlin. When Trump asserted that it was a "good thing" to have relations with Russia, the base quickly followed suit. By the end of 2017, numerous conservative personalities would be found to have made ties with pro-Moscow politicians. The money trail of donations from Russian billionaires started to expand from individuals into the coffers of the RNC. They moved via shadowy political action committees unleashed by the Citizens United ruling. Unlimited money meant unlimited chances for Russian oligarchs to make individual Americans willing assets for Russian intelligence.

In 1994, the Republican Party, under the leadership of Newt Gingrich, won a major electoral landslide. They gained 54 House seats and took control of Congress. Unlike previous Congresses, this one was won outright on conservatism. The unabashed promise to remake America into a slightly more authoritarian and thus safer country won them votes. Their first act was to attack the Democratic Party machine and damage it. They impeached President Bill Clinton and opened a wave of investigations to bring down the Democratic President. In the eyes of the American Republicans, the Democratic Party was no longer a loyal opposition but a plague on the American system of government to be attacked at every chance.

This hatred of the Democratic Party was extended to President Barack Obama, who was labeled a weak and ineffectual leader. Republicans assaulted his calm leadership style. Most of the criticism from the right came from hawks like Rep. Mike Rogers and Senators John McCain and Lindsey Graham, who wanted Obama to take decisive military action. Other Republicans called Obama weak on matters such as not carrying out the airstrike on Syria, or bringing Ukraine into NATO and arming them after the Russian invasion of Crimea, simply because he was a Democrat.

Former Alaska governor and Vice-Presidential candidate Sarah Palin was one of the first converts to the image of Vladimir Putin being the beacon of strongmen, although it was in the context of opposing Russia. After the Russian invasion of Ukraine in March 2014, Palin said,

> "Anyone who carries the common-sense gene would know that Putin doesn't change his stripes. He harkens back to the era of the czars and he wants that Russian empire to grow again, he wants to exert huge power and dominance....People are looking at Putin as one who wrestles bears and drills for oil. They look at our president as one who wears mom jeans and equivocates and bloviates. We are not exercising that peace through strength that only can be brought to you courtesy of the red, white and blue."

On Fox News, Rudy Giuliani reflected on how much he admired Putin's ability to provide orders and get things done. "Putin decides what he wants to do, and he does it in half a day, right? He decided he had to go to their parliament—he went to their parliament, he got permission in 15 minutes."[1]

From 2010, Putin's information agencies aligned themselves with the American conservative message to their own via Fox News and Russia Today. By 2012, the social media revolution would occur. Twitter, Facebook, and web alerts became the cruise missiles of the new war on democracy.

The Second Russia-Euro-American political war would not be limited to electronic systems. Traditional methods of using duped and recruited intelligence assets were employed. Russian intelligence agencies have a history of manipulating visiting American diplomats, politicians, and non-government organizations to seeing the world their way. One of the most infamous occurred in 1969. A. Allan Bates, President Lyndon Johnson's Director of the Office of Standard Policy in the Commerce Department, repeatedly claimed that the Soviet Union had been "the first and thus far only nation which has solved the problem of providing acceptable low-cost housing for its masses of citizens." While he could not provide data to back up his claims, he adamantly stated his personal experience in traveling through the Soviet Union convinced him that this was true. This impression by Bates filtered into his staff. Under Secretary of Commerce Howard Samuels stated, "The Soviet Union has far surpassed the United States in solving the low-cost housing needs of its people."[2] Unfortunately for him, his travels around Russia were guided by the KGB and scripted to give him this very exact impression with the intent of him bringing it back to the Western world and transmitting it as a "fact." As part of the plan, Soviet leader Leonid Brezhnev would make scripted comments that supported his KGB-inspired notions.

Bates was lucky that he was just a target of state manipulation. Yuri Bezmenov, the former KGB officer, described the actual targets of Russian intelligence recruitment as self-absorbed conservatives.

"This was my instruction: try to get into large-circulation, established conservative media; reach filthy-rich movie makers; intellectuals, so-called 'academic' circles; cynical, egocentric people who can look into your eyes with angelic expression and tell you a lie. These are the most recruitable people: people who lack moral principles, who are either too greedy or too [much] suffer from self-importance. They feel that they matter a lot. These are the people who KGB wanted very much to recruit."[3]

In fact, the Russians did not prefer recruiting from left-wing, Communist, or socialist groups. Bezmenov said that idealistically minded leftists were useless to the KGB. "Never barter with leftists. Forget about these political prostitutes....When they become disillusioned, they become your worst enemies."[4]

However, Russian intelligence was also carefully trying to deflect core messaging in America away from the mainstream media. Social media was quickly overtaking CNN, the *New York Times*, and *Yahoo!* news as the principal method of gaining news in America. Rational discourse, applied common sense, and thoughtful consideration of the facts were overpowered by the mainstreaming conspiracy theory insanity of Alex Jones's InfoWars and the slightly more mainstream Breitbart News. Using this, they began honing a positive image of Donald Trump.

The War on Gays

Although the Soviet Union fell in 1989, it would not be until 1993 when President Boris Yeltsin would sign a repeal of Article 121 of the Soviet-era Anti-Sodomy law. After this repeal, being openly gay in Russia was officially sanctioned. Gays felt a wave of openness and an ability to show their love publicly. Russia was still a conservative country with a newly rising Orthodox church, but gays were having their moment. This euphoria lasted until the second inauguration of Vladimir Putin in 2012. Then the gay community in Russia was filled with fear. The number of gay-bashing attacks, sanctioned by the Kremlin, exploded. Anti-gay religious groups called out the coming "demographic crisis"—a plunge in childbirth rates that they attributed to the freedom of gays to live their lives. One Duma member, Yelena Mizulina, told a news program that "Analyzing all the circumstances, and the particularity of territorial Russia and her survival...I came to the conclusion that if today we want to resolve the demographic crisis, we need to, excuse me, tighten the belt on certain moral values and information, so that giving birth and raising children become fully valued."

Putin's public partner in what became an open war on gays in Russia, and by extension the conservative movement worldwide, was the Russian Orthodox church. The Russian church had been suppressed for almost 100 years when Putin freed it from the stigma of the Communist era. Understanding that Russians were naturally conservative and religious, he fostered the church's place in post-Soviet society. This attracted the likes of then–Indiana Governor Mike Pence. Pence is a devout evangelical Christian. In May 2011, he would meet privately with Bishop Hilarion Alfeyev, Metropolitan of Volokolamsk and Chair of the Russian Orthodox Church (ROC). They met at Franklin Graham's convention on global persecution of Christians. Pence conversed with him about the two countries' focus on defeating ISIS.[5] It was a defining moment, as Pence was seen as the religious component of the Trump team. His relationship with evangelicals and religious leaders worldwide was Trump's point of entry into the religious community.

Back in 2014, John Aravosis, a writer for AMERICAblog, wrote about evangelical ties to Moscow:

> "Politically, the war over gay rights in America is over—while skirmishes remain, the gays have won, and the far right knows it. That's why America's religionists have moved their mission abroad, mostly to Africa, but also to Europe. And now, with Vladimir Putin's help, they've found a new, more powerful home in Moscow."[6]

In 2013, Brian Brown, the then-president of the National Organization of Marriage (NOM)[7], traveled to Moscow and testified in front of the Russian Parliament, at the same time Russia rolled out a draconian piece of anti-gay legislation and called the law "For the Purpose of Protecting Children from Information Advocating for a Denial of Traditional Family Values."[8] The legislation was a law prohibiting the open knowledge of gays, calling for a ban on "gay propaganda," allegedly because children were being exposed to knowledge that gays existed. Over 100 conservative groups worldwide signed petitions supporting the law.

Soon after the legislation passed, the World Congress of Families, an anti-LGBT organization, abandoned its traditional annual conference always held in Rockford, Illinois, to hold its 2014 convention in Moscow in support of their anti-gay agenda.

Around the same time, Buzzfeed obtained an email cache that had been released online to Shaltai Boltai (Russian for Humpty Dumpty), the blog of a Russian hacktivist group with a mission to leak illicit Kremlin documents. The tranche of documents related to the "pro-family" convention, initially slated to happen in the US but which ultimately took place in Russia on September 10-11, 2014, with a full list of "confirmed" attendees naming 20 American pro-life, pro-marriage, anti-gay organizations. This included Brian Brown. Brown said during his trip to Russia, "There was a real push to re-instill Christian values in the public square" and that activists from Russia and the US are "uniting together under the values we share."[9] Later in 2014, the American evangelicals would be drawn even closer to Moscow. Russia passed a ban for gays, single people, and unmarried people from adopting Russian children. American right-wingers were ecstatic. It seems like Russia was a bastion of Christendom they could finally admire.

Rabid anti-gay sentiment is a hallmark of all the nations in the Russo-European-American anti-globalist alliance. When Russia passed its anti-gay laws, right-wing groups all over Europe celebrated. In a wave of intimidation, Italian right-wingers put up posters of Putin in a Russian Navy fur hat with the slogan "*Io sto con Putin,*" or "I'm with Putin," all over gay neighborhoods in Rome. Others had a red, white, and blue Russian flag background with the words "Rome is with Putin. Obama is an Unwanted Guest." In Poland, right-wing marchers sang a nationalist song titled "We Want God." The European rallies were universally covered with Christian iconography. American evangelicals ate these rallies up and supported the Russian-backed outreach openly.

Scott Lively, a prolific evangelical anti-gay bigot, wrote of his time in Russia:

"Russia is today experiencing a Christian revival and is decidedly NOT communist. Some 30,000 churches have been built in the last year, and the ones in Moscow are reportedly overflowing with worshippers on Sundays. Most of the church is Orthodox, which is steeped in tradition, but at the same time relevant to the modern society."

He would go on to close with "how incredibly ironic it is that Russia is now our best hope for stopping the conquest of the world by the 'progressives.'"[10]

This was not the first time Lively wrote glowingly of Russia. In 2007, he wrote what his ministry called an Open Letter to the Russian People extolling their Christian spirit. The most noteworthy passage was his prediction that American evangelicals could soon be the next wave of Russian emigrés:

"While the United States and Europe continue to alienate their family-oriented citizens by following the destructive path of 'sexual freedom,' Russia could become a model pro-family society. If this were to occur, I believe people from the West would begin to emigrate to Russia in the same way that Russians used to emigrate to the United States and Europe. Russia might even win back the sympathies of its former states, such as Poland, Latvia and Lithuania, which are now chafing under the pro-homosexual demands of the European Union."[11]

Brian Brown would later be hired as President of the World Congress of Families (WCF), a group designated by the Southern Poverty Law Center as a hate group. They bill themselves as a pro-family, anti-gay organization involved in planning international conferences intended to spread their conservative values. Their deep ties to Moscow are a typical cross-section of Russo-American collaboration in the family values community.

The WCF Director at the time, Larry Jacobs, attended the first Russian Sanctity of Motherhood conference where he asserted, "Russians might be the Christian saviors of the world."[12] Jacobs also ties American-Russian Christianity into a weapon against liberalism. One of his acolytes, Jack Hanick, is a member of their planning committee who works for the Russian propaganda channel Tsargrad television. He is also an associate of Konstantin Malofeev and Aleksandr Dugin's Katehon think tank.[13] Hanick worked for Fox News from 1996 to 2011 as a producer, though he parades himself as a "founding employee" of the network.

Jacobs posited at this Moscow conference: "Russian [and] Eastern European leadership is necessary to counter the secular post-modern anti-family agenda and replace what I'm calling the cultural-Marxist philosophy that is destroying human society and in particular the family."[14]

It should be noted that right-wing Norwegian terrorist and mass-murderer Anders Breivik wrote extensively against liberalism using "cultural-Marxism," a code word for American and European liberal democracy and multiculturalism.

There have been several signs over the last decade that conservatives, specifically evangelicals and NRA gun owners, have demonstrated a significant change of attitude toward America's long-standing foe, Russia. The shift in attitude between the United States and Russia was occurring on many fronts, particularly as the two strategic opponents, President Barack Obama and Vladimir Putin, each ran and won their second terms. In the run-up to the 2012 election, Russia was reaching out to political opponents of Obama. One of the most favorably disposed Congressmen was Dana Rohrabacher (R-Calif.). In his estimation, "There has been a change in the views of hard-core conservatives toward Russia. Conservative Republicans like myself hated communism during the Cold War. But Russia is no longer the Soviet Union."[15] Many Republicans saw Russia as a capitalist society with a decidedly conservative bent that favored them. The mail-order bride business, which started in the 1990s, was still booming and lovely, educated Russian women were available and not indisposed to older men with money. Additionally, the global porn industry had moved away from the San Fernando Valley and right into Moscow. What Republicans previously saw as a nation of brutalist apartment blocks and rusted Lada cars was now a land of rich oligarchs and Mercedes G-Wagens. A dreamland where money could buy you a police escort and all the young women one desired. Their sexy Russian bride, they believed, would be waiting at home with a sparkling house and a martini in hand. It was the fantasy of a white Christian male paradise where everyone wanted to do business as long as the Tsarist motto "Orthodoxy. Autocracy. Nationality." was accepted along with vodka-laced hypocrisy. It was the land of 1950s values and home to the Kalashnikov rifle.

To capitalize on the Russian-Christian bastion, they sponsored these "code" conferences. In December 2015, during the presidential nomination process, Evangelist Franklin Graham, son of famed televangelist Billy Graham, met privately with Vladimir Putin at the Kremlin to discuss Russia's commitment to assist Graham with a "conference on persecution of Christians."[16] From the perspective of a former Russian human intelligence officer like Putin, this community could be easily co-opted. As Franklin Graham said about Putin, "He said he would do all he could from his office to help."[17] The Americans were practically throwing themselves at the Kremlin's feet.

The NRA and Russia

On December 14, 2012, Adam Lanza, a 20-year-old from the village of Newtown, Connecticut, had just murdered his mother with a bolt action Savage .22 rifle. He then took a Bushmaster AR-15-style .223 caliber rifle, loaded it, and took a large quantity of ammunition and drove to the Sandy Hook Elementary School. He entered the school's front door and massacred 20 children and six teachers. The attack stunned the nation. If an elementary school could be the target of an attack, then nowhere was safe. There was a national swell to impose some form of gun control, principally in restricting people with mental health issues from gaining access to guns. President Obama spoke on the matter and called on Congress to take action. This talk set off a national panic, a buying panic by gun owners who, by merely listening to the debate, assumed that America was about to seize or limit the purchase of firearms.

The Sandy Hook massacre occurred just weeks after Obama's electoral victory for his second term. In the five months afterward, 3 million more guns above the usual sales would be sold. Correspondingly, 60 gun owners and 20 children would die from accidental discharges of guns purchased in the same period.

The shooting and firearms world has always been wary of government encroachment into their right to bear arms. Yet it may have been two widely disparate events that gave them the greatest fear and may have moved them to join arms with the unseemliest of allies, the Kremlin of Vladimir Putin: a 1989 school shooting in California and the sanctions imposed against the head of the Russian defense industry in 2014.

In 1989, a shooting at an elementary school in Stockton, California, killed five children and wounded 30. All the victims were from the Asian community. The state of California acted swiftly and banned "assault weapons" or military-style weapons including the AK-47, which was used in the attack, and all AR-15-type weapons. For the gun community, this was a cause for outrage. Their principal complaint was that weapons such as the AK-47 were difficult to make "California legal." There was some logic to the hoops and hurdles the state was using to make guns difficult to own for legal owners, but for Wayne LaPierre, CEO of the National Rifle Association, it was nothing short of Communist tyranny.

In March 2014, President Obama sanctioned the Deputy Prime Minister of Russia and head of the Defense Industry, Dmitry Rogozin, over the Russian invasion of Crimea. The NRA strenuously opposed the sanctions because they believed it would cut off imports of Russian weapons and cheap factory-built AK-47 ammunition.[18] Kalashnikov ammo had already seen its price double from as low as 15 cents per round pre-Sandy Hook, to two to three times that amount afterward. The sanctions would make ammunition and authentic Russian spare parts more expensive. This, just a few months after the death of Mikhail Kalashnikov, was another outrage. The outrage brought about a withering number of articles in magazines such as *American Rifleman*, *Recoil*, *Guns and Ammo*, and *Soldier of Fortune*, all extolling the brilliance of the inventor of the AK-47 and disparaging the new restrictions on getting guns and parts. The glowing hagiography of Kalashnikov and the rise in AK ammo prices made American gun owners look admiringly toward Putin's Russia.

The California ban and the sanctions against Russian leadership, which had little to no effect on parts or ammunition, belied the fact that there were a growing number of Russian firearms classes entering the American shooting sports community. These included new models of Eastern European origin—Kalashnikovs from Bulgaria, the Czech Republic, and Romania, and even manufactured AK-47 variants. Popular in the US now is the Russian Izhmash Saiga-12 shotgun, which is a semiautomatic combat shotgun that can use 12- or 20-round drum magazines. There are also a myriad of Russian hunting shotguns. However, in Russia, virtually all these firearms are prohibited except for the criminals who buy them from the military black market. American shooters were in love with former Soviet weapons and developed an admiration of stereotypical Russian grit in combat. Dana Rohrabacher was right—in the shooting sports industry Russia was no longer the Soviet Union and they opposed liberals, which made them good enough for conservatives.

American admirers of Mikhail Kalashnikov, inventor of the AK-47 class of rifles and machine guns, appear unaware that there were just 6 million civilian-owned weapons in Russia compared to 270 million in America. 4.2 million are shotguns for hunting ducks or birds. Only 700,000 are non-military hunting rifles. The Constitution of the Russian Federation states "…each individual has the right to defend his/her rights and freedoms by all means not prohibited by law."[19] However, all weapons must be purchased and registered with the Russian government. There were no such restrictions on the American Second Amendment, even under President Obama, yet somehow the supporters of the American firearms industry found Russia to be a perfect bedfellow.

Aleksandr Torshin was a former Russian Senator in the upper chamber of the Russian Federal Assembly from 2001 to 2015. After leaving politics, he became the head of the Russian Central Bank. He was also suspected of having been tied to money laundering for the Russian mafia in St. Petersburg, the Taganskaya. In a brilliant exposé by the *Washington Post*, it was discovered that the Russian Federation had deep ties to the NRA. The first link came when Torshin was introduced to David Keene, the former president of the NRA, by G. Kline Preston IV. Preston was a Russian law expert who sported a porcelain bust of Putin in his Nashville office. He has been quoted as saying, "The value system of Southern Christians and the value system of Russians are very much in line."[20]

During the 2012 elections, Torshin came to Nashville accompanied by Preston to observe voting and the election process.[21] This is noteworthy because the American electoral process is well known around the world, but the street-level mechanics are also the most vulnerable. Any intelligence officer or surrogate would want to see it at the retail level to understand how money, politics, and influence affect votes.

Guns and religious evangelism run closely together in the United States. Most evangelicals are Southern and rural. They view guns as a God-given right. Torshin was also active in the Russian Orthodox church's outreach to the United States. He founded an international humanitarian organization, called Saint Sabbas the Presanctified, dedicated to preserving Christian shrines in Muslim-dominated Kosovo and Metohija (Western Kosovo). He was awarded a medal by the Serbian Orthodox church, the Order of Holy King Milutin.[22] That the two most powerful white Christian organizations in the US were brought to see Moscow's point of view would make for the basis of an unstoppable political bloc.

Torshin would set out with his 28-year-old assistant, Maria Butina. According to *Time* magazine, when Torshin recruited the lovely young woman she was a furniture salesperson in Siberia but moved to Moscow in 2011 to set up a pro-gun-rights group called Right to Bear Arms. This was the same time Torshin was publishing a pamphlet called "Guns Don't Kill. People Kill."[23] Butina captured the hearts of American gun enthusiasts in provocative photos. In them she presented sultry photos of herself with Saiga combat shotguns, holding Makarov pistols and standing over a dead boar.

In 2013, they reached out to David Keene and other pro-gun enthusiasts and invited them to come to an annual meeting in Moscow. According to the *Washington Post*, the founder of the US Second Amendment Foundation, Alan Gottlieb, and his wife attended this annual meeting in Russia. They said that Torshin and Butina presented them with gifts specific to their individual interests.[24] In April 2015, Butina and Torshin were invited to tour NRA headquarters in Fairfax, Virginia. They both attended the NRA National Convention and were introduced to Wisconsin Governor and presidential candidate Scott Walker.[25]

The ties to Donald Trump took a leap when MSNBC reported that Torshin sat with Donald Trump Jr. at the NRA convention during Donald Trump Sr.'s speech. Junior, along with his brother Eric, fancied themselves big trophy hunters. Donald Jr. was an enthusiast of large-caliber guns. Torshin told Bloomberg News he had a "friendly exchange with Trump [Jr.]." The Russian connections with the Trump campaign grew.[26]

In July 2015, a month after Donald Trump announced his candidacy for president, at the FreedomFest conference in Las Vegas, Maria Butina was the first to publicly ask Trump about US-Russia relations. "If you are to be president what is your foreign politics [especially in] the relationships with my country and do you want to continue the politics of sanctions that are damaging both [economies]?"[27] His response was, "I know Putin, and I'll tell you what, we get along with Putin."[28] She quickly tweeted in Russian: "Asked US presidential candidate Donald Trump about the position with respect to Russia. Trump talks about the easing of sanctions."[29]

Soon after that, the NRA donated as much as $30 million to Trump—triple the amount it gave Mitt Romney.[30]

The ties only increased as Trump started to become the sure frontrunner. In 2016, the NRA would send a delegation to Russia to meet with Dmitry Rogozin, the Deputy Prime Minister of Russia, and tour his Russian Shooting Federation headquarters. The attendees included David Keene, Milwaukee County Sheriff David Clarke, NRA leading donor Joe Gregory, and board member Peter Brownell, owner of the biggest online gun shop in America, Brownells.[31]

The young, beautiful Butina had many friends in the shooting sports industry. One, conservative operative Paul Erickson, befriended her and set up an LLC in his home state of South Dakota for her. He claims it was set up in case Butina, who was attending the American University graduate school, needed funding for classes. Erickson had met Butina and Torshin with David Keene at the Right to Bear Arms conference in Moscow.[32] Before May 2016, Erickson sent an email to Trump aide Rick Dearborn and Senator Jeff Sessions with the subject line: "Kremlin Connection." The email stated that he wanted to work out how to coordinate a meeting between Trump and Putin during the campaign.

> "Putin is deadly serious about building a good relationship with Mr. Trump....He wants to extend an invitation to Mr. Trump to visit him in the Kremlin before the election. Let's talk through what has transpired and Senator Sessions' advice on how to proceed."[33]

Moscow's long-range sniper shot using the gun industry had hit its mark. With Erickson's email, it was clear Russia's influence on the Trump campaign was paying off.

In August 2016, Spanish prosecutors sought the arrest of Torshin on money laundering charges. The Spanish Guardia Civil, the investigative paramilitary police, have 33 audio recordings of Torshin and Alexander Romanov plotting to launder 15 million euros through a hotel in Mallorca for the Taganskaya mafia gang. Romanov was convicted in Russia and sentenced to 4 years for money laundering. In the audio clips, Romanov refers to Torshin when he says, "the boss himself cannot buy the hotel, because he is a civil servant" and "godfather."[34] Torshin was supposed to be en route to Mallorca for further meetings when the Guardia Civil prosecutors were waiting with a 12-man team to arrest him. At the last minute, Torshin canceled his trip, as the Prosecutor General of Russia likely warned him that he was to be arrested.[35]

After Trump's election, Butina and Torshin attended Trump's first National Prayer Breakfast in D.C. As part of his evangelical outreach, Torshin had created a similar but monthly Prayer Breakfast in Russia. To get more American and European conservatives to attend, he made it an annual event.[36] Every year Vladimir Putin sends a greeting to the Russian event, a recognition of its value in allowing "Russian and American guests to come together under one roof in order to rebuild the relationship between the two countries that has degraded under the administration of President Obama."[37]

With Trump in the White House, Torshin was now one of the Russian point men in the Washington circles. He had successfully managed to link all branches of the American evangelical gun-owning right and Republican Party leadership with Moscow through bibles and guns. However, his star would burn out fast. Torshin was scheduled to meet with Trump at the National Prayer Breakfast but reports say the White House canceled the meeting when reports emerged from Spanish authorities that Torshin was wanted on connections to organized crime.[38]

The "Clenched Fist of Truth"

Once the presidency came under serious investigation by the Justice Department in 2017, the NRA created a series of web videos essentially threatening the potential for violence toward just about everyone who opposed Trump. Their spokesperson was Dana Loesch, a former writer and editor at Breitbart News, who had also worked on Glenn Beck's *TheBlaze*, a predecessor to Breitbart News. The NRA decided to take a page from the Russian playbook and stoke up tensions. The videos were designed to threaten the news media and the Democratic Party with gun-owning opponents. In the first video, titled "Freedom's Safest Place—Violence of Lies," she warned, "They use their media to assassinate real news, their schools to teach children that our President is another 'Hitler,' and they use their ex-President to endorse the 'resistance.' The only way we save our country and our freedom is to fight the left's violence of lies with the clenched fist of truth."

In a second video, titled "The Ultimate Insult," Loesch spelled out that the NRA is prepared to defend Trump's calumnies and made claims that the FBI, the Democratic Party, and the 65% of Americans who oppose him, are the real enemies of America.

> "These saboteurs, slashing away with their leaks and sneers, their phony accusations and gagging sanctimony, drive their daggers through the heart of our future, poisoning our belief that honest custody of our institutions will ever again be possible."

The NRA-Russian money cat would be out of the bag on January 18, 2018, when McClatchy news reported that the FBI was investigating Russian money ties to the NRA for the Trump campaign.[39] The NRA had funneled what was known to be $30 million to the Trump campaign but whispers that this number could be as high as $70 million, including contributions from Russian oligarchs, pro-Moscow businessmen, and the Kremlin itself, were now going to be spotlighted.

There were early hints through good news reporting that the FBI was on the Russian money trail for the Trump campaign through the NRA from as far back as 2015. In November 2016, Fusion GPS co-founder Glenn Simpson testified before the House Intelligence Committee. He told them he believed there was a "crime in progress" between the Kremlin and the NRA:

> "It appears as though the Russians, you know, infiltrated the NRA. And there is more than one explanation for why. But [it] appears the Russian operation was designed to infiltrate conservative organizations. And they targeted various conservative organizations, religious and otherwise, and they seemed to make a concerted effort to get in with the NRA."[40]

On February 28, 2017, President Trump signed legislation known as H.J. Resolution 40 that made it easier for the mentally ill to acquire guns.[41] One year later on February 14, 2018, Nikolas Cruz, a 19-year-old former student, entered Marjorie Stoneman Douglas High School and killed 17 students. He used an AR-15 rifle. Five of the seventeen victims were Jewish, and according to Rabbi Bradd Boxman at Kol Tivkah, a "huge number" of congregants attended the school.[42] Other victims were ethnic minorities, including one student of Asian descent.

Like clockwork Russian bots from the Internet Research Agency (RF-IRA) spewed out tens of thousands of anti–gun control tweets. They posted articles and lies demonizing the dead, the wounded student victims, and their parents who spoke out against guns. In one instance, mentions of an outspoken surviving student David Hogg had a 3,000% increase on Russian bot networks. The bot messages claimed he was not a student but a "crisis actor"—a conspiracy theory advanced by Alex Jones at InfoWars that there were no victims but actors claiming tragedies to force the seizure of guns. Other RF-IRA bots introduced the fake news narrative that the shooter was a member of the ultra-left anti-fascist activists (Antifa) and not a White Supremacist.

The NRA's Wayne LaPierre went on the attack simultaneously with the Russians. At the 2018 Conservative Political Action Committee convention days after the shooting, LaPierre said: "Their goal is to eliminate the second amendment and our firearms freedoms, so they can eradicate all individual freedoms. . . . They hate the NRA, they hate the second amendment, they hate individual freedom."

It should be noted this is the leader of an American group, who has Russian intelligence information warfare agencies broadcasting and defending his words from a country which does not have firearms freedom, led by an ex-KGB officer who is advised by a cabal of ex-KGB officers. What they have as a common cause is Putin's chosen leader—Donald Trump.

While the Americans were blind, the Spanish government was not. Spain could clearly see that Torshin was Moscow's man. The Spanish Prosecutor General's indictment against Torshin stated bluntly:

"The criminal organizations from the countries of the East have as their main characteristics the penetration of different state powers, such as politics, which is represented in this case by the figure of the First Vice-chairman of the Federation Council of the Federal Assembly of the Russian Federation, Alexander Porfirievich Torshin."[43]

On December 15, 2017, the *Dallas News* unveiled a blockbuster report on deep ties between Russian donors and high-ranking officials of the Republican Party. Author Ruth May penned this opening explanation:

"Buried in the campaign finance reports available to the public are some troubling connections between a group of wealthy donors with ties to Russia and their political contributions to President Donald Trump and a number of top Republican leaders. And thanks to changes in campaign finance laws, the political contributions are legal. We have allowed our campaign finance laws to become a strategic threat to our country."[44]

Campaign finance reports show numerous Russian donors to Trump and the Republicans including Len Blavatnik, a dual US/UK citizen who was one of the top donors in the 2016 campaign. Considered the wealthiest man in the UK—net worth $20 billion—who, according to the Federal Election Commission (FEC) data, donated a combined $462,552 between 2009 and 2014. In 2015, he donated $6.5 million to GOP Action Committees including millions to Mitch McConnell, Marco Rubio, and Lindsey Graham.[45] After Trump's win, his holding company would donate $1 million from Access Industries to President Donald Trump's Inaugural Committee. An Access Industries spokesperson stated the donation did not represent support for Trump.[46]

Rep. Adam Schiff (D-Calif.), the ranking Democratic leader on the House Intelligence Committee, told ABC News: "Unless the contributions were directed by a foreigner, they would be legal, but could still be of interest to investigators examining allegations of Russian influence on the 2016 campaign. Obviously, if there were those that had associations with the Kremlin that were contributing, that would be of keen concern."[47]

Other donors include Andrew Intrater and Alexander Shustorovich, the chief executive of IMG Artists, who donated $1 million to Trump's Inaugural Committee.[48] He had a $250,000 donation rejected by the George W. Bush campaign due to ties with the Russian government.[49] Simon Kukes, a Russian-born US citizen and oil magnate who was made CEO of Yukos after it was seized from Putin critic Mikhail Khodorkovsky, was also a major donor.[50] According to the *Dallas News*, in just one election cycle Blavatnik, Intrater, Shustorovich, and Kukes donated $10.4 million, with 99% going to Republicans.[51]

A word of caution: There is absolutely nothing wrong with American citizens donating money to political campaigns and political action committees for the purpose of winning elections and having their concerns and issues heard. That is the system we want to protect. The issue at hand is the fact the Republican Party vehemently denies that there is any contact with Russia, Russian interests, or people associated with the Russian government. Those denials are clearly inoperative.

Former Republican Congressman Joe Scarborough wrote an op-ed in frustration, "As a storm gathers over Washington and the world, Donald Trump's Republican Party remains complicit in his frenzied efforts to undermine the American institutions and established values that conservatives once claimed to share."[52] How did this happen? Was it just a matter of money?

It would be Paul Erickson, friend of Maria Butina and one of numerous Americans who tried to engineer a meeting between Putin and Trump, who would succinctly explain what was happening to the party of Ronald Reagan's hard-line anti-Communism. He told *Time* magazine, "There is a huge school within the conservative movement and the Republican Party that says you can't look at these people through the same lens of the Cold War."[53] Now that Russia had money, supported the Second Amendment, and loved the same Jesus, they were allies to be protected. The overwhelming body of evidence indicates Putin tasked Russian intelligence agencies to support whatever conservative cause was supported by Trump, including evangelicals and now a fifth column—the "Alternative Right."

CHAPTER 13

The American Fifth Column

I f chaos was the new normal in the United States after the disman-
tling of the Soviet Union, then the world standing of the United
States as a global power was greatly diminished at the end of 2016.
To those who saw the power and prestige of the Shining City on a Hill
waning, the Alternative Right (alt-right) movement was joyful that the
242-year American experiment was finally going to fail.

As the conservative movement grew stronger within the United
States, they pushed the traditional Republican platform off the cliff.
Gone were the days when balanced budgets and personal responsibility
were the party's hallmark. The party started to shift with Russia's assistance. The Republicans became more concerned with white grievance
like their European brethren. And like their cousins overseas, the alt-
right appeared to relish doing the work of the Kremlin in the same way
that the European Nationalists were aligning themselves with the United
Russia Party. Aleksandr Dugin cheered the rise of this new conservative
movement, "Out of the shadows has emerged a second America."[1]

Many European Nationalists, especially in Eastern Europe, have
used the internal systems of democracy to create chaos with endless
debates on austerity, blaming gypsies for societal ills, and scapegoat-
ing all non-whites and foreigners not of European descent. Alt-right
Americans are no different. Countries ranking lowest on the Democracy Index or nearing the gamut of flawed democracies have entered

such debates unwittingly and almost never emerge unscathed. American disunity and diminishment of global standing were the pinnacles of Vladimir Putin's wish list.

Alt-right is a short name for "Alternative Right." It is considered a "moderating" umbrella term for the white right-wing conservatives including neo-Nazis and others who view white supremacy and ethno-nationalist tribalism as natural. Though there are many wings of the alt-right, the most outspoken are the Ku Klux Klan and the American neo-Nazis. Nazi leader Richard Spencer believed that "White People need to be just as activist as Black People." A self-proclaimed White Nationalist, Spencer is the freshly shaved, clean-cut, baby face preppy image of the alt-right. Others, like Mike Tokes, co-founder of The New Right, are the tough New Right competition. Spencer believed that diversity was against white identity instead of being inclusive of everyone. Richard Spencer and the alt-right were against AIPAC, most Jews and Muslims, and against political correctness, feminism, and immigration from third-world countries.

The goal of the alt-right is to bring White Supremacist and neo-Nazi ideology together with bigotry, racism, and xenophobia, but with a milder, kinder image. When they march they wear polo shirts and khaki pants. They project that they are normal and that it is both masculine and chic to be a gentleman race hater. A strange version of this is Breitbart writer Milo Yiannopoulos. He is an unabashed English gay man who constantly brags of his well-endowed black male lovers. However, he spews the most incredible racism and misogyny. To claim that the alt-right had diverse white men who are gay and cavort with blacks made him a superstar on Twitter with well over a million followers. He was eventually banned for harassing African American actress Leslie Jones and has been banned from speaking on many college campuses. However, he acts as a protest touchstone because when his speeches are shut down, alt-righters prepare to start riots with the opponents.

The father of the alt-right is Trump Presidential Campaign CEO and former Trump Presidential Advisor Steve Bannon. He credited Breitbart, the online web news channel for extremist youth, as being their natural home and "the voice of the alt-right."

Younger conservatives are generally referred to as the New Right. Traditionalist worthies include the late William F. Buckley Jr., Barry Goldwater, Phyllis Schlafly, and President Ronald Reagan. Until Donald Trump, they and their college republican wing, Young Americans for Freedom, represented old-school conservatism at its finest. They formed in the 1950s and did not believe that skin color was the defining issue for conservatism—those were tax cuts and national defense. Mike Tokes, a young YouTube champion of the tie-wearing tribe, stated that "White people are the majority and to reject people based on skin color is wrong." Others who make up the main force of the alt-right are not so altruistic or liberal. They are represented by some of the most hated groups in American history.

After the Civil War, ex-Confederate officers founded a white terror group called the Ku Klux Klan during the Reconstruction era as a way to intimidate freed blacks. As democracy in the South was under construction by White Union Republicans (today's Democrats), organizations like the Klan were designed to ensure that Southern resistance to black progress never faded. The Ulysses S. Grant Administration eradicated the Ku Klux Klan in the 1870s, but they resurfaced nostalgically in 1915 with the help of D.W. Griffith's silent film *The Birth of a Nation*. By the 1920s and 30s the Klan had progressed to the point of being nearly mainstream as a fraternal social club, displaying vehement xenophobic hatred toward Catholics, Jews, and foreigners, in addition to their hostility toward African Americans and Civil Rights movements later in the 1950s and 60s. Currently, David Duke stands at the helm of the KKK despite being a "retired KKK wizard." Duke states that he does not support violence, yet his hate speech incites riots and validates the lack of social conscience for many of his followers, who view him as financially successful and, therefore, stable.

Neo-Confederates long for the days of traditional, yet archaic, race and gender roles. In that ethnocentric, White Supremacist fantasy world, there is a longing for an historical revival of the days of slavery or the Reconstruction era, where emancipated slaves had rights but could only partake in the possibility of a meager constitutional democracy as "Americans." This historical narrative is what distinguishes the Neo-Confederates from all other far-right racists. Klansmen like David Duke feel inferior in the present day and strive to conquer by their own outdated terms, submerged in futile nostalgia.

White Supremacists, also known as White Nationalists, believe that they are biologically superior due to their European blood, which they consider the highest pedigree. White Supremacists gravitate toward genealogical evidence. They do not wish to remove multicultural societies because they feel that they are at the top of the hierarchy and enjoy the privilege of being white. White Nationalists believe that they are genetically superior to minorities and so believe in a white ethno-state devoid of other cultures.

Neo-Nazis, like the original Nazis, hate Jews, non-whites, people with disabilities, and LGBT people. Neo-Nazis appeared in the United States after WWII as WUFENS (World Union of Free Enterprise National Socialists), founded by George Lincoln Rockwell in 1959, who later renamed it the ANP (American Nazi Party), hoping to attract more followers. In 1967, George Rockwell was assassinated after changing the name of the American Nazi Party to the National Socialist White People's Party (NSWPP), which alienated even more followers—as they were misperceived as Socialist. After the assassination of George Rockwell, the name changed back to the American Nazi Party.

Comprised of several different factions of WUFENS, the American Nazi Party is now headquartered in Arlington, Virginia, and although current neo-Nazi support is low, there are more right-wing terrorist organizations in the US than left-wing terrorist organizations, according to the Southern Poverty Law Center.

One very dangerous neo-Nazi paramilitary group, known as Atomwaffen Division, was founded in 2015 by Brandon Russell in Tampa, Florida. The name *Atomwaffen* means atomic weapons in German. It boasts over 80 members in 2018. Russell was arrested by the FBI and the Tampa Police Department when they found explosive devices made with hexamethylene triperoxide diamine, and the radioactive compounds thorium and americium, in his garage. Other members of Atomwaffen include Devon Arthurs, a man who considered the 2016 Orlando shooter at Pulse Nightclub a hero and later converted to Islam.

In May 2017, he murdered two Atomwaffen members and was arrested after a hostage barricade. Vinlanders Social Club, founded in 2003, is a large skinhead gang with their highest enrollment numbers in Arizona and Indiana. Their enrollment has decreased in Minnesota according to the SPLC.[2]

The Charlottesville Riots

Even after the election of Donald Trump there was no unifying organization or event to mark the coming out of the new American power base in the extremist world. That would be corrected when all wings of the alt-right showed up to make a demonstration of power at the Unite the Right rally in Charlottesville, Virginia. The rally was scheduled for Saturday, August 12, 2017. It was billed as a national unifying event and as a protest of the removal of Confederate statues across the South. This theme brought together all branches of the white right. They were making their stand at the scheduled removal of the Robert E. Lee statue in Charlottesville, home of Thomas Jefferson's Monticello and his educational legacy, the University of Virginia. The SPLC summarized the motivations of the protesters' leadership—like in Europe, they originated in Russia:

> "...unabashed in its open admiration of Russia's authoritarian strongman president, Vladimir Putin, and the nationalist agenda he has promoted both in Europe and in the United States. A number of alt-right figures [have] well-documented connections to the Russian regime, which also has played a major role in underwriting far-right movements in Europe. It later emerged after the 2016 election that Russia's propaganda machine had a powerfully symbiotic relationship with the alt-right in spreading its ideology and memes through social media during the campaign."[3]

The protests started after a cryptic text message from neo-Nazi leader Richard Spencer on Friday, August 11, 2017. The text stated "I'd be near campus tonight, if I were you. After 9 p.m. Nameless field."[4] The alt-right had congregated to protest in Charlottesville, but they had come armed for a race war. They were a hot-headed mix of white America's rebellion against the establishment's vision of a diverse democracy. At 9 p.m. hundreds of khaki-wearing, white polo–shirted White Supremacist protesters lined up in two-by-two formation, carrying tiki torches and chanting "White Lives Matter," "Jews will not replace us," "You will not replace us," and interestingly "Russia is our friend!"[5] Some included English renditions of Nazi Germany's most fervent chant "Blood and Soil." But the most noteworthy was the oft-repeated "Hail Trump!" Black and white students surrounded the statue of Robert E. Lee to counter the nighttime protest. The fuse was lit. The protest died overnight but the next morning by 11 a.m., the alt-right would fill the protest route that was supposed to start at 5 p.m.

The right-wing extremists had been coordinating with German and other European White Supremacists using the Discord chat app on their phones. The Europeans gave them pointers on equipment and riot tactics. The alt-right came armed with "legal" weapons. Flagpoles were thick and solid because they were really designed to be clubs. Somehow the police allowed plastic riot shields. Many wooden and Plexiglas shields were decorated to look like Norse warrior rune symbols. Many alt-righters view Viking and Celtic medieval symbols, from braided beards to horned helmets, as part of their own legacy. Others brought more traditional weapons such as pepper spray, and an armed contingent walked boldly with AR-15 assault rifles and pistols.

At 11 a.m. the dam broke. The White Supremacist marchers formed ranks and charged the opposition protesters. Widespread violence broke out. Bottles, pepper spray, and rocks flew. In one instance, a concealed firearm was shot at protesters in the thick of the fight while police stood aside and watched for about 30 minutes. At 11:22, the police broke up the two sides but running fights continued throughout the day. The violence took an ominous turn at 1:22 p.m., when a car driven by James Fields Jr., a 20-year-old member of the White Nationalist group Vanguard America, drove at high speed down a street and directly into a crowd of student protesters. He backed up and drove back through them to escape. When the attack was over, a young paralegal named Heather Heyer lay crushed to death and 19 others were seriously injured.[6] Fields was quickly found and arrested. When interviewed, he stated "he was scared" and drove through the crowd to escape, but the police chief said at the official press conference that the death of Heather Heyer was not an accident but a planned attack.

Outrage at the alt-right and their violence burned across the nation. Politicians of all sides condemned the violence, but when Donald Trump was asked about it, he spent an inordinate amount of time blaming the anti-fascist resistance Antifa. When pressed, Trump summed it up as "there are very fine people on both sides." He could not understand why people were furious at that remark. The Ku Klux Klan and neo-Nazis were delighted. The alt-right understood that Trump stood on their side.

As right-wing organizations throughout Europe were forming their alliances, the far-right nationalists in America were also being fueled by Russian ethno-state propagandists. It helped to have a newly elected President align himself with these racist groups. Their rise and his narcissism led to the elite of America being believers in the white genocide conspiracy theories. With Trump's Twitter feed active, these xenophobic views were becoming part of the mainstream media dialogue in America. The alt-right and mainstream Republicans adopted the European-Russian mantra of hatred toward immigrants. For years, Republicans had used the false belief that immigration from Mexico was the reason why Americans were jobless. But this was different. The organizer of the Charlottesville protest, Jason Kessler, had a BA degree in psychology from the University of Virginia. He had held a myriad of low-paying jobs including as a dishwasher, gym technician, truck driver, and handyman. Kessler was also a failed poet, novelist, screenwriter, and journalist. The rally attracted people like him—members of the KKK, American neo-Nazis, neo-Confederates, White Supremacists, White Nationalists, neo-Paganists, and alt-right followers. The biggest organizations that participated included:

- Traditionalist Worker Party
- Ku Klux Klan
- Vanguard America

- League of the South
- Identity Europa
- Proud Boys[7]

Why was the rally called? Matthew Heimbach and Jason Kessler of the Unite the Right Rally convinced themselves that "white genocide" was occurring. They believed wholeheartedly in the conspiracy theory propagated by White Supremacists that natural foreign immigration and the ability of white women to have abortions are plots by Jews and the superrich to snuff out the white race. The ACLU had facilitated Kessler's right to hold the rally because of his First Amendment constitutional right to free speech. Heimbach convinced his fellow members of the Traditionalist Worker Party to participate and be ready to attack counterprotesters.[8]

One of Trump's biggest fans was the former Grand Wizard of the Ku Klux Klan, David Duke. Duke often tried to bring his racism to the political arena starting in 1975, when he ran for Louisiana Senate and again in 1979. He ran for President in 1988 and 1992, first as a Democrat, then as a Republican. He successfully ran for a seat in the Louisiana State House of Representatives in 1988 and served from 1989 to 1992. He ran for a seat as US Senator for Louisiana in 1990 as a Republican against J. Bennett Johnston Jr. and lost. This was followed by a run for Governor of Louisiana in 1991. Duke lost again. In 1992, he ran again for US Senate and came in fourth in the primaries, but the election ultimately saw the victory go to Mary Landrieu. He ran again in 1999 for a seat in the US House of Representatives but lost. He ran again in 2016 for US Senator from Louisiana but barely received 3% of the vote in a race that was won by Republican candidate John Neely Kennedy.

On November 16, 2000, David Duke's home in Louisiana was searched by the FBI while he was in Russia. The FBI search warrant was based on information received that political donors were concerned that funds were gambled in casinos and used to fix up his home. Duke had been accused for years of pocketing money from supporters. Ultimately, he was charged for tax fraud and sentenced to prison and fines for back taxes.

Duke turned to Europe for acceptance—as America increasingly rebuked racists. He found allies around Europe and was given a doctorate from a Ukrainian university, the Interregional Academy of Personnel Management, reputed for its promotion of anti-Semitism.[9] Despite the appearance of a degree, the institution has no accreditation. This didn't stop Duke from teaching anti-Semitism there as "Dr. David Duke, PhD."

Duke has a fondness for Russia and has proclaimed, "In my opinion, Russia and other Eastern countries have the greatest chance of having racially aware parties achieving political power."[10] Russia loves him back. In fact, Duke's book *The Ultimate Supremacism: My Awakening on the Jewish Question* was for sale at the Duma in Russia for $2.00.[11] Duke owned a condo in Russia that he rented out to a fellow White Supremacist Preston Wiginton,[12] who was, according to the Southern Poverty Law Center, "a key white power activist in Russia and the US."[13]

Duke was not the only Russia-loving racist in the South. Sam Dickson, a wealthy White Supremacist lawyer in Atlanta who wrote about Abraham Lincoln being both a "myth" and a "demagogue," was a passionate admirer of Vladimir Putin.[14] Dickson had a reputation for bullying African Americans into undesirable real estate transactions, along with defending White Supremacist and White Nationalist individuals and groups.[15] In 2015, he gave a speech at a Rodina (aka Motherland) Party conference of the worldwide White Nationalists network in St. Petersburg, titled "International Russian Conservative Forum." He ended his speech with "God save the Czar." Dickson possessed a very romantic view of Russia, which could also be attributed to his longtime admiration and association with David Duke. Dickson said, "I admire the Russian people. They are the strongest white people on earth."[16]

Dickson's website had a 2017 Easter Message in which he spoke of the history of Moscow's Cathedral of Christ the Saviour and how it had been destroyed by "Bolsheviks" (what many White Supremacists view as liberal Jews and minorities that they accuse of controlling the media). Dickson described how the poor, after the collapse of the Soviet Union, funded the restoration as the first church to be rebuilt in Russia. He wrote in his blog:

"How I wish the White Russians I knew in my youth in Atlanta could have lived to have seen the day when the Head of State in Russia would attend Easter ceremonies in this shrine! Happy Easter! We can rejoice that Lenin's work like his projected shrine and statue are gone."[17]

Preston Wiginton is a neo-Nazi who believes Russia is "the only nation that understands RAHOWA," or the racial holy war. He leases David Duke's apartment in Moscow.[18] Wiginton has been allied with Russian radicals like Alexander Belov of the anti-Semitic Pamyat group,[19] Wiginton romanticized Russia's white ethno-state and was known for inviting Russian ultranationalist Aleksandr Dugin to Texas A&M University in April 2015, after the United States government had imposed sanctions on Dugin. The lecture was titled "American Liberalism Must Be Destroyed: Insights from Professor Aleksandr Dugin, Kremlin Insider and Informal Adviser to President Putin." Seventeen people attended.

It is worth noting that the same conference organized by the nationalist Russian party known as Rodina was attended not only by Sam Dickson and Preston Wiginton but also by Matthew Heimbach, Jared Taylor, and David Duke, and amounted to approximately "150 far-right leaders from the United States, Russia, and Western Europe, including politicians linked to neo-Nazi, anti-Semitic, and xenophobic views." It was a remarkably successful joint international effort by Russia to discredit the United States and other Western nations for their position on the annexation of Crimea and the Kremlin's subsequent attempt at Christian traditional values propaganda.[20] Wiginton takes a dramatic view toward Moscow: "Russia is under third world invasion. Luckily Russia is the only nation that understands RAHOWA.... Because of this immigrants [sic] think twice about coming to Russia."[21]

Wiginton likely moved to Moscow in late 2006, when Stormfront moved its server to Russia after Google dismantled it. It was there that he met Aleksandr Belov, who runs the Movement Against Illegal Immigration, a group well traveled by several far-right masterminds: Wiginton, Duke, Heimbach, Taylor, Spencer, and the nearly 200 other far-right Americans who attended the International Russian Conservative Forum. In the spring of 2007, Wiginton returned to America to protest the possibility of the African American Presidential candidate, Barack Obama. He hosted a series of lectures by White Nationalists and

White Supremacists, co-sponsored by the CCC (Council of Conservative Citizens, a racist think tank). One of the lecturers at Clemson University (which actually gave this racist initiative its blessing), the chairman of the BNP (British National Party—known for harboring Holocaust deniers) Nick Griffin, showed up to lecture not only at Clemson but also at Texas A&M. He subsequently traveled to Michigan State University to lecture MSU's Young Americans for Freedom (who had sponsored that leg of Nick Griffin's tour) on October 26.[22] Wiginton often encouraged White Nationalists to find Russian women as wives and to avoid Americans: "Real Russian women, not half-breeds or Jews, want real Russian men."[23]

Jared Taylor is the leader of right-wing extremist group New Century Foundation, and founder of the White Supremacist magazine, *American Renaissance*. He claims he created the phrase "alt-right," but whether he did or not he is still a hardcore White Nationalist who has tried to normalize his extreme racism through pseudo-science. Taylor is a Yale University graduate with a degree in philosophy. He describes himself as a "racial realist" like his former colleagues at the National Policy Institute, an organization founded by William Regnery II and led by Richard Spencer.

As with other racists in the West, Taylor has found a home in Russian support. Jared Taylor was not only invited to the International Russian Conservative Forum organized by Rodina leader, Aleksey Zhuravlyov, the *Wall Street Journal* reported that his travel and lodging were also paid for by the organizers.[24] Taylor told his Russian audience of the "American disease" of multicultural integration.[25] Taylor claims on the American Renaissance site that Russia and the United States have never fought a war against each other, which fails to see the amount of blood spilled in proxy wars and the century of spying and active measures.

Notably, he used his role to conduct robocalls on behalf of Donald Trump in the 2016 election.[26] And while some campaigns can't control who may advocate for them, Taylor was validated when he was retweeted by Trump before Twitter suspended Taylor's account.[27]

Taylor called the United States "the greatest enemy of tradition everywhere."[28] He has said that "There is a worldwide awakening of nationalism among European countries—and I include the United States in that."[29]

WHITE NATIONALIST MATTHEW Heimbach was active in trying to make his racist views go mainstream for several years before he became well known for his role in the Unite the Right rally in Charlottesville. Heimbach founded the White Student Union at Towson University, where he also created a chapter of the Youth for Western Civilization in 2011.[30] Heimbach and Matt Parrott, Heimbach's father-in-law, founded the Traditionalist Youth Network (TYN) in May 2013. The TYN also opened a chapter in Bloomington, Indiana, at Indiana University under the leadership of Thomas Buhls.[31] Heimbach was training director of the League of the South group, a neo-Confederate group, beginning in late 2014. The primary group associated with Heimbach is the Traditionalist Worker Party (TWP), which he founded with Parrot and Tony Hovater in January 2015. In 2017, Matthew Heimbach's group notoriously attended the Charlottesville rally. The group joined the Nationalist Front, a coalition of White Nationalists and neo-Nazis, on April 22, 2016. Other members are the National Socialist Movement, League of the South, and Vanguard America. The Nationalist Front was responsible for the October 2017 rally called "White Lives Matter" in Murfreesboro and Shelbyville, Tennessee.

Heimbach believes he is part of a counter-revolutionary effort in that the Western dynamic has been successfully overtaken by a revolution that displaced God, traditional values, and, most importantly, white power. Further, he believes that his group's views are not crazy, fringe, or extreme. However, he's also been spreading messages like, "the Jew does not care if you're pagan. The Jew does not care if you're Christian. The Jew does not care if you are a national socialist or a libertarian because they want to destroy us all."[32]

Matthew Heimbach shared this same Putinesque worldview. He had praised Putin as the best European leader of the 21st century.[33] Heimbach said that Russia under Putin became "kind of the axis of nationalists." Heimbach said, "I really believe that Russia is the leader of the free world right now," in an interview with *Business Insider*. He said that Putin was "supporting nationalists around the world and building an anti-globalist alliance, while promoting traditional values and self-determination."[34] To Heimbach, this is a battle he wants to take to the global stage in his war against "globalism." Heimbach compares the modern nationalism drive from Russia to the Comintern and sees it as an opportunity for racists around the world to unite through networks of nationalism. This would include moral support, financial support, aligned actions, and breeding to expand the size of the movement. Echoing the language of the former Soviets, "see what our comrades are doing around the world," he once preached to a small audience of supporters.

Heimbach says he sees Putin as leader of the free world and Russia as "our biggest inspiration."[35] "The Cold War is over. The Soviet Union has fallen and now Russia has become the bastion of traditionalism, of nationalism, and Christianity," and that it was important for American nationalists to align themselves with Russia against the United States. In Heimbach's view, the globalist evil of the world comes from Washington, D.C., Brussels, and Tel Aviv. To Heimbach, the battle is globalism versus nationalists.

He associated himself with racist groups around Europe like Golden Dawn and with neo-Eurasianist Aleksandr Dugin. Quoting Dugin, who once said, "If you support globalism, you are my enemy," Heimbach said, "Globalism is the poison, nationalism is the antidote."[36]

To Heimbach, "America is the problem." America is the Roman Empire and the nationalists are "the new barbarians." "By flying the American flag, by supporting generic American nationalism, you're actually waving the flag of the regime that wants to destroy you." Dugin even sent Heimbach a video speech for one of his meetings launching the Traditional Worker Party, called "To My American Friends in Our Common Struggle."[37] On his honeymoon, Heimbach met with Golden Dawn, the Czech Workers Party, and Romania's New Right. He's a member of the World National Conservative Movement, a Russian-created group aligned with the Russian Rodina Party and the Russian

Imperial Movement. According to the *New York Times*, by December 2016, Heimbach had had three trips to Europe for fundraising and organizing strategies.[38] He said his visits taught him how to turn his movement into "a real political force" that would be part of a worldwide network. Heimbach said, "Russia has already taken its place on the global stage by organizing national movements as counterparts to the Atlanticist elites," which is a full echo statement of Aleksandr Dugin. "Intellectually, they've shown us how it works."[39]

"The internet is the greatest thing given to our movement," said Heimbach, but he expressed that it should ultimately lead to meeting others, planning actions, and taking efforts "to the streets" as he saw in Europe when he went to visit Golden Dawn and as he sees in the success of anti-racist groups like Black Lives Matter.[40]

Heimbach lays out his plans to followers who will listen, essentially presenting them a plan that reads as follows:

- Find aligned people for his movement
- Use propaganda on the street and internet
- Move to the same general area

White Nationalists need to reach out to women since the movement has been dominated by males. Yet he believes women should be taught modesty by men, and to promote virtue and honor to reject the "American slut culture." Heimbach teaches the need of "cultural secession" to return to traditional values. He says the new racists will not ask for permission and they will not ask for forgiveness. "Their agenda is to make us all slaves on the international plantation." He believed that his peers should protest anti-racist activist Tim Wise. "We shall never betray our patrimony," he said defiantly.

RICHARD SPENCER HARDLY matches the profile of a downtrodden white American male. Instead, he was born into a wealthy family and sent to the finest schools. As a White Supremacy advocate,

Spencer runs a White Nationalist institute with the goal of "peaceful ethnic cleansing" via policy positions, but not all White Nationalists are nonviolent in achieving their objectives. He became president of the National Policy Institute, created by William Regnery II in 2005. Regnery is the financial backer of Richard Spencer.[41]

After quitting Duke University as a PhD student, Spencer began working to spread his extremist views. First, he worked for *American Conservative* magazine, becoming an editor in 2007, but he was fired by Scott McConnell for being "a bit extreme for us."[42] He then went on to work for *Taki's Magazine* in 2008. He founded the website AlternativeRight.com in 2010, the foundation of the term "alt-right," according to Spencer. In 2011, he was hired as executive director of the Washington Summit Publishers (WSP), a White Nationalist publisher created by Louis Andrews in 2006.[43] The WSP published articles by notable racists like American psychologist Kevin MacDonald, White Nationalist Samuel Francis, British psychologist Richard Lynn, Finnish politician/professor Tatu Vanhanen, and white separatist Michael Hart. WSP published Spencer's *Radix Journal*, beginning in 2012.

Days before the election of Donald Trump, on Martin Luther King Jr.'s birthday, Spencer launched a new website dedicated to the alt-right audience, AltRight.com. It was an outlet that featured the works of notable racist columnists including Jared Taylor and Swedish White Supremacist Henrik Palmgren and, like Spencer's other projects, was funded by William Regnery II.

But two events highlight Spencer's influence on the American White Supremacist movement, and both occurred in Charlottesville, Virginia. The town had voted to remove a statue of failed Confederate traitor Robert E. Lee, which provoked racists around the country to defend their heroes. On May 13, 2017, Spencer led a group of White Supremacists with torches in chants including "Russia is our friend" as they descended on Lee Park.[44]

Spencer would do this again in August for the infamous Unite the Right rally that saw a convergence of White Supremacists from around the nation on August 11, 2017. He returned yet again on October 7,

2017, to more chanting of "You will not replace us," but with far fewer numbers than the disastrous events in August.[45]

He may find friends in Dugin and other racists, but the global community hasn't been so keen to accept Spencer's views. Spencer was kicked out of Hungary like other racists who sought refuge there.[46] Under a treaty agreement established in 1985, dubbed the Schengen Agreement, Spencer subsequently is banned in 26 countries covered in the Schengen area. They include Austria, Belgium, the Czech Republic, Denmark, Estonia, Finland, France, Germany, Greece, Hungary, Iceland, Italy, Latvia, Liechtenstein, Lithuania, Luxembourg, Malta, the Netherlands, Norway, Poland, Portugal, Slovakia, Slovenia, Spain, Sweden, and Switzerland.

His visits to college campuses have sparked protests, including visits to Vanderbilt University in Nashville, Tennessee, in 2010; Providence College in Rhode Island in 2011; Texas A&M in College Station, Texas, in 2016; University of Florida in September 2017; Louisiana State University in 2017; Michigan State University in 2017; and Ohio State University in 2017. The block to speak at University of Florida led to a lawsuit resulting in the court's ruling in favor of Spencer, and he subsequently spoke to a mixed audience of supporters and campus students on October 19, 2017. But the event was met with a large protest and the cost of security for the event was estimated to be around $600,000.

Additionally, the social media platform Twitter had provided a verification check mark to Spencer's account. The blue mark was often seen as a status symbol. The verification mark was revoked in November 2017 and Twitter announced it would be reviewing its use of the verification status for all future accounts.

Spencer was married to Nina Kouprianova, a Russian-Canadian citizen. Kouprianova was also known as a Kremlin troll who wrote under the name Nina Byzantina, whose Twitter handle @NinaByzantina states that "This account is personally protected by Putin and [Chechen warlord, Ramzan] Kadyrov."[47]

Kouprianova is also Aleksandr Dugin's translator. She is a well-known "Moscow mouthpiece" who spreads #disinformation stories that clearly benefit the Kremlin on her blog and on Twitter. Her husband touts the same political ideology as Aleksandr Dugin: stay out of NATO, say no to the UN, play nice with Bashar al-Assad (Syria's President), and say no to globalism in general.

Spencer's online magazine, *Alternative Right*, has Aleksandr Dugin as a contributor. Spencer has called Russia the "sole white power in the world." Spencer said, "I think we should be pro-Russia because Russia is the great white power that exists in the world."[48]

Jason Kessler was the primary organizer of the Unite the Right rally in Charlottesville. He wrote an op-ed that was published by Chuck Johnson's Gotnews.com titled, "ANALYSIS: #Russia Will Be One Of America's Greatest Allies During The Trump Administration."[49] In the piece, Kessler argued that Russia was a natural ally to the United States in the area of nationalism. Andrew Auernheimer fled to Ukraine.[50] He worked with Andrew Anglin to create forums for The Daily Stormer, a neo-Nazi website.

The Secessionists

Louis Marinelli, a native of Buffalo, NY,[51] was an English teacher who found his path to Russia through the California secessionist movement and helped found Sovereign California. In 2004, he worked as a volunteer for the John Edwards campaign. Later, he was involved in supporting anti–gay marriage campaigns before changing views in 2010 to a more moderate stance. He said he voted for Trump in 2016. He announced a bid for office in 2015 as he attempted to run for a seat in the California assembly in the 2016 elections. He picked up just over 4,000 votes. When that failed, he repeatedly filed various ballot proposals, all aimed at splitting California away from the United States. Every one of them failed. Marinelli launched the movement called Yes California Independence Campaign in 2014 after the Scottish Independence Referendum of 2014.[52] The resulting campaign also picked up a hashtag, #Calexit after the British effort Brexit that succeeded in getting the UK to break away from the European Union. He was invited to a separatist conference in Russia on September 25, 2016, sponsored by the Rodina-aligned front group, Anti-Globalization Movement of Russia.

The ADR, as it is known in Russia, was created on March 15, 2012, and listed as a Russian NGO. The ADR is funded by a Kremlin-based grant of $50,000 from the National Charity Fund.[53] The ADR is a one-man operation under Alexander Ionov.[54] Ionov is the leader of the Anti-Globalization Movement of Russia, and CEO of Ionov Transcontinental, LLC. He's been involved with other outreach efforts, including a meeting called "Syria and Russia: Peace to unbreakable friendship," in February 2014. He was co-chair of the Committee for Solidarity with the Peoples of Syria and Libya, under former Rodina member Sergey Baburin. The group has bestowed honorary memberships to Mahmoud Ahmadinejad and Bashar al-Assad. Marinelli's trip to Russia was paid for by the Russian group. They even gave him free office space. The Moscow-based event was organized under the name of the International Congress of Separatists. The conference was dubbed "Dialogue of Nations: The Right of Peoples to Self-Determination and Building a Multipolar World." The attendees of the conference promoted separatists from California, Hawaii, Texas, Puerto Rico, Ireland, Catalonia, Western Sahara, and Donetsk.

In previous conferences, the ADR hosted the American organization United National Antiwar Coalition (UNAC), led by Joe Lombardo. In December 2014, the group invited members of the Texas Nationalist Movement (TNM) to attend a meeting but the FBI raided the TNM's offices. On June 2, 2016, the ADR worked with Rodina to create other events like the "Human Rights Movement for Indians in the US." The event featured Mashu White Feather of the Cherokee tribe. Also in attendance was Doreen Bennett of New Zealand, from the radio station "Voices of Indigenous People." Rodina member Fedor Biryukov (also co-chair of the Stalingrad Club) was joined by Ionov.

Despite all the ties to Kremlin initiatives, Marinelli stated, "We don't have any communication with or contact with or receive any support of any kind from the Russian government or any Russian government officials."[55] Ironically, Vladimir Putin signed a law in January 2014 outlawing spreading separatist views inside of Russia.

The punishment could be up to five years in jail. In December 2016, Russia Today was eager to cover Marinelli's opening of the "California Embassy" in Moscow.[56] Despite these welcoming arms, Marinelli refused donations from out of state. "The People of California alone should determine their own future."[57] However, Marinelli echoes the Kremlin's lines better than Putin himself, "The people in Washington are the enemy," and "those people in Washington are masters of propaganda."[58] As if the Russian support wasn't enough for Marinelli, he also sought to get a boost from Julian Assange after WikiLeaks backed the separatists in Catalonia.[59]

In 2016, when Marinelli sought to return to Russia, his now-wife Anastasia was unable to travel with him after they moved to San Diego because her visa had expired. Fearing a 10-year ban for the violation, Marinelli was forced to travel without her as he moved to Yekaterinburg, Russia, near Siberia in 2016.[60]

Texas separatist Nate Smith told a Russian newspaper during a trip to Moscow that "We [Texas] need independence, because we are different." Smith was the Executive Director of the Texas Nationalist Movement. Smith bragged to Russian newspaper *Vzglyad* that his group had 250,000 people supporting the movement, which led the newspaper to state that when it comes to Texas independence, the group was "the largest and most important organization in America." He additionally claimed, "we have no reason to stay in the US," and "We have a completely different way of life."[61] When Smith spoke to the Russian newspaper he said he was invited to come to Moscow because of the Anti-Globalization Movement of Russia and that it was his second trip. He also stated that a large number of military members from Texas are supportive of Texas independence. He falsely stated that "Texas has its own army," referring to the Texas National Guard. He told the Russian newspaper that "Texas receives nothing from the US federal government. Nothing." But this is clearly not true. For instance, the comptroller of Texas said the state received 35.5 percent of its net revenue from the federal government in 2016.[62]

Smith stated that despite local-, state-, and federal-level governance, "there are simply no people who represent the interest of Texans." In fact, Texas has two senators like all other states and 36 members in the House of Representatives. At the state level there are 150 members of the Texas House of Representatives and 31 members of the Texas Senate.

Smith addressed the education system in Texas by stating that "the federal government is artificially trying to create an American identity," even though the US identity is older than even that of a notion of an independent Texas. Smith argued that the movement wanted to teach "our children to study the history of Texas," which is indeed taught statewide.

Like Louis Marinelli of the Yes California secession group, Smith was working with Alexander Ionov of the Anti-Globalization Movement of Russia.

THE DAILY STORMER in many ways is the evil little brother of the first White Supremacist site, Stormfront. In the early days of the internet, there was Stormfront, established by Don Black, an ex-con Alabama Klansman who put his prison schooling in computers to really poor use. Black, who was in prison for conspiring to invade an island in the Caribbean dominated by blacks (the race and not his surname), had launched and christened Stormfront just weeks prior to the Oklahoma City bombing that left nearly 200 people (predominantly children) dead.

The Daily Stormer became the Stormfront for a new generation of little Nazis. After the Unite the Right rally in Charlottesville reminded the world about the danger of neo-Nazis and White Supremacists, a backlash ensued against tech companies giving safe harbor to the sites, forums, and social media profiles. As a result, The Daily Stormer was booted from GoDaddy servers and it wound up on servers in Russia.[63] The site emerged as dailystormer.ru. Additionally, alt-right groups were banned from Facebook and Twitter and began to seek community in the arms of the Russian social media platform VKontakte.[64]

CHAPTER 14

A Treasonous Aspect

Any final assessment by a trained intelligence professional would conclude that Trump was a spy's dream. His poor personal characteristics and indifference to anything or anyone but himself would be exploitable. Perhaps as far back as 1987, Russia had their sights on Trump as a potential asset. Little did they realize that as President he would become almost as effective as a witting trusted agent.

When 45th President of the United States Donald J. Trump speaks, little comes from his mouth that was not put there by Russians shaping actions and experiences, carefully planned to benefit the Russian Federation. There is a reason for that. It is not just his personal disposition toward Putin and his affiliation with the pan-European conservative network that motivates him. It is not brainwashing per se. It's that Trump has really come to embody Russia's interest. He believes what he is doing will benefit his base, which includes seeking the approval of Vladimir Putin and the Russian people, who made him feel more welcome than the people who did not vote for him.

That the Russians established a plan to hijack the perceptions of the American public and steer it to the benefit of Donald Trump in order to make him President of the United States is now without question. However, the combination of the Directorate of National Intelligence's estimate on the hacking, and the Mueller indictment of the Internet

Research Agency, along with Trump's own words and actions, would give any intelligence analyst high confidence that he was complicit in this plan.

To the public, the jury is out on the level of culpability and cooperation he has provided to the Russian Federation, though the circumstantial evidence is overwhelming. One could allow that he may have been an unwitting asset when he sent his first tweet in 2012 promising to Make America Great Again, but by 2018 it was clear he was no longer unwitting.

In the parlance of an intelligence professional, he is a Witting Asset. In the legal arena, he has betrayed his oath to protect and defend the Constitution. In the words of the common person on the street, he is considered by many to be a traitor.

How Trump's Decisions Were Made for Him

NATO practitioners in Russian active measures and cyberwarfare are given a study so that they understand their ideological opponents in the information warfare battle space. *The Handbook on Russian Information Warfare* is a brilliant study which introduces the practitioner to the formerly Soviet, now Russian, concept of "Reflexive Control." NATO defines it as "...the practice of predetermining an adversary's decision in Russia's favour, by altering key factors in the adversary's perception of the world."[1] The Russian General Staff changed the name of this process to "perception management."

The Russians have been applying perception management against the United States on a near-continuous basis since 2010. But, in 2012 to 2013, they focused their strategy to impact the 2016 election. The Russians decided that they would be the ones to set the parameters for what American citizens and their choice for President should be seeing. Done correctly, Russian perception management ensures that situations that confront American leadership would be seen through a lens that the leader believes is his own formulation. In fact, when Russian political, propaganda, and information warfare are applied correctly, the leader actually sees the situation through the lens that is crafted for him. In other words, if the leader sees the world through rose-colored glasses, the Russian information dominance process will not only give him the rose-colored lenses, they will have also created the circumstances where the leader will believe that it was his decision to put the rose glasses, not the yellow ones, on in the first place. This is performed by creating metanarratives—framing a situation on a strategic level well before the opponent enters the equation. The NATO handbook states: "Control of an opponent's decision is achieved by means of providing him with the grounds by which he is able logically to derive his own decision, but one that is predetermined by the other side."[2]

British information warfare analyst Charles Blandy noted a Ukrainian study, *The Fog of War: Russian Strategy of Deception and the Conflict in the Ukraine*, in which the stages of shaping a perception management campaign around an opponent after applying force (or in peacetime, a lack of force) can be achieved in four major stages:

> "By assisting the opponent's formulation of an appreciation
> of the initial situation.
> By shaping the opponent's objectives.
> By shaping the opponent's decision-making algorithm.
> By the choice of the decision-making moment."[3]

Since the rise of Putin as the leader of the Russian Federation, Russian perception management is a key psychological warfare component of Russia's intelligence preparation of its new information battlefield. When Putin would decide to implement this policy would depend on several factors, the most important of which was the American political environment, especially the level of intensity of the opposition to Presidents George W. Bush and Barack Obama, the will of the President to understand and oppose Russia's moves in the information domain, and the level of legitimacy that Russian PM techniques could be given through the global media. On the whole, George W. Bush was a tough President, and he was surrounded by the National Security staff of his father, an ardent anti-Communist. Though Bush saw "Putin's soul" and nicknamed him "Pooty-Poot," he would have been a poor choice with whom to try to craft the right environment to change US policy toward Russia. President Barack Obama and Hillary Clinton tried to reset tough relations with Russia after their interference in Georgia and Estonia, and their constant hacking attempts on the American administration. They were even worse choices. As the run-up to the American elections began, it was clear that Russia had managed to see that they could operate against Washington in the information sphere with their state media achieving parity with US cable news. WikiLeaks was still a credible "transparency" organization. Julian Assange hated Hillary Clinton, so combined with the incessant Republican attacks on her truthfulness and her emails, he could be helpful.

The Republican field had many players, but only one would fit all the parameters of Charles Blandy's perception management matrix. And he was very well known to Russian intelligence.

Creating a global change by introducing Russia's metanarratives into the mind of an American Presidential prospect would require him to be handled by Russia's Spymaster-in-Chief personally. With every asset, witting or unwitting, would come an evaluation as to his or her suitability to be handled by the human intelligence officers of the FSB and SVR. As Yuri Bezmenov said, the old KGB (and now the new clandestine service) preferred self-centered conservative narcissists who are greedy and lacked moral principles. Those vulnerabilities and character flaws of a perfect ideological blank slate who would do whatever was whispered in his ear by the Russian leader and his oligarchy were written all over the most egotistical person in the Western Hemisphere: Donald J. Trump.

Trump was historically known as a transactional leader who would do whatever it took to benefit himself. He was ready to make a deal no matter how bad. Several times Trump had proven that he was, in fact, an extremely poor businessman—the man had managed to bankrupt a casino! He failed at every venture he had taken part in. Had it not been his inheritance of up to $200 million from his father, he would be a destitute braggart.

Recruiting Trump by Chasing MICE

The basic recruiting methodology used by intelligence officers around the world to recruit an unwitting person to become a spy or asset is an acronym that spells MICE.[4]

Naveed Jamali, a US naval intelligence officer and former FBI double agent, was recruited by Russian intelligence to spy on America. For three years, he was supervised by a GRU officer, a Russian Navy captain assigned to the Russian Embassy in New York City. Jamali said, "The goal [of the Russian agent] is to cultivate a source and begin a relationship with them. As the relationship progresses it moves from overt to covert with the handler directing the asset to complete [his or her] operational tasking." This explains Trump's relationship with Putin— how would Trump come to know what Putin was up to? How would he ever believe anything other than that Putin was his friend? Russia scholars Fiona Hill and Clifford Gaddy accurately assessed the folly of this endeavor: "The most obvious reason we cannot take any story or so-called fact at face value when it comes to Vladimir Putin is that we are dealing with someone who is a master at manipulating information, suppressing information, and creating pseudo-information."[5]

M—Money. No matter if the person wants to or not, once cash or another form of payment changes hands, they have become an asset to an intelligence agency. If the person decides to ally themselves and join with the agency and sign a contract of service, they are an agent. One can be tricked into thinking they are working for law enforcement and still be an agent of a hostile intelligence service, which we call a false-flag. In 1986, Ronald Pelton was arrested by the FBI for espionage. He was an NSA Russian-speaking analyst who sold secrets to Russia for five years. Pelton was deeply in debt. Though he had left the NSA, he contacted the Russians and sold Top Secret national security information for a total of $37,000. The CIA's spy in Russia, Vitaly Yurchenko, became privy to this and exposed Pelton.

In the case of Donald Trump, the Russians had long known that he was in fact one of the worst dealmakers in the world. He was in a near-constant quest for money. None of his inheritance, or his many endeavors from Trump steaks to Trump wines, could ever bring him to the level of respect he thought he deserved. He always fell back on real estate. Russia made up a major part of his portfolio and the Kremlin tested if he was a suitable MICE. They first tested his level of avariciousness. Trump sold a Palm Springs mansion to Russian oligarch Dmitry Rybolovlev for $91 million. He made a 130% profit off the deal. It was a perfect cash dangle to see what Trump would do for money.[6]

This is what makes Trump such a perfect target to be influenced by a foreign power. Trump exercises no impulse control, and this makes him easily manipulated by the Russian formula for assets that watches his every action and move. A good agency can see where opportunity arises. Recklessness and impulsivity can give Russian diplomats, oligarchs, and spies a chance to step in to take market shares away from America and into Putin's coffers.

I—Ideology. Recruited assets often become agents due to their desire to become useful to the nation or cause with which they are ideologically aligned.

Aras Agalarov, billionaire investor in the Crocus Group, organizer of the Miss Universe pageant, and Russian oligarch was also the owner of the Nobu restaurant in Moscow. In November 2013, Agalarov quietly arranged a private two-hour meeting between Trump and a dozen of Russia's richest men. They were sequestered with Trump and spent that time presenting to him Russia's worldview. The group, including Herman Gref, CEO of the Russian state bank, Sberbank, and German Khan, the banking and oil magnate, opposed the Atlantic-European axis. Their perspectives, allied with those of the American conservatives, would create an impenetrable sphere of anti-global sentiment, which Trump would adopt. Jamali revealed that "The targeting of an asset by Russian intel often starts with overt and legitimate meetings. These early interactions are both innocuous and butter up the target by stroking their ego." During this meeting, Trump heard, and appears to have adopted, the positions of Russia in the way a compliant puppy relishes the food and treats given to him. In a room with the global elite—multibillionaires who were close personal friends of

Vladimir Putin, the man who could OK his lifelong dream project, Trump Tower Moscow—Trump would have adopted any position he saw as beneficial to himself. Assets tend to become pliant when both money and ideology converge with people they admire and who could facilitate their dreams; Trump would have sold his own child for Moscow at this point. The Nobu meeting was likely the point where Trump accepted his witting subornation by Moscow.

C—Coercion/Cooption/Compromised. Once an asset starts operations it is quite possible that the handlers will explain the gravity and seriousness of the betrayal, that many will come to fear that they have been caught in something, and that their family will be left destitute from exposure. This approach ensures compliance from the asset. It can also be followed with death threats or threats of physical torture. In many instances, the intelligence officer will have Kompromat, compromising information on the person, which could be used to threaten exposure or public humiliation.

As far back as 1988, Soviet and the Communist Czechoslovakian intelligence agencies were told by informants that Trump harbored presidential aspirations. According to German news magazine *Bild*, and Czech Television 24, the Czechs had been tasked with collecting information on Trump, starting in 1977.[7] Documents marked Top Secret were drafted by the Czechoslovakian State Security Agency, the StB (*Státní Bezpečnost*). Czech agents were monitoring Trump and his wife Ivana, who was born in Czechoslovakia. She would take Trump to visit her father, Miloš Zelníček, in the 1970s and 80s, before they divorced.[8] The StB reported directly to the KGB. They would receive all of this information and fuse it with intelligence on Trump that was collected in the United States and during his 1988 trip to Russia. These high-value target intelligence dossiers would be in a state archive at the Lubyanka Headquarters of the KGB when Putin was director of the FSB. These dossiers were automated and available for exploitation teams. When Trump visited Moscow in 2013 for the Miss Universe pageant, numerous Russians had done business with him. Trump had people friendly to Moscow on his staff and was desperate to seek an audience with Putin. All of this was very well known. Trump was a business competitor with the Russian oligarchs whether he knew it or not. Trump would have been designated a Special Collections Target (HVP-SCT). SCTs are usually reserved for heads of state or extremely wealthy businessmen like Bill Gates or George Soros. They were also reserved for CIA officers and former intelligence agency visitors. Having handled national level high-value targets, it's been my personal experience that these targets required special handling. They would target Trump's personal telephone and other voice communications. They would collect wiretaps on telephones in his hotel and from wires worn by people designated to collect private conversations with the celebrity. The FSB would have been reading Trump's activities and reporting in real time to the Kremlin anything of significance. The FSB would have had an Imagery Collections Team (aka Kompromat Evidence Team) operating independently with still and video cameras, both hidden and embedded into the walls to catch Trump in any compromising situation that could be used for exploitation. Every woman he kissed was videotaped. Every ass he pinched was recorded. Every sweet nothing he said to a mistress or side deal was the property of the Russian Federation. Being coerced is evidenced by the very fact that Trump would never, ever disparage or insult President Putin. The only credible explanation is that Moscow has information or evidence that could bring down the only thing Trump cares about—the Trump financial empire. This form of coercion would be revealed to Trump openly and blatantly so that there would be no confusion about the role that he is expected to play. It has been joked that Putin obviously has a non-disclosure agreement that Donald Trump will never ever violate. Considering the ability of Russian intelligence to gain virtually any information that Trump would have tried to hide while in Moscow, Trump would be trapped. Many former US intelligence analysts in the news media have publicly assessed that Trump's behavior as President validates this assessment.

E—Ego/Excitement. With an ego like Trump's, he could be led anywhere to do almost anything, given the right amount of compliments and promises of riches. The excitement of the game is a huge part of what Trump thrives on. He is his own Chaos Agent. He thrives on chaos—the excitement of his attacks on personalities, the back-and-forth with his enemies, and the adoration of the masses. Stroke his ego and he rolls over like a compliant puppy. Trump operates without a true political strategy as a form of excitement. He lacks impulse control and indulges beliefs he holds without any basis or grounding. It makes for a personally interesting world to watch people jump through his hoops. This irrationality makes him easily manipulated by foreign leaders and their spies who can guarantee certain words and actions that can throw him into a Twitter rage, or issue compliments that turn him into a puddle of obsequiousness.

Trump would think every idea put in by Moscow was his own brilliant thought in his big, beautiful mind. One cannot give Putin credit for controlling every aspect of this strategy. There are too many variables and the Kremlin would have to roll sevens every time. But he tasked the FSB/SVR to try it, and in 2013 after learning that Trump was serious about a Presidential run, they threw the dice.

The Russian intelligence metanarrative they would be tasked to push would be simple—convince Trump to believe that he already believed that:

1. NATO was strangling Russia with military bases and aggressively encroaching on its borders.
2. Russia was a new, rich, glorious empire with a strong fearless leader whose personal relationship could help Trump join the global elite oligarchy where borders mean nothing—only money matters.
3. The European Union, with its immigrant Muslim hordes, was finished—help start a new white ethno-nationalist conservative alliance worldwide with Moscow's help.

They buttered Trump up and convinced him that he could be one of the boys; that his country was poor and he could make a difference. Other methods of shaping his initial impression of the situation was contact through his more extreme allies in the NRA, and supporters of the American Evangelical movement, who would be repeating the same metanarrative he was hearing at Miss Universe and every conversation after that—Russia was an ally.

An additional aim of the Russian perception management strategy is "Shaping the Opponent's Objectives"—meaning that an information sphere is created in which the opponent adopts goals already crafted for him by Russian propagandists.

During the 2016 campaign, Trump adopted positions that would shock his allies and surprise the news media. He questioned NATO's usefulness and how NATO nations were not paying the United States for their defense. He did the same on the viability of the European Union and shared Marine Le Pen's desire to break it up.

While Russia invaded Crimea on March 18, 2014, and the world condemned Russia, Trump was complimenting Putin and criticizing Obama. Just 72 hours after Crimea had been seized by Russian army troops, on March 21, 2014, Trump tweeted, "Putin has become a big hero in Russia with an all-time high popularity. Obama, on the other hand, has fallen to his lowest ever numbers. SAD."

Trump would also tweet, "I believe Putin will continue to re-build the Russian Empire. He has zero respect for Obama or the U.S.!" The phrase "Russian Empire" are the very same words used by the Russo-European alt-right. It embraces the Russian Federation's imperial goals. It was now Trump's view of the world.

After the defeat of Mitt Romney by Barack Obama, Trump had tweeted on November 6, 2012, that "We can't let this happen. We should march on Washington and stop this travesty. Our nation is totally divided!" On November 19, 2012, Donald J. Trump for President, Inc., his nonprofit organization, registered the "Make America Great Again Political Action Committee."

The Miss Universe pageant would provide a perfect backdrop for convincing Trump he had a major role in changing the East-West dynamic. On the surface, it appeared that he was primarily interested in getting a deal to build a Trump Tower. He would tweet after leaving Russia "@AgalarovAras I had a great weekend with you and your family. You have done a FANTASTIC job. TRUMP TOWER-MOSCOW is next. EMIN was WOW!"[9]

Trump Tower Moscow was a treasure he had been wanting since 1988. They would even propose to name the spa *Ivanka*. In intelligence parlance, Trump Tower Moscow, an object Trump could not acquire for 15 years, could be called "a dangle." This is when the spy who is handling you offers you something made of that rare metal "unobtainium." It's the shiny object that lures the fish right onto the hook. As noted before, Trump had been briefed by the Russian oligarchy at the Nobu dinner about their objectives for him should he become America's leader. Likely after that discussion, and a pledge for their underground support, he decided definitively to run for President.

This is further evidenced by the fact that on January 22, 2014, a Kremlin apparatchik, Yulya Alferova, who lists her role as "Advisor to the Minister of Economic Development of the Russian Federation," tweeted a picture of herself next to Trump. She is in fact the ex-wife of Artem Klyushin, a Russian oligarch closely tied to Putin. It was taken at the Miss Universe pageant planning meeting the previous June. Her tweet said, "I'm sure @realDonaldTrump will be great president! We'll support you from Russia! America needs ambitious leader!"[10] This was a statement of support made completely out of the blue.

Interestingly, in June 2013 in Las Vegas, she was present at a private dinner hosted for Trump by Aras Agalarov and his wife, Irina, and attended by his son, Emin; the 83-year-old billionaire Phil Ruffin, who is married to the 36-year-old former Miss Universe Oleksandra Nikolayenko; British promoter Rob Goldstone; and Trump's bodyguard Keith Schiller. After that meeting, Alferova was hired to work for the pageant organization.

Trump most likely told her he intended to run for President before January 22, 2014. As a Kremlin apparatchik, if she knew it, Russian intelligence knew it before her tweet was even sent. They would have passed it directly to Vladimir Putin.

Another piece of evidence that Russia deeply impacted Trump's decision-making came in an indictment by the US Justice Department's Special Counsel, Robert Mueller, who wrote that the entire senior management of the FSB's Internet Research Agency was a criminal enterprise designed to influence the American election.

One piece of evidence that Russia was preparing for Trump was also in the indictment issued against the IRA. It stated that the first hires for the "translator project," a team of 90 English-fluent social media analysts that would shape the American public's perception of Russia and Trump, were in August 2013, just 60 days after the Miss Universe pageant was announced. In January 2014, about the time of Miss Alferova's tweet, they went into strategic cyber planning to change the perception of the American public, by using fictitious US profiles on social media to favor Donald Trump.[11]

When Trump started looking into running for President in late 2012, it was likely provisional. For almost two years, he never mentioned it on Twitter or even gave a hint that this was a possibility. Though Trump may have been busy, it's no coincidence that Russian intelligence, including Vladimir Putin's chief propagandist, had already organized a system to seize both Twitter and Facebook and harness the exponential power of social media to assist him.

In September 2014, Trump announced he was going to run for President. He tweeted: "I wonder if I run for PRESIDENT, will the haters and losers vote for me knowing that I will MAKE AMERICA GREAT AGAIN? I say they will!"[12]

It may have been Trump's idea to run but the actual decision would be based on a mechanism in place to get him elected. Trump does not realize that he only made the decision well after it was made for him.

A Trump Conspiracy with Russia?
Rykov's Confession

There have been many accusations rendered about the level of cooperation that Donald Trump and his campaign may have accepted from the Russian Federation but most of those are built on desire rather than fact. As the special prosecutor moves through his investigation, the facts may implicate Trump as not only being aware of the Russian plan to impact the American election, but he may also have been an active coordinator of the plot to outright hijack the thoughts of the American public and bring the country into the Russian fold.

Two days after the election of Donald Trump, Konstantin Rykov, former member of the Duma in Putin's United Russia Party, wrote what would amount to a confession of how Russia elected Donald Trump. Prior to the indictment of the Internet Research Agency this account was generally dismissed as puffery. Now it had essentially been corroborated by the details of the IRA's internal workings.

Rykov is best known for being Vladimir Putin's TV and media propagandist. He was head of cybermedia for Channel One, Russia's principal television network and the first channel allowed to broadcast in the post-Soviet Russian Federation. He also established a network of Russian political websites and became an internet celebrity for his fiery tweets and Facebook posts including posting on Facebook under the nom de plume of "Jason Foris." It is alleged that he is the creator of the Russian Craigslist for escorts, Dosug.

The night after the election of Barack Obama in 2012, Donald Trump tweeted that he was disgusted with the result that the African American President was reelected. In his fury and frustration, he tweeted, "We should march on Washington!"

Minutes after Trump's tweet, Rykov claims he sent a private direct message (DM) to Trump offering to bring Russia's assistance to helping him become President. Trump responded with a DM photo showing him on a private jet giving the thumbs-up. The only way to DM on Twitter is if the two parties follow each other, which is an informal way of giving permission to send private messages. Trump had given Rykov that permission earlier.

In 2016, Rykov wrote a Facebook post, in Russian, which started "It's time for great stories. I'll tell you about it now, as Donald Trump and I have decided to free America and make it great again."[13]

The schedule Rykov noted was a planning period that went from November 6, 2012, to November 8, 2016, the span of the second term of Obama's presidency. It was during this time that the FBI's investigation reported that the RF-IRA was being organized and almost 100 people were hired to manipulate the election though social media. Rykov confirmed the strategy should be to conduct a Russian Intelligence–style perception management campaign using the best minds he could find. Rykov continued: "What was our idea with Donald Trump? In four years and two days. It was necessary to get into the brain and seize all possible means of mass perception of reality. Ensure Donald's victory in the US President's election. Then create a political union between the United States, France, Russia (and other states) and establish a new world order.

Four years and two days is a very long time, and the other is very small. Our idea was crazy, but feasible."[14]

Rykov claimed that Trump somehow made him aware of the efforts of the British scientists at Cambridge Analytica. He said that "British scientists from Cambridge Analytica offered to make out of 5,000 existing human psychotypes [psychological profile]—the 'perfect image' of Trump's possible supporter. Then put that image back on all the [psychological profiles] and thus find the universal key to anyone and everyone."[15]

Rykov implies that Trump himself briefed him on this matter. "Donald has decided to invite the special science division of Cambridge University for this task." Additionally, he claims that Trump secured these services for $5 million. "But! He got into his hands a secret super weapon," said Rykov. Rykov said that they started searching for the best people who could "upload these data to information flows and social networks." They were assisted in what he called a "couple of hacker factions, civil journalists from WikiLeaks and political strategist Михаил Kovalev [Mikhail Kovalev]." They then took steps so that foreign intelligence agencies and "NSA" could not interfere.[16]

The Russians gamed out how to universalize the platform so that "Even people [who] do not speak each other's language, could exchange information faster than everyone, understand each other completely, feel trends and influence their development...."

According to Rykov, the social media hijack bot programs took a year to write the code between 2013 and 2014. He also says it took a year to beta test and perfect a working weaponized social media system (2014-2015). According to the Mueller indictment of the RF-IRA, these dates match the employment and operations records of their staff. Rykov notes that the botnet and "media-filter" were launched on Trump-2016.com on August 18, 2015. About the same time the GRU,

Russian military intelligence's FANCY BEAR, was savaging the servers of the Democratic National Committee.

Trump Made the Kremlin Great Again!

In democracies, it is the laws which usually manage to act as guardrails to the tendencies of autocrats and tyrants. However, laws can only act as a defensive line to limit abuse by leaders when they are strictly enforced, and compliance is safeguarded by a moral and ethical political class. If the leader is rooted solely for self-enrichment or the creation of a personal family dynasty, then the laws and political class must provide a hard check or suffer their dissolution.

In my opinion, Trump is willingly working with Putin to pull America down to capitalize on the Trump Organization's investments. There is ample evidence that Russia and Trump seek an American single-family and money-based autocracy with all the trappings of the original republic but without the force of law to affect or investigate anything but what the ruling family desires. Intelligence agencies of China, Russia, Iran, and North Korea find Trump easily understood and his recklessness offers chances to economically exploit the US and manipulate Trump to behave in a way that damages America but helps them. In each case the American interest generally does not align with the Trump family interest, unless there is money in it.

Trump campaigned for removing the United States from the Trans-Pacific Partnership (TPP)—a massive trade agreement that would give America an advantage to entering the markets of every nation with a coast in the Pacific—Trump declared it a "potential disaster." He pledged over and over to immediately remove the US from the agreement. Outgoing Secretary of Defense Ash Carter noted that the TPP was important due to its ability to create powerful financial leverage and the ability to control blocs within the Asia-Pacific market. On his fourth day as President, Trump signed an order to withdraw. Yet while he was publicly destroying America's ability to trade openly on the Asian market, his son-in-law and daughter were secretly dealing with China.

In April 2017, Chinese President Xi Jinping visited Trump at Mar-a-Lago. On the same day Chinese regulators awarded Ivanka Trump, now a US government employee, with valuable trademark approvals. Although she claimed to have separated her business from her government work, it appeared to have been in lip service. Ivanka's trademarks could make her even more wealthy, but should have run afoul of the Criminal Conflict of Interest Statute. By May 2017, Jared Kushner's sister, Nicole Kushner Mayer, was found to be selling access to Trump while pitching Chinese investors to come to the US for US EB-5 visas. These controversial visas offered foreigners permanent residency for investing in American businesses. She mentioned how much their investment would mean to her "…and her family."[17] In both instances the Trump administration did nothing to punish his children for trading on America's interest using the Trump name.

If the leader of a populist movement cites "the will of the people" as allowance for crimes, then there is nothing that a tyrant cannot do. When the mind of the voter is the target of a hacking, then all illicit actions and behaviors for that nation are permissible.

As a political analyst, I once joked that Trump appeared to have a Russian Autocrat Advisory Team (a RAAT?) assigned to the White House. That may not be far from the truth. In the whirlwind of controversy about his ties to Moscow, on multiple occasions he met with the Russian Foreign Minister, Russian Ambassador, Vladimir Putin, and other Russian dignitaries and oligarchs while under FBI investigation for conspiracy.

The day after the firing of FBI Director James Comey, Trump met with Foreign Minister Lavrov and Ambassador Kislyak in the Oval Office. In a meeting closed to the American press, he stated that he fired the FBI Director to get pressure off of him over the Russia investigation. He also coordinated with Putin and made an announcement of his desire to create "an impenetrable Cyber Security unit" with Russia to get to the bottom of the election hacking.

In January 2018, the directors of the FSB, SVR, and GRU secretly met with their American counterparts in Washington at Trump's request, even though the country was under US sanctions. When Trump wants an opinion, he gets one he can trust... from Moscow.

Trump adopted the tools and methods of the Kremlin that got Putin and other autocrats elected for multiple terms. He sees what works and what does not in European states such as Poland, Hungary, and Austria. From his actions it's clear he understands that deliberately sowing divisiveness within the citizenry is good for him personally. A divided voting base won't focus on a specific issue like the conservative authoritarian-leaning voters. His base will vote for the leader, not saving the whales, keeping streets clean, or gun control. Whatever he says goes and they vote that way. The others are just single-issue voters who can be ignored. By splitting the opposition, through a wave of divisiveness, he can isolate the two-thirds of the country who are thinking democratically from a unified remainder who are his loyalists. Loyalists get rewarded, opponents get punished. That Trump and his base have essentially adopted the Communist/fascist moves of the KGB is not surprising.

His most dictatorial trait is the embracing of violence against his political opponents. Trump openly expressed his desire for the arrest and imprisonment of those who dare cross him personally. During the 2016 campaign, Donald Trump threatened to arrest Hillary Clinton at every turn. When in office, he demanded (but did not get) investigations into every Democrat who defied him including Clinton, Obama, Comey, Congressman Adam Schiff, Senator Chuck Schumer, Congresswoman Nancy Pelosi, and MSNBC host and former Republican Congressman Joe Scarborough. He set the stage to bring about a shift in the minds of his voters—enemies are to be abused, attacked, and degraded. At his rallies, protesters were beaten, spat on, and insulted. Trump would urge his supporters to beat up protesters and promised to pay the legal fees of anyone who did. When it happened, Trump ignored the assailant's pleas for financial help. Still, he promised the American system would be changed so that people who are racially, culturally, and politically different can be confronted, harmed, and tossed from our midst. Trump did not limit himself to insulting

Hillary Clinton. He has similarly insulted Barack Obama, Joe Biden, Paul Ryan, Mitch McConnell, John McCain, Senator Lindsey Graham, his own Attorney General, Jeff Sessions, his National Security Advisor, General H.R. McMaster, the entirety of the FBI, the CIA, the Democratic Party, 65% of America, the Pope, and Oprah Winfrey. In his estimation, they are all "haters and losers." On the other hand, he did not dare criticize two people on this planet: Vladimir Putin... and MSNBC's Rachel Maddow.

Since George Washington, every president has had issues with the news media. Donald Trump is no different. But from the first day he announced his candidacy to his January 20, 2017, inauguration, he has been critical of his news coverage. That coverage often portrayed him as a buffoon and his behaviors did not challenge that impression. However, once he won the election his ire took a dark turn. Trump openly declared war on the American TV media and print press, declaring them enemies of the American people. He started to describe any accurate news reporting that did not please him as "fake news." For example: "The FAKE NEWS media (failing @nytimes, @NBCNews, @ABC, @CBS, @CNN) is not my enemy, it is the enemy of the American people."[18] Trump generally makes assertions without any evidence, tweeting that most major media stories are fake news well over 100 times.

This brings to mind the question as to whether Trump is aware that the press is specifically protected under the First Amendment of the same Constitution he swore an oath to protect. The First Amendment to the US Constitution guarantees the freedom of religion, of speech, to assemble, and the right to petition the government for redress—that includes printed and spoken words. Trump apparently decided to disregard this freedom and substituted in its place "the right to determine what is free speech."

Trump is in fact executing a tried-and-true policy of psychological and propaganda warfare: If you control what is the "Truth," then you determine what is real and what is not. Trump understands and is aware of the Kremlin playbook and immediately started creating an exclusive information bubble his followers would listen to. For it to be successful, he must discredit everything outside of that bubble. It is information control of the highest order. It's the tool of a tyrant.

On the surface, Trump's calling it "fake news" is a way to maintain support from his voters by dismissing reports that are contrary or have a negative image toward him. The danger of this is that Trump is well aware that he essentially makes his followers believe what he says over empirical fact. This is demagoguery.

CNN's global reach in the news world is a primary reason that Trump attacks their coverage above all other networks. CNN is the go-to news channel for national crises and international breaking news. CNN's investigative reporting and critical eye toward the wave of quantifiable lies that come from Trump meant that their force of journalistic integrity had to be discredited.[19] Trump tweeted "@FoxNews is much more important in the United States than CNN, but outside of the U.S., CNN International is still a major source of (fake) news, and they represent our Nation to the WORLD very poorly. The outside world does not see the truth from them!"[20]

The media to Trump is strictly a weapon of disinformation—a platform for disseminating his hard-right ideological views. He is equally an easily misled consumer of fake news. Unless it comes from what he believes is a trusted source, it is a lie.

Trump is known to watch the morning show *Fox and Friends* to get talking points on whatever he hears that he agrees with and then later on pass these "original thoughts" on his Twitter account, as if he conceived of them himself. It's the way a five-year-old sees the world. All is original once it crosses his mind.

Trump is certainly aware of how Putin attacked his news media detractors directly and won. In fact, Putin used the FSB and his state media agencies to turn his anger against the few independent news organizations and almost completely eliminated independent media in Russia.

In 2017, Trump wondered aloud why the public airwaves were allowing his critics to criticize him and if something could be done about it. He tweeted "Fake News coming out of NBC and the Networks, at what point is it appropriate to challenge their licenses?" He also had the Justice Department state that they were looking into CNN interfering with the Time Warner merger. Trump also pulled his signature move to wonder aloud if he should sue CNN. He told an audience, "These are really dishonest people. Should I sue them? I mean, they're phonies. Jeff Zucker, I hear he's going to resign at some point pretty soon. I mean these are horrible human beings."[21] Former US Ambassador to Russia Michael McFaul noted that this was familiar. "[It is] exactly what Putin did in Russia in 2000."[22]

The Kremlin had no problem taking heat for the hacking or electing of Trump. Their state media, WikiLeaks, and Trump's American allies gave them a reasonable level of deniability. Putin could maintain the fig leaf of being a strategic opponent or even adversary. America remains a military power whose projection across the Middle East, Asia, and Europe is a force that he could use to keep the Russian people supporting the Kremlin's new global adventurism and increases in defense. All of Russia's opposition to Trump was far more Potemkin village than Kabuki theater. A Potemkin village is a fake facade hiding dirt and grime, whereas Kabuki is precision, art, and beauty. That was not Putin's game. His game was action. Like a low-key street fighter from St. Petersburg, Putin's government was operating more like an industrial robot forging steel in a foundry. Covered in grime and immersed in heat, it was ruthlessly efficient and not dependent on human intervention when set to task. Although his plan took a lot of luck, it was well planned and factored in all the foibles of the Americans' current bout of self-hatred.

Putin was sure that Trump would eventually lift sanctions and give Russia an economic breakout while the United States descended into political chaos. It was in Russia's interest to keep Trump in office even with some friction. Trump believed in Putin's worldview, not Washington's or Reagan's...and not Barack Obama's.

From the beginning of Trump's rise one question loomed over his administration that eclipsed all others. *Why?* Why did Russia appear to pull out all the stops short of war to support a man who could barely read a TelePrompTer and whose sanity would be openly questioned? It was a word that every journalist, pundit, postman, and seamstress asked themselves each time Donald J. Trump sent an early-morning tweet storm, made a seemingly unhinged decision, or ranted about himself lovingly on television. Why did he behave the way he did? It is an intriguing question. Based on what was has happened, and what could happen, one would not be faulted for assessing that American democracy has entered a great period of peril because no one could seem to answer the question *Why?* To old spies and mafia bagmen the answer was simple: Trump was in debt.

The Debt

The personal and financial debt owed by Trump on November 9, 2016, was not a mere humbled obligation to return a polite courtesy to the Russian leader and his allies who kept the faith. No—the election was fixed to benefit him personally. Russia set up for four years to put Trump in the position to win by the smallest of margins. They expended large quantities of illegal, covertly appropriated money; they used a large part of its clandestine and covert intelligence services and the power and goodwill of Vladimir Vladimirovich Putin himself. Donald J. Trump was now a debtor. He owed Moscow, who bought for him Cambridge Analytica, Julian Assange's WikiLeaks, the evangelicals, and even more money from the NRA than all before him. Moscow had its hands shaping the global support for Trump that would make him the leader of the alternative to the Atlantic alliance. He is the first American populist president and it is all owed to Moscow. It is a debt in the manner of a drug dealer who owes millions to a Colombian drug lord or Mafia chief. Like a gambling addict is indebted to a loan shark. Putin made the debt with so high a payoff that, as long as Trump can survive each day without decisive evidence on how much he really owes Putin, he can look forward to surviving the next day. Like all who survive such morally deadly people, they feel exuberant until they have to wake up and do their master's bidding for another 24 hours. Every day, debtors like Trump rejoice when they have been spared the collection of their mortal souls, particularly when their most cherished asset is their self-made reputation. This is not just about traditional financial insolvency. That is easy to remedy. When faced with bankruptcy to a bank or other traditional lender, the elite rich laugh on their way to Monaco and forget they ever had a payment to make.

Trump has placed his bet on the number given to him by a corrupt casino owner and has taken home a massive jackpot—yet the spoils are not his. Having won the presidency, Trump became a vessel for Russia. He would carry any amount of water they chose to give him. Would there be a reckoning of the engineered luck? Yes, like all who make a deal with the devil, there must be repayment with interest. That's the devil's bargain.

The sword of Damocles that hangs over Trump's head is surely more than the fact that Moscow elected him President. His complete and total political and financial survival depends on Vladimir Putin keeping his mouth shut and his vaults inaccessible to US Intelligence. Clearly Trump is working extra hard to make his payments on time every time, especially when he owes his own life, liberty, and pursuit of happiness to the Pirate King who leads a global den of thieves.

Speculation in the news media as to why President Trump aligns himself so closely to Vladimir Putin falls into one of three categories: 1) Was he the Manchurian candidate, a foreign agent infiltrated as a brainwashed drone to do Putin's bidding? 2) Was he a Fellow Traveler, who had read, heard, and adopted the neo-Eurasian ideology and believes exactly as the Kremlin? Or 3) Was he just an idiot who could be told anything by people of influence, and when he saw money he would fervently stay as close to it as possible?

One thing is certain; he is not the Manchurian candidate. It is clear to all who see that Donald Trump is in fact a willing participant in Russia's plans to break up global democracy. The Russians spent years crafting a pro-Moscow perception bubble so that when he was ready to run for President or participate in American politics, he would already have been indoctrinated in where he should enter foreign policy—the correct worldview would come from the Kremlin's worldview. His interactions with Russian money, women, politicians, and fake news had already shaped his perception of who and what Russia was—a personal ally. As he rose to prominence, the perceptions and data he was taking in were run through his own personal perception filter. That filter was also crafted in Moscow, as it was built from his experience with Russians. Much of the news Trump receives about Russia, if from American alt-right conservative news (Breitbart Media and Fox News), has already been run through the fuel interjectors of Russian propaganda warfare distribution systems. By 2016 Russia could run virtually any anti-Hillary Clinton story and have it on Trump's lap in hours. All there is to know about Donald Trump and Russia is that he had no other frame of reference by which to form an opinion. He hated mainstream news media. As a functional illiterate he never read papers, and now as President he must have intelligence reports briefed to him. He eschews anything that smacks of political and foreign policy literacy that he did not form from his own personal experiences.

Bottom line: In his own estimation, anyone who opposes Russia opposes Trump. Anyone who opposes Trump is his enemy. What we have witnessed is peak psychological warfare. Unless Russia moves against Trump personally in a blatant betrayal, such as releasing some form of embarrassing Kompromat that disables his Presidency, he will be loyal to his friends in Red Square. This willful participation in Putin's clique shows Donald Trump is far from being a Manchurian candidate. If anything, he is a product of the first successful global cyber propaganda campaign to seize control of an enemy's leadership. He is a Cyberian candidate.

Moscow's Man in Washington

Donald J. Trump never really won his seat in the Oval Office—he is a cardboard cutout for the real power behind him, the former Russian KGB spymaster turned American Republican. Trump could possibly fill the role of President, but Vladimir Putin would always be the shadow broker that put him into power. This thought so terrifies Trump that he would spend every waking day of his time in office refuting the accusation that he and his campaign had worked with Russia to betray the nation to seize power. His most utterly terrifying thought must be that even as one of the most powerful men in the world, everyone believes he was owned lock, stock, and barrel by the Kremlin. He was right.

Testifying before the House Intelligence Committee, former Director of the CIA John Brennan spoke on the matter of how Russia handles its assets and agents: "They have been able to get people—including inside of the CIA—to become treasonous, and frequently, individuals who go along that treasonous path do not even realize they're along that path until it gets to be a bit too late...."[23]

Trump has definitively convinced me that he transitioned from an unwitting asset of Vladimir Putin to a witting asset working in league with the Russian Federation. Which of the following could provide the key bit of data for that assessment? Was it his thumbs-up photo to Konstantin Rykov's offer to assist his campaign in 2012? Was it his telling Rykov that Cambridge Analytica was working on voter profiles and somehow they fell into the hands of the RF-IRA? Was it his numerous meetings with Aras Agalarov? Was it the private two-hour dinner with the Russian oligarchy and his subsequent belief that Trump Tower Moscow was happening? Was it his casual comments to Yulya Alferova on his run for President in 2014? Was it his public endorsement of Russia's invasion of Crimea? Was it his son's desperation to meet with the lawyer Natalia Veselnitskaya to get dirt on Hillary Clinton in violation of numerous laws? Was it that he orchestrated lie after lie to the American people about his son meeting with Russian agents? Was it his openly begging Russia to hack and release Hillary Clinton's emails? Was it his professed love of WikiLeaks's crimes? Was it keeping his son-in-law cleared after it was learned that he had met with a Russian spy bank, sought loans from Qatar, or asked the Russian Ambassador for Special Communications to be hidden from the CIA?

Keep in mind that Trump has publicly complimented Putin over 100 times in a year in which he insulted over 425 people.

The *New York Times* reports that former CIA Director John Brennan made some informed speculation "...the fact that [Trump] has had this fawning attitude toward Mr. Putin, has not said anything negative about him, I think continues to say to me that he does have something to fear and something very serious to fear...."[24]

As President, the *New York Times* would write about Trump's inability to comprehend the meaning of the words Top Secret. It said Trump "simply did not possess the interest or the knowledge of the granular details of intelligence gathering to leak specific sources and methods of intelligence gathering that would harm American allies." This is almost the definition of a man unfit to be President of the United States. It would also be the definition of the perfect unwitting fool, the simpleton with a security clearance whose personal need to massage his ego and garner flattery, adulation, and approval from richer men than he exceeded the fundamental security needs of his nation.

Trump ordered his National Security Council staff to investigate the possibility of removing American troops from Europe as a reward to Putin. He also ordered the Director of National Intelligence and the CIA to meet with the three heads of Russian Intelligence, one of whom was under sanctions, in secret and in Washington. Either one of these would be the basis for an indictment for Conspiracy against the United States.

A thought experiment: Replace the word "Russia" with "ISIS" in the above-listed activities. If any person in the United States had this same level of communication, coordination, and complicity in an active conspiracy with a threatening group such as ISIS, al-Qaeda, or even Chinese Intelligence, there would have been a warrant for their arrest issued in record time. At the very least, an American with suspicious contacts with overseas agents entering government would have had federal investigators start a process to determine if there was in fact a secret desire to act as an espionage agent for a foreign power, if others were involved, and how deep it went.

Even Trump has reluctantly come to find out that no American is above the law or so high that they are above suspicion—even the President. Enter the Special Counsel, former FBI Director, Robert Swan Mueller III.

As further information emerges from the Mueller investigation, the level of Trump's complicity will determine if it was all coincidence or a plot to commit treason.

"Freedom Is a Light"

We Are Outgunned. Out manned. Out numbered.
Out planned.
We Gotta Make an All Out Stand!"

—GEN. GEORGE WASHINGTON,
Hamilton, the Musical

As a boy I used to solve my most taxing and vexatious problems on a bench behind Independence Hall in Philadelphia. Next to the statue of Commodore Barry, I would try to understand why my family cared so much about this nation. Why did my father show me how deeply he loved this country, even though as a black man he was disrespected at every turn in his life? Why did his father, my grandfather, volunteer to fight in the Great War and break his back offloading munitions and loading the dead in France? Why did his brother, my granduncle, run horse-drawn caissons filled with explosives to the front and back with dead white boys? Why did their father, my great-grandfather, run away from his plantation in Tennessee and take up arms in a regiment of US Colored Troops? I discovered the answer one day walking from Independence Hall. I had walked past Washington Square a thousand times in my youth but never stopped there until I was in the Navy. I learned that it was originally a cemetery for slaves and that during the Revolution it became a burial ground for perhaps a thousand or more unnamed soldiers who died in the war.

Above the mass grave turned park stands a statue of George Washington. In front of him is an eternal flame above the grave of the original unknown soldier. It reads, "Beneath this stone rests a soldier of Washington's army who died to give you liberty."

I wonder now how would Washington, the father of our country, the first in war, the first in peace, first in the hearts of his countrymen, feel about the divided United States today? I offer that he would weep with shame. He would shake in anger and stand up and raise his voice to oppose all threats to this great nation—both foreign and domestic. Like me, he would wonder if again in the life of this country will we toy with surrendering all that was won in blood, treasure, and love of liberty for the rule of the mob and the parseltongue of the billionaire tyrant.

Many of Trump's most ardent supporters wrap themselves in the flag and Constitution to argue for the destruction of that document's protections. Others say that the situation in America, crafted from their own ignorance, xenophobia, and an incessant feeding of Russian-backed propaganda, under an incredibly mild-mannered and even-keeled President Barack Obama, has led America to the brink of economic and cultural destruction. This is a horrible fantasy, which no one who espouses it could find a true documentable example. In fact, many feel that the greatest disasters of the early 21st century—the government's horrific response to Hurricane Katrina, the death toll of the Iraq War, the 2008 economic collapse, and the origin of the terrorist group ISIS—were all the responsibility, if not outright evil scheme, of the first African American President. Needless to say, none of those incidents had their origins or presented themselves during his presidency. The fact that he inherited them and resolved those issues somehow inflamed the lower-class white voter even more. And why not? The Republican Party and Fox News were there at every turn telling them that the black President had destroyed America. No one ever went to the window to check if the nation was actually destroyed. Like the Soviet and Russian propaganda campaigns that steered these fantasies into the internet, the Trump voter believes all the negative propaganda must be true if other people within their information warfare bubble believe them as well. It's beyond confirmation bias; it is in fact a case of national brainwashing à la the Soviet system.

This amazing turn away from American democracy while maintaining the trappings of the democratic legacy is astounding, not just because of its transparency, but in its bold assertion that what is happening is in fact American patriotism at its finest. So blinded by the Trump-Russian information stream, they think American patriotism is now defined by embracing the beliefs of a rich ex-Communist KGB officer and a con man who defrauded every blue-collar worker who ever laid eyes on him. Actor and activist Ron Perlman put it best when he said that Ronald Reagan's "Beacon on the Hill" has been replaced with an engine of hate.

That people have passion in their souls to achieve ambitions above the station of regular men and women is right and just. It is to be admired. But Donald Trump's life has been a case study of deceit in a man's heart, leading him to the ruin of the American experiment.

One of the most important statements in the entire national security debate was made by MSNBC's Joe Scarborough in an opinion editorial about Donald Trump's presidency. Scarborough noted: "While the framers of the Constitution foresaw the possibility of a tyrannical president, they never let their imaginations be darkened by the possibility of a compliant Congress."[1]

He is correct—the system was not designed to handle this level of corruption from two of the three branches of government. The founding fathers could never have conceived that their legacy, based on considered enlightenment truths, girded by science, and tempered by thoughtful discourse, of the American system of government would lose its way by willingly abdicating its role as three co-equal branches of government. Presidents and Congresses fight all the time. That was to be expected. It was a deliberate friction to incite debate and discovery. To compromise and advance legislation. To use the power of democracy to make the nation always great. Of course the framers assumed nation-states such as the great powers of Europe would attempt machinations, but the very size of the body of representation and the equal branches would put a check on that. Congress's ability to investigate chicanery stood the test even during the Civil War. But no one—not Jefferson, Franklin, Madison, Adams, Hamilton, or Washington—ever considered that the majority of the US Congress and its sustaining political party could come under the thrall of a President who gives Benito Mussolini a run for his money. It can be assured that they would have never thought of Americans bowing publicly and openly to a European adversary, whose spies had managed to seed the promise of enough gold that two-thirds of the government would consider the Constitution something of a secondary consideration—and George Washington would know, he ran numerous spy rings!

No matter what happens to Donald Trump, whether his presidency improves or collapses under its own weight, we are confronted by a party that no longer believes in the democracy that was formed by the founding fathers. For all the lip service to originalist American patriotism as it was conceived on July 4, 1776, Donald Trump has embraced policies, actions, and rhetoric that hew closer to those of King George III than George Washington.

Hold Fast!

So where do we go? What are the solutions? They are simpler than one would imagine. America was built on the lone volunteer citizen-solider, the Minuteman, standing up with whatever tools he had to hold his small part of the line of defense.

We are in an existential fight for our nation's soul. The opponents of America's historical tradition of temperate liberty are fellow citizens who accept the words of a nation whose only information source was once *Pravda*, a news source that figuratively stood for "fake news." We must stand and defend the accurate news media, the true stories that can be empirically counted. The one thing that all Americans have in equal share is their power to vote this travesty away. If every voter who voted for someone who embraced truth, decency, and dignity of our traditions (as opposed to a blustering xenophobe)—that's 65 million voters—were to bring just one person who had never voted to any election, there would be a massive tidal wave of opposition to the crisis that faces our great nation. Vote + 1 would bring to the polls 130 million voters. These numbers would reflect the real will of the American people. It is a time in American history where one must take a stand. Stand for the founding values of America. The anti-democratic opposition wants you to believe they hold the nation's values only in their hands by way of bumper stickers, the yellow Gadsden "Don't tread on me" flag, and AR-15 rifle decals with "Come and take it" adornments on their cars. That is not America or its true values. The issue is not about who owns guns, but about who loves the real American story—warts and all. This is not a debate of partisanship but one of patriotism, honor, and defense of the American national security infrastructure. If you need a refresher in that inspirational series of events, read *The Federalist Papers* or *The Debate on the Constitution*, watch the TV series *Turn: Washington's Spies*, or renew the love story of our founding fathers by listening to the soundtrack of *Hamilton*. Watch for the fault lines of the travesty and step into its face with your own voice. Discuss, protest, and make your voice heard. You must. A thought experiment: Imagine the stakes of what will be lost if you, the reader and lover of democracy, do not stand and place yourself between this new global fascism and the legacy of Philadelphia. You owe your children and, by extension, everyone who strives for a chance at democracy to have their voices heard.

Americans, Europeans, and all who cherish the promise of freedom and democracy must hold high their defense of these values. When confronted with a tyrant, like our founding fathers were, we must risk our blood, our treasure, and our very lives to resist and oppose such a corruption of those who have entered the people's house and made it a den of villainy and inequity.

2016 was a banner year for Russia. In a carefully choreographed cyberwarfare attack, the United States, France, Austria, and Montenegro would almost simultaneously fall into Moscow's sphere of influence. By January 2018, the European Union and NATO would have been on the brink of dissolution; if Trump and Le Pen both had won they would have removed their support. Montenegro would have fallen in a bloody coup, and Russia would acquire a naval base in the Adriatic.

Right-wing groups all over Europe would rise and force new elections. As Konstantin Rykov proclaimed, "It will be a new world order."

Only by the good sense of the citizens of France, a nation that saved America in the crib, through the election of Emmanuel Macron and the guardrails of American democracy, stopped the attack in its tracks. But like a bus teetering over the edge of a cliff on the Karakorum highway, it's the passengers' decision about what to do next that determines their survival. One more false step to the right and the balance of power in the world that has held the poisonous ideology of Nazism, fascism, and dictatorship at bay since 1945, may end.

One last reminder from General George Washington about who we are and what we stand for:

> "Citizens by birth or choice of a common country, that country has a right to concentrate your affections. The name of American, which belongs to you in your national capacity, must always exalt the just pride of patriotism more than any appellation derived from local discriminations. With slight shades of difference, you have the same religion, manners, habits, and political principles. You have in a common cause fought and triumphed together. The independence and liberty you possess are the work of joint councils and joint efforts—of common dangers, sufferings, and successes."

America and Europe are now joined by a common danger, a philosophy that could easily consume our enlightened histories. It is our duty to stand up to, and counterattack, this mortal threat to our freedom and liberty. All who love freedom and liberty as they were given to us at the birth of the herald of democracy must hold fast and shout out the maxim of the United States Army—"This I'll Defend"—the salvation of the greatest political democracy in the history of the world is in our hands. We are the cavalry we have been waiting for. Now stop reading. Go forth. Save democracy.

Acknowledgments

This book was made possible by the combined efforts of a dedicated team of researchers, fact checkers, global experts, and friends who gave their time and effort to making it a success. Special thanks to the PDD research team led by my friend and coauthor of *Hacking ISIS*, Chris Sampson. The principal researchers included Marina Gipps, Nicole Navega, Josh Manning, Robin Brenizer, and Heather Regnault.

To my MSNBC family, I am so proud to know each of you: Joy-Ann Reid, Brian Williams, Rachel Maddow, Chris Matthews, Chris Hayes, Lawrence O'Donnell, Katy Tur, Nicolle Wallace, Ali Velshi, Stephanie Ruhle, Joe Scarborough, Mika Brzezinski, and Phil Griffin. You are all patriots. Remember, history has its eyes on you. Stand firm. Stand fast. Stand true.

Many international experts and thought leaders gave me great insight about the inner machinations of the Russian Federation and American politics at a level far deeper than the level I have presented to make my points. The most notable were Ian Bremmer of the Eurasia Group and author Fred Kaplan, who in just one discussion revealed such a remarkable grasp of the Russian situation that the entire direction of the book was changed to better reflect the Kremlin's insidious need to influence the American elections. My friend David Frum, editor-in-chief of *The Atlantic*, and his lovely wife, Danielle, hosted roundtable discussions with some of the most noteworthy of

Washington's Trumpologists, which proved invaluable to the insights held within these pages. True experts on Russia and Donald Trump included journalists Julia Ioffe, Anne Applebaum, Tim O'Brien, Robert Costa, Sarah Kendzior, and Jonathan Alter. Their words and thoughts gave me a new lens through which to comprehend what is happening to this nation. My thanks to former NATO supreme allied commander Admiral James Stavridis in explaining the criticality of maintaining the Atlantic alliance and how we need to support our NATO allies now more than ever. Thank you to my friend ex-FBI double agent Naveed Jamali and the staff of the International Spy Museum for their assistance in clarifying the ways of Russian Intelligence. Special thanks to former CIA directors General Michael Hayden and John Brennan and, in particular, CIA officer Phil Mudd whose colorful, blunt assessments of the risks posed by Donald Trump will show in time to be historic warnings about a national threat.

Let's raise a glass to my friends in California who have helped me understand that patriotism lies within the hearts of all Americans regardless of profession and geography, in particular Rob and Michele Reiner, actor Ron Perlman, superstar talk show host Bill Maher (whose show *Real Time* finally got me recognized on the street in Oslo!) and his staff Scott Carter and Susan Bennett, radio diva Stephanie Miller, the comedy duo Frances Callier and Angela V. Shelton aka Frangela, and my buddy Jean Scally. In Philadelphia, my crew of originalist revolutionaries known as the "Grown-ups of the Resistance" for their stimulating political discussions during our morning meetings at the Mount Airy High Point Café, they include the notable Philadelphian Todd Bernstein as well as Randy, Doc Saeed, Mark, Peter (the Shah), Steve, Ken, and Bob.

My deepest thanks to my manager, Josanne Lopez, her soon-to-be-spy daughter Seblé, and my daughter Nadia, whose assistance has been invaluable to both this book and our sanity.

This book is dedicated to my wife, Maryse. Her guidance, love, companionship, and tough military spousal support helped navigate my career to the point where my opinion is not only valued but might even be called wise. Never thank me for my service, thank her.

Notes

Chapter 1: Shots Fired

1 Associated Press, Clinton Adviser Connects Trump's Long-Time Aide to WikiLeaks, Fortune, October 12, 2016, http://fortune.com/2016/10/11/clinton-john-podesta -roger-stone-wikileaks-russia/

2 Julian Hattem, Michelle Obama's passport, White House planning materials leaked, The Hill, September 22, 2016, http://thehill.com/policy/national-security/297207 -michelle-obamas-passport-white-house-planning-materials-leaked

3 Luke Harding, Stephanie Kirchgaessner, Nick Hopkins, British spies were first to spot Trump team's links with Russia, The Guardian, April 13, 2017, https://www.theguard ian.com/uk-news/2017/apr/13/british-spies-first-to-spot-trump-team-links-russia

4 William Mansell, Who Is George Papadopoulos? Read Indictment After For-mer Trump Aide Pleads Guilty, International Business Times, October 30, 2017, http://www.ibtimes.com/who-george-papadopoulos-read-indictment-after-former -trump-aide-pleads-guilty-2608099

5 Robert Windrem, Guess Who Came to Dinner with Flynn and Putin, NBC News, April 18, 2017, https://www.nbcnews.com/news/world/guess-who-came-dinner-flynn -putin-n742696

6 Rick Noak, How a Dutch intelligence agency secretly hacked into the Kremlin's most notorious hacking group, Independent, January 28, 2018, http://www.independent .co.uk/news/world/europe/netherlands-dutch-russia-kremlin-united-states-robert -mueller-intelligence-agencies-cozy-bear-aivd-a8181046.html

7 Huib Modderkolk, Dutch agencies provide crucial intel about Russia's inter-ference in US-elections, De Volkskrant, January 25, 2018, https://www.volksk rant.nl/media/dutch-agencies-provide-crucial-intel-about-russia-s-interference -in-us-elections~a4561913/

8 Mike Eckel, Ex-CIA Chief Brennan Complained to FSB Director in August Of Election Meddling, RadioFree Europe RadioLiberty, May 23, 2017, https://www .rferl.org/a/u-s-russia-brennan-fsb-election-meddling-collusion/28504859.html

9 Steve Benen, CIA warned lawmakers about Russia's pro-Trump efforts last summer, MSNBC, April 7, 2017, http://www.msnbc.com/rachel-maddow-show/cia-warned -lawmakers-about-russias-pro-trump-efforts-last-summer

10 Eric Bradner, Former top CIA official: Putin wants Trump to win, CNN, Sep-tember 11, 2016, http://www.cnn.com/2016/09/11/politics/michael-morell-donald -trump-putin-russia/index.html

11　Ellen Nakashima, U.S. Government Officially Accuses Russia of Hacking Campaign to Interfere with Elections, The Washington Post, October 7, 2016, https://www.washingtonpost.com/world/national-security/us-government-officially-accuses-russia-of-hacking-campaign-to-influence-elections/2016/10/07/4e0b9654-8cbf-11e6-875e-2c1bfe943b66_story.html?utm_term=.6409fb7871ab

12　Ellen Nakashima, U.S. Government Officially Accuses Russia of Hacking Campaign to Interfere with Elections, The Washington Post, October 7, 2016, https://www.washingtonpost.com/world/national-security/us-government-officially-accuses-russia-of-hacking-campaign-to-influence-elections/2016/10/07/4e0b9654-8cbf-11e6-875e-2c1bfe943b66_story.html?utm_term=.6409fb7871ab

13　Mike Eckel, Ex-CIA Chief Brennan Complained to FSB Director in August Of Election Meddling, RadioFreeEurope RadioLiberty, May 23, 2017, https://www.rferl.org/a/u-s-russia-brennan-fsb-election-meddling-collusion/28504859.html

14　Evan Perez, Shimon Prokupecz, Wesley Bruer, Feds Believe Russians Hacked Florida Election Systems Vendor, CNN, October 12, 2016, http://www.cnn.com/2016/10/12/politics/florida-election-hack/index.html

15　Mike Levine, Pierre Thomas, Russian Hackers Targeted Nearly Half of States' Voter Registration Systems, Successfully Infiltrated 4, ABC News, September 29, 2016, http://abcnews.go.com/US/russian-hackers-targeted-half-states-voter-registration-systems/story?id=42435822

16　Aaron Blake, The Final Trump-Clinton Debate Transcript, Annotated, The Washington Post, October 19, 2016, https://www.washingtonpost.com/news/the-fix/wp/2016/10/19/the-final-trump-clinton-debate-transcript-annotated/?utm_term=.c54ddc7619c6#annotations:10669010

17　Frank Newport Lisa Singh, Stuart Soroka, Michael Traugott, Andrew Dugan, Email Dominates What Americans Have Heard About Clinton, Gallup News, September 19, 2016, http://news.gallup.com/poll/195596/email-dominates-americans-heard-clinton.aspx

18　Andrew Solomon, Travel as Antidote to Xenophobia, The Boston Globe, May 12, 2016, https://www.bostonglobe.com/opinion/2016/05/11/travel-antidote-xenophobia/ZMwdqxXi24bSPbLUM0rMxI/story.html

Chapter 2: Reporting to Moscow

1　Alexander Hamilton, Enclosure (Objections and Answers Respecting the Administration), Founders Online, August 18, 1972, https://founders.archives.gov/documents/Hamilton/01-12-02-0184-0002

2　Michael S. Schmidt, Comey Memo Says Trump Asked Him to End Flynn Investigation, The New York Times, May 16, 2017, https://www.nytimes.com/2017/05/16/us/politics/james-comey-trump-flynn-russia-investigation.html

3　Reuters, Comey Infuriated Trump with Refusal to Preview Senate Testimony: Aides, Reuters, May 10, 2017, https://www.cnbc.com/2017/05/10/comey-infuriated-trump-with-refusal-to-preview-senate-testimony-aides.html

4　CNN, Trump's Letter Firing FBI Director Comey, CNN, May 10, 2017, https://www.cnn.com/2017/05/09/politics/fbi-james-comey-fired-letter/index.html

5　Erik Ortiz, Trump Defends Comey Firing, Mocks Democrats for Playing 'So Sad,' NBC News, May 10, 2017, https://www.nbcnews.com/politics/donald-trump/trump-defends-comey-firing-mocks-democrats-playing-so-sad-n757281

6　Erik Ortiz, Trump Defends Comey Firing, Mocks Democrats for Playing 'So Sad,' NBC News, May 10, 2017, https://www.nbcnews.com/politics/donald-trump/trump-defends-comey-firing-mocks-democrats-playing-so-sad-n757281

7　Erik Ortiz, Trump Defends Comey Firing, Mocks Democrats for Playing 'So Sad,' NBC News, May 10, 2017. https://www.nbcnews.com/politics/donald-trump/trump-defends-comey-firing-mocks-democrats-playing-so-sad-n757281

8 Doug Stanglin, Trump's Meeting with Russians Closed to U.S. Media, Not to TASS Photographer, USA Today, May 10, 2017, https://www.usatoday.com/story/news/2017/05/10/trumps-meeting-russians-closed-us-media-but-not-tass-photographer/101520384/

9 Matt Apuzzo, Maggie Haberman, Matthew Rosenberg, Trump Told Russians That Firing 'Nut Job' Comey Eased Pressure from Investigation, The New York Times, May 19, 2017, https://www.nytimes.com/2017/05/19/us/politics/trump-russia-comey.html

10 Sabrina Siddiqui, Ben Jacobs, Donald Trump 'Shared Highly Classified Information with Russian Officials,' Guardian, May 16, 2017, https://www.theguardian.com/us-news/2017/may/15/donald-trump-shared-classified-information-russia-white-house-report

11 NBC News, Lester Holt's Extended Interview with President Trump, NBC News, May 11, 2017, https://www.nbcnews.com/nightly-news/video/pres-trump-s-extended-exclusive-interview-with-lester-holt-at-the-white-house-941854787582

12 Ali Vitali, Corky Siemaszko, Trump Interview with Lester Holt: President Asked Comey If He Was Under Investigation, NBC News, May 11, 2017, https://www.nbcnews.com/news/us-news/trump-reveals-he-asked-comey-whether-he-was-under-investigation-n757821

13 Eugene Scott, Trump Threatens Comey in Twitter Outburst, CNN, May 12, 2017, http://www.cnn.com/2017/05/12/politics/donald-trump-james-comey-threat/index.html

14 Michael Schmidt, Maggie Haberman, Trump Ordered Mueller Fired, but Backed Off When White House Counsel Threatened to Quit, New York Times, January 25, 2018, https://www.nytimes.com/2018/01/25/us/politics/trump-mueller-special-counsel-russia.html?hp&action=click&pgtype=Homepage&clickSource=story-heading&module=a-lede-package-region&region=top-news&WT.nav=top-news

15 Peter Baker, Michael S. Schmidt, Maggie Haberman, Citing Recusal, Trump Says He Wouldn't Have Hired Sessions, New York Times, July 19, 2017, https://www.nytimes.com/2017/07/19/us/politics/trump-interview-sessions-russia.html

16 Katie Bo Williams, Declassified report: Putin ordered election interference to help Trump, The Hill, January 6, 2017, http://thehill.com/policy/national-security/313108-declassified-report-putin-ordered-election-interference-to-help

17 Natasha Bertrand, Paul Manafort, Rick Gates, indicted in Mueller probe, plead not guilty, Business Insider, October 30, 2017, http://www.businessinsider.com/paul-manafort-indicted-by-special-counsel-robert-mueller-and-told-to-surrender-2017-10

Chapter 3: Make Russia Great Again

1 Fiona Hill, Clifford G. Gaddy, Mr. Putin: Operative in the Kremlin, Brooking Institute press (Washington, DC, Brookings Institution Press, 2013), https://static.squarespace.com/static/538f6712e4b0c1af61fbb317/t/53d27f17e4b0498d331ad768/1406304023526/MrPutin.pdf

2 Andrei P. Tsygankov, Russia's Foreign Policy: Change and Continuity in National Identity (United Kingdom: Rowman & Littlefield Publishing Group, 2013), pg. 28

3 Fiona Hill, Clifford G. Gaddy, Vladimir Putin's Risky Ploy to Manufacture History, The Atlantic, January 12, 2012, https://www.theatlantic.com/international/archive/2012/01/vladimir-putins-risky-ploy-to-manufacture-history/251269/

4 Fiona Hill, Clifford G. Gaddy, Mr. Putin: Operative in the Kremlin (Washington, DC, The Brookings Institution, 2013), pg. 10

5 Michael Wines 'None of Us Can Get Out' Kursk Sailor Wrote, New York Times, October 27, 2000, http://www.nytimes.com/2000/10/27/world/none-of-us-can-get-out-kursk-sailor-wrote.html

6 Gleb Pavlovsky, Interview with Gleb Pavlovsky, The Putin Files, Frontline, July 13, 2017, https://www.pbs.org/wgbh/frontline/interview/gleb-pavlovsky/

7 Angela Stent, The Limits of Partnership: U.S.—Russian Relations in the Twenty-First Century (Princeton: Princeton University Press, 2014), pg. 82-96

8 D. Eglitis, The Baltic Countries: Changes and Challenges in the New Europe, in Central & East European Politics: From Communism to Democracy, eds. SL Wolchik & JL Curry (London: Roman & Littlefield, 2015), pg. 322

9 Angela E. Stent, The Limits of Partnership: U.S.—Russian Relations in the Twenty-First Century (Princeton: Princeton University Press, 2014), pg. 103-118

10 Samuel Charap, Timothy J. Colton, Everyone Loses: The Ukraine Crisis and the Ruinous Contest for Post-Soviet Eurasia, The International Institute for Strategic Studies (New York: Routledge, 2017), pg. 89

11 Christian Neef, Matthias Schepp, Medvedev's Betrayal of Russian Democracy, October 4, 2011, Spiegel Online, http://www.spiegel.de/international/world/the -puppet-president-medvedev-s-betrayal-of-russian-democracy-a-789767.html

12 Samuel Charap, Timothy J. Colton, Everyone Loses: The Ukraine Crisis and the Ruinous Contest for Post-Soviet Eurasia, The International Institute for Strategic Studies (New York: Routledge, 2017), pg. 91-94

13 Gleb Pavlosky, Interview with Gleb Pavlovsky, The Putin Files, Frontline, https://www .pbs.org/wgbh/frontline/interview/gleb-pavlovsky/

14 Samuel Charap, Timothy J. Colton, Everyone Loses: The Ukraine Crisis and the Ruinous Contest for Post-Soviet Eurasia (New York: Routledge, 2017), pg. 118-122

15 Gleb Pavlovsky, Interview with Gleb Pavlovsky, The Putin Files, Frontline, July 13, 2017, https://www.pbs.org/wgbh/frontline/interview/gleb-pavlovsky/

16 The Economist, Igor Sechin, head of Rosneft, is powerful as never before, The Economist, December 15, 2016, https://www.economist.com/news/europe/21711921-russian-oil-king-former-aide-vladimir-putin-and-friend-rex-tillerson-igor-sechin-head

17 Jack Farchy, Igor Sechin: Russia's second most powerful man, Financial Times, April 28, 2014, https://www.ft.com/content/a8f24922-cef4-11e3-9165-00144feabdc0

18 The Economist, Igor Sechin, head of Rosneft, is powerful as never before, December 15, 2016, https://www.economist.com/news/europe/21711921-russian-oil-king-for mer-aide-vladimir-putin-and-friend-rex-tillerson-igor-sechin-head

19 Al Jazeera, Russia's Vladimir Putin Sergei Ivanov, Al Jazeera, August 12, 2016, http://www.aljazeera.com/news/2016/08/vladimir-putin-dismisses-chief-staff -sergei-ivanov-160812111051560.html

20 Mikhail Fishman, Putin Closes Russia's Drug Agency, Casts Aside Longtime Supporter Ivanov, Moscow Times, May 19, 2016, https://themoscowtimes.com/articles/ putin-closes-russias-drugs-agency-casts-aside-longtime-supporter-ivanov-52936

21 Reuters Staff, Medvedev promotes another Putin KGB ally, Reuters, May 15, 2008, https://in.reuters.com/article/russia-ivanov-appointment/medvedev-promotes-another -putin-kgb-ally-idINL1581146420080515

22 Litvinenko Inquiry Report: Report into the death of Alexander Litvinenko, https:// www.litvinenkoinquiry.org/files/Litvinenko-Inquiry-Report-web-version.pdf, pg. 100

23 Susan B. Glasser, Minister No, Foreign Policy, March 29, 2013, http://foreignpolicy .com/2013/04/29/minister-no/

24 Anthony Cormier, Jeremy Singer-Vine, John Templon, Trump's longtime lawyer is defending Russia's biggest bank, BuzzFeed News, March 23, 2017, https://www .buzzfeed.com/anthonycormier/trumps-longtime-lawyer-is-defending-russias -biggest-bank?utm_term=.uvnz29Pbw#.qhYe35PA2

Chapter 4: Putin's Philosophy

1 Gleb Pavlovsky, Interview with Gleb Pavlovsky, The Putin Files, Frontline, July 13, 2017, https://www.pbs.org/wgbh/frontline/interview/gleb-pavlovsky/

2 Shaun Walker, Kremlin puppet master's leaked emails are a price of return to political frontline, The Guardian, October 26, 2016, https://www.theguardian.com/world/2016/ oct/26/kremlin-puppet-masters-leaked-emails-vladislav-surkov-east-ukraine

3 Constitution of the Soviet Socialist Republics, 1977, http://www.departments.bucknell
.edu/russian/const/77cons01.html.

4 Vladmir Illych Lenin, The Transition from Capitalism to Communism, The State and
Revolution, 1917, Marxists.org

5 Peter Pomerantsev, The Hidden Author of Putinism, The Atlantic, November 7, 2014,
https://www.theatlantic.com/international/archive/2014/11/hidden-author-puti
nism-russia-vladislav-surkov/382489/

6 Tatiana Stanovaya, The Fate of Nashi Movement: Where Will The Kremlin's Youth
Go?, The Institute of Modern Russia, March 26, 2013, https://imrussia.org/en/
politics/420-the-fate-of-the-nashi-movement-where-will-the-kremlins-youth-go

7 Peter Pomerantsev, The Hidden Author of Putinism, The Atlantic, November 7, 2014,
https://www.theatlantic.com/international/archive/2014/11/hidden-author-puti
nism-russia-vladislav-surkov/382489/

8 Andrei Soldatov, Irina Borogan, The Red Web: The struggle between Russia's digital dictators and the new online revolutionaries (United States: Public Affairs, 2015),
pg. 111

9 Viktor Jerofejev, A Suicide Novel, Central Europe Forum Salon, November 27, 2012,
http://salon.eu.sk/en/archiv/9151

10 Yuliya Komska, Can The Kremlin's Bizarre Sci-Fi Stories Tell Us What Russia
Really Wants?, Pacific Standard, April 15, 2014, https://psmag.com/social-justice/can
-kremlins-bizarre-sci-fi-stories-tell-us-russia-really-wants-78908

11 Shaun Walker, Kremlin puppet master's leaked emails are a price of return to political frontline, The Guardian, October 26, 2016, https://www.theguardian.com/
world/2016/oct/26/kremlin-puppet-masters-leaked-emails-vladislav-surkov-east
-ukraine

12 James Heiser, Putin's Rasputin: The Mad Mystic Who Inspired Russia's Leader,
Breitbart, June 10, 2014, http://www.breitbart.com/national-security/2014/06/10/
putin-s-rasputin-the-mad-mystic-who-inspired-putin/

13 Anton Shekhovtsov, The Palingenetic Thrust of Russian Neo-Eurasianism: Ideas of
Rebirth in Aleksandr Dugin's Worldview, December 2018, http://www.academia
.edu/194083/The_Palingenetic_Thrust_of_Russian_Neo-Eurasianism_Ideas_of
_Rebirth_in_Aleksandr_Dugins_Worldview

14 Jack Gilbert, We spoke to the man who's been labelled 'Putin's brain,' Vice, April 28, 2014,
https://www.vice.com/en_uk/article/3b7a93/aleksandr-dugin-russian-expansionism

15 Jack Gilbert, We spoke to the man who's been labelled Putin's Brain, Vice, April 28,
2014, https://www.vice.com/en_uk/article/3b7a93/aleksandr-dugin-russian-expan
sionism

16 Alexander Dugin, Eurasian Mission: An Introduction to Neo-Eurasianism (United
Kingdom: Arktos Media, 2014)

17 Alexander Dugin, Russian Geopolitician: Trump Is Real America, Katehon, February 02,
2016, http://katehon.com/article/russian-geopolitician-trump-real-america

18 Aleksandr Dugin, Dugin's Guideline—In Trump We Trust, Katehon Think Tank,
March 4, 2016, https://www.youtube.com/watch?v=aOWIoMtIvDQ

19 Aleksandr Dugin, Dugin's Guideline—In Trump We Trust, Katehon Think Tank,
March 4, 2016, https://www.youtube.com/watch?v=aOWIoMtIvDQ

20 Aleksandr Dugin, Donald Trump's Victory, Katehon Think Tank, November 10, 2016,
https://www.youtube.com/watch?v=uEQINJdR8jo

21 Aleksandr Dugin, Donald Trump's Victory, Katehon Think Tank, November 10,
2016, https://www.youtube.com/watch?v=uEQINJdR8jo

22 Aleksandr Dugin, Donald Trump's Victory, Katehon Think Tank, November 10, 2016,
https://www.youtube.com/watch?v=uEQINJdR8jo

23 Aleksandr Dugin, Dugin's Guideline—In Trump We Trust, Katehon Think Tank,
March 4, 2016, https://www.youtube.com/watch?v=aOWIoMtIvDQ

24 Owen Matthews, The Kremlin's Campaign to Make Friends, Newsweek, February 16, 2015, http://www.newsweek.com/2015/02/27/kremlins-campaign-make-friends -307158.html

25 Ionut Illascu, Russian hackers leak list of pro-Russian influence group made of high-profile European individuals, Softpedia News, December 4, 2014, http:// news.softpedia.com/news/Russian-Hackers-Leak-List-of-Pro-Russian-Influence -Group-Made-of-High-Profile-European-Individuals-466418.shtml

26 Andrew Osborn, As if Things Weren't Bad Enough, Russian Professor Predicts End of U.S, Wall Street Journal, December 29, 2008, https://www.wsj.com/articles/ SB123051100709638419

27 Andrew Osborn, As if Things Weren't Bad Enough, Russian Professor Predicts End of U.S, Wall Street Journal, December 29, 2008, https://www.wsj.com/articles/ SB123051100709638419

28 Andrew Osborn, As if Things Weren't Bad Enough, Russian Professor Predicts End of U.S, Wall Street Journal, December 29, 2008, https://www.wsj.com/articles/ SB123051100709638419

29 Robert O'Harrow, Jr., Shawn Boburg, During His Political Rise, Stephen K. Bannon Was a Man with No Fixed Address, The Washington Post, March 11, 2017, www.washingtonpost.com/investigations/during-his-political-rise-stephen-k -bannon-was-a-man-with-no-fixed-address/2017/03/11/89866f4c-0285-11e7 -ad5b-d22680e18d10_story.html?utm_term=.8b6a2ebf76fe.

30 Joshua Green, This Man Is the Most Dangerous Political Operative in America, Bloomberg Politics, October 8, 2015, www.bloomberg.com/politics/graphics/2015-steve-bannon/.

31 Shawn Boburg, Emily Rauhala, Stephen K. Bannon Once Guided a Global Firm That Made Millions Helping Gamers Cheat, The Washington Post, August 4, 2017, www.washingtonpost.com/investigations/steve-bannon-once-guided-a-global-firm -that-made-millions-helping-gamers-cheat/2017/08/04/ef7ae442-76c8-11e7-803f -a6c989606ac7_story.html?utm_term=.b148f97309bd

32 Steve Bannon's Would-Be Coalition of Christian Traditionalists, Yahoo, March 23, 2017, https://www.yahoo.com/news/steve-bannons-coalition-christian-traditionalists-085000579.html

33 Ronald Radosh, Steve Bannon, Trump's Top Guy, Told Me He Was 'a Leninist,' The Daily beast, August 22, 2016, https://www.thedailybeast.com/steve-bannon -trumps-top-guy-told-me-he-was-a-leninist

Chapter 5: A Rising Russia, a Failing America

1 Gary Kasparov, Twitter: @kasparov63, 2018, https://twitter.com/Kasparov63

2 Jack Farchy, Putin names NATO among threats in new Russian security strategy, Financial Times, January 2, 2016, https://www.ft.com/content/6e8e787e-b15f-11e5 -b147-e5e5bba42e51

3 Matthew N. Janeczko, The Russian Counterinsurgency Operation in Checnya Part 2: Success, But At What Cost? 1999-2004, Small Wars Journal, November 2, 2012, http://smallwarsjournal.com/jrnl/art/the-russian-counterinsurgency-operation-in -chechnya-part-2-success-but-at-what-cost-1999

4 Julia Ioffe, Why Many Young Russians See a Hero in Putin, National Geographic, December 2016, https://www.nationalgeographic.com/magazine/2016/ 12/putin-generation-russia-soviet-union/

5 The Economist, Putin's New Model Army, The Economist, May 24, 2014, https:// www.economist.com/news/europe/21602743-money-and-reform-have-given -russia-armed-forces-it-can-use-putins-new-model-army

6 John Simpson, Russia's Crimea Plan Detailed, Secret, and Successful, BBC, March 19, 2014, http://www.bbc.com/news/world-europe-26644082

7 Bettina Renz, Hanna Smith, Russia and Hybrid Warfare: Definitions, Capabilities, Scope, and Possible Responses, Finnish Prime Minister's Office, January 2016, https://www.stratcomcoe.org/download/file/fid/4920

8 Defense Intelligence Agency, Russia: Military Power, Building a Military to Support Great Power Aspirations, Defense Intelligence Agency, June 28, 2017, http://www.dia.mil/Portals/27/Documents/News/Military%20Power%20Publications/Russia%20Military%20Power%20Report%202017.pdf

9 Andrew Osborn, Putin, in Syria, Says Mission Accomplished, Orders Partial Russian Pull-Out, Reuters, December 11, 2017, https://www.reuters.com/article/us-mideast-crisis-syria-russia-putin/putin-in-syria-says-mission-accomplished-orders-partial-russian-pull-out-idUSKBN1E50X1

10 Carlo Jose Vicente Caro, Moscow's Historical Relations with Damascus: Why It Matters Now, Huffington Post, https://www.huffingtonpost.com/carlo-caro/moscows-historical-relati_b_9065430.html

11 Henry Austin, Russia Threatens to Retaliate Against U.S. Forces in Syria, Independent, September 21, 2017, http://www.independent.co.uk/news/world/russia-us-syria-war-putin-trump-target-forces-retaliate-latest-a7960376.html

12 Jeremy Bender, The Hazing Epidemic That's Holding Back Russia's Military, Business Insider, May 29, 2014, http://www.businessinsider.com/hazing-is-holding-back-russias-military-2014-5

13 The Economist, War Games, The Economist, October 29, 2009, http://www.economist.com/node/14776852

14 Ken Gude, How Putin Undermines Democracy in the West, Chapter and Verse, Newsweek, March 18, 2017, http://www.newsweek.com/how-putin-undermines-democracy-west-chapter-and-verse-568607

15 Yury E. Federov, Continuity and Change in Russia's Policy Toward Central and Eastern Europe, Communist and Post-Communist Studies 46 (2013), pg. 323

16 Eglitis, "The Baltic Countries: Changes and Challenges in the New Europe," pg. 336.

17 Yury E. Federov, Continuity and Change in Russia's Policy Toward Central and Eastern Europe, September 2013, pg. 323

18 Holly Ellyatt, CNBC, "Putin abandons United Russia party, will run as an independent in 2018 election," December 14, 2017, https://www.cnbc.com/2017/12/14/putin-to-run-as-an-independent-in-2018-election.html

19 Mikhail Zygar, All the Kremlin's Men: Inside the Court of Vladamir Putin (United States: Public Affairs, 2016), pg. 64

20 Arkady Ostrovskey, The Invention of Russia: The Rise of Putin and the Age of Fake News (New York: Penguin Books, 2015), pg. 30

21 Denis Grishkin, Rogozin's Rodina Party Reinstated, The Moscow Times, October 1, 2012, https://themoscowtimes.com/articles/rogozins-rodina-party-reinstated-18170

22 Casey Michel, Russia Wants Texas and Puerto Rico to Secede, Daily Beast, September 24, 2015, https://www.thedailybeast.com/russia-wants-texas-and-puerto-rico-to-secede

23 CDM, Rogozin's party seeks protection for Shishmakov and Popov, CDM, October 13, 2017, https://www.cdm.me/english/rogozins-party-seeks-protection-shishmakov-popov/

24 Ben Farmer, Surveillance photos show Russian officers plotting Montenegro coup, The Telegraph, August 29, 2017, http://www.telegraph.co.uk/news/2017/08/28/surveillance-photos-show-russian-intelligence-officers-plotting/

25 Julie Corwin, Radio Free Europe Radio Liberty, "Russia: A Youth Movement Needs a Leader," April 21, 2005, https://www.rferl.org/a/1058597.html

26 Andrew Osborn, Telegraph, "Pro-Kremlin youth group accused of plagiarizing Goebbels," November 15, 2010, https://www.telegraph.co.uk/news/world

news/europe/russia/8134688/Pro-Kremlin-youth-group-accused-of-plagiarising
-Goebbels.html

27 Charles Clover, Black Wind, White Snow (Yale, 2016), pg. 281

28 United States Treasury, "Treasury Announces New Designations of Ukrainian Sep-
    aratists and Their Russian Supporters," March 11, 2015, https://www.treasury.gov/
    press-center/press-releases/Pages/jl9993.aspx

29 Associated Press, "Inside the radical 'war camps' where Russian fighters are born,"
    October 18, 2016, https://nypost.com/2016/10/18/inside-the-radical-war-camps
    -where-russian-fighters-are-born/

30 Josephine Huetlin, Russian extremists are training right wing terrorists from
    Western Europe, The Daily Beast, August 02, 2017, https://www.thedaily
    beast.com/russian-extremists-are-training-right-wing-terrorists-from-western
    -europe

31 Andrew Roth, A right-wing militia trains Russians to fight the next war with or
    without Putin, The Washington Post, January 2, 2017, https://www.washingtonpost
    .com/world/europe/a-right-wing-militia-trains-russians-to-fight-the-next-war
    —with-or-without-putin/2017/01/02/f06b5ce8-b71e-11e6-939c-91749443c5e5
    _story.html?utm_term=.bebb7b794dcc

32 Interview with Stanislav Vorobyov, https://www.zaks.ru/new/archive/view/135459

33 Interview with Stanislav Vorobyov, https://www.zaks.ru/new/archive/view/135459

34 Anton Shekhovtsov, Russian fascist militants give money to Swedish counterparts,
    September 19, 2015, http://anton-shekhovtsov.blogspot.com/2015/09/russian-fascist
    -militants-give-money-to.html

35 Justin Spike, suspected neo-Nazi shoots, kills police officer near Gyor, Buda-
    pest Beacon, October 26, 2016, https://budapestbeacon.com/suspected-neo-nazi
    -shoots-kills-police-officer-near-gyor/

36 Dezso Andras, Szabolcs Panyi, Russian diplomats exercised with Hungarian cop
    killer's far-right gang, Index, October 28, 2016, https://index.hu/english/2016/10/
    28/russian_diplomats_exercised_with_hungarian_cop_killer_s_far-right_gang/

37 Pierre Sautreuil, Believe It or Not, Russia Dislikes Relying on Military Contrac-
    tors, March 9, 2016, War is Boring, warisboring.com/believe-it-or-not-russia-dis
    likes-relying-on-military-contractors/

38 Последний бой «Славянского корпуса, Fontanka.ru, November 14, 2013, http://www
    .fontanka.ru/2013/11/14/060/

39 Feral Jundi, Cool Stuff: A Russian Contractor Gives the Low Down on His Indus-
    try, Feral Jundi, July 30, 2015, http://feraljundi.com/2015/07/30/cool-stuff
    -a-russian-contractor-gives-the-low-down-on-his-industry/

40 Feral Jundi, Industry Talk: The Slavonic Corps–A Russian PMSC In Syria,
    Feral Jundi, January 14, 2014, http://feraljundi.com/2014/01/14/industry-talk
    -the-slavonic-corps-a-russian-pmsc-in-syria/

41 Pierre Sautreuil, Believe It or Not, Russia Dislikes Relying on Military Contrac-
    tors, March 9, 2016, War is Boring, warisboring.com/believe-it-or-not-russia-dis
    likes-relying-on-military-contractors/

42 Andrew E. Kramer, Russia Deploys a Potent Weapon in Syria: The Profit Motive, New
    York Times, July 5, 2017, https://www.nytimes.com/2017/07/05/world/middleeast/
    russia-syria-oil-isis.html

43 Zakharova Downplays Armed Clash with Americans in Syria, Kremlin-
    linked Audio Recordings Contradict Her Story, February 16, 2018, Polygraph
    .info, https://www.polygraph.info/a/us-wagner-russia-syria-scores-killed/29044339
    .html

44 Aaron Mehta, Mattis: Unclear if Russia Directed Attack Against U.S. Allies in
    Syria, Military Times, February 18, 2018, https://www.militarytimes.com/flash
    points/2018/02/17/mattis-unclear-if-russia-directed-attack-against-us-allies
    -in-syria/

45 Zakharova Downplays Armed Clash with Americans in Syria, Kremlin-linked Audio Recordings Contradict Her Story, February 16, 2018, Polygraph.info, https://www .polygraph.info/a/us-wagner-russia-syria-scores-killed/29044339.html

Chapter 6: Active Measures

1 Soviet Active Measures: Hearings before the Subcommittee on European Affairs of The Committee on Foreign Relations, United States Senate, Ninety-Ninth Congress, September 12 and 13, 1985, http://www.loc.gov/law/find/nominations/gates/ 017_excerpt.pdf

2 Christopher Andrew, Vasill Mitrokhin, The Sword and Shield: The Mitrokhin Archive and the Secret History of the KGB (New York, New York: Basic Books, 1999), pg. 10

3 Susan B. Glasser, Ex-Spy Chief: Russia's Election Hacking Was an 'Intelligence Failure,' Politico Magazine, December 11, 2017, https://www.politico.com/magazine/ story/2017/12/11/the-full-transcript-michael-morell-216061

4 Secret Police, Revelations from the Russian Archives: Internal Workings of the Soviet Union, Library of Congress, https://www.loc.gov/exhibits/archives/intn .html

5 Christopher Andrew, Vasill Mitrokhin, The Sword and Shield: The Mitrokhin Archive and the Secret History of the KGB (New York, New York: Basic Books, 1999), pg. 10

6 Amy Knight, The KGB, Perestroika, and the Collapse of the Soviet Union, Journal of Cold War Studies 5, no. 1 (Winter 2003), pg. 67-93.

7 Soviet Active Measures, Testimony before the House of Representatives Permanent Select Committee on Intelligence, 97th Congress, July 13, 1982, (statement of John McMahon), pg. 30.

8 Tennent H. Bagley, Spymaster: Startling Cold War Revelations of a Soviet KGB Chief (SkyHorse, 2013), pg. 171

9 Tennent H. Bagley, Spymaster: Startling Cold War Revelations of a Soviet KGB Chief (SkyHorse, 2013), pg. 172

10 Christopher Andrew, Vasill Mitrokhin, The Sword and Shield: The Mitrokhin Archive and the Secret History of the KGB (New York, New York: Basic Books, 1999), pg. 144

11 Christopher Andrew, Vasill Mitrokhin, The Sword and Shield: The Mitrokhin Archive and the Secret History of the KGB (New York, New York: Basic Books, 1999), pg. 144

12 Tennent H. Bagley, Spymaster: Startling Cold War Revelations of a Soviet KGB Chief (SkyHorse, 2013), pg. 167

13 Tennent H. Bagley, Spymaster: Startling Cold War Revelations of a Soviet KGB Chief (SkyHorse, 2013), pg. 167

14 John Barron, KGB: The Secret Work of Soviet Secret Agents (Bantam Books, 1974), pg. 226

15 Testimony of Stanislav Levchenko, Permanent Select Committee on Intelligence— House of Representatives, July 14, 1982, http://njlaw.rutgers.edu/collections/gdoc/ hearings/8/82603795/82603795_1.pdf

16 Soviet Active Measures, Testimony before the House of Representatives Permanent Select Committee on Intelligence, 97th Congress, July 13, 1982 (statement of John McMahon), pg. 35

17 Christopher Andrew, Vasill Mitrokhin, The Sword and Shield: The Mitrokhin Archive and the Secret History of the KGB (New York, New York: Basic Books, 1999), pg. 215

18 Ladislav Bittman, The KGB and Soviet Disinformation, An Insider's View (Pergamon-Brasseys International Defense Publishers, 1985), pg. 25

19 Ladislov Bittman, The KGB and Soviet Disinformation, An Insider's View (Pergamon-Brasseys International Defense Publishers, 1985), pg. 47

20 Ladislav Bittman, The KGB and Soviet Disinformation, An Insider's View (Permagon-Brasseys International Defense Publishers, 1985), pg. 29

21 Pete Earley, Comrade J: The Untold Secrets of Russia's Master Spy in America After the End of the Cold War (Penguin Books, 2007), pg. 195

22 Ladislav Bittman, The KGB and Soviet Disinformation, An Insider's View, (Pergamon-Brasseys International Defense Publishers, 1985), pg. 56

23 John Barron, KGB: The Secret Work of Soviet Secret Agents (Bantam Books, 1974), pg. 239

24 John Barron, KGB: The Secret Work of Soviet Secret Agents (Bantam Books, 1974), pg. 243

25 Pete Earley, Comrade J: The Untold Secrets of Russia's Master Spy in America After the End of the Cold War (Penguin Books, 2007), pg. 195

26 Ladislav Bittman, The KGB and Soviet Disinformation, An Insider's View (Pergamon-Brasseys International Defense Publishers, 1985), pg. 51

27 Ladislav Bittman, The KGB and Soviet Disinformation, An Insider's View (Pergamon-Brasseys International Defense Publishers, 1985), pg. 36

28 The Moscow Times, Shoigu, Lavrov Deny that Crimean Forces are Russian, The Moscow Times, March 5, 2014, https://themoscowtimes.com/articles/shoigu-lavrov-deny-that-crimean-forces-are-russian-32709

29 ABC News, Ukrainian defense ministry says Russian forces have seized missile defense units in Crimea, ABC News, March 5, 2014, http://www.abc.net.au/news/2014-03-05/russia/5301724

30 Christopher Andrew, Vasill Mitrokhin, The Sword and Shield: The Mitrokhin Archive and the Secret History of the KGB (Basic Books), pg. 33

31 Christopher Andrew, Vasill Mitrokhin, The Sword and Shield: The Mitrokhin Archive and the Secret History of the KGB (Basic Books), pg. 37

32 Christopher Andrew, Vasill Mitrokhin, The Sword and Shield: The Mitrokhin Archive and the Secret History of the KGB (Basic Books), pg. 17

33 John Barron, KGB: The Secret Work of Soviet Secret Agents (Bantam Books, 1974), pg. 245

34 Vanora Bennet, Russian Justice Minister Falls Victim to Sex Scandal, Los Angeles Times, June 23, 1997, http://articles.latimes.com/1997-06-23/news/mn-6203_1_justice-minister

35 Robyn Dixon, Kremlin Official Suspended Amid a Sex Scandal, Los Angeles Times, April 3, 1999, http://articles.latimes.com/1999/apr/03/news/mn-23855

36 Julia Ioffe, How State-Sponsored Blackmail Works in Russia, The Atlantic, January 11, 2017, https://www.theatlantic.com/international/archive/2017/01/kompromat-trump-dossier/512891/

37 Michael Idov, Ilya Yashin, Katya Garasimova, Russia's Amazing Drugs and Hookers Sex Scandal, The Daily Beast, March 23, 2010, https://www.thedailybeast.com/ilya-yashin-katya-gerasimova-and-russias-amazing-drugs-and-hookers-sex-scandal

38 Ilya Yashin, Улыбайтесь. Вас снимает скрытая камера, March 23, 2010, http://yashin.livejournal.com/894296.html

39 Julia Ioffe, Bears in a Honey Trap: The Sex Scandal That's Rocking the Russian Opposition, Foreign Policy, April 28, 2010, http://foreignpolicy.com/2010/04/28/bears-in-a-honey-trap/

40 Claire Berlinsky, Did Britain Fall into Putin's Trap in Prosecuting a Russian Dissident? National Review, May 11, 2016, http://www.nationalreview.com/article/435238/Russian-dissident-vladimir-bukovsky-sues-uk-government-libel

41 Court filing, Vladimir Bukovsky v Crown Prosecution Service, November 15, 2015, http://c2.nrostatic.com/sites/default/files/Bukovsky%20writ.pdf

42 CNN, U.S. calls purported sex tape 'doctored' and 'smear campaign,' CNN, September 24, 2009, http://www.cnn.com/2009/US/09/24/russia.us.sextape/

43 Gregory Crow, Seymour Goodman, S.A. Lebedev and the Birth of Soviet Computing (1994), Annals of History of Computing

44 Andrei Soldatov and Irina Borogan, The Red Web: The Kremlin's War on the Internet (Public Affairs, 2015), pg. 30

45 Andrei Soldatov and Irina Borogan, The Red Web: The Kremlin's War on the Internet (Public Affairs, 2015), pg. 30

46 Los Angeles Times, Hackers found guilty of selling codes, Los Angeles Times, February 15, 1990, http://articles.latimes.com/1990-02-15/news/mn-1231_1_hackers-guilty

47 Daniel Domscheit-Berg, Inside WikiLeaks: My time with Julian Assange at the world's most dangerous website (New York: Crown Publishers, 2011)

48 Newsweek, We're in the middle of a cyberwar, September 12, 1999, Newsweek, https://www.prnewswire.com/news-releases/newsweek-exclusive-were-in-the-middle-of-a-cyberwar-74343007.html

49 FBI Indictment, Most Wanted: Evgeniy Mikhailovich Bogachev, March 15, 2017, https://www.fbi.gov/wanted/cyber/evgeniy-mikhailovich-bogachev

50 FBI Indictment, Most Wanted: Alexey Belan, March 15, 2017, https://www.fbi.gov/wanted/cyber/alexsey-belan

51 FBI Indictment, Most Wanted: Dmitry Aleksandrovich Dukochaev, March 15, 2017, https://www.fbi.gov/wanted/cyber/dmitry-aleksandrovich-dokuchaev

52 Pavel Sudoplatov, Special Tasks, Little, Brown, 1994, pg. xxii

53 Pavel Sudoplatov, Special Tasks, Little, Brown, 1994, pg. 3

54 Pavel Sudoplatov, Special Tasks, Little, Brown, 1994, pg. 3

55 Natalya Shulyakovskaya, Korzhakov says bombings were Berezovsky's doing, Moscow Times, October 28, 1999, http://old.themoscowtimes.com/news/article/tmt/270814.html

56 Lizzie Dearden, Alexander Litvinenko: The three other times Russia suspected of involvement in killings on British Soil, Independent UK, January 22, 2016, http://www.independent.co.uk/news/uk/crime/alexander-litvinenko-the-three-other-times-russia-suspected-of-involvement-in-killings-on-british-a6826796.html

57 Andrew Monaghan, UK & Russia: A troubled relationship, Conflict Studies Research Centre, May 22, 2007, https://www.da.mod.uk/events/the-uk-russia-a-troubled-relationship-part-i

58 Alex Goldfarb, Marina Litvinenko, "Death of a Dissident: The Poisoning of Alexander Litvinenko and the Return of the KGB," Free Press, 2007

59 Editorial Staff, Boris Berezovsky wins Litvinenko poison spy libel case, BBC, March 10, 2010, http://news.bbc.co.uk/2/hi/uk_news/8559543.stm

60 Alex Goldfarb, Marina Litvinenko, Death of a Dissident: The Poisoning of Alexander Litvinenko and the Return of the KGB, Free Press, 2007

61 Yelena Dikun, Profile of Boris Nemtsov: Russia's newest deputy premier, Jamestown Foundation, April 18, 1997, http://jt.codingheads.com/program/profile-of-boris-nemtsov-russias-newest-first-deputy-premier/

62 BBC, Kremlin critic in ammonia attack, March 23, 2009, http://news.bbc.co.uk/2/hi/europe/7959819.stm

63 Staff, Sites of Nemtsov and Milov attacked after publication of new report, June 1, 2010, https://graniru.org/Internet/m.178982.html

64 Boris Nemtsov,"Why Does Putin Wage War on Ukraine," Kyiv Post, September 1, 2014, https://www.kyivpost.com/article/opinion/op-ed/why-does-putin-wage-war-on-ukraine-362884.html

65 Elana Milchanovska, Sobesednik.ru, "Полное интервью Немцова "Собеседнику": Если бы я боялся Путина, то…" February 29, 2015, https://sobesednik.ru/politika/20150228-polnoe-intervyu-nemcova-sobesedniku-esli-by-ya-boyalsya-puti

66 BBC, Boris Nemtsov murder: Who are the suspects?, BBC October 3, 2016, http://www.bbc.com/news/world-europe-31834026

67 Tom Peck, Vladimir Kara-Murza, a twice-poisoned Russian dissident, says: 'If it happens a third time, that'll be it,' Independent UK, March 18, 2017, http://

www.independent.co.uk/news/uk/politics/russian-dissident-vladimir-kara-murza
-poisoned-twice-democracy-campaigner-vladimir-putin-a7637421.html

68 Michele Berdy, Top Rosneft Exec Found Dead in Moscow, Moscow Times, December 26, 2016, https://themoscowtimes.com/news/top-rosneft-exec-found-dead-in-moscow-56649

69 Robert Mendick, Mystery death of ex-KGB chief linked to MI6 spy's dossier on Donald Trump, Telegraph UK, January 27, 2017, https://www.telegraph.co.uk/news/2017/01/27/mystery-death-ex-kgb-chief-linked-mi6-spys-dossier-donald-trump/

70 Steele Dossier, Company Intelligence Report 2016/94: Russia: Secret Kremlin Meetings Attended by Trump Advisor, Carter Page in Moscow July 2016

71 Rober Mendick, Telegraph, "Poisoned Russian spy Sergei Skripal was close to consultant who was linked to the Trump dossier," March 7, 2018, https://www.telegraph.co.uk/news/2018/03/07/poisoned-russian-spy-sergei-skripal-close-consultant-linked/

72 BBC, Russian spy: Highly likely Moscow behind attack, says Theresa May, BBC, March 13, 2018, http://www.bbc.com/news/uk-43377856

73 Shehab Khan, Independent UK, "Video re-emerges of Putin threat that 'traitors will kick the bucket,'" March 7, 2018, http://www.independent.co.uk/news/world/europe/vladimir-putin-traitors-kick-bucket-sergei-skripal-latest-video-30-pieces-silver-a8243206.html

74 NBC News, "Confronting Russian President Vladimir Putin," March 10, 2018, https://www.youtube.com/watch?v=z1pPkAOZI50

75 Mike Eckel, Radio Free Europe Radio Liberty, "Russian State TV host warns 'traitors' after Skripal poisoning," March 8, 2018, https://www.rferl.org/a/russia-skripal-poisoning-russia-tv-warning-traitors-kleimenov/29087407.html

76 Mark Sweney, The Guardian, "Russian broadcaster RT could be forced off UK airwaves," March 13, 2018, https://www.theguardian.com/media/2018/mar/13/russian-broadcaster-rt-hits-back-at-threat-to-uk-licence

Chapter 7: Fake News

1 Vladimir, Kvachov, Спецназ России, http://militera.lib.ru/science/kvachkov_vv/index.html

2 Conceptual Views Regarding the Activities of the Armed Forces of the Russian Federation in the Information Space, 2011, https://ccdcoe.org/strategies/Russian_Federation_unofficial_translation.pdf

3 Andrey Kartapolov, Lessons of military conflict and prospects for the development of means and methods for conducting them Vestnik Akademii Voennykh Nauk (Bulletin of the Academy of Military Science), No. 2 2015, pg. 28-29

4 Susan B. Glasser, Ex-Spy Chief: Russia's Election Hacking Was an 'Intelligence Failure,' Politico, December 11, 2017, https://www.politico.com/magazine/story/2017/12/11/the-full-transcript-michael-morell-216061

5 Soviet Active Measures, Testimony before the House of Representatives Permanent Select Committee on Intelligence, 97th Congress, July 13, 1982 (statement of John McMahon), pg. 43

6 Soviet Active Measures, Testimony before the House of Representatives Permanent Select Committee on Intelligence, 97th Congress (July 13, 1982) (statement of John McMahon), pg. 21

7 Arkady Ostrovsky, The Invention of Russia: From Gorbachev's Freedom to Putin's War (Viking, 2016) pg. 15

8 Christopher Andrew, Vitali Mitrokhin, The World Was Going Our Way: The KGB and the Battle for the Third World (Basic Books, 2005), pg. 340

9 Soviet Active Measures, Testimony before the House of Representatives Permanent Select Committee on Intelligence, 97th Congress, July 13, 1982 (statement of John McMahon), pg. 38

10 Ladislav Bittman, The KGB and Soviet Disinformation, An Insider's View (Pergamon-Brasseys International Defense Publishers, 1985) pg. 69

11 Christopher Andrew, Vitali Mitrokhin, The World Was Going Our Way: The KGB and the Battle for the Third World (Basic Books, 2005), pg. 330

12 Christopher Andrew, Vitali Mitrokhin, The World Was Going Our Way: The KGB and the Battle for the Third World (Basic Books, 2005), pg. 333

13 Ellen Mickiewicz, Changing Channels: Television and the Struggle for Power in Russia (Duke University Press, 1997)

14 Soviet Active Measures, Subcommittee on European Affairs of the Committee on Foreign Relations, United States Senate, Ninety-Ninth Congress, September 12-13, 1985, http://www.loc.gov/law/find/nominations/gates/017_excerpt.pdf

15 Gleb Pavlosky, The Putin Files, Frontline, https://www.pbs.org/wgbh/frontline/interview/gleb-pavlovsky/

16 Soviet Active Measures, Subcommittee on European Affairs of the Committee on Foreign Relations, United States Senate, Ninety-Ninth Congress, September 12-13, 1985, http://www.loc.gov/law/find/nominations/gates/017_excerpt.pdf

17 Rory Carrol, Russia Today news anchor Liz Wahl resigns live on air over Ukraine crisis, The Guardian, March 5, 2014, https://www.theguardian.com/world/2014/mar/06/russia-today-anchor-liz-wahl-resigns-on-air-ukraine

18 Jack Stubbs, Ginger Gibson, Russia's RT America registers as 'foreign agent' in U.S., Reuters, November 13, 2017, https://www.reuters.com/article/us-russia-usa-media-restrictions-rt/russias-rt-america-registers-as-foreign-agent-in-u-s-idUSKBN1DD25B

19 Jack Moore, 'We can't even hire a stringer,' Russia Today says its U.S. staff leaving in 'masses,' Newsweek, October 6, 2017, http://www.newsweek.com/we-cant-even-hire-stringer-russia-today-says-its-us-staff-leaving-masses-679380

20 Laetitia Peron, Russia fights Western 'propaganda' as critical media gets squeezed, Yahoo News, November 20, 2014, https://www.yahoo.com/news/russia-fights-western-propaganda-critical-media-squeezed-132033487.html

21 Andrew Feinberg, My life at a Russian propaganda network, Politico Magazine, August 21, 2017, https://www.politico.com/magazine/story/2017/08/21/russian-propaganda-sputnik-reporter-215511

22 Ben Nimmo, Question That: RT's Military Mission, Assessing Russia Today's role as an information weapon, Digital Forensic Research Lab, Atlantic Council, January 8, 2018, https://medium.com/dfrlab/question-that-rts-military-mission-4c4bd9f72c88

23 Ben Nimmo, Question That: RT's Military Mission, Assessing Russia Today's role as an information weapon, Digital Forensic Research Lab, Atlantic Council, January 8, 2018, https://medium.com/dfrlab/question-that-rts-military-mission-4c4bd9f72c88

24 Robert Donaldson, Joseph L. Nogee, Vidya Nadkarni, The Foreign Policy of Russia: Changing Systems, Enduring Interests (New York: Routledge, 2001) pg. 456

25 DFRL, #BalticBrief: Enhanced Anti-NATO Narratives Target Enhanced Forward Presence, The Atlantic Council's Digital Forensic Science, February 6, 2018, https://medium.com/dfrlab/balticbrief-enhanced-anti-nato-narratives-target-enhanced-forward-presence-fdf2272a8992

26 Macomb Daily, Protestors Throw Rocks at Selfridge Reservists, Macomb Daily, June 3, 2006, http://www.macombdaily.com/article/MD/20060603/NEWS01/306039996

27 Nick Paton Walsh, Protests Threaten NATO War Games, The Guardian, June 12, 2006, https://www.theguardian.com/world/2006/jun/12/ukraine.russia

28 Gregory Warner, Ukraine vs. Fake News, NPR, August 21, 2017, https://www.npr.org/templates/transcript/transcript.php?storyId=544458898

29 Christopher Paul, Miriam Matthews, The Russian "Firehouse of Falsehood" Propaganda Model: Why It Might Work and Options to Counter It, The RAND Corporation, pg1, https://www.rand.org/pubs/perspectives/PE198.html

30 Bettina Renz, Hanna Smith, Russia and Hybrid Warfare—Going Beyond the Label, Finnish Prime Minister's Office, January 2016, https://www.stratcomcoe.org/download/file/fid/4920

31 William Cook, Russian Fake News Is Causing Trouble in Latvia, The Spectator, December 2017, https://blogs.spectator.co.uk/2017/12/russian-fake-news-is-causing-trouble-in-latvia/

32 James Carstensen, Alleged Russian Hacks, Fake Sites Follow Opening of NATO-EU Center on Hybrid Threats, CNSN News, October 6, 2017, https://www.cnsnews.com/news/article/james-carstensen/alleged-russian-hacks-fake-sites-follow-opening-nato-eu-center-hybrid

33 Reuters Staff, Bulgaria Says Will Not Join Any NATO Black Sea Fleet After Russian Warning, Reuters, June 16, 2016, https://www.reuters.com/article/nato-bulgaria-blacksea/bulgaria-says-will-not-join-any-nato-black-sea-fleet-after-russian-warning-idUSL8N19835X

34 Stefan Meister, The "Lisa" Case: Germany as a Target of Russian Disinformation, Nato Review Magazine, https://www.nato.int/docu/review/2016/Also-in-2016/lisa-case-germany-target-russian-disinformation/EN/index.htm

Chapter 8: Internet Research Agency & Russian Cyber Weapons

1 Col. S.G. Chekinov, Lt. Gen. S.A. Bogdanov, The Nature and Content of a New-Generation War, Military Thought (English edition), No. 4, 2013, http://www.eastviewpress.com/Files/MT_FROM%20THE%20CURRENT%20ISSUE_No.4_2013.pdf

2 Max de Haldevang, Russia's troll factory also paid for 100 activists in the US, Quartz, October 17, 2017, https://qz.com/1104195/russian-political-hacking-the-internet-research-agency-troll-farm-by-the-numbers/

3 Andrey Soshnikov, "С политических троллей Кремля попытаются "сорвать маску" в суде "BBC, August 15, 2016, http://www.bbc.com/russian/features-37083188

4 RBC, Troll factory spent about $2.3 million to work in the US, October 17, 2017, https://www.rbc.ru/technology_and_media/17/10/2017/59e4eb7a9a79472577375776?from=main

5 Scott Shane, Vindu Goel, Fake Russian Facebook Accounts Bought $100,000 in Political Ads, New York Times, September 6, 2017, https://www.nytimes.com/2017/09/06/technology/facebook-russian-political-ads.html

6 Alex Stamos, Facebook, An Update on Information Operations on Facebook, Facebook News, September 6, 2017, https://newsroom.fb.com/news/2017/09/information-operations-update/

7 Alex Stamos, Facebook, An Update on Information Operations on Facebook, Facebook News, September 6, 2017, https://newsroom.fb.com/news/2017/09/information-operations-update/

8 Lorand Laskai, Year in Review: Tech Companies Grapple with Disinformation, Council on Foreign Relations, January 2, 2018, https://www.cfr.org/blog/year-review-tech-companies-grapple-disinformation

9 Konstantin Rykov, Facebook, November 12, 2016, https://www.facebook.com/konstantin.rykov/posts/10210621124674610

10 Nicholas Confessore, Danny Hakim, Data Firm Says, 'Secret Sauce' Aided Trump; Many Scoff, The New York Times, March 6, 2017, https://www.nytimes.com/2017/03/06/us/politics/cambridge-analytica.html?_r=0

11 REPORT: Hillary's Emails Hacked by Russia—Kremlin Deciding Whether to Release 20,000 Stolen Emails (VIDEO)

12 "Sorcha Faal," Kremlin War Erupts Over Release of Top Secret Hillary Clinton Emails, What does it mean.com, May 6, 2017, http://www.whatdoesitmean.com/index2036.htm

13 Betsy Woodruff, Trump Data Guru: I tried to team up with Julian Assange, The Daily Beast, October 25, 2017, https://www.thedailybeast.com/trump-data-guru-i -tried-to-team-up-with-julian-assange

14 Craig Silverman, Lawrence Alexander, How Teens in the Balkans Are Duping Trump Supporters with Fake News, Buzzfeed, November 3, 2016, https://www .buzzfeed.com/craigsilverman/how-macedonia-became-a-global-hub-for-pro -trump-misinfo?utm_term=.tr5A54RYG#.svVmBQ48d

15 Donie O'Sullivan, What Russian trolls could have bought with $100,000 on Facebook, CNN, September 7, 2017, http://www.cnn.com/2017/09/07/media/what -russian-troll-army-could-buy-facebook-ads/index.html

16 Team99, "Дела Людмилы Савчук. Команда 29 рассказывает о «фабрике троллей," January 1, 2017, https://team29.org/court/trolls/

17 Donie O'Sullivan, Russian trolls created Facebook events seen by more than 300,000 users, CNN, January 26, 2018, http://money.cnn.com/2018/01/26/media/russia-trolls -facebook-events/index.html

18 Ben Collins, Gideon Resnick, Kevin Poulsen, Spencer Ackerman, Exclusive: Russians Appear to Use Facebook to Push Trump Rallies in 17 U.S. cities, Daily Beast, September 20, 2017, https://www.thedailybeast.com/russians-appear-to-use -facebook-to-push-pro-trump-flash-mobs-in-florida

19 Donie O'Sullivan, Drew Griffin, Curt Devine, In an attempt to sow fear, Russian trolls paid for self-defense classes for African Americans, CNN, October 18, 2017, http:// money.cnn.com/2017/10/18/media/black-fist-russia-self-defense-classes/index.html

20 Sherdog, Omowale 'Black Panther' Adewale Assists Black Fist Self Defense Project (founder interviewed), Sherdog, March 7, 2017, http://forums.sherdog.com/threads/ omowale-black-panther-adewale-assists-black-fist-self-defense-project-founder -interviewed.3487585/

21 Robert Booth, Matthew Weaver, Alex Hern, Stacee Smith, Shaun Walker, Russia used hundreds of fake accounts to tweet about Brexit, data shows, The Guardian, November 14, 2017, https://www.theguardian.com/world/2017/nov/14/how -400-russia-run-fake-accounts-posted-bogus-brexit-tweets

22 Testimony of Sean Edgett, October 31, 2017, https://www.lgraham.senate.gov/ public/_cache/files/4766f54d-d433-4055-9f3d-c94f97eeb1c0/testimony-of-sean -edgett-acting-general-counsel-twitter.pdf

23 Twitter, Update on Results of Retrospective Review of Russian-Related Election Activity, January 19, 2018, https://www.judiciary.senate.gov/imo/media/doc/Edgett Appendix to Responses.pdf

24 Natasha Bertrand, Russia-linked Twitter accounts are working overtime to help Devin Nunes and WikiLeaks, Business Insider, January 19, 2018, http://www.business insider.com/release-the-memo-campaign-russia-linked-twitter-accounts-2018-1

25 Jason Schwartz, Russia pushes more 'deep state' hashtags, Politico, February 6, 2018, https://www.politico.com/story/2018/02/06/russia-twitter-hashtags-deep-state -395928

26 US Department of Justice, Louisiana Man Pleads Guilty to Federal Charges for Threatening Pizza Shop in Northwest Washington, January 13, 2017, US Department of Justice, https://www.justice.gov/usao-dc/pr/louisiana-man-pleads-guilty -federal-charge-threatening-pizza-shop-northwest-washington

27 Matthew Rosenberg, Trump Adviser Has Pushed Clinton Conspiracy Theories, New York Times, December 5, 2016, https://www.nytimes.com/2016/12/05/us/politics/ michael-flynn-trump-fake-news-clinton.html

28 Adrian Chen, The Agency, New York Times, June 2, 2015, https://www.nytimes .com/2015/06/07/magazine/the-agency.html

29 Andy Cush, Who's behind this shady propagandistic Russian photo exhibition? Gawker, October 10, 2014, http://gawker.com/whos-behind-this-shady-propagandistic-russian-photo-ex-1643938683

30 Euromaidan Press, Trolls on tour: How Kremlin money buys Western journalists, Euromaidan Press, August 20, 2015, http://euromaidanpress.com/2015/08/20/trolls-on-tour-how-kremlin-money-buys-western-journalists/#arvlbdata

31 Alex Jones, Twitter, https://twitter.com/realalexjones/status/959119134477955073

32 Sheera Frenkel, The New Handbook for Cyberwar Is Being Written by Russia, Buzzfeed, March 19, 2017, https://www.buzzfeed.com/sheerafrenkel/the-new-handbook-for-cyberwar-is-being-written-by-russia?utm_term=.ihoOrerjo#.uu4XK4KMg

33 Col. S.G. Chekinov, Lt. Gen. S.A. Bogdanov, The Nature and Content of a New-Generation War, Military Thought (English edition), No. 4, 2013, http://www.eastviewpress.com/Files/MT_FROM%20THE%20CURRENT%20ISSUE_No.4_2013.pdf

34 Hannes Grassegger, Mikael Krogerus, fake news and botnets: how Russia weaponised the web, The Guardian, December 2, 2017, https://www.theguardian.com/technology/2017/dec/02/fake-news-botnets-how-russia-weaponised-the-web-cyber-attack-estonia

Chapter 9: Hail Hydra!

1 Christian Gysin in Oslo, Simon Tomlinson, Victims were paralysed by fear as I fired: Breivik recounts island youth camp massacre in horrifying detail, The Daily Mail, April 20, 2012, http://www.dailymail.co.uk/news/article-2132656/Anders-Behring-Breivik-trial-Norway-killer-recounts-Utoya-island-massacre-horrifying-detail.html#ixzz5ABjPAJde

2 BBC, Joerg Haider: Key Quotes. BBC News, February 2, 2000, http://news.bbc.co.uk/2/hi/europe/628282.stm

3 Aleksandr Dugin, Donald Trump: The Swamp and Fire, Katehon Think Tank, November 16, 2016, https://www.youtube.com/watch?v=PRakmMpUJ24

4 Benjamin Haddad, Marine Le Pen ousts her dad, keeps his repulsive French Populist Party, Daily Beast, August 22, 2015, https://www.thedailybeast.com/marine-le-pen-ousts-her-dad-keeps-his-repulsive-french-populist-party

5 Eleanor Beardsley, France's Marine Le Pen Contends Populism Is the Future, NPR, January 6, 2017, https://www.npr.org/2017/01/06/508587559/frances-marine-le-pen-contends-populism-is-the-future

6 Eleanor Beardsley, France's Marine Le Pen Contends Populism Is the Future, NPR, January 6, 2017, https://www.npr.org/2017/01/06/508587559/frances-marine-le-pen-contends-populism-is-the-future

7 Translation, Marine Le Pen: France will withdraw from NATO, October 14, 2011, http://bibkatalog.ru/newsblog/2011/10/14/marine-le-pen-france-will-withdraw-nato

8 Moscow Times, Marine Le Pen's Party Asks Russia for €27 Million Loan, The Moscow Times, February 19, 2016, http://www.themoscowtimes.com/news/article/marine-le-pens-party-asks-russia-for-27-million-loan/560066.html

9 Gabriel Gatehouse, Marine Le Pen: Who's Funding France's Far Right?, BBC, April 3, 2017, http://www.bbc.com/news/world-europe-39478066

10 Suzanne Daley, Maia de la Baume, French Far Right Gets Helping Hand with Russian Loan, New York Times, December 1, 2014, https://www.nytimes.com/2014/12/02/world/europe/french-far-right-gets-helping-hand-with-russian-loan-.html

11 Gianluca Mezzofiore, Former 'London KGB agent' Yuri Kudimov 'lent €2m to FN's Jean-Marie Le Pen,' International Business Time, December 1, 2014, http://www.ibtimes.co.uk/former-london-kgb-agent-yuri-kudimov-lent-2m-fns-jean-marie-le-pen-1477450

12 Translation, Marine Le Pen: France will withdraw from NATO, October 14, 2011, http://bibkatalog.ru/newsblog/2011/10/14/marine-le-pen-france-will-withdraw-nato

13 Translation, Marine Le Pen: France will withdraw from NATO, October 14, 2011, http://bibkatalog.ru/newsblog/2011/10/14/marine-le-pen-france-will-withdraw-nato

14 Translation, Marine Le Pen: France will withdraw from NATO, October 14, 2011, http://bibkatalog.ru/newsblog/2011/10/14/marine-le-pen-france-will-withdraw-nato

15 Peter Allen, Jean-Marie Le Pen is found guilty of inciting racial hatred after he described a group of Roma gipsies as smelly, Daily Mail, January 28, 2017, http://www.dailymail.co.uk/news/article-4269450/Jean-Marie-Le-Pen-guilty-inciting-racial-hatred.html

16 Tessa Berenson, French Far-Right Leader Marion Maréchal-Le Pen Sounded a Lot Like Trump at CPAC, Time Magazine, February 22, 2018, http://time.com/5170730/marion-marechal-le-pen-cpac/

17 David Duke, Interview with EU Parliamentarian Bruno Gollnish, March 14, 2007, http://davidduke.com/interview-with-eu-parliamentarian-bruno-gollnisch

18 Jewish Telegraph Agency, French Politico faces firing for calling existence of gas chambers debatable, Jewish Telegraphic Agency, October 18, 2004, https://www.jta.org/2004/10/18/archive/french-politico-faces-firing-for-calling-existence-of-gas-chambers-debatable

19 Matt Wilding, Farage Slithered In; UKIP's Founder talks about the early days of the party, The Guardian, June 12, 2016, https://www.theguardian.com/politics/2013/sep/08/ukip-founder-new-leftwing-anti-eu-party

20 Nick Griffin, Nick Griffin expelled from British National Party, The Guardian, October 1, 2014, https://www.theguardian.com/politics/2014/oct/01/nick-griffin-expelled-from-bnp

21 William Booth, Karla Adam, Trump's retweets elevate a tiny fringe group of anti-Muslim activists in Britain, Washington Post, November 29, 2017, https://www.washingtonpost.com/world/trumps-tweets-elevate-a-tiny-fringe-group-of-anti-muslim-activists-in-britain/2017/11/29/02489a42-d515-11e7-9ad9-ca0619edfa05_story.html?utm_term=.3cc1e0e9c252

22 The Guardian, German far-right party calls for ban on minarets and burqa, The Guardian, May 1, 2016, https://www.theguardian.com/world/2016/may/01/german-far-right-party-ban-minarets-burqa-alternative-fur-deutschland

23 Anne Applebaum, Peter Pomeranstev, Melanie Smith, Chloe Colliver, Make Germany great again: Kremlin, Alt-Right and International influences in the 2007 German elections, Institute for Strategic Dialogue, http://www.isdglobal.org/wp-content/uploads/2017/12/Make-Germany-Great-Again-ENG-081217.pdf

24 Melanie Amann, Pavel Lokshin, German Populists Forge Ties with Russia, Spiegel Online, April 7, 2016, www.spiegel.de/international/germany/german-populists-forge-deeper-ties-with-russia-a-1089562.html

25 Stephen Brown, Lutz Bachmann, Founder of German Anti-Muslim Movement PEGIDA, Resigns After Posting Hitler Photo, Huffington Post, January 21, 2015, https://www.huffingtonpost.com/2015/01/21/lutz-bachmann-pegida-hitler-photo_n_6515542.html

26 Hana de Goeij, Rick Lyman, Czech Election Won by Anti-Establishment Party Led by Billionaire, New York Times, October 21, 2017, https://www.nytimes.com/2017/10/21/world/europe/andrej-babis-ano-czech-election.html

27 Patrick Strickland, Greece mourns slain anti-fascist rapper Pavlos Fyssas, Al Jazeera, September 15, 2017, http://www.aljazeera.com/indepth/features/2017/09/greece-mourns-slain-anti-fascist-rapper-pavlos-fyssas-170911080142110.html?xif=.

28 BBC, Joerg Haider: Key Quotes, BBC News, February 2, 2000, http://news.bbc.co.uk/2/hi/europe/628282.stm

29 Manès Weisskircher, Matthew E. Bergman, Austria's election: four things to know about the result, the London School of Economics and Political Science, October 16, 2017, http://blogs.lse.ac.uk/europpblog/2017/10/16/austrias-election-four-things-to-know-about-the-result/

30 Alison Smale, Austria's Far Right signs a cooperation pact with Putin's party, The New York Times, December 19, 2016, https://www.nytimes.com/2016/12/19/world/europe/austrias-far-right-signs-a-cooperation-pact-with-putins-party.html

31 Alison Smale, Austria's Far Right signs a cooperation pact with Putin's party, The New York Times, December 19, 2016, https://www.nytimes.com/2016/12/19/world/europe/austrias-far-right-signs-a-cooperation-pact-with-putins-party.html

32 Alison Smale, Austria's Far Right signs a cooperation pact with Putin's party, The New York Times, December 19, 2016, https://www.nytimes.com/2016/12/19/world/europe/austrias-far-right-signs-a-cooperation-pact-with-putins-party.html

33 Marthe van der Wolf, Dutch Far-right Leader Seeks Ban on Quran, Mosques, Voice of America, August 26, 2016, https://www.voanews.com/a/netherlands-wilders-mosque-quran-ban/3482009.html

34 Statement by Geert Wilders on Milan, January 29, 2016, https://www.pvv.nl/index.php/36-fj-related/geert-wilders/8931-milaan-290616.html

35 Lili Bayer, Exclusive: Controversial Trump aide Sebastian Gorka backed violent anti-semitic militia, Forward, April 3, 2017, https://forward.com/news/national/367937/exclusive-controversial-trump-aide-sebastian-gorka-backed-violent-anti-semi/

36 Lili Bayer, Exclusive: Controversial Trump aide Sebastian Gorka backed violent anti-semitic militia, Forward, April 3, 2017, https://forward.com/news/national/367937/exclusive-controversial-trump-aide-sebastian-gorka-backed-violent-anti-semi/

37 Anna Nemtsova, How Putin's Using Hungary to Destroy Europe, The Daily Beast, November 9, 2017, https://www.thedailybeast.com/how-putins-using-hungary-to-destroy-europe

38 DW, Hungary's European Parliament member Bela Kovacs charged with spying for Russia, DW, December 6, 2017, http://www.dw.com/en/hungarys-european-parliament-member-bela-kovacs-charged-with-spying-for-russia/a-41672171

39 DW, Hungary's European Parliament member Bela Kovacs charged with spying for Russia, DW, December 6, 2017, http://www.dw.com/en/hungarys-european-parliament-member-bela-kovacs-charged-with-spying-for-russia/a-41672171

40 Remi Adekoya, Xenophobic, authoritarian, and generous on welfare: How Poland's right rules, The Guardian UK, October 25, 2016, https://www.theguardian.com/commentisfree/2016/oct/25/poland-right-law-justice-party-europe

41 Rick Lyman, Joanna Berendt, "As Poland Lurches to Right, Many in Europe Look on in Alarm," New York Times, December 15, 2015, https://www.nytimes.com/2015/12/15/world/europe/poland-law-and-justice-party-jaroslaw-kaczynski.html

42 https://www.nbcnews.com/politics/donald-trump/here-s-full-text-donald-trump-s-speech-poland-n780046

43 La Corte di Putin in Italia, "Valerio Cignetti, la Fiamma Tricolore a scaldare Edia Rossiya," November 23, 2014, https://italianiputiniani.blogspot.com/2014/11/valerio-cignetti-la-fiamma-tricolore.html

44 Alan Cullison, Wall Street Journal, "Far-Right Flocks to Russia to Berate the West," March 23, 2015, https://www.wsj.com/articles/far-right-flocks-to-russia-to-berate-the-west-1427059613

45 The Guardian, "Italian Elections 2018 full results," March 5, 2018, https://www.theguardian.com/world/ng-interactive/2018/mar/05/italian-elections-2018-full-results-renzi-berlusconi

46 Stephanie Kirchgaessner, The Guardian, "Steve Bannon in Rome to 'support far-right candidate' in Italian Election," March 1, 2018, https://www.theguardian.com/world/2018/mar/01/steve-bannon-in-rome-to-support-far-right-candidate-matteo-salvini?CMP=edit_2221

47 Alan Cullison, Far-Right Flocks to Russia to Berate the West, Wall Street Journal, March 23, 2015, https://www.wsj.com/articles/far-right-flocks-to-russia-to-berate-the-west-1427059613

48 Alan Cullison, Far-Right Flocks to Russia to Berate the West, Wall Street Journal, March 23, 2015, https://www.wsj.com/articles/far-right-flocks-to-russia-to-berate-the-west-1427059613

49 Benjamin Hart, Bannon Tells France's National Front: 'Let Them Call You Racist,' NY Magazine, March 10, 2018, http://nymag.com/daily/intelligencer/2018/03/bannon-tells-national-front-let-them-call-you-racist.html

Chapter 10: The Axis of Autocracy

1 Andrea Kendall-Taylor, Erica Frantz, How Democracies Fall Apart: How Populism Is a Pathway to Autocracy, Foreign Affairs, December 5, 2016, https://www.foreignaffairs.com/articles/2016-12-05/how-democracies-fall-apart

2 Andrea Kendall-Taylor, Erica Frantz, How Democracies Fall Apart: How Populism Is a Pathway to Autocracy, Foreign Affairs, December 5, 2016, https://www.foreignaffairs.com/articles/2016-12-05/how-democracies-fall-apart

3 Andrea Kendall-Taylor, Erica Frantz, How Democracies Fall Apart: How Populism Is a Pathway to Autocracy, Foreign Affairs, December 5, 2016, https://www.foreignaffairs.com/articles/2016-12-05/how-democracies-fall-apart

4 Konstantin Strigunov, The Coco Revolution, Voyenno-promyshlennyy kur'er magazine, July 24, 2017, https://vpk-news.ru/articles/38011

5 Christiane Hoffman, Klaus Brinkbaumer, Germany's Foreign Minister 'We Are Seeing What Happens When the U.S. Pulls Back,' Spiegel Online, January 8, 2018, http://www.spiegel.de/international/germany/sigmar-gabriel-we-are-seeing-what-happens-when-the-u-s-pulls-back-a-1186181.html

Chapter 11: Operation GLOBAL GRIZZLY

1 Patrick Howell O'Neill, The cyberattack that changed the world, The Daily Dot, May 20, 2016, https://www.dailydot.com/layer8/web-war-cyberattack-russia-estonia/

2 Brian Krebs, Lithuania Weathers Cyber Attack, Braces for Round 2, The Washington Post, http://voices.washingtonpost.com/securityfix/2008/07/lithuania_weathers_cyber_attac_1.html

3 Sheera Frenkel, The New Handbook for Cyberwar Is Being Written by Russia, Buzzfeed, March 19, 2017, https://www.buzzfeed.com/sheerafrenkel/the-new-handbook-for-cyberwar-is-being-written-by-russia?utm_term=.ihoOrerjo#.uu4XK4KMg

4 Patrick Howell O'Neill, The cyberattack that changed the world, The Daily Dot, May 20, 2016, https://www.dailydot.com/layer8/web-war-cyberattack-russia-estonia/

5 Toby Helm, British Euroscepticism: A brief history, The Guardian, February 6, 2016, https://www.theguardian.com/politics/2016/feb/07/british-euroscepticism-a-brief-history

6 Toby, British Euroscepticism: A brief history, The Guardian, February 6, 2016, https://www.theguardian.com/politics/2016/feb/07/british-euroscepticism-a-brief-history

7 BBC, De Gaulle says 'non' to Britain—again, BBC, November 27, 1967, http://news.bbc.co.uk/onthisday/hi/dates/stories/november/27/newsid_4187000/4187714.stm

8 Sam Wilson, Britain and the EU: A long and rocky relationship, BBC, April 1, 2014, http://www.bbc.com/news/uk-politics-26515129

9 European Parliament, The Maastricht and Amsterdam Treaties, The European Parliament, http://www.europarl.europa.eu/atyourservice/en/displayFtu.html?ftuId =FTU_1.1.3.html

10 Gov.UK, Prime Minister's speech on EU, Gov.UK, November 10, 2015, https://www .gov.uk/government/speeches/prime-ministers-speech-on-europe

11 Legislation.Gov.UK, European Union Referendum Act 2015, http://www.legisla tion.gov.uk/ukpga/2015/36/crossheading/the-referendum

12 Gov.UK, PM Commons statement on EU reform and referendum: 22, February 2016, https://www.gov.uk/government/speeches/pm-commons-statement-on-eu-re form-and-referendum-22-february-2016

13 UKIP Leader Nigel Farage on the leave EU campaigns, UKIP, October 9, 2015, http:// www.ukip.org/ukip_leader_nigel_farage_on_the_leave_eu_campaigns

14 Better Off Out Website, Who We Are, http://www.betteroffout.net/about/who -we-are/

15 Jack Sommers, Nigel Farage interviewed by George Galloway, Who agreed with everything they discussed, Huffington Post, February 17, 2016, http://www.huffing tonpost.co.uk/2016/02/13/nigel-farage-george-galloway-eu-sputnik_n_9227554 .html

16 Carole Cadwalladr, Arron Banks: Brexit was a war. We won. There's no turning back now, The Guardian, April 2, 2017, https://www.theguardian.com/politics/2017/ apr/02/arron-banks-interview-brexit-ukip-far-right-trump-putin-russia

17 Matthew Nitch Smith, Jo Cox's alleged killer was a 'dedicated supporter' of an American Neo-Nazi group, Business Insider, June 17, 2016, http://www.business insider.com/jo-cox-killer-and-american-neo-nazi-national-alliance-2016-6

18 The Lisbon Treaty, Article 50, http://www.lisbon-treaty.org/wcm/the-lisbon -treaty/treaty-on-European-union-and-comments/title-6-final-provisions/137 -article-50.html

19 Michael McFaul, How Brexit is a win for Putin, KyivPost, June 27, 2016, https:// www.kyivpost.com/article/opinion/op-ed/michael-mcfaul-how-brexit-is-a-win-for -putin-417252.html

20 Robert Booth, Matthew Weaver, Alex Hern, Stacee Smith, Shaun Walker, Rus-sia used hundreds of fake accounts to tweet about Brexit, data shows, The Guardian, November 14, 2017, https://www.theguardian.com/world/2017/nov/14/how-400 -russia-run-fake-accounts-posted-bogus-brexit-tweets

21 United States Senate Committee on the Judiciary, Testimony of Sean J. Edgett, October 31, 2017, https://www.lgraham.senate.gov/public/_cache/files/4766f54d -d433-4055-9f3d-c94f97eeb1c0/testimony-of-sean-edgett-acting-general-counsel -twitter.pdf

22 United States Senate Committee on the Judiciary, Testimony of Sean J. Edgett, October 31, 2017, https://www.lgraham.senate.gov/public/_cache/files/4766f54d -d433-4055-9f3d-c94f97eeb1c0/testimony-of-sean-edgett-acting-general-counsel -twitter.pdf

23 Robert Booth, Matthew Weaver, Alex Hern, Stacee Smith, Shaun Walker, Rus-sia used hundreds of fake accounts to tweet about Brexit, data shows, The Guardian, November 14, 2017, https://www.theguardian.com/world/2017/nov/14/how-400 -russia-run-fake-accounts-posted-bogus-brexit-tweets

24 United States Senate Committee on the Judiciary, Testimony of Sean J. Edgett, October 31, 2017, https://www.lgraham.senate.gov/public/_cache/files/4766f54d -d433-4055-9f3d-c94f97eeb1c0/testimony-of-sean-edgett-acting-general-counsel -twitter.pdf, pg.6

25 Adam Payne, Russia used a network of 150,000 Twitter accounts to meddle in Brexit, Business Insider, November 15, 2017, https://amp.uk.businessinsider.com/russia -used-twitter-accounts-to-meddle-in-brexit-investigation-shows-2017-11

26 Robert Booth, Matthew Weaver, Alex Hern, Stacee Smith, Shaun Walker, Russia used hundreds of fake accounts to tweet about Brexit, data shows, The Guardian, November 14, 2017, https://www.theguardian.com/world/2017/nov/14/how-400-russia-run-fake-accounts-posted-bogus-brexit-tweets

27 Karla Adam, William Booth, Rising alarm in Britain over Russian meddling in Brexit vote, The Washington Post, November 17, 2017, https://www.washington post.com/world/europe/rising-alarm-in-britain-over-russian-meddling-in-brexit -vote/2017/11/17/2e987a30-cb34-11e7-b506-8a10ed11ecf5_story.html?utm _term=.39ba2dfafd54

28 Robert Booth, Matthew Weaver, Alex Hern, Stacee Smith, Shaun Walker, Russia used hundreds of fake accounts to tweet about Brexit, data shows, The Guardian, November 14, 2017, https://www.theguardian.com/world/2017/nov/14/how-400 -russia-run-fake-accounts-posted-bogus-brexit-tweets

29 Agence France-Presse, UK cyber security chief blames Russia for hacker attacks, Security Week, November 15, 2017, https://www.securityweek.com/ uk-cyber-security-chief-blames-russia-hacker-attacks

30 Andrew Picken, Revealed: Bogus accounts' 400,000 tweets on Scottish independence, The Sunday Post, November 19, 2017, https://www.sundaypost.com/ fp/bogus-accounts-400000-tweets-on-independence/

31 Staff, Theresa May accuses Russia of interfering in elections and fake news, The Guardian, November 14, 2017, https://www.theguardian.com/politics/2017/nov/13/ theresa-may-accuses-russia-of-interfering-in-elections-and-fake-news

32 Laura Daniels, How Russia hacked the French election, Politico, April 23, 2017, https:// www.politico.eu/article/france-election-2017-russia-hacked-cyberattacks/

33 US Department of State, Soviet Influence Activities: A Report on Active Measures and Propaganda, 1986-87, August 1987, https://www.globalsecurity.org/intell/library/ reports/1987/soviet-influence-activities-1987.pdf

34 Alex Hern, Macron Hackers linked to Russian-affiliated group behind US attack, The Guardian, May 8, 2017, https://www.theguardian.com/world/2017/ may/08/macron-hackers-linked-to-russian-affiliated-group-behind-us-attack

35 Bethany Palma, Was the French Election Hacked by Russia? Snopes, May 10,2017 https://www.snopes.com/2017/05/10/french-election-russian-hack/

36 Andy Greenburg, The NSA Confirms It: Russia Hacked French Election 'Infrastructure,' Security, May 9, 2017, https://www.wired.com/2017/05/nsa-director-confirms -russia-hacked-french-election-infrastructure/

37 Digital Attack on German Parliament: Investigative Report on the Hack of the Left Party Infrastructure in Bundestag, Netzpolitk, June 19, 2015, https://netzpolitik .org/2015/digital-attack-on-german-parliament-investigative-report-on-the-hack -of-the-left-party-infrastructure-in-bundestag/

38 Jennifer Baker, Ruskies behind German govt cyberattack—Report, The Register, June 4, 2015, https://www.theregister.co.uk/2015/06/04/ruskies_are_behind _german_government_cyber_attack/

39 Alice Bota, Merkel and the Fancy Bear, De Zeit Online, http://www.zeit.de/ digital/2017-05/cyberattack-bundestag-angela-merkel-fancy-bear-hacker-russia/ seite-6

40 Fabian Reibold, Is Moscow Planning Something? Germany Prepares for Possible Russian Election Meddling, Spiegel Online, September 7, 2017, http://www.spiegel .de/international/germany/how-germany-is-preparing-for-russian-election-medd ling-a-1166461.html

41 Constanze Stelzenmüller, The impact of Russian interference on Germany's 2017 elections, testimony to US Senate Select Committee on Intelligence, Brookings Institution, June 28, 2017, https://www.brookings.edu/testimonies/the-impact-of -russian-interference-on-germanys-2017-elections/

42 Constanze Stelzenmüller, The impact of Russian interference on Germany's 2017 elections, testimony to US Senate Select Committee on Intelligence, Brookings Institution, June 28, 2017, https://www.brookings.edu/testimonies/the-impact-of-russian-interference-on-germanys-2017-elections/

43 Anne Applebaum, Peter Pomeranstev, Melanie Smith, Chloe Colliver, Make Germany great again: Kremlin, Alt-Right and International influences in the 2007 German elections, Institute for Strategic Dialogue, 2017, http://www.isd global.org/wp-content/uploads/2017/12/Make-Germany-Great-Again-ENG -081217.pdf

44 Anne Applebaum, Peter Pomeranstev, Melanie Smith, Chloe Colliver, Make Germany great again: Kremlin, Alt-Right and International influences in the 2007 German elections, Institute for Strategic Dialogue, 2017, http://www.isd global.org/wp-content/uploads/2017/12/Make-Germany-Great-Again-ENG -081217.pdf

45 Anne Applebaum, Peter Pomeranstev, Melanie Smith, Chloe Colliver, Make Germany great again: Kremlin, Alt-Right and International influences in the 2007 German elections, Institute for Strategic Dialogue, 2017, http://www.isdglobal.org/wp-content/uploads/2017/12/Make-Germany-Great-Again-ENG-081217.pdf

46 Anne Applebaum, Peter Pomeranstev, Melanie Smith, Chloe Colliver, Make Germany great again: Kremlin, Alt-Right and International influences in the 2007 German elections, Institute for Strategic Dialogue, 2017, http://www.isdglobal.org/wp-content/uploads/2017/12/Make-Germany-Great-Again-ENG-081217.pdf

47 Karsten Schmehl, Ryan Broderick, A German YouTuber Tried to Make His Far-Right Hashtag Go Viral and It Was a Huge Flop, Buzzfeed, September 4, 2017, https://www.buzzfeed.com/karstenschmehl/these-secret-chats-show-who-is -behind-the-meme-att?utm_term=.ch3O13E6a#.mhggMkKxJ

48 Blake Hester, Discord Shuts Down Its Alt-Right Server After Charlottesville Protests, Rolling Stone, August 15, 2017, https://www.rollingstone.com/glixel/news/discord-shuts-down-alt-right-server-after-charlottesville-w497856

49 German elections 2017: Full results, The Guardian, September 25, 2017, https://www.theguardian.com/world/ng-interactive/2017/sep/24/german-elections-2017 -latest-results-live-merkel-bundestag-afd

50 John Henly, Russia waging information war against Sweden, study finds, The Guardian, January 11, 2017, https://www.theguardian.com/world/2017/jan/11/russia -waging-information-war-in-sweden-study-finds

51 John Henly, Russia waging information war against Sweden, study finds, The Guardian, January 11, 2017, https://www.theguardian.com/world/2017/jan/11/russia -waging-information-war-in-sweden-study-finds

52 John Henly, Russia waging information war against Sweden, study finds, The Guardian, January 11, 2017, https://www.theguardian.com/world/2017/jan/11/russia -waging-information-war-in-sweden-study-finds

53 John Henly, Russia waging information war against Sweden, study finds, The Guardian, January 11, 2017, https://www.theguardian.com/world/2017/jan/11/russia-waging-information-war-in-sweden-study-finds

54 Andrew Rettman, Lisbeth Kirk, Sweden raises alarm on election meddling, EU Observer, January 15, 2018, https://euobserver.com/foreign/140542

55 Ben Farmer, Surveillance Photo's Show Russian Intelligence Officers Plotting, The Telegraph, August 29, 2017, http://www.telegraph.co.uk/news/2017/08/28/surveillance-photos-show-russian-intelligence-officers-plotting/

56 Ben Farmer, Reconstruction: Full Incredible Story Behind Russia's Deadly Plot, The Telegraph, February 16, 2017, http://www.telegraph.co.uk/news/2017/02/18/reconstruction-full-incredible-story-behind-russias-deadly-plot/

57 Kate McCann, Boris Johnson claims Russia was behind plot to assassinate Prime Minister of Montenegro as he warns of Putin's 'dirty tricks,' The Telegraph, March 12, 2017, http://www.telegraph.co.uk/news/2017/03/12/boris-johnson-claims-russia -behind-plot-assassinate-prime-minister/

58 Mark Landler, Maggie Astor, U.S. Embassy in Montenegro Is Attacked, but Only Attacker Is Killed, The New York Times, February 21, 2018, https:// www.nytimes.com/2018/02/21/world/europe/montenegro-embassy-attacked .html?ribbon-ad-&mtrref=undefined&gwh=013097E02EA2E624E007F6D 71C760869&gwt=pay

Chapter 12: Russia's American Beachhead

1 Elias Isquith, Rudy Giuliani: Unlike Obama, Putin is "what you call a leader," Salon, March 4, 2014, https://www.salon.com/2014/03/04/rudy_giuliani_unlike _obama_putin_is_%E2%80%9Cwhat_you_call_a_leader%E2%80%9D

2 John Barron, KGB: The Secret Work of Soviet Secret Agents (Bantam Books, 1974), pg. 231

3 Yuri Bezmenov, Soviet Subversion of the Free World Press: A Conversation with Yuri Bezmenov, Youtube, 1984, https://www.youtube.com/watch?v=Cnf0I2dQ0i0

4 Yuri Bezmenov, Soviet Subversion of the Free World Press: A Conversation with Yuri Bezmenov, Youtube, 1984, https://www.youtube.com/watch?v=Cnf0I2dQ0i0

5 Elizabeth Dias, Vice President Mike Pence met with Top Russian Cleric, Time Magazine, May 12, 2017

6 John Aravosis, Vladimir Putin and the Falwell Bloc, AmericaBlog, December 29, 2014

7 J. Lester Feder, Susie Armitage, Emails show 'Pro-Family' activists feeding contacts to Russian Nationalists, Buzzfeed, December 8, 2014, https://www.buzzfeed .com/lesterfeder/emails-show-pro-family-activists-feeding-contacts-to-russian?utm _term=.cbqLgjxOA#.xmprdq84o

8 Rosalind Helderman, Tom Hamburger, Guns and Religion: How American Conservatives grew closer to Putin's Russia, The Washington Post, April 30, 2017, https://www.washingtonpost.com/politics/how-the-republican-right-found-allies -in-russia/2017/04/30/e2d83ff6-29d3-11e7-a616-d7c8a68c1a66_story.html?utm _term=.2a65c1e738c9

9 Rosalind Helderman, Tom Hamburger, Guns and religion: How American Conservatives grew closer to Putin's Russia, The Washington Post, April 30, 2017, https://www.washingtonpost.com/politics/how-the-republican-right-found-allies -in-russia/2017/04/30/e2d83ff6-29d3-11e7-a616-d7c8a68c1a66_story.html?utm _term=.7a4fb6933752

10 Scott Lively, Kevin Abrams, The Pink Swastika: Homosexuality in Nazi Germany, 5th ed, http://www.scottlively.net/tps/

11 Scott Lively, Letter to the Russian people, October 15, 2007, http://www.defendthe family.com/pfrc/archives.php?id=5225300

12 Natasha Bertrand, A model for civilization: Putin's Russia has emerged as 'a beacon for nationalists' and the American alt-right, Business Insider, December 10, 2016, http:// www.businessinsider.com/russia-connections-to-the-alt-right-2016-11

13 Natasha Bertrand, A model for civilization: Putin's Russia has emerged as 'a beacon for nationalists' and the American alt-right, Business Insider, December 10, 2016, http:// www.businessinsider.com/russia-connections-to-the-alt-right-2016-11

14 Erasmus, The Axis between Russian Orthodox and American Evangelicals is Intact, The Economist, July 14, 2017, https://www.economist.com/blogs/erasmus/ 2017/07/praying-together-staying-together

15 Rosalind Helderman, Tom Hamburger, Guns and religion: How American Conservatives grew closer to Putin's Russia, The Washington Post, April 30, 2017,

https://www.washingtonpost.com/politics/how-the-republican-right-found-allies
-in-russia/2017/04/30/e2d83ff6-29d3-11e7-a616-d7c8a68c1a66_story.html?utm
_term=.929ff427df5b

16 Rosalind Helderman, Tom Hamburger, Guns and religion: How American Conservatives grew closer to Putin's Russia, The Washington Post, April 30, 2017,
https://www.washingtonpost.com/politics/how-the-republican-right-found-allies
-in-russia/2017/04/30/e2d83ff6-29d3-11e7-a616-d7c8a68c1a66_story.html?utm
_term=.929ff427df5b

17 Alex Altman, Elizabeth Dias, Moscow Cozies Up to the Right, Time, March 10, 2017,
http://time.com/4696424/moscow-right-kremlin-republicans/

18 Mak, Tim, Top Trump Ally Met with Putin's Deputy in Moscow, The Daily
Beast, March 7, 2017, https://www.thedailybeast.com/top-trump-ally-met-with
-putins-deputy-in-moscow

19 Constitution of the Russian Federation art. 45.2, http://www.constitution.ru/en/
10003000-01.htm

20 Rosalind Helderman, Tom Hamburger, Guns and religion: How American Conservatives grew closer to Putin's Russia, The Washington Post, April 30, 2017,
https://www.washingtonpost.com/politics/how-the-republican-right-found
-allies-in-russia/2017/04/30/e2d83ff6-29d3-11e7-a616-d7c8a68c1a66_story.html
?utm_term=.57f40de12c26

21 Rosalind Helderman, Tom Hamburger, Guns and religion: How American Conservatives grew closer to Putin's Russia, The Washington Post, April 30, 2017,
https://www.washingtonpost.com/politics/how-the-republican-right-found-allies
-in-russia/2017/04/30/e2d83ff6-29d3-11e7-a616-d7c8a68c1a66_story.html?utm
_term=.57f40de12c26

22 Order of Holy King Milutin to Mr. Alexandar Torshin, www.spc.rs/eng/order
_holy_king_milutin_mr_alexandar_torshin

23 Alex Altman, Elizabeth Dias, Moscow Cozies Up to the Right, Time, March 10, 2017,
http://time.com/4696424/moscow-right-kremlin-republicans/

24 Rosalind Helderman, Tom Hamburger, Guns and religion: How American Conservatives grew closer to Putin's Russia, The Washington Post, April 30, 2017,
https://www.washingtonpost.com/politics/how-the-republican-right-found-allies
-in-russia/2017/04/30/e2d83ff6-29d3-11e7-a616-d7c8a68c1a66_story.html?utm
_term=.85cd6ef20f19

25 Rosalind Helderman, Tom Hamburger, Guns and religion: How American Conservatives grew closer to Putin's Russia, The Washington Post, April 30, 2017,
https://www.washingtonpost.com/politics/how-the-republican-right-found
-allies-in-russia/2017/04/30/e2d83ff6-29d3-11e7-a616-d7c8a68c1a66_story.html
?utm_term=.85cd6ef20f19

26 Peter Stone, Greg Gordon, FBI Investigating Whether Russia Money Went to
NRA to Help Trump, McClatchy DC Bureau, January 18, 2018, http://www
.mcclatchydc.com/news/nation-world/national/article195231139.html

27 Transcription by author, YouTube, July 13, 2015, https://www.bing.com/videos/
search?q=maria+butina+question+trump+freedom+fest&&view=detail&mid=
A63FC0A0957CFA913D0AA63FC0A0957CFA913D0A&&FORM=VRDGAR

28 Rosalind Helderman, Tom Hamburger, Guns and religion: How American Conservatives grew closer to Putin's Russia, The Washington Post, April 30, 2017,
https://www.washingtonpost.com/politics/how-the-republican-right-found
-allies-in-russia/2017/04/30/e2d83ff6-29d3-11e7-a616-d7c8a68c1a66_story.html
?utm_term=.85cd6ef20f19

29 Maria Butina, Twitter, @Maria_Butina, https://twitter.com/maria_butina/status/
619961053170958336

30 Peter Stone, Greg Gordon, FBI Investigating Whether Russia Money Went to NRA to Help Trump, McClatchy DC Bureau, January 18, 2018, http://www.mcc latchydc.com/news/nation-world/national/article195231139.html

31 Tim Mak, Top Trump Ally Met with Putin's Deputy in Moscow, The Daily Beast, March 7, 2017, https://www.thedailybeast.com/top-trump-ally-met-with-putins -deputy-in-moscow

32 Peter Stone, Greg Gordon, FBI Investigating Whether Russia Money Went to NRA to Help Trump, McClatchy DC Bureau, January 18, 2018, http://www.mcclatchydc .com/news/nation-world/national/article195231139.html

33 Peter Stone, Greg Gordon, FBI Investigating Whether Russia Money Went to NRA to Help Trump, McClatchy DC Bureau, January 18, 2018, http://www.mcclatchydc .com/news/nation-world/national/article195231139.html

34 Peter Stone, Greg Gordon, FBI Investigating Whether Russia Money Went to NRA to Help Trump, McClatchy DC Bureau, January 18, 2018, http://www .mcclatchydc.com/news/nation-world/national/article195231139.html

35 Jose Maria Irujo, The Spanish connection with Trump's Russia scandal, El Pais, April 3, 2017, https://elpais.com/elpais/2017/03/31/inenglish/1490984556_409827.html

36 Rosalind Helderman, Tom Hamburger, Guns and religion: How American Conservatives grew closer to Putin's Russia, The Washington Post, April 30, 2017, https://www.washingtonpost.com/politics/how-the-republican-right-found-allies -in-russia/2017/04/30/e2d83ff6-29d3-11e7-a616-d7c8a68c1a66_story.html?utm _term=.85cd6ef20f19

37 Rosalind Helderman, Tom Hamburger, Guns and religion: How American Conservatives grew closer to Putin's Russia, The Washington Post, April 30, 2017, https://www.washingtonpost.com/politics/how-the-republican-right-found -allies-in-russia/2017/04/30/e2d83ff6-29d3-11e7-a616-d7c8a68c1a66_story.html ?utm_term=.85cd6ef20f19

38 Rosalind Helderman, Tom Hamburger, Guns and religion: How American Conservatives grew closer to Putin's Russia, The Washington Post, April 30, 2017, https://www.washingtonpost.com/politics/how-the-republican-right-found -allies-in-russia/2017/04/30/e2d83ff6-29d3-11e7-a616-d7c8a68c1a66_story.html ?utm_term=.85cd6ef20f19

39 Peter Stone, Greg Gordon, FBI Investigating Whether Russia Money Went to NRA to Help Trump, McClatchy DC Bureau, January 18,2018, http://www.mcclatchydc .com/news/nation-world/national/article195231139.html

40 Elizabeth Dias, Vice President Mike Pence met with Top Russian Cleric, Time, May 12, 2017, http://time.com/4776717/mike-pence-russian-cleric-hilarion-alfeyev/

41 Laura Strickler, White House refuses to release photo of Trump signing bill to weaken gun law, CBS News, February 15, 2018, https://www.cbsnews.com/ news/white-house-refused-to-release-photo-of-trump-signing-bill-to-weaken-gun-law/

42 Eric Cortellessa, Stuart Winer, Five members of Jewish community among 17 killed in Florida massacre, The Times of Israel, February 15, 2018, https:// www.timesofisrael.com/five-members-of-jewish-community-confirmed-among -17-killed-in-florida-massacre/

43 Jose Maria Irujo, The Spanish connection with Trump's Russia scandal, El Pais, April 3, 2017, https://elpais.com/elpais/2017/03/31/inenglish/1490984556_409827.html

44 Ruth May, How Putin's Proxies Helped Funnel Millions into GOP Campaigns, The Dallas News, Dec 15, 2017, https://www.dallasnews.com/opinion/ commentary/2017/12/15/putins-proxies-helped-funnel-millions-gop-campaigns

45 Ruth May, How Putin's Proxies Helped Funnel Millions into GOP Campaigns, The Dallas News, Dec 15, 2017, https://www.dallasnews.com/opinion/ commentary/2017/12/15/putins-proxies-helped-funnel-millions-gop-campaigns

46 Ruth May, How Putin's Proxies Helped Funnel Millions into GOP Campaigns, The Dallas News, Dec 15, 2017, https://www.dallasnews.com/opinion/commentary/2017/12/15/putins-proxies-helped-funnel-millions-gop-campaigns

47 Ruth May, How Putin's Proxies Helped Funnel Millions into GOP Campaigns, The Dallas News, Dec 15,2017, https://www.dallasnews.com/opinion/commentary/2017/12/15/putins-proxies-helped-funnel-millions-gop-campaigns

48 Ruth May, How Putin's Proxies Helped Funnel Millions into GOP Campaigns, The Dallas News, Dec 15, 2017, https://www.dallasnews.com/opinion/commentary/2017/12/15/putins-proxies-helped-funnel-millions-gop-campaigns

49 Max de Haldevang, Trump's Inaugural Committee Took $1 Million from Russian-Americans Whose Money the GOP Rejected, Quartz, Apr 20, 2017, https://www.dallasnews.com/opinion/commentary/2017/12/15/putins-proxies-helped-funnel-millions-gop-campaigns

50 Ruth May, How Putin's Proxies Helped Funnel Millions into GOP Campaigns, The Dallas News, Dec 15, 2017, https://www.dallasnews.com/opinion/commentary/2017/12/15/putins-proxies-helped-funnel-millions-gop-campaigns

51 Ruth May, How Putin's Proxies Helped Funnel Millions into GOP Campaigns, The Dallas News, Dec 15, 2017, https://www.dallasnews.com/opinion/commentary/2017/12/15/putins-proxies-helped-funnel-millions-gop-campaigns

52 Joe Scarborough, Even now, Republicans are ignoring the storm clouds. The Washington Post, January 26, 2018, https://www.washingtonpost.com/opinions/even-now-republicans-are-ignoring-the-storm-clouds/2018/01/26/a6b727e6-02d9-11e8-8acf-ad2991367d9d_story.html?utm_term=.03885b6a8bba

53 Alex Altman, Elizabeth Dias, Moscow Cozies Up to the Right, Time, March 10, 2017, http://time.com/4696424/moscow-right-kremlin-republicans/

Chapter 13: The American Fifth Column

1 Aleksandr Dugin, Donald Trump's Victory, Katehon Think Tank, November 10, 2016, https://www.youtube.com/watch?v=uEQINJdR8jo

2 David Holthouse, Preston Wiginton emerges in Russia promoting race hate, Southern Poverty Law Center, May 20, 2008, https://www.splcenter.org/fighting-hate/intelligence-report/2008/preston-wiginton-emerges-russia-promoting-race-hate

3 David Neiwert, When White Nationalists chant their slogans, what do they mean?, Southern Poverty Law Center Hatewatch, October 10, 2017, https://www.splcenter.org/hatewatch/2017/10/10/when-white-nationalists-chant-their-weird-slogans-what-do-they-mean

4 Joe Heim, Recounting a day of rage, hate, violence and death, The Washington Post, Aug 14, 2017, https://www.washingtonpost.com/graphics/2017/local/charlottesville-timeline/?utm_term=.cffae5b50678

5 Joe Heim, Recounting a day of rage, hate, violence and death, The Washington Post, Aug 14, 2017, https://www.washingtonpost.com/graphics/2017/local/charlottesville-timeline/?utm_term=.cffae5b50678

6 Tom Porter, Charlottesville: Heather Heyer named as anti-racist killed in car ramming at alt-right demo, Newsweek, August 13, 2017, http://www.newsweek.com/heather-heyer-named-woman-killed-car-ramming-alt-right-counter-demo-650220

7 Southern Poverty Law Center, The people, groups and symbols of Charlottesville, Southern Poverty Law Center, August 15, 2017, https://www.splcenter.org/news/2017/08/15/people-groups-and-symbols-charlottesville

8 Robert King, Indiana white nationalist called the 'next David Duke' isn't stopping with Charlottesville, Indystar, August 27, 2017, https://www.indystar.com/story/news/2017/08/27/indiana-white-nationalist-called-the-next-david-duke-isnt-stopping-charlottesville/573817001/

9 Nathaniel Popper, David Duke offers Antisemitism 101 at a Ukrainian university, Forward, November 3, 2006, https://forward.com/news/7416/david-duke-offers-antisemitism-101-at-a-ukra/

10 CBS News, David Duke, To Russia with Hate, CBS News, February 2, 2001, https://www.cbsnews.com/news/david-duke-to-russia-with-hate/

11 Natasha Bertrand, 'A model for civilization': Putin's Russia has emerged as 'a beacon for nationalists' and the American alt-right, Business Insider, December 10, 2016, http://www.businessinsider.com/russia-connections-to-the-alt-right-2016-11

12 Natasha Bertrand, 'A model for civilization: Putin's Russia has emerged as 'a beacon for nationalists' and the American alt-right, Business Insider, December 10, 2016, http://www.businessinsider.com/russia-connections-to-the-alt-right-2016-11

13 David Holthouse, Preston Wiginton emerges in Russia promoting race hate, Southern Poverty Law Center, May 20, 2008, https://www.splcenter.org/fighting-hate/intelligence-report/2008/preston-wiginton-emerges-russia-promoting-race-hate

14 Sam Dickson, Shattering the Icon of Abraham Lincoln, Journal of Historical Review, http://vho.org/GB/Journals/JHR/7/3/Dickson319-344.html

15 Alexander Zaitchik, How Klan lawyer Sam Dickson got rich, Southern Poverty Law Center, October 19, 2006, https://www.splcenter.org/fighting-hate/intelligence-report/2006/how-klan-lawyer-sam-dickson-got-rich

16 Alan Feuer, Andrew Higgins, Extremists turn to a leader to protect Western Values: Vladimir Putin, The New York Times, December 12, 2016, https://www.nytimes.com/2016/12/03/world/americas/alt-right-vladimir-putin.html?mcubz=0

17 Sam Dickson, Easter Message, April 17, 2017, http://www.sam-dickson.com/Easter 2017.htm

18 Natasha Bertrand, A model for civilization: Putin's Russia has emerged as 'a beacon for nationalists' and the American alt-right, Business Insider, December 10, 2016, http://www.businessinsider.com/russia-connections-to-the-alt-right-2016-11

19 David Holthouse, Preston Wiginton emerges in Russia promoting race hate, Southern Poverty Law Center, May 20, 2008, https://www.splcenter.org/fighting-hate/intelligence-report/2008/preston-wiginton-emerges-russia-promoting-race-hate

20 Deana Kjuka, Link Exposed Between Charleston Killer and Hater's Convention in Russia, Radio Free Europe Radio Liberty, June 24, 2015, https://www.rferl.org/a/charleston-dylann-roof-russia-conservative-forum-citizens/27091137.html

21 David Holthouse, Preston Wiginton emerges in Russia promoting race hate, Southern Poverty Law Center, May 20, 2008, https://www.splcenter.org/fighting-hate/intelligence-report/2008/preston-wiginton-emerges-russia-promoting-race-hate

22 David Holthouse, Preston Wiginton emerges in Russia promoting race hate, Southern Poverty Law Center, May 20, 2008, https://www.splcenter.org/fighting-hate/intelligence-report/2008/preston-wiginton-emerges-russia-promoting-race-hate

23 David Holthouse, Preston Wiginton emerges in Russia promoting race hate, Southern Poverty Law Center, May 20, 2008, https://www.splcenter.org/fighting-hate/intelligence-report/2008/preston-wiginton-emerges-russia-promoting-race-hate

24 Alan Cullison, Far-Right Flocks to Russia to Berate the West, Wall Street Journal, March 23, 2015, https://www.wsj.com/articles/far-right-flocks-to-russia-to-berate-the-west-1427059613

25 YouTube video, "Race Situation in America—Jared Taylor in Russia," May 12, 2015, https://www.youtube.com/watch?v=vbA4OSAezfI

26 Stephen Piggot, White Nationalists Continue to Support Trump Through Robocalls, Southern Poverty Law Center, January 12, 2016, https://www.splcenter.org/hatewatch/2016/01/12/white-nationalists-continue-support-trump-through-robocalls

27 Hayley Tsukayama, Twitter purge suspends account of far-right leader who was retweeted by Trump, The Washington Post, December 18, 2017, https://www.washingtonpost .com/news/the-switch/wp/2017/12/18/twitter-purge-suspends-account-of-far-right -leader-who-was-retweeted-by-trump/?utm_term=.b1a59a6aed55

28 Natasha Bertrand, A model for civilization: Putin's Russia has emerged as 'a beacon for nationalists' and the American alt-right, Business Insider, December 10, 2016, http:// www.businessinsider.com/russia-connections-to-the-alt-right-2016-11

29 Alan Feuer, Andrew Higgins, Extremists turn to a leader to protect Western values: Vladimir Putin, The New York Times, December 3, 2016, https://www.nytimes .com/2016/12/03/world/americas/alt-right-vladimir-putin.html?mcubz=0

30 ADL, Traditionalist Youth Network, ADL, https://www.adl.org/education/resources/ backgrounders/traditionalist-youth-network

31 ADL, Traditionalist Youth Network, ADL, https://www.adl.org/education/resources/ backgrounders/traditionalist-youth-network

32 Matthew Heimbach, YouTube, "Matthew Heimbach at Camp Comradery 2015: Our Struggle, Our Future," September 19, 2015, https://www.youtube.com/ watch?v=N-BU2UFdkWQ

33 Casey Michel, US hate group forging ties with the 'Third Rome,' Eurasianet, July 15, 2016, https://eurasianet.org/node/79686

34 Natasha Bertrand, A model for civilization: Putin's Russia has emerged as 'a beacon for nationalists' and the American alt-right, Business Insider, December 10, 2016, http:// www.businessinsider.com/russia-connections-to-the-alt-right-2016-11

35 Alan Feuer, Andrew Higgins, Extremists turn to a leader to protect Western values: Vladimir Putin, The New York Times, December 3, 2016, https://www.nytimes .com/2016/12/03/world/americas/alt-right-vladimir-putin.html?mcubz=0

36 Alan Feuer, Andrew Higgins, Extremists turn to a leader to protect Western values: Vladimir Putin, The New York Times, December 3, 2016, https://www.nytimes .com/2016/12/03/world/americas/alt-right-vladimir-putin.html?mcubz=0

37 Vegas Tenold, The Little Fuhrer: A day in the life of the newest leader of white nationalists, Al Jazeera, July 26, 2015, http://projects.aljazeera.com/2015/07/hate -groups/

38 Alan Feuer, Andrew Higgins, Extremists turn to a leader to protect Western values: Vladimir Putin, The New York Times, December 3, 2016, https://www.nytimes .com/2016/12/03/world/americas/alt-right-vladimir-putin.html?mcubz=0

39 Alan Feuer, Andrew Higgins, Extremists turn to a leader to protect Western values: Vladimir Putin, The New York Times, December 3, 2016, https://www.nytimes .com/2016/12/03/world/americas/alt-right-vladimir-putin.html?mcubz=0

40 Matthew Heimbach, YouTube, Matthew Heimbach at the Maryland Council of Conservative Citizens, April 2, 2015, https://www.youtube.com/watch?v=nVpnwDIxlB8

41 Aram Roston, Joel Anderson, The Moneyman Behind the Alt-Right, Buzzfeed, July 23, 2017, https://www.buzzfeed.com/aramroston/hes-spent-almost-20 -years-funding-the-racist-right-it

42 Josh Harkinson, Meet the White Nationalist Trying to Ride the Trump Train to Lasting Power, Mother Jones, October 27, 2016, https://www.motherjones.com/ politics/2016/10/richard-spencer-trump-alt-right-white-nationalist/

43 Southern Poverty Law Center, A fresh crop of 'intellectuals' joins the radical right, Southern Poverty Law Center, August 11, 2006, https://www.splcenter .org/fighting-hate/intelligence-report/2006/new-racialists

44 CBS News, Mayor: Torch-lit protest in Charlottesville, VA 'harkens back to the days of the KKK, CBS News, May 15, 2017, https://www.cbsnews.com/ news/charlottesville-protest-richard-spender-kkk-robert-e-lee-statue/

45 Trevor Hughes, Far right's Richard Spencer returns to Charlottesville, tiki torch in hand, USA Today, October 7, 2017, https://www.usatoday.com/story/news/ nation/2017/10/07/white-nationalists-charlottesville-again/743624001/

46 Martin Gelin, White Flight, Slate, November 13, 2014, http://www.slate.com/articles/news_and_politics/foreigners/2014/11/jared_taylor_richard_spencer_and_american_white_supremacists_in_europe_why.html

47 Natasha Bertrand, A model for civilization: Putin's Russia has emerged as 'a beacon for nationalists' and the American alt-right, Business Insider, December 10, 2016, http://www.businessinsider.com/russia-connections-to-the-alt-right-2016-11

48 Joan Walsh, Islamophobes, White Supremacists, and Gays for Trump—The Alt-Right Arrives at the RNC, The Nation, July 20, 2016, https://www.thenation.com/article/islamophobes-white-supremacists-and-gays-for-trump-the-alt-right-arrives-at-the-rnc/

49 Jason Kessler, ANALYSIS: #Russia Will Be One of America's Greatest Allies During the Trump Administration, Got News, January 11, 2017, http://gotnews.com/analysis-russia-will-one-americas-greatest-allies-trump-administration/

50 Ben Schreckinger, GOP researcher who sought Clinton emails had alt-right help, Politico, July 11, 2017, https://www.politico.com/magazine/story/2017/07/11/gop-researcher-who-sought-clinton-emails-had-alt-right-help-215359

51 Adam Taylor, He's the founder of a Californian independence movement. Just don't ask him why he lives in Russia, The Washington Post, February 19, 2017, https://www.washingtonpost.com/news/worldviews/wp/2017/02/19/hes-the-founder-of-a-californian-independence-movement-just-dont-ask-him-why-he-lives-in-russia/?utm_term=.c70d5dfed85c

52 The Scotsman, Yes Scotland logo adopted by California independence movement, The Scotsman, February 24, 2016, https://www.scotsman.com/news/yes-scotland-logo-adopted-by-california-independence-movement-1-4037382

53 Melody Gutierrez, Advocate's Russian ties cause concern in state secession movement, San Francisco Chronicle, February 3, 2017, https://www.sfchronicle.com/politics/article/Advocate-s-Russian-ties-cause-concern-in-state-10907521.php

54 Melody Gutierrez, Advocate's Russian ties cause concern in state secession movement, San Francisco Chronicle, February 3, 2017, https://www.sfchronicle.com/politics/article/Advocate-s-Russian-ties-cause-concern-in-state-10907521.php

55 Katie Zezima, California is a nation, not a state: A fringe movement wants a break from the U.S., The Washington Post, February 18, 2017, https://www.washingtonpost.com/politics/california-is-a-nation-not-a-state-a-fringe-movement-wants-a-break-from-the-us/2017/02/18/ed85671c-f567-11e6-8d72-263470bf0401_story.html?utm_term=.a3595e742220

56 RT, Calexit: Yes California movement opens embassy in Moscow, RT, December 18, 2016, https://www.rt.com/usa/370698-calexit-california-embassy-moscow/

57 Andrew Kramer, California Secession Advocate Faces Scrutiny Over Where He's Based: Russia, The New York Times, February 21, 2017, https://www.nytimes.com/2017/02/21/us/yes-california-calexit-marinelli-russia.html

58 Melody Gutierrez, Advocate's Russian ties cause concern in state secession movement, San Francisco Chronicle, February 3, 2017, https://www.sfchronicle.com/politics/article/Advocate-s-Russian-ties-cause-concern-in-state-10907521.php

59 Natasha Bertrand, California separatist leader: We welcome vocal support of Julian Assange, Business Insider, October 9, 2017, https://www.businessinsider.nl/california-exit-secession-leader-calexit-julian-assange-2017-10/

60 Adam Taylor, He's the founder of a Californian independence movement. Just don't ask him why he lives in Russia, The Washington Post, February 19, 2017, https://www.washingtonpost.com/news/worldviews/wp/2017/02/19/hes-the-founder-of-a-californian-independence-movement-just-dont-ask-him-why-he-lives-in-russia/?utm_term=.c70d5dfed85c

61 Patrick Reevell, Texas, California Separatists Attend Kremlin-Funded Conference, ABC News, September 27, 2016, http://abcnews.go.com/International/texas-california-separatists-attend-pro-kremlin-conference/story?id=42395066

62 Kevin McPhearson, Bruce Wright, Texas, Federal Funding in Texas, Comptroller Texas, https://comptroller.texas.gov/economy/fiscal-notes/2017/november/federal-funding.php

63 Angelo Young, Matthew Sheffield, Neo-Nazi blog The Daily Stormer tries to move to Russian domain, Salon, August 16, 2017, https://www.salon.com/2017/08/16/neo-nazi-blog-the-daily-stormer-tries-to-move-to-russian-domain/

64 Katie Zavadski, American Alt-Right Leaves Facebook for Russian Site VKontakte, The Daily Beast, November 3, 2017, https://www.thedailybeast.com/american-alt-right-leaves-facebook-for-russian-site-vkontakte

Chapter 14: A Treasonous Aspect

1 Keir Giles, The Handbook of Russian Information Warfare, NATO Defense College (Rome, 2016) pg. 19

2 Keir Giles, The Handbook of Russian Information Warfare, NATO Defense College (Rome 2016) pg. 20

3 K. Pynnöniemi and A. Rácz, Fog of Falsehood: Russian Strategy of Deception and the Conflict in Ukraine, FIIA Report No. 45, pg. 38

4 Randy Burkett, An Alternative Framework for Agent Recruitment: From MICE to RASCLS, CIA Center for Study of Intelligence, Studies in Intelligence Vol 57. No.1, March 2013, https://www.cia.gov/library/center-for-the-study-of-intelligence/csi-publications/csi-studies/studies/vol.-57-no.-1-a/vol.-57-no.-1-a-pdfs/Burkett-MICE%20to%20RASCALS.pdf

5 Fiona Hill, Clifford Gaddy, Mr. Putin: Operative in the Kremlin (Washington, D.C., Brookings Institution Press, 2013), pg. 7, https://books.google.com/books/about/Mr_Putin.html?id=ND8PBAAAQBAJ&printsec=frontcover&source=kp_read_button#v=onepage&q&f=false

6 The Huffington Post, Trump Sells $100M Palm Beach Mansion, Huffington Post, May 25, 2011, https://www.huffingtonpost.com/2010/01/26/trump-flips-100m-palm-bea_n_437234.html

7 Kate Connelly, Czechoslovakia spied on Donald and Ivana Trump, communist-era files show, The Guardian, December 15, 2016, https://www.theguardian.com/us-news/2016/dec/15/czechoslovakia-spied-on-donald-trump-ivana-files

8 Archivy StB: Trump se chtěl stát prezidentem v roce 1996, Ceskatelevize 24, December1,2016,http://www.ceskatelevize.cz/ct24/domaci/1970461-archivy-stb-trump-se-chtel-stat-prezidentem-v-roce-1996

9 Donald J. Trump, Twitter, November 11, 2013, https://twitter.com/realDonaldTrump/status/399939505924628480

10 Yulya Alferova, Twitter, January 22, 2014, https://twitter.com/alferovayulyae/status/426103699572678656?lang=en

11 Robert Muller, U.S. v. Internet Research Agency, et al, February 16, 2017, https://www.scribd.com/document/371672481/U-S-v-Internet-Research-Agency-et-al

12 Donald J. Trump, Twitter @realDonaldtrump, September 24, 2014, https://twitter.com/realDonaldTrump/status/515635087275474944

13 Konstantine Rykov, Facebook, November 12, 2016, https://www.facebook.com/konstantin.rykov/posts/10210621124674610

14 Konstantine Rykov, Facebook, November 12, 2016, https://www.facebook.com/konstantin.rykov/posts/10210621124674610

15 Konstantine Rykov, Facebook, November 12, 2016, https://www.facebook.com/konstantin.rykov/posts/10210621124674610

16 Konstantine Rykov, Facebook, November 12, 2016, https://www.facebook.com/konstantin.rykov/posts/10210643558675446

17 Marilyn Geewax, Jackie Northam, Kushner Family Business Pitch in China Prompts Questions About Investor Visas, National Public Radio, May 8, 2017, https://www

.npr.org/2017/05/08/527451591/kushner-family-business-pitch-in-china-prompts-questions-about-investor-visas

18 Donald J. Trump, @realDonaldTrump twitter, February 17, 2017, https://twitter.com/realdonaldtrump/status/832708293516632065?lang=en

19 Jonathan Easley, War between Trump, media set to intensify, The Hill, December 28, 2017, http://thehill.com/homenews/administration/366608-war-between-trump-media-set-to-intensify

20 Lisa de Moraes, CNN video blasts Donald Trump's new attack on international journalists, Deadline, November 27,2017, http://deadline.com/2017/11/cnn-responds-donald-trump-attack-international-video-1202215030/

21 Aric Jenkins, President Trump Calls CNN Staff 'Horrible Human Beings' in Leaked Audio From RNC Fundraiser, Time Magazine, July 1, 2017, http://time.com/4842997/donald-trump-cnn-horrible-human-beings/

22 McFaul, Michael Ambassador, Twitter @McFaul, https://twitter.com/McFaul?ref_src=twsrc%5Egoogle%7Ctwcamp%5Eserp%7Ctwgr%5Eauthor

23 Kate Irby, Former CIA head explains how Russia lures people to commit treason without knowing it, McClatchy News, May 23, 2017, http://www.mcclatchydc.com/news/politics-government/article152136047.html

24 Veronica Stracqualursi, Ex-CIA boss says Russians could have personal dirt on Trump, CNN on MSN.com, March 21, 2018, https://www.msn.com/en-us/news/politics/ex-cia-boss-says-russians-could-have-personal-dirt-on-trump/ar-BBKw9ML?OCID=ansmsnnews11

Epilogue: "Freedom Is a Light"

1 Joe Scarborough: A Storm Is Gathering, December, 29, 2017, Hartford Courant, http://www.courant.com/opinion/op-ed/hc-op-ed-scarborough-trump-churchill-20171229-story.html

Index